COLLEGE OF MARIN LIBRARY
KENTFIELD, CALIFORNIA

P9-DTM-749

KIERKEGAARD

The Arguments of
the Philosophers

EDITOR: TED HONDERICH

Reader in Philosophy, University College London

The group of books of which this is one will include
an essentially analytic and critical account of each of
the considerable number of the great and the
influential philosophers. The group of books taken
together will comprise a contemporary assessment and
history of the entire course of philosophical thought.

Already published in the series

Plato	J. C. B. Gosling
Meinong	Reinhardt Grossman
Santayana	Timothy L. S. Sprigge
Wittgenstein	R. J. Fogelin
Hume	Barry Stroud
Descartes	Margaret Dauler Wilson
Berkeley	George Pitcher
Kant	Ralph Walker
The Presocratic Philosophers (2 vols)	Jonathan Barnes
Russell	Mark Sainsbury
Socrates	Gerasimos Xenophon Santas
Sartre	Peter Caws
Karl Popper	Anthony O'Hear
Gottlob Frege	Hans Sluga
Schopenhauer	David Hamlyn
Karl Marx	Allen W. Wood

KIERKEGAARD

Alastair Hannay

Routledge & Kegan Paul
London, Boston, Melbourne
and Henley

First published in 1982
by Routledge & Kegan Paul Ltd
39 Store Street,
London WC1E 7DD,
9 Park Street,
Boston, Mass. 02108, USA,
296 Beaconsfield Parade, Middle Park,
Melbourne, 3206, Australia and
Broadway House,
Newtown Road,
Henley-on-Thames,
Oxon. R69 1EN
Set in Garamond by
Cambrian Typesetters, Farnborough, Hants
and printed in Great Britain by
Hartnoll Print
Bodmin, Cornwall
© Alastair Hannay 1982
No part of this book may be reproduced in
any form without permission from the
publisher, except for the quotation of brief
passages in criticism

Library of Congress Cataloguing in Publication Data

Hannay, Alastair.
Kierkegaard.

(The arguments of the philosophers)
Includes bibliographical references and index.
1. Kierkegaard, Søren, 1813–1855.
I. Title.   II. Series.
B4377.H348   198.9   82-5362

ISBN 0-7100-9190-7   AACR2

To the memory of
ERSKINE HANNAY
(1900—56)

Contents

Satan, saint, or Socrates . . .

As a spiritual type, in a wide sense, Kierkegaard belongs to the
Mephistopheles category. Like that devil's chargé d'affaires in
Goethe, he is possessed of a superior intellect, which he deploys
with the same supple facility and tirelessness. They are both, in
their at once witty, impudent, and dazzling ways, irresistible. In
fact, Kierkegaard goes one better than the devil, being without
rival in the art of attacking reason with its own weapons. He is
not just Mephistopheles, he is at the same time Mephistopheles's
victim, man, Faust. It is not only against others that he turns his
weapons, in the end he turns them without mercy on himself. . . .
[While] Mephistopheles simply dissolves in a smoke of brilliant
conversation . . . Kierkegaard is the dire sufferer of his own
satanism. He is, one might say, the tragic satan. . . .

> *The Doomed Fiddlers*, by William Heinesen,
> Gyldendal, Copenhagen, 1965, p. 144,
> my translation

Kierkegaard was by far the most profound thinker of the last
century. Kierkegaard was a saint.

> Ludwig Wittgenstein, in private correspondence
> with M. O'C. Drury, in *Acta Philosophica Fennica*,
> vol. 28, nos 1–3 (1976), North-Holland Publishing
> Company, Amsterdam, 1976

People think the world needs a new republic, a new social
order, and a new religion, but it never occurs to anyone that
what the world now needs, confused as it is by much knowing,
is a new Socrates.

> Søren Kierkegaard, *The Sickness unto Death*,
> *Samlede Værker*, vol. 15, pp. 144–5, my translation

Preface

This book, in compliance with the aims of the series, attempts to provide a comprehensive and critical account of Kierkegaard's thought. In the case of a writer so complex, prolix, and so little concerned with the logical presentation of his own thought, it is perhaps inevitable that the exegetical side of this task should overshadow the critical. The reader will find that I have adopted a kind of compromise. If we can think of criticism as combining with exegesis in two different ways, either as appraisal of expounded doctrine or as an appraising way of expounding doctrine, this book mostly exemplifies the second way. Instead of erecting a body of doctrine on its supporting arguments and then subjecting it to a critical bombardment, I have tried to construct my account of Kierkegaard in a more critical, or argumentative, way, as well as one that is more compendiously coherent, than Kierkegaard's own. Those who like their criticism destructive, or more especially those who expect it to be so in the case of Kierkegaard, will be largely disappointed, and may even see in my efforts to state the sense and reason in Kierkegaard's concepts and views some hint of a misplaced piety, something which the Series Editor has explicitly asked us to avoid. I do not think I have been pious. Certainly in the course of writing this book I have acquired an increasing respect for the depth, range, and unity of Kierkegaard's thought, but I do not claim to be a Kierkegaardian in any other sense than that. I would prefer the reader to regard this work as an attempt to locate and exploit the intellectual resources of Kierkegaard's writings with a view to giving his thought a better philosophical showing than it usually receives. If I have succeeded, the critical reader will at least have an improved basis for making his or her own assessment of the philosophical value of Kierkegaard's claims and concepts.

Another feature of this work calling for explanation is the amount of reference made to other philosophers' views. There is a lot of Hegel, a fair amount of Kant, some Feuerbach and Marx, and a bit of Wittgenstein. The purpose of these references is wholly expositional. I found that the most effective way of bringing out the latent structure and logical content of Kierkegaard's writings was to compare and contrast his views with those of accredited philosophers whose thought is better known and more accessible.

Third, I have taken it to be a primary and not merely an additional task to identify and account for the unifying framework of Kierkegaard's thought. The fact that the framework is a religious one gives, in many philosophers' eyes, Kierkegaard's contentions and arguments, as well as his insights, a gratuitous ideological bias. This is no doubt one reason why modern philosophers tend to have only a passing or piecemeal acquaintance with his writings, and why there is a tendency in modern commentary (except that by Kierkegaardians) to assume that Kierkegaard's contribution to philosophy can only be measured once the main discussions have been separated from the framework and placed in more neutral settings. Clearly, such an approach would defeat the purposes of a series devoted to the doctrines and arguments of the thinkers themselves.

I am grateful to the Series Editor for this opportunity to renew and greatly improve my own acquaintance with Kierkegaard, as well as for his much tested patience, and not least for helpful advice in the preparation of the final draft. I would also like to thank Vincent Hope and Helge Høibraaten for valuable comments on parts of earlier drafts. I owe a special debt to Bente Børsum for help in translation and for much besides.

The leave which enabled me, after many interruptions, to complete the book was supported by the Norwegian Research Council for Science and the Humanities, which also covered the cost of typing the final draft. This assistance is gratefully acknowledged.

A.H.
Agios Sostis

I

A Kind of Philosopher

A poetic and philosophical nature has been set aside
in order [for me] to become a Christian.[1]

1 Life and influence

Although facts of biography say that Kierkegaard is a nineteenth-
century thinker, he had no impact whatever on that century's
thought. And prompted though his writings were by a rejection of
prevailing moral and intellectual patterns, as far as their influence
on those patterns was concerned they might have been published
on another planet. The fact alone that Kierkegaard wrote exclusively
in Danish prevented the spread of his ideas beyond Scandinavia in
his lifetime. Besides, Denmark itself, as he often complained, was a
cultural backwater; the chances of his work having any influence
even there were remote. But there is also the fact that Kierkegaard's
thought was at its time genuinely innovative, just too novel for its
implications to be immediately appreciated even beyond the limited
horizons of Copenhagen's intelligentsia.

There is, however, another factor. A recent biographer refers to
the 'penchant for secrecy and deceptiveness' that runs 'as a
constant thread through [Kierkegaard's] life and work', and to a
life-long 'urge to bait, seduce, and offend his public'.[2] Kierkegaard's style is not that of one who wants to influence people by
making friends. It is that of a polemicist taking on the cultural
world as a whole, hoping to open its eyes to the fact of its own
moral and intellectual torpor. Temperamentally incapable of
adapting himself to prevailing bourgeois norms, and regarding the
facility with which others did so as due to a self-serving super-

1

ficiality and lack of critical judgment on their part, Kierkegaard turned his brilliant intellect and considerable literary talent to the task of informing his public of its well-protected complacency. A quasi-biographical passage in *Concluding Unscientific Postscript* reads:

> Out of love of mankind, as well as despair at my embarrassing situation, seeing I had not accomplished anything and had been unable to make anything easier than it had already been made, [and] from a genuine interest in those who make everything easy, I conceived it my task to make difficulties everywhere.

Not a programme with a great deal of built-in consumer appeal. In referring ironically to those who 'make everything easy', Kierkegaard was thinking not of those who benefit mankind through technological innovation, whether in communications ('omnibuses, steamships, telegraphy') or the storage of information ('easily understood compendia and digests of everything worth knowing'), but of 'the age's true benefactors' whose contribution had been to 'make spiritual existence systematically easier, and nevertheless more and more meaningful, on the basis of thought'.[3] To a reading public for whom it was a congenial orthodoxy that collective human progress went hand in hand with the growth of a universal science of spirit, the obstacles Kierkegaard wished to put in its path were unlikely to be grasped as favours.

Kierkegaard's books were translated, quite soon after his death, into German. Initially, however, they created little stir even there. It seems, for instance, that Nietzsche, thirty-one years Kierkegaard's junior, although he had heard of him and in spite of obvious coincidences of view, never read him.[4] When recognition did dawn in Germany, it was primarily as a religious writer that he found readers. Even Heidegger, whose debt to Kierkegaard is considerable, suggests that his importance lies more in the religious aspect of the authorship than in any positive contribution his works make to philosophy as such.[5]

Kierkegaard (an earlier spelling of the Danish 'Kirkegaard', or 'Churchyard', but carrying in Danish as in English the primary connotation 'graveyard') was born in Copenhagen on 5 May 1813. Some of the relevant cultural statistics for that year would include the following. Hegel was forty-three years old and the year saw the publication of the second of the two books forming the section on 'Die objektive Logik' in his *Wissenschaft der Logik*. Schelling, whose lectures Kierkegaard was to attend in Berlin twenty-eight years later, was thirty-eight. Schelling, though Hegel's junior, had been an important influence in the latter's earlier development, and in his own later writings was to anticipate many of the themes of existentialist philosophy. Although a generation younger than Schelling, Kierkegaard was to survive him by only a year. Schopenhauer, in whose views Kierkegaard, not long before his death, was to see much in common with his own, was twenty-five. The year 1813 was also, incidentally, that of the birth of Richard Wagner, as well as of the father of his critic, Nietzsche, who was himself born in the year Kierkegaard published his first philosophical and psychological works. Karl Marx, who was to attend Schelling's lectures at about the same time as Kierkegaard, was five years younger. Feuerbach, to whom Marx owed much and whose work also occupied Kierkegaard, was eleven years older. In 1813 Hamann and Lessing, neither of them a professional philosopher but both important influences on Kierkegaard, had been dead for, respectively, twenty-five and thirty-two years. Fichte, the ethical idealist whose work interested Kierkegaard as a student, died the following year, while the previous year (to relieve the Teutonic landscape) had seen the birth of Charles Dickens. In 1813 John Stuart Mill was seven years old. Charles Darwin was four, and Kierkegaard was Herbert Spencer's senior by seven years.

Søren Aabye was the youngest of seven children born to Michael Pedersen Kierkegaard and his second wife Anne (formerly maid to the first wife who had died childless after only two years of marriage). A brother and a sister died before he was nine.[6] His two surviving sisters, a brother, and his mother all died not long before he was twenty-one (the brother in the USA). Søren came firmly to believe that he himself would not live to be more than thirty-three. He was born and brought up in Copenhagen, attending the strictly run Borgerdydskole (School of Civic Virtue), where he gained a reputation for sharpness of wit and a quick tongue, and later the university, where he enrolled in the autumn of 1830. His chosen subject was theology, but his studies included the liberal arts and science and in all he spent seven years as a student. The theological studies were not completed until the summer of 1840.

Before then, however, a number of significant events, which in most people's lives would be considered fairly normal occurrences, became for Kierkegaard the catalyst which set in motion his comparatively short but extraordinarily productive career as an ethical, philosophical, and religious writer. Three years previously, in 1837, he had met Regine Olsen. Regine, the daughter of a respected dignitary, was then only fourteen years old. Within three years, however, and after Kierkegaard's much delayed degree examination, they were engaged. To put these facts into perspective we must probe into the near and more distant past. A year subsequent to his meeting Regine, Kierkegaard's father had died, aged eighty-one. Until about three years prior to his father's death, Kierkegaard had been under the strict moral thumb of this elderly autodidact, a self-made man who had grown literally from serfdom to riches. (Kierkegaard senior's family had worked the land of their local priest in Jutland in a feudal arrangement which gave them their name, but the priest released Michael when he was twenty-one. By that time he had already moved to Copenhagen to work in an uncle's hosiery business, and later became a wealthy wholesaler of imported goods on his own account.) In 1835 something happened to release the son from the father's influence. Whatever it was — according to Kierkegaard himself it involved some profound disillusionment — the outcome was an attempt to recapture the spontaneity his contagiously melancholic father had wrested from him in early childhood[7] and, parallel to this, a growing disenchantment with Christianity, which by 1835 he was describing as 'debilitating'.[8] (There are interesting parallels in the life of John Stuart Mill, except that in his case the virtues brought to bear were intellectual and the doctrine put in question a secular one, namely Benthamism.) The rebellion clearly left a gap. In the August of that year he wrote that he needed an idea to 'live and die' for.[9] (Mill's quest led him to the world of poetry and higher feeling.) Freed from the immediate influence of his father, for the next three years Kierkegaard forsook his studies and led outwardly the life of a rich young man about town, aesthete, and wit. But entries in his journal from that time testify to a deepening despair, inner isolation, and lack of direction or definition of self.

> I have just now come from a party where I was its life and soul; witticisms streamed from my lips, everyone laughed and admired me, but I went away — yes, the dash should be as long as the radius of the earth's orbit _____
> _____ and wanted to shoot myself.[10]

From 1837 we read: 'Sadly my life is all too much in the subjunctive mood. Would to God that I had some indicative power.'[11] At twenty-four Kierkegaard was already tired of life;[12] evidently the attempt to recapture spontaneity had failed. In 1838, some years after freeing himself from the religious straitjacket his father had placed upon him, something the latter confided in him gave his depression a sombrely religious twist. His father told him how, as an eleven-year-old tending sheep on a windswept Jutland heath, he had once cursed God for the monotony, loneliness, and misery in which he was placed, and that he had come to regard the fortune that subsequently favoured him as a preparation for divine punish-ment.[13] The idea was transmitted to Kierkegaard that the deaths in his family (in a period of less than two-and-a-half years some few years earlier he had lost his mother, two brothers, and both his sisters) were indeed a divine punishment for the father's sin, to be visited also upon himself. But soon after this a recovery seems to have been anticipated. Two months before his father's death he writes of an 'indescribable joy', not directed at anything in particular, simply 'a full-bodied shout of the soul'.[14] The shout was uncharacteristic and short but heralded a reconciliation with his father, and soon after the latter's death Kierkegaard was saying that 'Christianity explains the world'.[15] It seems that at last he felt that he had a task to fulfil, a religious task to which he could devote his talents; the world had a place for him. In spite of inheriting a considerable fortune, enough to make the degree examinations so long postponed no longer a practical necessity, he decided to resume his studies and completed them within a year. Then came the engagement to Regine and all seemed set for a life of civic virtue. Kierkegaard was, in the phrase of his ethical spokes-man, Judge William in *Either/Or*, about to 'realize the universal', that is to say, to engage in human affairs by establishing a family and taking a position of responsibility. The year following the engagement was spent dutifully preparing for this civic future. Kierkegaard underwent the necessary practical training for a career in the Danish State Church, and, possibly with an academic career in mind, began work on his doctoral thesis (*The Concept of Irony with Constant Reference to Socrates*). He preached his first sermon.

The civic future was not to be. Well before the end of that year, in August 1841, Kierkegaard had returned Regine's engagement ring. By November, and not long after the successful defence of his thesis, the break was final and he was on his way to Berlin. He remained there for four months and attended Schelling's lectures. The background for this turn of events, if not obscure, is at least complex. The crux seems to be Kierkegaard's inability to fulfil the *personal* conditions of civic life, in particular those involved in being husband and father. There seems also to have been a growing need – perhaps even in the form of a sense of personal mission, though it is natural to suggest also a need to administer his own therapy – to put words to his own suffering, at any rate to apply his hyperactive mind to this difficulty of 'realizing the universal', a problem which he now linked with the profligacy of the life he had led previous to his 'recovery'. In retro-spect Kierkegaard even suggests that the period of the engagement

5

was in fact a kind of pause in a development begun before his father's death, and which he postponed by letting Regine's existence 'twine itself' around his.[16] At any rate there followed the flood of pseudonymous works, beginning in February 1843 with *Either/Or* (in two volumes, each of over 400 pages), followed eight months later by *Repetition* and *Fear and Trembling* – all three on the theme of realizing the universal – and at the same interval (in June 1844) by *Philosophical Fragments* and *The Concept of Anxiety*. These latter four were comparatively slim volumes, but then ten months later came the substantial *Stages on Life's Way*, followed by the 'dialectical' *tour de force, Concluding Unscientific Postscript*, with its 'humorous' treatment of the final stage by an author who sees that there is more to it than philosophy can account for. In parallel with this already impressive production Kierkegaard also published twenty-one religious ('edifying' and 'Christian') discourses under his own name.

This period of intense activity was broken by three brief spring visits to Berlin in 1843, 1845, and 1846. Immediately prior to the turn of the latter year, Kierkegaard provoked a feud with a satiric weekly called *Corsair* (*Corsaren*), the consequence of which was to reinforce his isolation. It originated in a reply to an attack on *Stages on Life's Way* by an ambitious young intellectual in a collection of criticism edited by the attacker himself, whom Kierkegaard knew privately also to be an occasional anonymous editor of *Corsair*. In a published reply Kierkegaard made known the critic's connection with this disreputable tabloid and in passing wondered, invitingly, why he himself had been singled out as the only author of note to be spared its abuse. (His work had in fact received what Kierkegaard may have regarded as the embarrassing compliment of being treated sympathetically in *Corsair*, whose main editor had some respect for him.) In the following months *Corsair* made amends with a vengeance, and by the summer of 1846 Kierkegaard, with his odd, jerky gait and growing reputation as an author of peculiar books, was an object of public ridicule. His journals reflect on his fate in respect of his reading public. While *Concluding Unscientific Postscript* received no reviews and 'sold perhaps fifty copies', with the result that its publication cost him 'including the fee for the proof-reading . . . about 400 to 500 rd. besides [the] time and trouble, yet', notes Kierkegaard,

> I am portrayed in a muckraking weekly which in the same little country has 3000 subscribers, and another journal (also with a wide circulation) *Flyveposten*, continued the discussion about my trousers.[17]

'They have poisoned the atmosphere', he wrote, and complained that he was now deprived of the relaxation of being 'alone in the crowd', so important to him in his 'depression and enormous effort'.[18]

The isolation persisted for the remainder of his life. In his final years Kierkegaard brought even greater notoriety upon himself by attacking the State Church and its more eminent functionaries with an acerbity which the editors of *Corsair* would have envied. This was the culmination of the final period of his activity, the period beginning, he said in retrospect, when he became conscious of being a religious author concerned with 'the individual'. The crucial event was the completion of the *Postscript*, a work which he described as a 'turning point' because in it he had first clearly stated '*the* problem' of his authorship, the problem of how to become a Christian[19] (or, in a version that better captures the polemical point, how to become a Christian *within Christendom*).[20]

In February 1846, Kierkegaard seems to have had second thoughts. While the *Corsair* affair was at its height and three weeks before the *Postscript* was to appear, a journal entry suggests that he had given up the idea of writing altogether and was once more planning to become a priest; he says it had 'by now been clear' to him, even 'for some time', that he should 'no longer be an author',[21] the only literary chore still to complete being the proof-reading of a review of a book called *Two Ages*, a review in which he may have felt that he had rounded off his work by spelling out its social and political implications. But whatever the actual sequence of events, by January of the following year he was dismissing these plans for the priesthood as a lapse of nerve and the author was soon in full spate again.[22] In that same year, 1847, he published *Edifying Discourses in Different Spirits* and the substantial *Works of Love*, followed in the spring of 1848 by *Christian Discourses* and in 1849 *The Lilies of the Field and the Birds of the Air* and *Three Discourses at Communion on Fridays*. There then followed the works of a new pseudonym, Anti-Climacus: *The Sickness unto Death* (1849) and *Practice in Christianity* (1850). These two works really form the coping-stones of the presentation of the general view expressed in the earlier pseudonymous writings. But they are natural coevals of the religious discourses among which they appeared (and more of which were to follow). They exploit the ambitious spiritual level of the discourses in order to cast new light on the themes of the earlier pseudonyms. *The Sickness unto Death* returns to the theme of *The Concept of Anxiety*, and *Practice in Christianity* to that of *Philosophical Fragments*.

In the next few years Kierkegaard wrote little until unleashing his culminating attack on the State Church, which he now saw clearly as the real root and bastion of spiritual complacency and compromise. During these years he lived in increasingly straitened circumstances and the remainder of his inheritance (it had amounted to something in excess of £200,000 in today's currency)[23] went to financing the final assault, amongst other things through the publication of his own broadsheet, *The Instant* (*Øieblikket*; for the significance of this title, see Chapter V, below). This went through nine issues before Kierkegaard fell ill. On 2 October 1855 he collapsed in the street and died in hospital on 11 November, probably of an infection of the lungs. Despite the earlier obsession with death,[24] or perhaps because of it − the extra time being 'borrowed' or even granted as a form of reprieve − its immediate certainty at the age of forty-two seems not to have depressed him. On the contrary, we are told that he expressed himself as happy and content at having accomplished something. He was 'sad' only that he could not 'share [his] happiness with anyone'.[25] When his boyhood friend Emil Boesen, now a pastor and the only member of the church he would allow to his sickbed, not excluding his own brother, asked him if there was anything he still had not said but wanted to, Kierkegaard first replied: 'No', but then said 'Yes, remember me to everyone. I was much attached to them all.' He added:

> tell them that my life is a great, and to others unknown and incomprehensible suffering; it all looked like pride and vanity, but it wasn't. I'm no better than others. I've said that and never anything else. I had my thorn in my flesh, and therefore I did not marry and could not take on an official position.[26]

Kierkegaard's funeral was the occasion of a demonstration led by his student nephew, who protested the church's insistence on officiating at the committal proceedings, contrary to the deceased's wishes.[27]

2 Paraphilosopher?

Readers may think this volume calls for a justification unnecessary in the case of its fellows in the series. Whatever his historical importance as cultural innovator or iconoclast, Søren Kierkegaard is not normally reckoned among the major philosophers. He is not even widely held to be a philosopher at all, or not a very good one, least of all by those for whom the hallmark of true philosophy is the systematic and economical statement of a well-defined thesis and supporting argument. Compared with a Hume, a Kant, or ever a Hegel, Kierkegaard may seem too volatile and prolix, even too passionate and ironic, a writer to be counted in the same company. He had a significant influence certainly, and for his pioneer statements and analyses of the central concepts of what came to be known as existentialism, meriting the scattered acknowledgements to be found in the works of those, such as Heidegger, Jaspers, and Sartre, who are indebted to him; but hardly a reputable philosopher in his own right.[28]

Kierkegaard nevertheless receives his accolades from philosophers. We read, for example, that 'Kierkegaard's brilliance as a writer and critic [of Hegelian idealism] more than makes amends for his magnificent philosophical failure'.[29] And one author, with Kierkegaard particularly in mind, has proposed a special category for thinkers of importance to philosophy which does not correlate this importance with academic or professional proficiency. He calls them 'paraphilosophical thinkers'. 'Kierkegaard came into his own, as an important paraphilosophical thinker, through our gradual recognition and use of his writings and life style in their bearing upon the living issues of our day.' That he was not a philosopher in the unqualified sense is due to his being primarily a religious thinker, and thus one whose 'chief orientation and activities lead him toward some other sphere of creativity'. Nevertheless, the judgment of history must be that the influence of his thought in reshaping 'methods and questions, concepts and living springs of evidence in modern philosophy' qualifies him as one of those 'men of genius' who 'fit uncomfortably into the minor and middling categories for formal philosophers'.[30]

Now it is all very well, and justified in Kierkegaard's case, to accord a thinker a qualified status within philosophy on the basis of his influence. But it would be a disservice both to history and to him to let the bestowal of the title 'paraphilosopher' settle the question of whether he was a philosopher, good or bad, also in an *un*qualified sense. In fact, the assumption that Kierkegaard's creative energies were chiefly directed towards a non-philosophical goal seems to me premature, even if initially it may seem obviously to be the case and Kierkegaard apparently admits as much himself. Of his own work he says, in retrospect, that it has required a 'poetic and philosophical nature [to be] set aside in order [for him] to become a Christian'.[31] We have already seen that the *Postscript* was a turning point which clearly identified the central questions of his work as being how to become a Christian. In the posthumously published *The Point of View of My Work as an Author* he even tells us that the entire production, almost from the very beginning, has been under divine guidance or management

(*Styrelsen*).[32] It seems quite clear, then, that Kierkegaard himself saw his primary role as being that of a religious author, according to criteria which he himself recognized prevented him also being classified as a philosophical one.

But the issue is less clear-cut. Clearly, it is not impossible for someone to be a philosophical thinker in virtue of the very same criteria which make it appropriate to call him a religious one. Furthermore, Kierkegaard had a special reason for denying that as a religious thinker he was also a philosophical one: it is a crucial tenet of his anti-Hegelianism that religion and ethics fall outside the realm of Hegelian science. Yet Kierkegaard's denial that he was a Hegelian in this respect does not force us to say that there is no useful sense at all in which *qua* religious thinker he might also be called a philosophical one. That is, even if in this one sense Kierkegaard would by no means want to be interpreted as combining a philosophical with a religious role, it might still be possible to see him as fulfilling some or other philosophical role precisely in respect of, and not as distinct from, his prior commitment to religion.

What philosophical role? One possibility is that of philosopher of religion. But if by that is meant one who applies himself to the general philosophical questions that arise in respect of religion as such and its concepts, Kierkegaard is not a philosopher *of* religion. Nor indeed would it normally be appropriate to describe a philosopher of religion as, without further ado, a religious thinker. This designation is usually reserved for someone who takes the truth, or at least the special significance, of a particular religious doctrine for granted, and not just as one of a set of religious contentions to be analysed and assessed. It is clear, furthermore, that Kierkegaard *is* indeed a religious thinker in this sense; that he does in fact argue on the assumption that it is correct, or in some way appropriate, to be interested in a particular religious doctrine, namely Christianity, or more specifically in the doctrine of incarnation that is distinctive of that religion. Philosophy is for him a method of clarifying an interest in just this doctrine, an interest that he thinks all people will have if only they see their situation aright, though also a method, indeed a polemical weapon, for undermining beliefs about the nature of religion that dissipate this interest by distorting what it is that he finds significant about that doctrine.

It seems, therefore, that whatever basis there is for calling Kierkegaard a philosopher must be found in specific features of the grounds there are for correctly calling him a religious thinker in the above sense. As to what those specific features are, one suggestion might be that perhaps Kierkegaard's concern for

10

religion was 'philosophical' in the popular sense in which any insightful and articulate preoccupation with ultimate questions deserves that title. But clearly that would not be enough. It is certainly true to say that Kierkegaard's adult life was an uninterrupted preoccupation with matters of good and evil, of life, death, and eternity, and also that these are the unifying themes of his writings. But this alone cannot warrant the characterization of the thought-products of his main 'sphere of creativity' as contributions to the development of philosophy as such. And of course, even if there were such warrant, one would need further justification for assigning him a similar standing within the ranks of the accredited contributors. There are a number of requirements that have to be satisfied, not least formal ones. Thus, to count as a significant contributor to philosophy at all, a thinker should have articulated his insights in a way (for instance, with a surface texture open enough to lay bare, but not so open as to dissipate, an underlying logical and argumentational structure) that makes it possible to offer them in propositional form for systematic scrutiny and appraisal. In this respect Kierkegaard's credentials will strike many as very shaky indeed. In sharp contrast to the above-board, scientific approach now expected of the professional philosopher, and just as totally removed from the orderly aphoristic style of permitted exceptions like Wittgenstein, Kierkegaard's philosophical writings seem oddly casual, and not clearly distinguishable, in either theme or style, from the remainder of his heterogeneous corpus of literary works, psychological treatises, and moral and religious discourses. Indeed, what is generally considered the philosophical 'core' of his work consists of the pseudonymous writings of a self-styled humorist, which even suggests that Kierkegaard does not intend us to take this part of the corpus seriously. Of course, as the category of 'paraphilosophical thinker' is intended to allow, neither this nor the literary and rhetorical style of the writings as a whole need be taken to entail any denial of the philosophical relevance of the corpus in whole or part. But they do tend to indicate a basis for denying that Kierkegaard's contribution to philosophy has been a philosophical contribution, and that therefore the description of Kierkegaard as a paraphilosopher is substantially correct.

There is, however, another suggestion. Although philosophy for Kierkegaard was a limited enterprise whose terms of reference did not extend to the solution of the ultimate questions which concerned him, we are, of course, nowadays well prepared to accept that the view that philosophy is limited is a philosophical view. Or better, a metaphilosophical view. Unlike paraphilosophy which carries the connotation of a project 'beside' or 'beyond' philosophy,

11

metaphilosophy takes philosophy itself as its province and has just as good reason to be called philosophy as has, say, philosophy of religion, politics, logic, or whatever. Thus, although Kierkegaard's thought as a whole is correctly regarded as being directed towards a *para*philosophical goal, it does not follow, nor is it true, that it has no philosophical aspect or indeed basis. What the alternative suggestion also indicates is why, although setting limits to philosophy, Kierkegaard's work can be regarded as containing philosophy within those limits. It does so because, although philosophy on Kierkegaard's terms is a limited enterprise, it is also – in a sense that modern philosophers should be well able to grasp – one with its own functions. Finally, the suggestion also explains why, in respect of what ancillary ends philosophy is suited to serve, it is understandable that the style of the philosophy in Kierkegaard should diverge so conspicuously from that normally required of 'good' philosophy. Which is not, however, to deny that the philosophy has suffered from Kierkegaard's preoccupation with a paraphilosophical goal.

3 Preview

To give substance to the above, and as background for the course of the discussion to follow, it will be useful to give a preliminary sketch of the principal components of what we may take to be Kierkegaard's metaphilosophical position. They are given here together with some slight indications both of the more obvious objections and of ways of responding to them.[33]

First, there is a basic epistemological thesis, a negative thesis, to the effect (1) that essential truth not only lies outside our theoretical grasp, but can be accepted as truth only in defiance of absolute standards of rationality. To this the rationally responsible reply is surely: so much the worse for essential truth; the proper conclusion to draw from (1) is that essential truth is a myth, and it is only to be deplored that so luminously intelligent a writer as Kierkegaard clung, for whatever personal and perhaps psychoanalysable reasons, to this form of expression. Kierkegaard's rejoinder would be based on another, though again not very promising, thesis: that (2) human beings are 'infinitely' concerned for their own eternal blessedness; in other words for the existence of some cosmological state of affairs – a theoretically and practically possible state of affairs – the (in both senses) 'obtaining' of which would imply that the merely finite and apparently accidental nature of human life are in some sense illusions.

So what, replies the critic. Even if this psychological claim were true — and surely in our own day it would encounter massive dis-confirmation — the correct philosophical response would be to deplore the fact as a sign of human frailty and self-deception, and at least take steps to ensure that it was untrue of oneself.

Kierkegaard would reply that, on the contrary, (3) it is precisely in trying to exempt oneself from (2) that one betrays human frailty and self-deception. That is to say, first, the fact that there can be no objective basis for believing that the said cosmological state of affairs obtains should not itself be accepted as a reason for believing that it does not; and second, to accept it as that would be a sign of frailty and self-deception — in short, the proper course, in spite of (1), is to retain the aspiration of (2).

For the present purposes we can point briefly to two factors that may help to undermine the easy assumption that (3) is an entirely arbitrary thesis.

First, (2) itself is not intended as an ordinary psychological claim. For instance, that people — even an overwhelming number — claimed exemption from it would not necessarily count against its truth — not necessarily even in their own cases, since Kierke-gaard identifies among those who reject the aspiration of (2) typical personality configurations which harbour its concealed acceptance. But even if the aspiration were genuinely and widely absent, this would not show that it was not a 'proper' aspiration for a human individual to have. It *might* be argued, more or less convincingly, that the state in which a person has the aspiration is less a state of weakness and self-deception than one in which he lacks it. Which is not, however, to say that certain states in which he has some form or version of the aspiration might not be states of weakness and self-deception.

Second, and taking up this latter point, positivists (to use a convenient label for those who oppose Kierkegaard on (3)) often advertise their own doctrines precisely as cures for socially de-structive human weakness and self-deception. They point, for example, to the undoubted barbarities perpetrated in the names of religion and romantic idealism, and suggest that these — or even, though less plausibly, that *such* — barbarities would not have occurred had the corresponding aspirations been absent. But Kierkegaard, too, would hold that the aspirations people have actually held were destructive. His difference with the positivists is not in his diagnosis but in his cure. For him the solution of these ills lies not in removing the ideals of which actual historical beliefs have almost always, in Kierkegaard's view, been the disastrously inadequate expressions, but in pressing on to a more adequate conception of them — to a genuinely ethical form of practice. If

13

this could be backed by the suggestion that the positivist cure is designed to remove but one symptom of the disease and not the disease itself, who would say that *that* was an altogether arbitrary claim? Or that in criticizing his contemporaries for their com-placency Kierkegaard would have shown deeper insight into long-term human interests had he advocated root and branch removal of the ideals upon which this complacency focuses?

The next thesis is that (4) Christianity is the only doctrine that encompasses the possibility of the individual's eternal blessedness. It says that if we accept (3), i.e. the aspiration of (2), then the necessary conditions of that aspiration's fulfilment are provided exclusively by basic tenets of Christian belief. 'Exclusively' is strong, and in trying to justify Kierkegaard here his apologists must steer clear of the tautology-generating hazards of writing too much that is specially Christian into the aspiration. If there is to be any philosophical point in (4) it seems that this thesis must be based on claims about the general form rather than the specific content of Christian doctrine: claims, for example, to the effect that Christian doctrine, properly conceived, has the form of an objectivist but non-intuitionist ethics, in which the content of true ethical judgments (or the moral law) is given by an outside and uncertifiable authority; that the content of these judgments is only properly grasped, or the true ethical situation only obtained, in a special form of practice the exemplar of which has been provided; and that that form of practice, the true ethical situation, constitutes the fulfilment of the aspiration — eternal blessedness — referred to in (2) and (3). If Christianity can be construed in this way as a form of Kantianism in which the highest good is conceived as coincidental with moral practice, then the contention of (4) may be narrowed down to the genuinely philosophical issue of the indispensability of the specifically Christian amendment to Kantian ethics: the idea that moral content is identified by concrete example rather than by an abstract moral principle. Further, it would indicate a plausible interpretation of 'eternal blessedness' in the context of Kierkegaard's writings, as well as the form in which the 'infinite' concern for that state could be claimed to be a strength rather than a weakness.

Then finally, a fifth component. This is the doctrine of the aesthetic, ethical, and religious stages. It is a theory of the develop-ment of a 'genuine' individual, or a self-integrated, autonomous person who retains his infinite concern for eternal blessedness in clear and full realization of the fact and implications of the truth of (1). In lifting himself out of the aesthetic into the ethical stage he achieves integration by taking on duties, roles, responsibilities, by virtue of which he first presents a 'self' to the world at large. Then in the religious stage he realizes that if his conscientious life is to have moral content, its goal cannot be *his* goals, that is, temporal goals designed to satisfy the self, but infinite goals in which self-satisfaction, including any self-satisfying form of eternal blessedness, plays no part. The genuine individual is therefore one who not only fully realizes there is no basis for accepting the only doctrine that offers him this 'highest good', but also understands that to secure this good he must so effectively remove all vestiges of self-regard from the motivational complex out of which he acts that even the goal of eternal blessedness itself must provide no incentive. In short, virtue must be its own reward.

In the light of these five components let us now review the obstacles we mentioned earlier to Kierkegaard's enrolment as a philosopher. One was that he is primarily a religious thinker. But we can see that for someone whose position is that outlined by (1) and (4) the religious question that in fact forms the basis of his thought — how to become a Christian — must be a very relevant topic; in the special senses suggested for these terms on the basis of (1) and (4), becoming a Christian is the necessary and sufficient condition of grasping essential truth. Whether the theses in their turn are acceptable is another matter, but at least no reader of Kierkegaard's philosophical pseudonym, Johannes Climacus, can accuse Kierkegaard of neglecting to state and by all means clarify the meaning and importance of these and other assumptions and principles which form the background of his activity as a writer — something that cannot always be said even of the most professional philosophers.

Another obstacle was the general absence of any systematic, i.e. ordered, statement of thesis and argument. But Kierkegaard's critic has to stress 'systematic', and to interpret the word in a rather strict way, for thesis and argument are by no means lacking and in the longer term Kierkegaard's presentation is very systematic. But let us also ask ourselves what purpose the, in a strict sense, systematic statement of thesis and argument might serve for a philosopher whose position is the one outlined. Certainly not the establishment of essential truths, such as the existence of God or the content of the moral law. These are excluded by (1). But then what about rational self-criticism? We briefly invoked the name of Kant. If Kierkegaard's ethics is as close to Kant's as the above outline suggested, why do we find nothing in Kierkegaard corresponding to Kant's attempt to establish the rational basis of a metaphysic of morals? Surely if one believes, as in fact Kierkegaard claims, that 'ethical reality is the only reality', one should at the very least try to show that the notion of ethics makes good sense. Here there are two points to make on Kierkegaard's behalf. First, Kierkegaard seems to have excluded Kant (as he also generally excludes the Greeks) from his attack on 'philosophy' — not, of course, because he did not regard Kant as a philosopher, but because the attack was directed at the 'theocentric' and therefore 'fantastic' turn taken by philosophy since it left, as Kierkegaard puts it, Kant's 'honest way'.[34] Why then did not Kierkegaard go that way himself? Not necessarily, I think, because he regarded Kant's labours as misdirected in their own terms, but rather because, on his own different conclusions about the ethical, he must certainly have seen them as seriously deficient. Which brings us to the second point. Kant's moral philosophy lacks what since Hegel we have called the 'historical' or 'dialectical' dimension — we could equally call it the genetic aspect. This is partly because Kant's theory allows the moral component in an action to be identified by applying a general formula available in principle to anyone at any time. But partly also because of Kant's exclusively theoretical interests as a writer on ethics: he did not see it as part of his task to cultivate a *sense* of morality in his reader. This, however, is precisely what Kierkegaard did see as his task, since on his view genuine identification of the moral (and the true) can only occur in properly moral practice, and that is an outcome of a process of self-integration and moral growth. The various steps of this growth are plotted in the doctrine of the stages. The significance of (5) is its description of the birth and self-education of the ethical subject, relating the forms of existence characteristic of the various stages of development to one another in a dialectical progression with parallels in that depicted by Hegel in his *Phenomenology*.

The discussion in the following chapters will show in what way Kierkegaard himself conceives his writings to be the appropriate means for the task at hand. Here, however, it will be useful to summarize the role of the four main categories of the writings. First, there are what Kierkegaard himself refers to as his 'aesthetic' works. Including notably his early literary masterpiece *Either/Or*, these are expressions 'from the inside' of the forms of existence appropriate to the genesis of a person willing to make something of himself in terms of roles, duties, and responsibilities, yet without having yet clearly seen what the ethical as such is and demands. Since this genesis occurs not in thought alone but in living practice it cannot be brought about by treatises or drill books. The reader of the 'aesthetic' works is being confronted with the only kind of enlightenment that can help him, the actual choice of remaining where he is — with attendant consequences, still 'from the inside' — or of literally pulling himself together ethically. The aesthetic works are discussed in Chapter III.

Second, there are the 'dialectical' works of Johannes Climacus — though acknowledged as Kierkegaard's own as under his 'editor-ship'. These are aimed at a philosophically literate audience and attempt with considerable art, irony, *and* argument to present the anti-Hegelian substance of the position outlined in (1) to (5) in such a way that it is genuinely understood as an alternative to Hegel and not as a position that Hegelians might be tempted to judge or appropriate in their own terms. *Philosophical Fragments* is Kierkegaard's introduction of his position to an Hegelian audience. As we have already noted, the *Postscript* (to *Fragments*) is his first clear presentation, in fact analysis, of the central problem (becoming a Christian). These works are discussed in Chapter IV.

Third, there are the psychological works, also pseudonymous. These systematically map the attitudes and personality types corresponding to successively unambiguous and conscious re-nunciations of the choice of the good. Their aim is apparently to provide the faltering individual with a diagnosis of his present condition, and a prediction as to its further course if the ethical choice is not either made or resumed. These works are the fruit of Kierkegaard's own odyssey in the realms of anxiety and despair. They are discussed in Chapter V.

Fourth, there are the non-pseudonymous and moralizing discourses published parallel with the pseudonymous works. Here Kierkegaard assumes his reader has accepted the ethical alternative, and the author drops his pseudonymity in order to communicate directly on a mutually understood topic of ethics, namely sin, in the mood proper to that topic, namely seriousness — perhaps we should say moral earnestness as opposed to what Kierkegaard considers the inappropriately contemplative and thereby trivializing attitude of a 'philosophy' of ethics. The aim of these works is to show their reader how easy it is, even having adopted the ethical goal, to deceive oneself with regard both to the nature of the goal and to the extent to which one's actual moral practice approxi-mates it. These works are discussed in Chapters VI and VII.

However much in Kierkegaard's work may deserve the title 'philosophy', and in whatever sense or senses, there is certainly justice in the allegation that Kierkegaard is not a 'good' philosopher. He read carelessly and wrote rapidly. Witticism often does for argument, and the arguments themselves often dissolve in finesse and entertainment. His own assessment, that to pursue the course

17

that had been set for him he had been compelled to set aside a philosophical nature (as well as a poetic one), if true, suggests that although Kierkegaard was capable of constructing his works with greater attention to the availability of their logical structure and argumentational role, in the event he has sacrificed these philosophical virtues to the urgencies of his own paraphilosophical goals — as well, perhaps, as to the pleasures of indulgence in his imaginative and literary gifts as a writer.

If so, our task here may be seen as that of developing that side of Kierkegaard's work which, in the light of what for him were more compelling motivations, he himself found it inexpedient to develop further. Developing it, be it noted, in the photographer's rather than the constructor's sense. If successful, we should be bringing to light a latent philosophical image which is already there, not 'reconstructing' the parts into a philosophical portrait which Kierkegaard himself would not recognize as his own. A first step in this task is to 'fix' the Hegelian framework which Kierkegaard aims to undermine, but from which he nevertheless borrows the philosophical terminology and conceptual tools with which to do so.

II

Turning Hegel Outside-in

The unhappy person is one who has his ideal, the
content of his life, the fullness of his consciousness,
the essence of his being, in some manner outside
himself.[1]

1 Preliminary

In a paper delivered to a Hegel congress in 1933, Jean Wahl pointed
out how deeply influenced the young Hegel (of the *Early Theological Writings*) had been, as Kierkegaard was to be later, by the
Sturm und Drang and by Hamann.[2] In fact, according to Wahl, the
young Hegel was 'more of a pre-Kierkegaardian than a pre-Hegelian'.
But despite the irony in Hegel's having been a precursor of the
'most violent anti-Hegelianism ever formulated', Wahl detects even
in Hegel's early years an 'abyss which separates them': 'in the
young Hegel', he says, 'there is a sense of . . . victory, a note of
triumphant joy not to be found in Kierkegaard'; 'Kierkegaard',
says Wahl, 'is an unhappy consciousness.'[3]

Kierkegaard would not have liked the description. The label is
Hegel's and to be called an unhappy consciousness is already, at
least for Hegelians, to be placed in the 'System' Kierkegaard so
violently opposed; it is to diagnose the condition it ascribes to him
as one whose solution is found in *philosophy*. In Hegel's
Phenomenology the thought-paradigm (*Gestalt*) called 'the unhappy
consciousness' is the one out of which speculative reason is supposed to emerge to assure consciousness of its oneness with all
being, thereby resolving its unhappiness. Kierkegaard's main
objection to Hegel is precisely the latter's attempted vindication of

19

the idea that resolving the unhappiness, or equivalently, attaining the traditional goal of a highest good, is to be identified as a philosophical event, as a property of the world of ideas.

How are we to understand such fundamental differences? Are we to interpret the mature Hegel's writings and those of his most violent opponent as nothing but divergent expressions of two fundamentally opposed natures — an irrepressible optimism on one side of the abyss and an incurable melancholy, a soul in torment, on the other, each reconstructing the world after its own image? Or does one of these natures provide its owner with a better vantage-point than the other; so that one of them captures more of reality? If so, which? The optimistic, healthy-minded Hegel, or the sickly, self-centred Kierkegaard? And on what common ground could this be decided, or even argued?

More relevant than either of these considerations in the present context, are certain expositional advantages afforded by Wahl's characterization of Kierkegaard as an unhappy consciousness — if it is correct, as will be argued in the following section. The advantages of its being so are three in number. First, if Kierkegaard, in his person and writing, really does represent the position Hegel calls the unhappy consciousness, then there is a sense in which the two fundamentally opposed philosophies do in fact share a common ground: they are agreed about the general structure of the unhappy consciousness and *can* be agreed about the range of attitudes accommodated by that structure; the disagreement concerns the framework in which the unhappy consciousness is to be embedded if there is to be a solution to which it stands as the problem. Hegel sets the unhappy consciousness in a philosophical framework because the solution he envisages is, in the peculiarly Hegelian way, a conceptual one. Not accepting such a solution, Kierkegaard offers his paraphilosophical 'framework' instead, in which the solution promised is practical. Whatever conclusions are reached about this solution, at least the shared ground allows us to see more clearly where the differences begin and the real issue lies. Second, the conciseness and detail of Hegel's account of the unhappy consciousness can be used with advantage as a blueprint for assembling the *disjecta membra* of Kierkegaard's own much less systematic presentation into something like the lineaments of a co-ordinated and distinctive philosophical point of view. Finally, the comparison with Hegel brings to the fore something which too much attention to Kierkegaard's nearly always critical remarks on Hegel can easily lead one to lose sight of: namely that although Kierkegaard limits philosophy (or 'dialectic') to an ancillary role in relation to his paraphilosophical ends, the role he intends for the paraphilosophy itself is as embracing in its scope as that intended by Hegel for his philosophy.

This raises a further point. As a quotation in the previous chapter testifies, it is sometimes supposed that the main value of Kierkegaard's thought lies in its criticism of Hegel. This can have an unfortunate result. When it is found that Kierkegaard, either by ignorance or wilfully, frequently misses Hegel's point and has to be classified as a 'bad' philosopher in this regard, the supposed absence of any other significant regard can easily lead one to lose interest in him as a philosophical writer altogether. But the supposition is wrong, as is the frequent assumption that all one ever need know about Kierkegaardian philosophy is to be found in the works of the pseudonym Johannes Climacus, perhaps supplemented by the two main psychological works (*The Concept of Anxiety* and *The Sickness unto Death*). It is true that these four contain in concentrate most of the main ideas (in fact, the *Postscript* alone offers a synoptic view of the whole range of Kierkegaard's thought); and it is also true that in these works we come as close as we ever do in Kierkegaard to finding clear conceptual statements couched in a terminology suited to philosophically educated readers. But to limit oneself to these is to gain a false impression of the breadth and unity of Kierkegaard's writings. It is therefore important to appreciate that the point of view from which these works are written is indeed intended to have the same scope as Hegel's, and to provide solutions to the same range of questions concerning human life and society. To do justice to Kierkegaard we have to take the full compass of his writings into account. Of the forty or so volumes of the collected works and papers none can truthfully be said to be irrelevant to a presentation of his thought. Some, however, are clearly more suited than others as sources for a systematic presentation. For this purpose I have reduced the focal literature here to approximately ten separate titles.

Finally, before embarking on a brief (and therefore regrettably abstract) outline of Hegel's account of the unhappy consciousness, it is worth remarking that although Kierkegaard shows (in the passage from which the present chapter's motto is taken)[4] that he was familiar with that account, he never points to any parallels between it and the theoretical framework of his own writings. There is a plausible explanation for this. In Hegel's philosophy the unhappy consciousness defines a situation that is inherently problematical; its solution, happiness, requires a change in the framework. For Kierkegaard, however, the framework Hegel uses to describe the unhappy consciousness is the one that has to provide the solution. The happy consciousness has to be put together with pieces that for Hegel, however you arrange them, inevitably spell 'unhappiness' and 'problem'. Thus one good reason why Kierkegaard might not want such parallels to be drawn is that in Hegelian eyes the concept of the unhappy consciousness implies that unless a person transcends the religious viewpoint he cannot be happy.

2   The unhappy consciousness

Hegel's *Phenomenology of Spirit* (*Phänomenologie des Geistes* (1807), sometimes translated as 'The Phenomenology of Mind') describes a quasi-logical succession of thought paradigms, beginning with immediate experience and culminating in an all-embracing science. In this notion of an all-embracing science Hegel offers us an ideal picture of man as universal self-consciousness. He presents it as the conclusion of a logical sequence recapitulating the actual development of conscious spirit. Many philosophers, even – perhaps particularly – those who reject the picture, have found a rich source of ideas in Hegel's analyses in the *Phenomenology* of what he calls 'universal [forms] of the world-spirit'.[5] Although attention has been mainly focused on Hegel's brilliantly imaginative discussion of the so-called dialectic of master and slave, his accounts of the forms which he calls 'Stoicism', 'scepticism', and 'the unhappy consciousness' are if anything even richer sources of philosophical analysis, and in their way just as compelling.

The unhappy consciousness is 'the consciousness of self as a dual-natured, merely contradictory being'.[6] This paradigm follows upon scepticism in a kind of logical succession, and scepticism is preceded in its turn by Stoicism, which represents the form of freedom characteristic of emergence from the state of bondage in which the slave has been bound in all externals to the master. Common to scepticism and Stoicism is that the terms of the dual nature are not posed consciously in opposition to one another, but are taken in turn (inevitably in vain) as *the* foundation of consciousness. In their cases, therefore, the contradiction does not emerge. In the sceptical paradigm, for example, which is the one immediately preceding and leading into the unhappy consciousness, consciousness 'keeps the poles of . . . its contradiction apart' through 'lack of thought about itself'.[7] The unhappy consciousness distinguishes itself as that transparent mode of consciousness for which 'both [terms] are [seen to be] equally necessary and contradictory'.[8]

What is the contradiction? In abstract terms it is the simultaneous attribution of the properties 'infinite' and 'finite' to one and the

22

same thing, namely consciousness. But this answer does not take us very far. To understand what the terms imply, as well as why it should be thought necessary to attribute either or both of the corresponding properties, we must briefly retrace our philosophical steps and rehearse the reasons why Hegel thought his own philosophy an improvement upon that of Kant.

By 'finite' Hegel means in the traditional way 'delimited'; not only temporally, in the sense in which 'temporal' is opposed to 'eternal', but in the general sense of being delimited in respect of, or definable in exclusion from, and in at least that sense in opposition to, other things. Being finite in this sense is essential to being a distinguishable something subject to the logical laws of exclusion — what Hegel elsewhere calls the either—or of the understanding.[9] Correlative to this idea of the systematic differentiation of things among themselves is the idea of a whole, the totality of differentiated things not itself differentiated from anything. By 'infinite' Hegel means this totality, but not conceived as just an aggregation. If it were that the whole would be merely adventitious: there would be no reason why it might not have been, or later become, a different whole. In short, the whole would simply be a function of the parts. Idealist philosophy conceives the parts as dependent upon the whole, the latter providing their rationale, the clue to their true nature, possibilities, and correct ordering, and to the fact that they could not be more or less or otherwise. The idea of the whole is the scholastic notion of the conditioning but unconditioned ground, or principle of the unity, of all things. Hegel's 'infinite' is a variant of this notion of the limitless as the absolute or self-contained and self-explanatory totality. What distinguishes Hegel's notion from the traditional one is that the self-containedness and self-explanatoriness it appeals to are not timeless Platonic characteristics accessible at any time to pure thought; they evolve *in* time and their evolution in time constitutes the course of history, which Hegel regards as the process of the embodiment or incarnation of the 'absolute mind'.

Hegel saw Kant's philosophy as crucially defective because, according to it, the principle of unity remains outside the reach of reason. Kant opposes the finite to the infinite because he identifies the finite world with the world of sense experience and conceives the 'ground' of the finite as something that falls outside that experience. Kant's *a priori* concepts of reason have no empirical reference. His notion of the Absolute, therefore, as that of the totality of the *a priori* conditions of empirical experience, is of a totality which thought is incapable of grasping, even if, as Kant believes, thought cannot help but be motivated by an ambition to do so. Hegel complained of the tradition represented by Kant ('the metaphysic of subjectivity') that for it,

> [t] he world as thing is transformed into the system of phenomena or of affections of the subject, and actualities believed in, whereas the Absolute as [proper] matter and absolute object of Reason is transformed into something that is absolutely beyond rational cognition.[10]

Kant's distinction between appearances or phenomena and their cognitively inaccessible ground − that in which the objects of discourse are 'things-in-themselves' − categorically excludes the possibility of things appearing to consciousness in their natures or essences. Given that phenomena are finite, and natures or essences have to be grounded in the infinite in the senses explained, it is logically impossible for the predicate 'infinite' to apply to objects of experience. It is indeed contradictory to assume that they do.

Similarly, then, with the contradiction of the unhappy consciousness. There is on the one hand a finite particular, the individual human being in its 'separate existence', and on the other a universal, its objective 'ground' or essence. Only here it is not the essence or nature of things or events in the physical world which escapes rational cognition, but the essence or nature of the cognizer. The finite particular is the self conceived as 'a particular individual', also characterized by Hegel as the 'protean changeable'; while the infinite universal is the self's conception of its own essence or true nature, or, correspondingly, of itself as 'the simple unchangeable'.[11] (The opposition between 'unchangeable' and 'changeable' corresponds to the traditional distinction, allied to the infinite/finite distinction, between eternity and temporality, the latter concept implying successiveness and so exposure to change.) The problem for the unhappy consciousness is that it finds itself unable to dispense with either of these opposing conceptions of itself.

It might seem at first glance that the difficulty here was simply a special case of the general logical problem of the relation of particular to universal. Thus, granting the observation (Plato's) that universals are immutable in a sense in which the things exemplifying them are not, Hegel's unhappy consciousness might be conceived simply as the special case in which the particular asks the question of itself and finds that no answer is conceivable.

This, however, does less than justice to the problem Hegel is describing. The question is not how, in the case of a particular exemplifying those universals it undoubtedly does exemplify, i.e. as a human individual of this or that character, standing, and circumstance, these or any such exemplifications are logically possible — as specific conjunctions of particular changeable and universal unchangeable. The question facing the unhappy consciousness is rather, how, as a 'protean' particular *merely* but already exemplifying this, that, or the other universal, or exemplifying mutably a succession of universals, it can conceive itself, in its entirety, as something *immutable*. The notion of 'universal' here has the Aristotelian sense of 'essence' or 'nature', and not simply of 'general characteristic as such'. The essence of something in this sense is, roughly speaking, the determinate (and determinable) content of the concept under which something is identified as what, actually or potentially, it is 'in itself'. The essence of a thing, in Hegel's usage, is said to 'transcend' the particulars whose essence is; and they, by 'realizing' their essence, by the same token transcend their 'mere' particularity, in two complementary senses: first, in conforming to their universal natures they cease to be merely independent particulars and become also instantiations or examples; and, second, by the same token they become 'one' with all those particulars with which they share a universal nature.

According to this concept of essence or nature, it is essential that, whatever historical processes and changes are involved in realizing an essence or nature, the latter itself cannot change. Essences are objectively given in the order (though not necessarily, or immediately, or all at once in the discernible nature) of things. If it is found that as a matter of historical fact our conceptions or general characterizations of things change, these changes are never to be construed as changes of essence. At best they can only represent a greater profundity in our discernment of essences, or a progressive conformity of things (and selves) *to* their true essences. And so with diversity in general: variety and differentiation do not of themselves imply a corresponding complexity, multiplication, or volatilization of natures; they are the surface manifold which thought must penetrate in order to grasp the unifying concepts which underlie and generate all diversity and change. If we equate surface diversity here with 'accident' in the traditional sense, and the underlying principle of unity with 'essence', or 'substance', we can say that for Hegel what thought aims to grasp are the irreducible, or 'simple', thus unchangeable, essences comprising the transformational possibilities to which surface diversity and mutability in fact correspond.

This now invites an alternative interpretation of the problem facing the unhappy consciousness. The problem might seem to be that of penetrating beneath the personal diversity and change in order to find the principle underlying them. But this is not how

25

Hegel characterizes the problem. According to Hegel, the unhappy consciousness does not have to *find* the principle, because it already has it in its grasp. Or rather, it knows what its own immutable essence is, for this Hegel believes is already contained in the idea of its being a consciousness; consciousness, says Hegel, recognizes that it is '*itself* a simple, hence unchangeable, consciousness', and, because of this, is 'aware that this consciousness is its own essence'.[12] Here Hegel seems to be arguing that in all the diversity of consciousness's modes (and objects), or what corresponds to the 'protean changeable', there is one thing that does not change and that is the particular consciousness itself as the subject pole of thought and experience. The notion of the identity of consciousness here sounds not unlike Kant's *formal* unity of consciousness, the transcendental apperception which, we note, Kant too describes as a 'pure original *unchangeable* consciousness'.[13]

The problem of the unhappy consciousness, then, is not that it has no idea of its immutable essence but that it cannot conceive this essence as being the principle of the unity of its unchangeable, finite self. This is because the unchangeable aspect cannot (yet) be conceived as belonging within the same category as the finite changeable; there is no way in which this consciousness can conceive the unity of its changeableness in the changeableness itself. It can try neither, like Hegel's stoic, to seek its freedom by 'steadfastly withdrawing from the bustle of existence . . . into the simple essentiality of thought', nor, like the sceptic, to deny that there is an objective, determinable reality (or 'other') from which to withdraw in the first place and *a fortiori* any relationship, cognitive or otherwise, in which consciousness itself stands to such a reality.[14] It recognizes both aspects, its 'essential' capacity to determine natures (including its own) and its merely particular existence, as inescapably its own, but is compelled to conceive them as incompatible. In effect, it cannot conceive the transcendence of its own particularity except as loss of that particularity, knowing full well that as an inescapable particular existence it cannot lose it.

An individual aware of itself as being merely particular and (perhaps thereby) able to entertain the thought of its transcendence of this clearly deficient status, obviously seeks to translate this thought into reality. For Hegel the attempt to do so involves a 'movement' (*Bewegung*) of thought, which if successful amounts to a 'scientific' progression from one view of particular things, of their confinement to their particularity, to another in which their particularity is transcended. But because the unhappy consciousness lacks the conceptual wherewithal to take this crucial step, that is to make the movement whereby its finite character can be 'comprehended' in the thought of its infinite nature, it postulates an 'unattainable beyond' into which it projects the ideal it seeks, and thus comes by the notion of an eternal and infinite God; in its intellectual despair consciousness, or that part of its nature which recognizes itself as the eternal and unchangeable in man, is 'forced to take flight to the Deity', as Hegel expresses it elsewhere.[15] However, since this deity represents the fulfilment of the individual's goal, but is at the same time so conceived as to be absolutely distinct from the untranscendable individual, in its enforced flight *to* the deity, consciousness in fact places the particular and finite part of its nature at an infinite remove *from* that deity. Before this God, consciousness in its finite aspect becomes as nothing, and because the 'infinite' aspect lacks the *conceptual* means to repair the breach, *its* relationship to the ideal, instead of being one of 'pure thinking' is only 'a movement *towards* thinking', i.e. a mere attitude of respect for, and so 'devotion' (*Andacht*) to, pure thinking, but not an actual exercise of it. Hegel calls it

> a musical thinking that does not get as far as the Notion . . . [a] pure inner feeling [which] does indeed come into possession of its object [which, however] does not make its appearance in conceptual form . . . as something . . . comprehended, and appears therefore as something alien.[16]

Hegel thinks this alienation can be overcome in *thought*. But how? One might suspect that if, as was suggested, the unchangeable aspect is analogous to Kant's formal 'I think', the solution might lie in that notion. But no, Kant's conception of the unity of consciousness combines the variety of 'representations' into the experience of a single (Kant also says: 'simple') 'I' only in a formal way. Kant's 'I think' is merely a logical condition of there being a consciousness at all. What Hegel's unhappy consciousness requires is a principle of the unity of consciousness as a concretely embodied consciousness, identified by the finite, changeable characteristics it possesses as a particular living being. Where Kant's solution puts the principle of the unity of these characteristics outside the range of human knowledge (so that it manifests itself only in the form of rules), what Hegel's unhappy consciousness seeks is a grasp of the unity of its actions, achievements, and satisfactions *within* this changing, finite world.

How does Hegel think this unity can be grasped? In effect by a simple inversion of Kant's conception of the relationship of experience to the objective world, of appearances to things-in-themselves. Instead of the absolute ground of all possible experience lying outside the range of human cognition, Hegel's 'mind' discovers that it is itself the ground. Hegel refers to this as consciousness's discovering itself as reason.[17] Kant's absolute, the conditioning but unconditioned ground of all appearances, is related to appearances only as their transcendental condition; it is not to be found in the appearances themselves. Accordingly, no knowledge of things as they are can be gained from their appearances. For human cognition, the 'infinite' and 'finite' for ever exclude one another. Hegel's philosophy of spirit is based on the contrary assumption that it *is* possible to discern the essences of things in their appearances. The discovery of this possibility is the emergence in consciousness of the idea of the 'true' infinity (*die wahrhafte Unendlichkeit*) which is not 'a negation of a finite' but an aspect in virtue of which infinite and finite, or universal and particular, are identical.[18] The true infinity is something Hegel also calls the 'absolute idea', which represents the point of view of 'speculative' reason. That the absolute idea is of the identity of infinite and finite does not mean that speculative reason is absolved from the laws of logic. It means that, in the absolute idea, speculative reason grasps the overriding principle of the absolute unity of all things. This principle then becomes the new and proper reference of the word 'infinite', still in its original sense of 'un(de)-limited', but now with the impossibility removed of its application to the 'natures' or 'essences' of finite things.

For Hegel, then, it is spirit's discovery of itself as reason that effects the resolution of its formerly apparent dividedness. It does so as a consequence of the general discovery that it is itself the medium of the infinite. Consciousness's idea of reason, as Hegel puts it, is that of 'the certainty, that, in its particular individuality, it has being absolutely *in itself*, or is all reality'.[19] With that discovery and this certainty it is able in principle to identify its own particular existence, action, etc., with the absolute reality which it now grasps itself as being. As Hegel says, the idea of reason is that of the action and being of a particular consciousness being *action* and *being* 'in themselves'. To say of action and being that they are action and being in themselves is to say both of two things: first, that some particular actions of finite individuals and (thus) the actual finite existences of the agents themselves have intrinsic value; and second, that they do not acquire this value from a transcendent source, as it appears from the point of view of the unhappy consciousness. Since the finite world and infinite being are no longer conceived as opposites, but the latter is seen to be necessarily manifested in the former, the projects and goals

28

which individuals encounter in the world will constitute the resource of possibilities from which whatever is to be called 'human fulfilment' (amongst other things self- or inner certainty, freedom and happiness) is to be drawn. This is an 'immanentist' position with regard to the source of absolute human values. As such it is — and Kierkegaard, too, calls it this and means it negatively — a form of humanism. Its basic assumption is that some (finite) forms of action and being are in themselves what is properly meant by 'human fulfilment'.

What forms of action and being? Since the medium in which the reconciliation of finite and infinite is achieved is consciousness, itself conceived as the capacity for conceptualization and systematic thought, the modes of fulfilling action and of fulfilled being (or of being fulfilled) will be those in which the goals and purposes can be called 'common', 'collective', and 'communal', and the motivating interests ones that are shared by all mankind and therefore mutually understood.[20] In short, they will be actions whereby individuals transcend their individuality in the ways mentioned earlier: by appropriating their universal nature, their 'humanity', on the one hand, and by finding themselves unified in generic solidarity with all other humans on the other. Herein lies the basis of Hegel's social and political philosophy, with its principle that actions which go beyond private interest by being rationally co-ordinated in the pursuit of social goals will be *found* to be free and fulfilling.

Since what is essential to human beings, however, is the ability of consciousness to become aware of itself as being *all* (not just social and political) reality, the unity which the once apparently isolated individual ultimately achieves is that of being 'at one' with the world itself. This is, of course, a widely accepted specification of human fulfilment, more especially nowadays in its psychological aspect as the sense of a particular kind of satisfaction, often claimed to be an essential ingredient in mental health. The 're-conciliation' of consciousness's individuality with the universal described in the *Phenomenology* has its psychological aspect, too: once 'assured in itself [consciousness] is at peace'.[21] And, naturally enough, the psychological state of peace has a counterpart in the state of longing which anticipates it. Hegel's general view seems to have been, however, that this form of anticipation belongs to a spiritually inferior, religious frame of mind; the infinite longing 'that yearns beyond body and world'[22] is religious in character and represents an immaturity of spirit in which consciousness attempts to accomplish in feeling what it cannot yet achieve in thought. Where 'intellect . . . sees nothing but finitude in the truth of being', says Hegel in *Faith and Knowledge*, 'alongside [it] religion has its sublime aspects as feeling [*Empfindung*], the love filled with eternal longing'. 'Religion, as this longing,' he adds, 'is subjective', even though 'what it seeks and what is not given to it in intuition, is the absolute and the eternal'.[23]

Hegel's view is that what cannot be given in religion, with its limited, quasi-pictorial form of thought, can be given in philosophy, the highest expression of absolute mind and spirit. There the notion of supreme happiness or highest good (*summum bonum*) takes the form of the idea of reason as the reconciliation of individual and universal. Consequently, the happiness which Hegel's unhappy consciousness lacks is not the one it longs for; 'highest bliss' is to be construed at the level of philosophy as 'highest idea'.[24] '[I] f highest bliss is highest idea', says Hegel, with an unmistakable hint of that note of triumphant joy referred to by Wahl, 'then rational action and highest enjoyment, ideality and reality, are equally contained in it and are identical.'[25]

Consciousness's unhappiness, in summary then, is its inability to grasp itself as the self-same something to which both of the predicates 'infinite' and 'finite' (alternatively, 'unchangeable' and 'changeable') are applicable. The impossibility is logical: the terms in question are contradictory and subject to the 'either/or of understanding'. Concretely this means that consciousness cannot *see* the conceptual solution to its apparently accidental nature, its isolation, and transitoriness in the world of rational action and experience. So it divides the world into an immanent 'here' and a transcendent 'beyond', sets the 'inner' self apart from the conceptualizing self as the proper point of contact, and addresses, to this beyond, its wish to overcome these unsatisfactory limitations from the private, inner world of the 'heart'. For Hegel, however, this is because consciousness fails as yet to see 'the true identity of the inner and outer'.[26] Unable to eternalize the finite, external world, religion 'builds its temples and altars in the heart of the individual', the single individual who 'seeks . . . in sighs and prayers . . . for the God whom he denies to himself in intuition'.[27] The individual sees it as sacrilege to identify the sacred and eternal object of its longing with any finite thing or person.

However, with the emergence in consciousness of the 'true' infinity as the identity of the infinite and finite, the inner world of subjectivity becomes superfluous. Granting itself now the possibility in principle of the 'highest cognition', namely that of 'what that [not merely finite] body is wherein the individual would not be single [and separate], and wherein longing reaches perfect vision and blissful enjoyment',[28] it no longer has any grounds for supposing that the infinite is *contaminated* by contact with the external and finite. And the idea of the infinite, which the separate domain of subjectivity was designed to protect from such contamination, proves to have been a false idea since it was *not* that of an infinite which could 'consume and consummate finitude [*die Endlichkeit aufzuzehren*]'.[29]

3 'Becoming infinite'

In a posthumously published 'report to history', and the only place where he openly addresses an audience wider than that of his local readership, Kierkegaard explains why he abandoned the career of a literary author:

> I broke with the public . . . because I was conscious of being a
> religious author and as such concerned with 'the individual',
> a thought in which ('the individual' as opposed to 'the public')
> is concentrated a whole life-view and world-view.[30]

Kierkegaard places this break shortly after the publication of the (well-received)[31] *Either/Or*, that is to say, early on in the production and, in fact, with the exception of *Either/Or*, prior to all the works to be discussed in any detail here. We are therefore dealing with a self-avowed religious author, moreover one who asks his reader 'constantly to bear in mind that the unifying thought [*Total-Tanke*] of the whole authorship is: becoming a Christian'.[32] Given that Hegel's account of the unhappy consciousness deliberately attempts to reconstruct a mode of consciousness characteristic of Christianity (and Judaism), a considerable similarity between Hegel's account and the 'life-view' or 'world-view' underlying Kierkegaard's writings is only to be expected.

In fact, much of what directly emerges of Kierkegaard's underlying view reads not only like a one-to-one confirmation of the accuracy of Hegel's account but as a source of supplementary detail. To list some of the essential points: first, Kierkegaard stresses an 'absolute distinction [or difference]' between man and God,[33] ensuring that the 'essence' of the former, in Hegel's words, appears as an 'unattainable beyond',[34] and thus denies that man possesses the means of his own self-fulfilment. Second, pursuit of fulfilment involves, correspondingly, taking God's side *against* man and thus entails a converse estrangement from the *finite* world: 'the individual is a stranger in the world of the finite,' says Kierkegaard, 'he lives in the finite, but does not have his life in it'.[35] This estrangement extends naturally enough to man's own body: 'the inwardness of spirit' says Kierkegaard, 'is always as a stranger and

foreigner in a body'.[36] Note that, in spite of this second estrangement's being a response to the first, it cannot be understood as an
attempt to replace it. The growth of 'spirit' is marked in Kierkegaard's account by ever greater clarity about the absoluteness of
the distinction between God and man, so the net result is not one
estrangement cancelling another but a double estrangement from
both the poles, the 'changeable protean' and 'simple unchangeable', of Hegel's dichotomy. Thus man in pursuit of his fulfilment
is left hovering between the familiar, protean, and finite world,
which is found incapable of supplying fulfilment, and a totally unknowable, unchanging infinite which, instead of coming closer,
becomes conceptually increasingly remote.

Third, there is the quasi-pictorial personification of the infinite:
'the infinite itself . . . is a subject' (which presumably implies some
limitation upon the absoluteness of the distinction between God
and man — Kierkegaard himself writes of the difficulty of preserving both the difference and the quasi-personal relationship in
the case of prayer).[37] And there is, fourth, the mode of the
relationship to God, devotional, affective, yearning; the 'pure
inner feeling', which in Hegel's unhappy consciousness 'possesses
its object' (but not conceptually), is echoed in Kierkegaard's talk
of the individual's relationship to the (essential) truth as 'an
appropriation-process of the most passionate inwardness'.[38] As for
the subjectivity with which Hegel says this 'longing' infects religion,
and the inner world with which religion protects the infinite from
contamination with the finite and external, if there is one main
message in Kierkegaard's writings it is that subjectivity and the
distinction between outer and inner should be preserved and
cultivated at all costs. 'Becoming subjective', he says, 'is the task
[indeed the 'highest task'] proposed to every human being'.[39]
Correspondingly, the tendency to obliterate the distinction between
inner and outer is something he consistently deplores.[40]

Finally, like Hegel, Kierkegaard describes unhappiness in terms
of contradiction. He also says that happiness depends on an ability
'to resolve contradictions', though obviously not in the sense that
Hegel intends, and in the psychological context Kierkegaard talks
of the contradiction not as unhappiness, but as 'despair', and of
happiness as 'health'.[41] Despair is a contradiction in the form of a
'sickness unto death'. Or rather two forms, a weaker and a stronger,
only the second of which corresponds to the unhappiness of
Hegel's unhappy consciousness. The weaker form is that in which
'death is the last thing'.[42] This corresponds to the inability to
validate the overordinate term in the synthesis, that referring to
the infinite or eternal aspect. We can understand the contradiction

here most literally as the logical conflict between certainty that death is the end and the proposition that it is not, the latter representing the situation desired by one who wants to believe that death is *not* the last thing but is (despairingly) forced to believe that it is. Crucially, however, sickness unto death *proper* is said to be the 'agonizing' (*qvalfulde*) converse contradiction between certainty that death is *not* the end and the proposition that it is. The latter proposition here, too, represents a situation desired by one who is (despairingly) forced to believe that the situation cannot obtain, the despair now corresponding to the inability to *in*validate the overordinate term in the synthesis; the despairer wants in this case to believe that death *is* the end.

How can such a desire be understood? It might stem from rationalist scruples, a desire to obey the dictates of reason, which we can assume issue in the imperative: believe that death is the end! The desire to obey this dictate may even be over-determined; it might be in obedience to the further dictate, no doubt also reason's: do not entertain contradictory desires (that death be the end and that it be not the end)! In other words, it could be part of an attempt to resolve the contradiction, a typically rationalist attempt which involves removing the one term (the infinite or eternal aspect) which it seems in practice *can* be dispensed with. The despair would then arise through the intractability of a countervailing irrational desire that death be *not* the end. (The despairer continues, say, to listen intently rather than disaprovingly to those who say it is not.)

This, however, is clearly not how Kierkegaard understands it. The unhappy man, Kierkegaard's despairer proper, is one who in some sense *knows* (whatever else his reason might try to dictate) that death is not the end but cannot, in the face of the exorbitant demands made, and the degree of self-estrangement incurred, by his 'knowledge', give up a desire that it *be* the end. It is not that he cannot, through an unquenchable desire to overcome the limitation of death, bring his desire into line with the rational belief that he will not overcome it; it is rather that he cannot bring his desire into line with what he fundamentally *knows* because of an unquenchable desire to *avoid an unpleasantness* implicit in the *ability* to overcome that limitation. This sounds strange if not implausible. What is this 'knowledge'? Some kind of inextinguishable belief? An innate idea? Or at least one that sits indefeasibly once it occurs? The answer is not easy to give, or if it is (the matter is expounded at greater length in Chapter V), easy to justify. It will not do, for example, to say that the idea sits because it has been chosen, though this could provide a framework for one

33

or more not so implausible interpretations (so long as one remains committed to the idea, the desire to avoid its implications will necessarily engender despair; or alternatively, once having chosen it, the desire to avoid its implications becomes an akratic threat to the morale of a self of whom the choice is in some sense constitutive). These interpretations are excluded by Kierkegaard's consistently talking of despair as a failure to accept and measure up to what one really knows, and not just to what one has chosen to believe. For Kierkegaard faith, as we shall see later, is accepting an idea that is offered, not constructed; and sin (absence of faith or, equivalently, despair) is refusal to accept the idea. Whatever the difficulties, however, it is at least clear that Kierkegaard's interpretation preserves the parallel with Hegel's unhappy consciousness. Hegel's divided consciousness also *knows* itself in both its aspects, but cannot reconcile them.

The reference to sickness unto death is of course biblical. In St John's Gospel Jesus says that Lazarus's sickness, though mortal, was 'not unto death'; not because he was subsequently to revive Lazarus, as in the story he does, but because even if Lazarus had stayed dead the sickness that led to his death was still 'for the glory of God, that the son of God might be glorified thereby'.[43] From the Christian point of view, 'death is by no means the last thing of all, it too is only a little event within that which is all [namely] an eternal life'.[44] The sickness of *despair*, however, which *is* unto death, is not to face death in the expectation of eternal life; it is to face it in the manner of one who lies mortally ill and is 'burdened with death' (*trækkes med Døden*), of one who wants to but 'cannot die'.[45] Unlike an ordinary sickness, however, in the case of despair the impossibility is not, says Kierkegaard, for the time being, it is for ever. The 'sickness in the self is eternally to die, to die and yet not to die, to die [one's] death' or, alternatively, to 'live through it'.[46]

On most conventional interpretations expressions like 'eternally dying' and 'living through one's death' express contradictions and so cannot represent possible states of affairs; they assert what they at the same time deny. Of course, the fact that one thing is both asserted and denied is not itself contradictory; if it were there could be no disagreement. And the disagreement may even be with oneself, in the sense that one rejects or suspends beliefs one *has* held, or is inclined now and then to hold. One may even hold two inconsistent beliefs simultaneously without being aware of the implicit contradiction. But what one cannot do is consciously and consecutively to affirm two propositions knowing them to be contradictory. This, however, is not what either Kierkegaard or

Hegel claims. According to Hegel it is precisely the *inability* to affirm two contradictory propositions, in the full knowledge that they are contradictory, that characterizes 'consciousness of self as a dual-natured, merely contradictory being'.[47] The attempt to affirm the one proposition is frustrated by the felt necessity of affirming the other. In the case of Hegel's sceptic, the self divides into two positions, each attempting to assert its half of the contradiction, only to be confronted with the other's refutation, which is again refuted by the first. Of sceptical self-consciousness, the one that through 'lack of thought keeps the poles of its contradiction apart' (see above), Hegel says that its 'talk' is 'like the squabbling of self-willed children, one of whom says *A* if the other says *B*, and in turn says *B* if the other says *A*, and who by contradicting *themselves* buy for themselves the pleasure of continually contradicting *one another*'.[48] The unhappy consciousness sees through this deceit and is forced to try to embrace both positions as elements in a single consciousness which 'must for ever have present in the one consciousness the other also'.[49] So also with Kierkegaard's despairing self whose contradictory nature is contained in the 'dialectical fact that the self is a synthesis in which the one factor is constantly the opposite of the other'.[50] The self's attempt to assert its infinitude (for Hegel, 'unchangeableness') is frustrated by its 'knowledge' that it is merely finite (changeable), and the attempt to make do with finitude is frustrated conversely by the 'knowledge' (conviction, ineradicable desire to believe, or whatever) that it is not merely finite.

The resolution of the contradiction in Kierkegaard's case lies not in knowledge but in faith. The individual can only be rid of despair, or unhappiness, by *choosing* to believe that, as with the Christian view of Lazarus's physical sickness, though mortal, this 'sickness' is nevertheless *not* unto death. In other words, the self has to side with the position which affirms that it is more than finite, thus ceasing to believe that it is merely finite and so deliberately removing the frustration that this 'knowledge' presents. It has to be *willing* to affirm its infinitude, in such a way as to abandon its fear of its 'spiritual destiny', so that it no longer really prefers the position which 'knowledge' (conviction, ineradicable desire to believe, etc.) of its infinitude frustrates. But it has to do this without objective certainty,[51] indeed, as we shall see in the next section, from a position where it does not believe it has, as a finite particular, *any* affinity with a possible 'beyond'.[52]

In short, Kierkegaard's solution to the contradiction is an act of will, the choice to 'become infinite' by 'risking everything'.[53] Clearly, acts of will or decisions do not literally resolve contradictions. So the solution, however one construes it, is not one that satisfies the human intellect. Indeed the choice involves 'venturing to believe against understanding'.[54] In other words, the 'everything' one must risk includes 'one's thought'.[55] The decision to affirm one's infinitude is an 'act of daring' (*Vovestykke*) performed in the full realization that 'in a finite sense' it is 'madness'.[56]

In order to grasp the precise significance of this act of daring, and the way in which its outcome, 'becoming infinite', is supposed to function in the resolution of the contradiction, we must introduce a further element in Kierkegaard's philosophy, namely his account of the three (in effect four) stages or 'spheres' of life or existence.[57] These are analogous (with important disanalogies to be discussed) to what we have called Hegel's thought-paradigms. Kierkegaard also calls them 'existence interpretations'.[58] They consist of the aesthetic, ethical, and religious stages, the latter subdividing into religiousness A and religiousness B. Their importance here is that, towards the end of the *Postscript*, Kierkegaard explicitly defines these paradigms in relation to the contradiction between finite and infinite. It is only at the final stage, religiousness B, that the contradiction emerges in consciousness in the way necessary for the individual's 'act of daring' to have 'becoming infinite' as its consequence.

The notion of becoming infinite is itself fraught with contradictions, and most self-respecting philosophers would drop it like a hot brick. Not so Kierkegaard. Although he admits the unintelligibility of the notion, he is still willing to make it the cornerstone of his practical solution. The formal difficulty with the idea of 'becoming infinite' is that, on the one hand, in order to satisfy it something must initially *not* be infinite, while, on the other, in its technical sense being infinite implies being an undelimited whole, and as such the determinant *of* differentiation and change, not something subject *to* differentiation and change. As Kierkegaard points out in respect of the correlative idea of 'becoming eternal',[59] the 'dialectic of the eternal' is such that 'as soon as [something] is it, it must have been it'. This, he rightly says, is 'inaccessible to all thought'.[60] It is nevertheless the applicability of this notion in the case of religiousness B that distinguishes that paradigm from the other members in the sequence. This is because it is only in religiousness B that the individual abandons altogether the assumption that it possesses an 'eternal determinant';[61] i.e. it no longer assumes that by virtue of some specific exercise of thought or action, or by the adoption of some specific attitude to itself and the world, it is capable of realizing some latent 'kinship' (*Slægtskab*) with the eternal.[62] In Kierkegaard's expression, religiousness B, unlike the preceding paradigms, does not assume that 'each individual is in essence equally adapted to eternity and essentially related to the eternal'.[63] It therefore 'places the conflict [*Modsætningen*] absolutely between existence [as a whole] and eternity'.[64]

What typifies the two intermediate spheres, the ethical and religiousness A, is that they do assume the individual's essential relationship to the eternal. They both therefore represent what Kierkegaard calls 'immanent' points of view; which simply means that they rest on the belief that the unity of the finite and infinite comes within the scope of human thought and experience, not beyond it as one who adopts a 'transcendent' position believes. In the ethical sphere the unity is taken to consist in the exercise of civic and social responsibility. Since it therefore depends on the decision to accept such responsibility, Kierkegaard says that the problem presented by the contradiction is conceived here as a matter of 'self-assertion'.[65] He means this in two senses: first, in so far as it is up to the individual to establish the unity; and second, in so far as, by accepting responsibility, a person first 'chooses' himself and 'reveals a self to the world'.[66] The rationale of this position is exhaustively presented in the second volume of *Either/Or*, which in the concept of 'equilibrium' (*Ligevægt*) expresses the view that a life of civic virtue, with its stress on generality, principle, and continuity, far from depriving its exponent of the opportunity to savour the diversity of the world, adds a new depth and richness to the experience of diversity. One who chooses this life, says its spokesman (appropriately a judge), will not only see how 'difference casts light on the general', but will actually be instrumental in '[transfiguring] difference in the general'.[67] The exercise of conventional moral and civic responsibility 'brings [one] into harmony with the whole of existence [*med hele Tilværelsen*]'.[68] The contradiction is thus understood as lying within existence and as resolvable there. We shall return to the ethical sphere in the next chapter.

Where the ethical sphere sees the resolution as a matter of self-assertion, religiousness A sees it as a matter of self-*annihilation*. From this point of view not only does conventional morality no longer appear as an adequate means of bringing the individual into harmony with the whole of existence, nothing in the public, finite world can be identified as having that function. To secure the possibility of its harmony with the whole of existence, the individual must have recourse to the Deity. The position is still an immanent one, however, because, although existence *contains* no adequate means of bringing the individual into harmony with the

whole of existence, existence itself *as a whole* is conceived as being
'borne by' eternity. Thus although eternity is nowhere to be
grasped, it is nevertheless conceived as being everywhere: 'the
eternal is *ubique et nusquam*'.[69] The finite individual therefore
retains an essential relationship to the eternal. But the eternal
itself and the relationship to it can only be conceived negatively;
though the source of the finite's intrinsic value, it is itself something 'other' than the finite, and the relationship to it, the means
of access to that value, involves the self-renunciation (and 'consciousness of guilt')[70] which involves what Kierkegaard calls living
in the finite but not having one's life in it. The individual is
'dialectically defined within himself in self-annihilation before
God'.[71]

Kierkegaard contrasts these intermediate interpretations of
existence with, on the one hand, the initial, aesthetic sphere in
which the individual lives 'outside' the contradiction and is therefore not 'defined dialectically' *within* himself at all (the position is
also referred to as 'immediacy'),[72] and, on the other, religiousness
B in which, as noted, the contradiction is 'placed' between eternity
and existence as a whole. The latter contrast is the crucial one
here, that is to say between acceptance and rejection of the
'immanence' of the eternal, though we should also note Kierkegaard's comments on speculative philosophy in this connection: it
'abrogates . . . the distinction between "here" and "beyond"
absolutely . . . in the pure being of eternity', in which existence
itself becomes a 'vanishing and abrogated moment', and it can
only conceive of existence as the *past*, as 'having existed', which
'explains why speculative philosophy wisely steers clear of ethics
and makes a fool of itself whenever it embarks upon it'.[73]

The break with immanence typifying religiousness B implies
that the individual now accepts that it has no reason whatever to
believe it possesses an 'eternal determinant', i.e. any form of
cognitive contact or other form of communion ('fundamental
kinship') with the eternal. (Though presumably, strictly, it cannot
express this by saying that it lacks any such kinship with *the*
eternal, since the assumption that there is an eternal at all with the
desired foundational properties would itself have to be based on
some postulated cognitive achievement on the part of the individual.)
As Kierkegaard says, there is now no 'calling the eternal to mind'
or 'reflection' on it 'in time'.[74] In other words, the unity of finite
and infinite cannot be conceived as a pre-established harmony
which finite thought (or action) has the capacity to represent (or
re-enact).

The impossibility of conceiving it in this way is not to be understood as due to an impossibility in principle of conceiving the unity of finite and infinite, in abstraction from the circumstances of human existence; it is to be understood as due to the open-ended nature of human existence itself, and the realistic requirement that the problem of the opposition of finite and infinite be grasped from the existing individual's point of view. It is when the individual identifies the finite term in the opposition with itself, and locates the problem of unity in the field of choice and action, that the logical impossibility of the solution's being found in the form of a completed intellectual system first emerges. This impossibility, however, does not prevent the finite individual's choices and actions having some unifying function in respect of their determining, or even creating, the *future*. Nor does the total opacity of the eternal from the finite point of view contradict this possibility, for even if the finite individual is impotent as far as consciously bestowing this function on its own choices and actions is concerned, the infinite or eternal itself need not be thus impotent. It is still possible, Kierkegaard assumes, and as we shall see his practical solution depends on the assumption, that finite choice and action could be seen and intended from an *infinite* point of view to perform this function. But if this intention is to be relevant to the finite agent's problem, the latter must still be able to identify the choices and actions which have the function in question. Granted the total opacity of the eternal from the finite point of view, this requires that the method of identification be given in time. Thus, to solve the contradiction within the sphere of religiousness B requires the absolutely paradoxical situation (see Chapter IV below) that the eternal come into the world Religiousness B is the 'paradox religiousness'; the individual is 'paradoxically dialectical [*in* itself]', 'every trace of original immanence is annihiliated and all connection cut off' so that 'the individual is reduced to the extremity of existence'.[75] Unlike religiousness A, in religiousness B the individual 'does not come to relate itself *in time* to the eternal, or to call [or recall (*besinde sig paa*)] its relationship to mind'; it comes instead 'to relate itself *in time* to the eternal-*in-time* . . . a relationship which is just as contrary to all thought whether one reflects on the individual or on the Deity'.[76]

The individual's decision to believe, in spite of the unthinkableness of the identity, that its relation to something in time is a relation to the eternal-in-time, is what Kierkegaard means by the individual's 'becoming' infinite (or eternal). In the interests of consistency this cannot, of course, mean that by this decision the individual in fact acquires an 'eternal determinant'; the break with immanence is definite and the practical solution has to be found within the framework established by that break. What Kierkegaard seems to intend here is this: by making the decision, the individual is siding with a notional and totally alien eternal, or, to put it in another way, accepting an identity apart from and overordinate to the finite and temporal, on the 'mad' speculation that, although 'there is . . . no fundamental kinship between the temporal and the eternal, . . . the eternal itself has entered time and wants to constitute the kinship there'.[77] The choice does, however, effect a material change in the individual. In fact, Kierkegaard says the individual becomes 'a different individual'.[78] He is not clear about what this change concretely amounts to, but we can presume that it is to be described in the terms used to contrast the individual's new interpretation of existence with the old; that is to say, in terms of the individual's rationally unjustifiable determination to persist with the project of reconciliation in the only way possible once it is clear that the existential vantage-point itself and its repertoire of possibilities opens no path to it.

4 *Two sub-paradigms*

Kierkegaard generally writes as though the notions of an infinite point of view and divine intention were not inherently contradictory or otherwise problematic. Thus although he repeatedly criticizes the speculative philosopher's (e.g. Hegel's) ideal of 'immanence-theory', according to which the absolute becomes realized in time, because it represents a contemplative, i.e. inactive, point of view, appropriate for 'worshipful professors and their friends and relations' but in fact no more than a delusion, he does say that the point of view is (uniquely) proper to God.[79] And although existence (*Tilværelse*) 'cannot be a system for an existing [*existerende*] spirit, [it *is*] a system [with all the completeness and finality that implies] for God',[80] for whom the 'conformity of thought with being . . . *is* realized'.[81] And his answer to the question, Who is the systematic thinker, '[that one] who is outside existence and yet in existence, who is in his eternity for ever complete, and yet includes existence within himself'?, is — 'It is God'.[82]

Hegel's 'true infinity' grounds the finite in consciousness or thought; but only when consciousness has resolved its inner conflict by discovering itself as reason. In Hegel's account, it is reason which achieves the 'mediation' of infinite and finite. The discovery of consciousness of itself as reason is therefore tantamount to the coincidence of the ideal, or infinite, point of view

40

with that of human reason. But it is important for Hegel that what is discernible from this point of view is not an abstract, theoretical principle from which the unity of the finite in experience can somehow be intellectually derived; it is the evolving, discernible unity itself. The unity in which the finite is grounded in the infinite is not a 'unity *behind* manyness', but a unity in the concrete here and now which 'manyness makes out of itself'.[83]

Kierkegaard, of course, denies that any such unity is discernible by human reason (though sometimes his claim seems to be the apparently weaker one that if human *reason* could discern it, this merely conceptual or theoretical unity would not have any real, i.e. practical, application). But he does not deny that there is something in *practice* which can amount to the unity which manyness makes out of itself. In his non-pseudonymous writings, which fall under the general title of 'religious discourses', Kierkegaard analyses (amongst other things) the requirements of a good will, or what in another context he refers to as a will that succeeds in becoming 'concrete in the same degree that it is abstract'.[84] The fact that these writings are *called* religious (sometimes just 'edifying', at others either 'ethico-religious' or 'Christian') and are not pseudonymous has a special significance. It means that they assume the correctness of the Christian viewpoint and presuppose the reader's freely made ('freely' also in the sense of being rationally unjustifiable) decision in favour of it. The works in question elaborate in detail both the form and content of the concrete will as a will fitted for the agency of the good. What the account of such a will amounts to is a prescription of the kind of will the finite individual must form in itself if the actions flowing from it are to qualify as manifestations in time (and finite 'manyness') of eternity and infinity — actual instances of the good in the sense of the creation, in a genuinely practical way, of the unity of the infinite in, and out of, manyness.

The question arises how such a view accords with the earlier claim that Kierkegaard's position is essentially that of Hegel's unhappy consciousness. Is not the idea of a finite will, capable of creating the unity of the infinite, incompatible with that absolute distinction between finite and infinite which appears to be an essential feature of the paradigm described by Hegel? And if so, is not the promotion of this as a Christian idea inconsistent with Hegel's intention that his notion should *define* the prevailing Christian attitude? Or can the distinction be 'overcome' in the way Kierkegaard's solution requires without resolving the conflict in a manner which would imply a departure from the basic structure of the unhappy consciousness? And in that case are we to allow, after all, that the unhappy consciousness admits, through this way of overcoming the conflict, the possibility of overcoming its own unhappiness?

To answer these questions let us begin by distinguishing between two putative alternative sub-paradigms of the unhappy consciousness, one in which there is no breach of the distinction and another in which there is such a breach. The first sub-paradigm claims the absolute transcendency of the infinite and gives it thereby a monopoly of intrinsic value. According to such a view the individual's interest in fulfilment would have to focus exclusively on the prospect of a life after death, or at least in some form of release from the finite state. The appropriate attitude of the finite individual towards the infinite here is one of total alienation and unreciprocal dependence. Eternal happiness is conceived as immortality in a 'hereafter' or a 'beyond', and virtue or 'good work' at best a labour by which one earns reprieve from this transitory and contemptible life on earth. The absolute transcendence of God goes hand in hand with the absolute worthlessness of man in his natural state.

This looks very like the basic structure of Hegel's unhappy consciousness. The divided consciousness tries to overcome its futile situation, in which the attempt to grasp *itself* as unchangeable requires it to turn away from its 'particular individuality', by assembling the *notion* of an 'unchangeable individuality' which obviates this requirement; that is to say, the idea of a being at once unchangeable *and* particular. Since it is characteristic of this consciousness, however, not to be able to grasp itself (or indeed any finite thing or person) as instantiating this idea, it is led, as we saw, to conceive the unchangeable individuality in which the idea of its own fulfilment ('intrinsic being') is invested, as something alien and transcendent. The identification of its ideal of harmony in a transcendent 'other' then also leads the divided consciousness to conceive of its own finite part, the part encompassing its actions and enjoyments, as inherently worthless. In its continued quest for harmony it then, as Hegel's account has it, surrenders its power of decision, will, goods, and satisfaction, along with the power of these to confirm its 'actuality', to the 'other'.[85] This recalls the self-annihilation before God characteristic of Kierkegaard's religiousness A; and its further extension in the breaking with 'immanence' as such in religiousness B.

According to the second sub-paradigm, the infinite is not (even though from an inadequate point of view it may seem to be) absolutely or in principle transcendent. Here the infinite is not the sole possessor of value; its value is bound up with, and can invest the finite. A conceptual basis of views like this that accept the infinite as the source of intrinsic value and yet deny its ultimate transcendence, is typically the idea that the infinite is itself dependent upon the finite; that it can only 'realize' its own value by revealing, diversifying, 'unfolding' itself, or some such, in the world of finite particulars. So the finite individual's fulfilment is bound up with the individual's performing an intrinsically valuable function of the infinite, namely its achievement of its own value in finite 'action and being'.

Initially it looks as if the two sub-paradigms neatly distinguished the Kierkegaardian from the Hegelian position. And it is certainly true that much of Kierkegaard reads as if the first sub-paradigm applied in his case, while the second obviously contains at least the seeds of Hegel's solution. On the one hand, the notions of sin, self-renunciation, and surrender are typically Kierkegaardian, while, on the other, that of nature and human history (the 'world') as the means by which alone God can perfect himself, and of human fulfilment as achieved through the accomplishing of God's purpose on earth, is quintessentially Hegelian.[86] But we have seen that Kierkegaard also has some of this: 'the eternal', according to his solution, 'has entered time and wants to constitute the kinship there'. The difference is that for Hegel the religious account, so far as it preserves a *distinction* between divine purpose and human interest, is merely provisional; it is to be replaced by the non-metaphorical philosophical language of the 'true infinity' which destroys the basis for the distinction both here and *a fortiori* in the former, more extreme sub-paradigm. For Kierkegaard, on the contrary, the religious account is true precisely to the extent that it does preserve the distinction. But not, it now seems, in such a way as to enforce the absolute demarcation of the more extreme sub-paradigm. In specifying a kind of will fitted for the agency of the good, Kierkegaard is clearly admitting the more congenial possibilities that arise from the notion of a mutuality of interest on the part of finite and infinite.

In Kierkegaard's solution, however, there is no knowing that what flows from a will fitted for the agency of the good is in fact the fulfilment in time of a divine intention. No specification of the will, or any other prescription for ethical performance, will provide what is recognizably or authoritatively a *description* of the Good. Such a description could only be derived from the eternal point of view, and no human being could ever have that. So not only does Kierkegaard not know, or suppose he or anyone could ever acquire, this point of view, he does not know or suppose there could be any reason for anyone to believe that there *is* such a point of view.

Thus we find in the *Postscript* the denial that he has 'at all under-taken to prove that there *is* [such a good]'. Partly, he says, because it isn't *his* business but that of Christianity which preaches it', but also, more germanely, because 'if it could be proved, it most certainly would not exist, since the existence of the absolute ethical good can only be *proved* by the individual's expressing its existence in his'.[87] We shall take up the problematic use of the notion of 'proof' in this context later. The important thing to stress here is that the problem of the *Postscript* is not 'the truth of Christianity', but 'the individual's relation to Christianity'.[88] Kierkegaard's pseudonymous author does not even claim to have 'understood Christianity', beyond grasping that 'it wants to make the individual eternally happy' and (importantly) presupposes 'as a *conditio sine qua non*' of the reader's attention an interest in this happiness on the part of the individual.[89] The truth of Christianity is not something to be established (according to Part One of *Postscript* there are in fact no objective procedures for establishing it — see Chapter IV below); but it is a necessary condition of the individual human being's fulfilling an interest in an eternal happiness. The assumption is that individual human beings do indeed have this interest, and furthermore — as remarked in the previous chapter — that it is natural, or fitting, that they should have it, even if there are those, even a majority, who claim that they do not.

It is to be remarked here that although Kierkegaard's rejection of the Hegelian view, that religious truths are inadequately concep-tualized *philosophical* truths, might lead one to suppose that he regarded Hegelian philosophy as also claiming to cater to the individual's interest in eternal happiness, in fact he considers speculative philosophy to be incapable of addressing itself to the *individual's* interest at all. 'For the speculating [philosopher] the question of his personal eternal happiness cannot present itself, just because his task consists in getting more and more away from himself and becoming objective, and thus in vanishing from himself and becoming the contemplative power of philosophy itself.'[90] The fulfilment offered by speculative philosophy is addressed to 'humanity at large' (*Menneskeheden*) irrespective of the particular identities of individual human beings.[91] Christianity, on the other hand, professes to cater for the eternal happiness of each individual irreplaceably. Kierkegaard argues the appropriateness of this 'infinite passionate interest' in a 'personal eternal happiness' on the grounds that it 'definitely [*bestemt*] expresses the synthesis [or that juxtaposition of the temporal and the eternal character-istic of existence and the individual]'. 'Speculative happiness' is an illusion', because the speculator 'wishes to be *merely* eternal in time'.[92] A later passage in the *Postscript*, where Climacus compares a position he calls pantheism (favourably) with speculative philosophy, can throw some light on this remark. The pantheist '[takes himself] by way of recollection out of existence *back* into the eternal, whereby all existential decisions become a mere shadow-play over against what is eternally decided from behind'.[93] The 'pantheist', in other words, is a determinist who suspends belief in the efficacy and significance of decision and choice, and assumes a universal order which nothing in time can change, but which can be recaptured in recollective contemplation: he is 'eternally put at ease backwards, [and for him] that moment in time of existence, the three-score years and ten, is infinitesimal [*et Forsvindende*]'. The speculative philosopher, on the contrary, tries impossibly to accept at once both the efficacy and significance of decision and choice on the one hand, and a universal order which embraces the individual's, and thus also his own, existence on the other: he wants to 'be an individual . . . who exists *sub specie aeterni*'.[94] Unlike the pantheist (idealist, Platonist, or pre-determinist), who consciously turns his back on the concrete and the temporal, the speculative philosopher gives himself the 'illusory', because impossible, project of incorporating these, and thus also himself, intact, within an abstract system of thought.[95] The synthesis is a juxtaposition of *irreconcilable* terms. Placed concretely in time, as one is, one's interest in a personal eternal happiness can only be associated with the open-ended and un-determined realm of choice, decision, and action. Or, to put the point in a way that captures what is the specific objection to speculative philosophy, an interest in a personal eternal happiness can only be associated with the (existential) realm of choice, decision, and action as *genuinely* open-ended and undetermined. In claiming, then, that Christianity's presupposition of an 'infinite passionate interest in a personal eternal happiness' is appropriate to the synthesis, and that its conception of this goal is therefore 'higher' than that of the speculative philosopher, Kierkegaard clearly means that, unlike the latter, Christianity takes realistic account of the actual situation of the individual. Characteristic of that situation is the individual's confinement to a temporal, finite reality in which he is ineluctably in a state of 'becoming'.[96] The completeness, finality, and stability of the eternal could never be *found* attaching to finite reality, which from the point of view of human knowledge can never be more than, in Hegel's term, the 'protean changeable'. The individual's interest in acquiring those qualities of the eternal, in becoming *also* the 'simple unchangeable', must therefore focus on a goal which transcends the finite; not, however, in such a way as to involve a disregard for, or an (impossible) flight from, the finite. The interest is one which the individual has *while* existing finitely, and is directed *upon* his or her own finite existence. It is an interest in the possibility that this finite existence, notwithstanding the systematic elusiveness of the quality of the eternal from the finite point of view, might nevertheless in principle acquire that value. What this interest amounts to, if our interpretation is correct, is first of all an interest in the existence of that other, eternal point of view.

The finite agent can only believe, never know, that its action is an instance of the unfolding of the unity of the infinite. But the belief is sufficient for the sense of participation in the fulfilment of the infinite which, it becomes clear, is what Kierkegaard means by the attainment of an eternal happiness — or, as Hegel puts what is essentially the same thing, of 'the self-satisfaction or blessed enjoyment' which 'the action of a particular individual' acquires when it is 'an absolute action', and the agent's existence and action are confirmed as 'being and action in *themselves*'.[97]

However, Hegel claims that the best that the unhappy consciousness can achieve is not enough. The reason is that the only assurance to be received there has to come from outside (the 'mediation' being in the as yet imperfect form of a 'counsellor' or 'mediating minister'); the unhappy consciousness never actually *knows* that its own action is (ever) absolute action. Not yet having discovered itself as reason, its certainty is 'still incomplete', and its action brings it 'self-satisfaction or blessed enjoyment' only 'in principle'.[98]

Must this not apply equally on Kierkegaard's assumption? Not exactly. Kierkegaard's view seems to be that once a person is clear that the quest for epistemological certainty on essential matters is misguided, the way is open for another, immediately available and more personally engaging form of certainty. This is a self-certainty which, instead of depending upon some conclusive evidence or argument (which it must wait upon and which will in any case always be open to revision), is immediately available in a self-guaranteeing form: that of a performative product of the agent's own independent decision. Clearly there is no logical connection between believing something to be the case and its actually being the case, and in this sense whatever happy assurance follows, in some quasi-performative way, from a decision to believe something, remains happiness only 'in principle'. There could be said to be one point in favour of Kierkegaard's version, however: the desired property in its case is not something like a piece of property one categorically fails to possess but hopes to obtain, it is something one hopes to be possessing already, though with the impossibility in principle of knowing whether one does. (If we recall Kierkegaard's remark, in connection with the notion of 'becoming eternal', that since according to the 'dialectic of the eternal' whatever is eternal must (always) have been so, the notion is in fact unthinkable; we might turn this point to Kierkegaard's advantage by noting the compatibility of this 'dialectic' with the idea that from an *eternal* point of view the finite individual does indeed have its 'eternal determinant' and *a fortiori* has it eternally.)[99]

We shall note later that Kierkegaard nevertheless uses a traditional epistemological terminology ('proof', 'objectivity', and 'knowledge') in connection with the non-epistemological certainty resulting from autonomous choice. But we shall also see that he uses the corresponding words in an extended sense designed to show that, at least in regard to essential matters, their proper field of application is not that of propositional content — which Kierkegaard refers to as 'the what' — but of the quality of the individual's relationship to the content, of 'the how', as he puts it. Applying epistemological criteria in such a case is, as he himself says, to 'manoeuvre [*spille* — lit. 'play'] the matter into [the realm of] knowledge and talk'. Kierkegaard ridicules 'the serious man' who concedes that if only he could be certain about an eternal happiness 'in store' — 'so as to know it is really there' — he could 'risk everything for its sake'. His certainty would *prevent* him from risking 'everything'.[100]

A final point. We said earlier that on Kierkegaard's view a description of the good can only be derived from the point of view of the good — a point of view from which, if indeed it exists, human consciousness is absolutely excluded. But assuming there is such a point of view, as one who aspires to an eternal happiness passionately hopes, then it must — according to our second sub-paradigm — be possible for descriptions of finite actions *also* to be descriptions of the good, even if no one could ever substantiate a particular claim of this kind, or even justify a claim as to where to look for those special actions that might qualify as 'absolute' actions. But unless this possibility is to be of only academic interest, such claims must at least be made. Christianity proposes that the actions in question are those that conform with the teachings of Christ. The Christian doctrine of the incarnation is important in this respect. It is in fact important at two levels. First, it claims that Christ is the eternal in time (Christianity is thus religiousness B, or paradox-religiousness). It therefore admits the possibility in principle of the finite's being a manifestation of the

47

infinite. Given this possibility the finite individual may then hope that, by 'becoming infinite (or eternal)' in the way described, it can become in itself such a manifestation. In this way the life of Jesus is an historical event upon which the individual can ground the belief in the genuine possibility of an eternal happiness. The implications of the Christian claim that 'an eternal happiness is decided in time through the relationship to something historical' are the topic of *Philosophical Fragments*, and dealt with more explicitly and at length in the *Postscript*. Both works (to be discussed in Chapter IV) are directed (the first indirectly) against Hegel, for whom the doctrine of the incarnation is also central, but only as a provisionally quasi-pictorial way of representing Infinite Being's manifestation of itself in the infinite, a way which according to Hegel fails to capture the philosophical truth that Infinite Being is *necessarily* manifested in the finite. But second, the doctrine of the incarnation is also important because, on its assumption that the life of Jesus does manifest the infinite, that life can be taken to contain a record of finite actions which are also 'absolute' actions, i.e. actions descriptions of which *are* therefore also descriptions of the good, and of statements indicating what it is about such actions that qualifies them as descriptions of the good.

5 The journey inwards without itinerary

In the *Phenomenology* Hegel talks of a 'path of natural consciousness'. It is, he writes, 'the way of the soul which journeys through the series of its own configurations as though they were the stations appointed for it by its own nature, so that it may purify itself for the life of the Spirit'.[101] In Hegel spirit (or mind) is a collective notion comprising a developing series of prevailing modes ('configurations') of self-understanding – thought-paradigms as we have called them – in a broad respect which includes what might be called a mode's characteristic philosophy of the relation of the self, that is any self that comes under that mode, to the objective world. The configurations have also their characteristic expressions in social and political life. In its progression through the series the soul 'presses forward' through what appear to it to be its appointed stations to 'true knowledge'. The aim, or at any rate outcome, of the journey is to provide the soul with a 'completed experience of itself', in which it finally achieves the 'awareness of what it really is in itself'.[102] The content of this awareness is nothing less than reality. 'This last shape of Spirit', writes Hegel,

is absolute knowing . . . Spirit that knows itself in the shape of
Spirit . . . a *comprehensive knowing* [*begreifendes Wissen*]
. . . [where] truth is not only *in itself* completely identical
with certainty, but . . . also has the shape of self-certainty. . . .
Truth is the *content*, which in religion is still not identical with
its certainty . . . [but] is now a fact, in that the content has
received the shape of the Self. As a result, that which is the very
essence, viz. the Notion . . . has become the *form of objectivity*
for consciousness. Spirit, *manifesting* or *appearing* in consciousness in this element, or what is the same thing, produced
in it by consciousness, *is Science*.[103]

In other words, whatever may at first appear to transcend the self
as something radically external to it has been reduced without
remainder to conceptual content. 'External' here must not, of
course, be interpreted in the classical empiricist sense as a problematic physical, 'outer' counterpart to the 'inner', or 'immediate',
psychological domain of sense-experience and imagery, a sense in
which a 'reduction' of the external takes the form of phenomen-
alism. The sense in question is that in which the external is what is
'extra-mental' in the sense of resisting representation in concepts:
anything which can at best only be *referred* to indirectly and mis-
leadingly by concepts, perhaps even in the form of a contradiction,
but cannot be genuinely represented in or by them, for instance
God, Infinite Being, Kant's *noumenon*, or any metaphysical sub-
stratum. In this sense the external is not the common public world
in which we all live, move, and meet. It is whatever there might be
about or distinct from the world, in any geographical, biological,
psychological, social or political aspect, that escapes systematic
understanding. To say that the 'external' can be reduced without
remainder to *conceptual*, as distinct from experiential or empirical,
content is to say that in the long run no aspect of human life has
to be understood in terms of principles which human reason
cannot grasp and justify. An important aspect of the soul's ability
to 'reduce' the external, indeed its very *modus progrediendi*, is, on
Hegel's account, elimination of whatever in the world appears
initially in the form of a limitation on the soul's freedom. Central
in the present context is its elimination of the limitation consisting
of a felt disproportion between its merely finite, natural existence
and the goal of freedom and fulfilment: the problem of the unhappy consciousness.

Now Kierkegaard also talks of 'spirit'. He says that 'man is
spirit'.[104] He also talks of a spiritual destiny: man is that special
case of the 'synthesis' that is 'so constructed as to be spirit'.[105]

49

He sometimes even employs forms of expression suggesting, like Hegel, that spirit proceeds according to a pre-arranged itinerary via 'appointed stations': 'The whole development of the world tends in the direction of the absolute significance of the category of singleness.'[106] However, Kierkegaard's term 'spirit' does not refer to a collective mode of self-understanding, something which actual selves or individuals share. It refers to the individual as such, as a unique self. Thus by 'man' in 'man is spirit' Kierkegaard means 'each separate human being'.[107]

There is a sense, as we have seen, in which spiritual progress for Kierkegaard is natural, as Hegel's talk of 'stations appointed by nature' suggests it is in his conception too; it is natural in the sense of being motivated by an appropriate or 'fitting' interest in an eternal happiness. But once it is borne in upon a person that essential truth lies beyond human comprehension, that the 'contra-diction' is between existence as a whole and the eternal, and provided the person does not succeed in ignoring *this* truth, the pull of the prospect of an eternal happiness is neutralized by the 'offence' of the paradox.[108] It must give way to the 'passion of the infinite' (*Uendelighedens Lidenskab*),[109] in which effective pursu-ance of this interest can only be sustained by an act of will in, as Kierkegaard says, 'an appropriation-process of the most passionate inwardness'.[110]

It is also true to say that for Kierkegaard, as with Hegel, the 'problem' of the unhappy individual consists in the disproportion between finite existence and what is understood as being needed for freedom and fulfilment. In Kierkegaard's case, however, the problem is an inescapably *practical* one. The 'synthesis' of soul and body does not conform *itself* to 'the [eternal] determinant of spirit',[111] it has to be brought actively into conformity with that determinant (*Bestemmelse*, category or 'characteristic' in the strong sense of 'defining characteristic', but also in the sense of an inherent possibility that ought to be realized, or which it is the destiny of the human soul/body synthesis to realize). Far from it being the case that human beings will conform to it as a matter of course, 'not many even make an attempt at [the] life [of spirit], and of those who do, most soon run off'.[112]

Not surprisingly. Not only is the flesh *naturally* unwilling to accept the constraints imposed on instinct by the life of spirit, so that the natural life remains in any case a problem requiring the individual's active intervention; the individual has no reason to believe that, in respect of an eternal happiness, the intervention will have the desired effect. There may not be any, and indeed there is every *reason* to believe there is no, eternal happiness in store, and the decision in favour of the belief that there is has to be made in full realization that 'in a finite sense' the choice is 'madness'.

Eternal happiness, however, is not the only consideration. In Kierkegaard, again as in Hegel, there is a social side to the life of spirit, corresponding to Hegel's notion of the embodiment of spirit in the institutions of a civilized state. But here, too, there is a crucial difference. For Hegel sociality — the fact of free social cohesion — is the result of a willing acceptance of tasks and responsibilities imposed by an already established social unity, namely the state. The individual accepts the task and responsibilities willingly once he or she is able to recognize the necessity of the state as a constituent in personal freedom: both as a constraint on any destructive potentialities of the pursuit of private interest in general, and as the means of turning private interests into public advantage. This insight, when properly assimilated, signals the arrival of spirit at that most important of the stations 'as though appointed for it by its own nature', namely the one affording it experience of itself as a *social* and *political* self. The insight and experience will come with the provision of effective means for the cultivation of civic virtue.

For Kierkegaard, however — and perhaps it was an insight born of his own experience of a School of Civic Virtue — this procedure is radically misguided. Sociality, if it is to exist at all, must be a direct product of an ability to judge the rightness or wrongness of one's own actions independently of the prescriptions of civic duty. The authority that is to be willingly accepted is not that of the state but a transcendent moral authority; and the individual accepts this authority willingly not because of its social consequences but because it is hoped that doing so will enable him or her to acquire intrinsic value personally, and because this notion of an intrinsic personal value is practically linked with that of the notion of *individuals* being the only possible way of impressing the value-giving unity of the infinite upon the diversity of finite nature. The unity ensuing from the elimination of any destructive tendencies of the private will has to be a function of the individual will itself, in its deference to an 'absolute' goal; and the same is required of the transformation of self-interest into an interest in the advantage of others.

Feuerbach criticized Hegel for personifying human characteristics and capacities, as if they themselves were capable of reactions, purposes, plans, and initiatives. Hegel's concept of spirit, he pointed out, was a personification of the human capacity for thought. This, objected Feuerbach, is to invert the real state of affairs. It is not

51

thought that thinks, it is individuals who do so. Feuerbach proposed that the terms referring to these characteristics and capacities be treated not as substantives referring to mythical universal agents but as predicates qualifying the activities of particular persons. This reformatory procedure, known as 'standing Hegel on his head', became the basis of Marx's better known and more radical critique of Hegel.

Kierkegaard, too, stands Hegel on his head in this way. One instance is his use of the basic term 'spirit' to refer to a potentiality of the individual, not of man or 'consciousness' in general. Another is his criticism of the speculative idealist's 'abstract' way of talking of thought as 'thought with no thinker' and without reference to a particular topic, time or place.[113] In fact, Hegel's *Phenomenology* lends itself particularly well to this form of objection. Hegel is constantly describing thought as such in terms of intentions, strategies, responses, inevitable frustrations, and the like, all obviously borrowed from human psychology. Indeed, many of his descriptions anticipate Kierkegaard's. Thus,

> in positing . . . a single particular . . . [consciousness establishes] the beyond . . . [and in this way] suffers . . . violence at its own hands, [spoiling] its own limited satisfaction. When consciousness feels this violence, its anxiety may well make it retreat from the truth, and strive to hold on to what it is in danger of losing. But it can find no peace. If it wishes to remain in a state of unthinking inertia, then thought troubles its thoughtlessness, and its own unrest disturbs its inertia. Or, if it entrenches itself in sentimentality. . . . [etc.] .[114]

Feuerbach says that what is upside-down in speculative idealism is its conception of the path of philosophy as being 'from the abstract to the concrete, from the ideal to the real'. The starting-point should be the finite, without which 'the infinite cannot be conceived'.[115] Feuerbach observes that '[t]he transition from the ideal to the real takes place only in *practical* philosophy'.[116] Whatever Feuerbach means by practical philosophy,[117] it is clear that Kierkegaard also holds *both* the view that the proper direction is the reverse of Hegel's, *and* the view that Hegel's problem of moving from the ideal to the real is a practical one, a problem of the finite individual's *creating* the unity of the ideal rather than discovering it. In respect of this practical problem Kierkegaard prescribes a path that is not only the reverse of Hegel's by virtue of its having the particular and finite as its beginning and the universal and infinite as its goal, but is its reverse in another respect too: Hegel's journey goes from private to public, from inner to outer, from individuality to a consummation in 'publicity' that 'consumes' individuality by prescribing social tasks which have their moral labels already attached to them for all in their right civic minds to see. The progress is outward from an 'immediacy' ('sense-certainty') to a public domain where spirit finds itself completely at home, and in relation to which any pockets of privacy in the public fabric are wrinkles to be flattened out in further extensions of a common vision of objective truth. Kierkegaard's journey is inwards, as greater insight reveals the inherent inability of the public world to provide for the individual's consummation or the attachment of moral labels, and as the roles of will ('heart') and personal choice are revealed as the resources with which the finite agent must secure any consummation that may be in store for it. The force of Kierkegaard's injunction that we should become 'subjective', and that this is the 'highest' task confronting every individual,[118] is that, apart from having to be stood on his head, Hegel also has to be turned outside-in.

III

The Knight of Faith's Silence

The relief of speech is that it translates me into the universal.[1]

1   *The aesthetic works*

The metaphors at the conclusion of the previous chapter invite misinterpretation. There is a particular danger of distortion in the description of Hegel's ideal as one of a common 'vision' of objective truth, even though the visual metaphor is one that Hegel himself uses. It sounds as if the 'highest bliss' which truth affords is for Hegel a state of contemplation, as in Aristotle's original version of the idea; that is, as though the truth were some ultimately satisfying vista upon which the eyes of the enlightened are rapturously fixed. The danger is compounded by Hegel's describing his ideal not only as a vision but as a scientific one.[2] But it is essential to an understanding of Hegel that the topic of his science not be conceived as an objective reality 'outside' the self, or subject, to which the self stands opposed; the topic of this science *is* the self and its fulfilling activities and goals. In other words, it is in forms of the self's *action* that 'consciousness' is afforded the satisfying experience of being at one with all reality.

It is important to stress this, because the point at issue between Hegel and Kierkegaard is not whether the *active* self and its interests are *at all* to be taken into account — Hegel would certainly agree that they should — but whether these interests can be accounted for in the framework of 'systematic' science. Kierkegaard is, of course, flatly opposed to the assumption that there can be a *science* of human goals and that the active experience of oneness with all reality can be *knowledge*.

54

But the visual metaphor also misrepresents Hegel in another way. It fails to convey that the 'self-knowledge' in question is conceptual, not empirical, and that in the transition from religion to philosophy it is, as Hegel says, truth as *content* that has now received the 'shape of the self'.[3] The special relevance of this both here and for the following chapter lies in the fact that the science Hegel affirms and Kierkegaard denies is one whose envisaged outcome is a community forged by a *shared* and *common* knowledge of what constitutes self-fulfilling activity. Our focus will be turned upon a very significant corollary of Kierkegaard's denial of a *science* of self-fulfilment: namely the rejection of the idea that the path to self-fulfilment is one of convergence upon some common location (called 'truth') in an objective world of thought.

The consequences for the notions of objectivity and truth (both of which Kierkegaard contentiously wishes to retain in connection with self-fulfilment) will be discussed in the next chapter. Here, partly in order to preserve the actual chronology of Kierkegaard's own discussion, we shall consider first his denial that the goal of becoming properly human, of being 'reconciled' in the oppositions, or of being a fulfilled self, is essentially linked to knowledge and mutual understanding. This, as will appear, involves a crucial question of interpretation: whether, and if so in what sense, Kierkegaard claims not just that the goal is not necessarily linked to *shared* content, but that there is something essential to attaining it which is not 'content' at all.

As an introduction to our topic let us formulate an, at this level of analysis, admittedly crude and facile inference which places it usefully in the context of the closing metaphors of the previous chapter. If the idea of an objective world is that of a shared world, which is in turn a world of shared meanings, then the more subjective a person becomes in some respect (say, self-fulfilment) the less meaning that person shares in that respect with others; and at an extreme of subjectivity there will be *nothing* that the person can say in this respect which others will understand. Now this extreme position seems to be the one Kierkegaard ascribes to his 'knight of faith'. The knight of faith, portrayed in a version of the Genesis story of Abraham's willingness, on God's command, to sacrifice his son Isaac as proof of his faith, is someone who acts in 'absolute isolation'.[4] Whatever Abraham might say in explanation of his action, he cannot convey why he should be willing to do just this in order to prove his faith. From the Hegelian point of view Abraham is a radically recalcitrant wrinkle in the public fabric, a man forced to be silent on something essential.

The knight of faith has to be approached by way of an explanation both of the overall purpose of the 'aesthetic production', in which he is a key figure, and of its *general* topic. The former explanation is given by Kierkegaard himself in the *Point of View*, and the latter is expounded at length in the first of the aesthetic works, the well-known *Either/Or*.

In distinguishing his 'aesthetic' from his 'religious' production (to which we shall turn in Chapters VI and VII) Kierkegaard says that the works of the latter are straightforward in a way in which the aesthetic works are not. The aesthetic production is in a way, he says, 'a fraud'; not, be it said, because it defrauds the reader *of* the truth, but because it is designed to cheat the reader *into* the truth. The 'aesthetic' works are so called because they are designed to lead the reader '*back* from the aesthetic', that is to say from a life ensnared in or dedicated to immediacy. The characteristic which sets them most obviously apart from the religious works is their pseudonymity; and the recourse to pseudonyms is to be explained by this deliberate deception. 'What does it mean to deceive?' asks Kierkegaard:

> It means that one doesn't begin *directly* with what one wants to communicate, but . . . going along with the other's delusion. Thus (to keep to the present work's topic) one begins by saying, not 'I'm a Christian, you are not', but 'You are a Christian, I am not'. Not by saying 'It is Christianity I preach, and the life you lead is purely aesthetic [the life of immediacy] ', but by saying 'Let's talk about the aesthetic'. The deception is that one does this precisely in order to come to the religious. But according to the assumption, the other is also under the delusion that the aesthetic is the Christian, since he thinks he is a Christian and yet lives the life [of immediacy] .[5]

In other words, the aesthetic works are addressed to self-professing Christians who are under the false impression that the life they lead is a Christian one. In order to put them on the right track the author enters into the spirit of the delusion which is preventing them from embarking on it, concealing from the reader that this is what he is doing, and why. The reason? Because in the grip of their false picture of the Christian life, they are not in a position to grasp the point of an instruction, as it were, from above. To lead someone on to a definite destination, says Kierkegaard, you have 'first and foremost to take steps to find where *he* is, and begin from there'. He may not accompany you to the destination, but there is always one thing you can do for him, and that is 'force him to pay attention'. Where false pictures paralyse a person's will and understanding, any form of direct communication is useless.

One must first apply a 'corrosive'; 'but this corrosive is the negative, and in communication the negative is precisely to deceive'.[6]

Kierkegaard's pseudonymity is a controversial theme, regarding both the motives behind the particular choices of pseudonym and the reasons for the recourse to pseudonymity in general. Not everyone accepts Kierkegaard's retrospective explanation as the last word. Perhaps at the time of writing the aesthetic works the distance between the opposites 'I am a Christian' and 'you are not' was less evident in his own case than it later became; at that earlier time Kierkegaard may himself have been more actively searching for that path which he later says he has tried to hoodwink his readers into taking, so that the aesthetic works are partly to be understood as expressions of consciously transitional or experimental points of view also on the side of their author. However, the niceties of the debate need not detain us here. It suffices for our purposes to note that Kierkegaard has told *us* that the works are all his, that at the time this was something most people quickly knew in any case, and that the pseudonyms are never ones that could possibly deceive his readers into identifying them as the names of actual persons. This in addition to an important consideration mentioned in a 'First and [although, as it turned out, not] Final Explanation [*Forklaring*]' which Kierkegaard appends to the *Postscript*, and in which he acknowledges that he is 'as one says, author of *Either/Or . . .*' etc.; namely that the reason for his 'polyonymity' is that it absolves him from *responsibility* for the views portrayed in the works in question: something which makes his own relationship to these works more extreme even than that of a poet, who at least produces his *own* prefaces. In this respect 'in the pseudonymous books there is not a single word [written] by [him] self'.[7] By transferring ownership of the works and their prefaces to fictitious authors Kierkegaard has acquired a combination, so to speak, of the reporter's freedom from having to answer personally for the views he passes on, and of the fiction-writer's freedom to create the persons (and perspectives) of whom (and which) the views are expressions. The advantages of this for someone who wants the views to take effect without consideration of their author's real intentions are obvious.

The aesthetic production begins with *Either/Or*. Its two parts represent a clash of life-views. The second part consists of letters addressed by a civic official, William, to a younger man, the author of the papers comprising the first part. William (or 'B'), by occupation a judge (*Assessor i Retten*), speaks for an ethical life-view. The papers of his young friend (referred to simply as 'A') 'contain a variety of attempts at [rendering] an aesthetic

57

life-view'. The 'editor' of both parts, one Victor Eremita, suggests that the attempt to give any 'single, coherent' account of the aesthetic view of life will be in vain.[8] He also suggests that both parts may be read as though written by the same person, someone who has practised or at least reflected upon both life-views. The title 'Either/Or' is chosen to dissuade the reader, having read both parts, from asking which view wins, 'whether A became in fact convinced and repented, whether B won, or whether it all ended with B's going over to A's opinion'.[9] We are even allowed to entertain the possibility that A wrote his part *after* receiving B's letters. The work, says the editor, 'has no ending' — something which he considers 'fortunate', since 'when the book has been read A and B are forgotten, only the views remain directly opposed to each other and await no final decision in particular personalities'.[10] A further likely prejudice *not* mentioned by the editor may also have to be suspended. The fact that A, the problem child of *Either/Or*, is not a self-professing Christian may strike us as inconsistent with Kierkegaard's retrospective claim that the aesthetic works are addressed to people in that category — unless we allow the possibility that B, too, is being shown the way back from the aesthetic.

The point of view of the second part is that of one who has succeeded in 'realizing the universal'. The expression is B's own,[11] and it can be said to express the general topic of the aesthetic production. The Danish term translated as 'the universal' here has the more everyday meaning of 'the general' (*det Almene* — as opposed to 'det Universelle' which Kierkegaard uses only occasionally).[12] It is not to be understood in a strict or abstract philosophical sense. Realizing the universal for B is not, for example, conforming his intentions to the abstract Kantian principle: 'Act according to a maxim which can at the same time make itself a universal law.'[13] Judge William has not bent his will to the requirements of an ideal kingdom of ends (to conceive which requires one, as Kant says, to 'abstract from the personal differences of rational beings, and likewise from all the content of their private ends').[14] Nor has he 'realized his essence' in an Aristotelian sense, i.e. brought to fruition an innate capacity to perform in a specifically human way. It is nevertheless true that he has conformed himself to something, and that this something is linked to the idea of his proper nature. He has adapted himself to the social world around him in the belief both that individual freedom requires the maintenance of a civil state, and that the most humanly fulfilling activities are those in which this result is most directly achieved — that is, from positions of civic and political responsibility. More generally, and disregarding the privileges which have given William access to these especially fulfilling (though perhaps also especially taxing) activities, he has become an effective participant in an already existing and hetero-geneous community with its pre-existing system of moral and legal obligations.

The ethical life which B recommends to his young friend A is therefore that of Hegel's *Sittlichkeit*, a public morality or con-formity to an already spontaneously existing ethical state of affairs (as opposed to *Moralität*, or Kant's concept of ethics as the obligation to 'realize' what does not exist).[15] The recommendation focuses on the virtues (and rewards) of marriage and of having a job (or 'position'). We recall Kierkegaard's deathbed regret: 'I had my thorn in my flesh, and therefore I did not marry and could not take on an official position.'[16] That Kierkegaard himself failed to realize the universal does not mean that he rejected Judge William's view that to do so is a good thing. All it means is that Kierkegaard himself was unable to put the recommendation into practice. It is relevant that *Either/Or* and the pseudonymous works following it are the product of the intense activity which began *after* the breaking off of his engagement and the abandonment of the idea of an academic or clerical career. The possible nature of the problems preventing his successful accommodation to the life of civic virtue were hinted at in Chapter I. These problems, particularly those surrounding his decision not to marry, are the recurring themes of *Either/Or* (1843), *Fear and Trembling* (1843), *Repetition* (1843), and *Stages on Life's Way* (1845).

It would be wrong to interpret these works merely as attempts to make philosophical and literary capital out of a banal circum-stance; just as it would be misleading to think of them as no more than elaborate attempts to excuse himself in his own eyes, those of his ex-fiancée, or of the prevailing *Sittlichkeit*. Certainly, he does try in these works to explain the conditions under which the failure of this particular attempt to realize the universal might nevertheless be justified, and to examine (in *Fear and Trembling*) the different ways in which a relationship to the universal can be *lost*, and what is required for it to be *regained*. But the project can be more profitably interpreted as a penetrating critique of the ethics of *Sittlichkeit* as such. Rather *because* than *in spite* of their autobiographical origin, Kierkegaard's reflections on his own exceptionality have the force of elevating his own case into a demonstration of the inadequacy of a public morality (a morality based on the 'universal-human')[17] as a foundation for human fulfilment, and thus, in effect, of giving his own case the status of

59

a counter-example to the theory that it *is* an adequate foundation. As a counter-example it can, of course, be the more significant the greater the reason for supposing the circumstances surrounding it to be 'banal', that is, common.

2 *Equilibrium*

B's (Judge William's) recommendation of the universal is couched in terms which give no hint that there might be insuperable difficulties in realizing it.

> He who has chosen and found himself ethically has determined himself in all his concreteness. He then has himself as an individual with these capacities, these passions, these inclinations, these habits, as one under these outside influences, who is swayed in one direction thus, in another thus. Here then he has himself as a task, which virtually amounts to arranging, shaping, moderating, arousing, suppressing, in short bringing about a proportionality [*Ligelighed*] in the soul, a harmony which is the fruit of the personal virtues. The end of his activity here is himself, but it is not an arbitrarily fixed end, for he has himself as a task which is set *for* him, even though it has become his by his choosing it. But although he himself is his end, this end is nevertheless also another, for the self which is the end is not an abstract self which fits in everywhere and so nowhere, but a concrete self which stands in living interaction with these particular surroundings, these conditions of life, this order of things. This self which is the end is not merely a personal self but a social, a civic [*borgerligt*] self. He has, then, himself as a task for an activity whereby as this particular personality he intervenes in the conditions of life. Here his task is not to shape himself but to exert an influence, and yet he cultivates himself at the same time. . . .[18]

Judge William assumes a happy coincidence of personal fulfilment and civic virtue. By cultivating the latter one is *thereby* promoting the former, analogously to Kant's 'Stoic' and 'Epicurean' positions as the views, respectively, that happiness is a product of virtue and virtue a product of happiness.[19] Like Kant, except that the appeal here is to a bureaucratic, not a categorical imperative, William even insists that one must not think of what one actually achieves by engaging in the primary activity; one must simply do one's job: 'what I accomplish follows upon my work as a piece of good luck in which I may well take delight but which I dare not impute absolutely to myself'.[20] A person must just focus on that particular part of the fabric of society which it is his (or her) 'concrete' lot to be able to maintain. Although Judge William is a conservative in that he does not envisage the need to alter the structure of society, and indeed opposes 'all revolutionary radic-alism',[21] the issue he primarily addresses is not political. William is trying to impress upon A, the aesthete, the error of supposing that *individual* fulfilment must consist in rising *above* the universal, in becoming exceptional, a misfit from the universal, i.e. general, point of view. A's mistake is to assume that the universal and the particular cannot be reconciled and that to be a self, a particular person, a free individual, one must eschew the category of the universal with its duties, roles, and responsibilities. William is saying that A will find the personal fulfilment he is after, indeed first *become* a self, by choosing the ethical sphere. This, according to William, is not to do away with difference, to ignore all that by which one is individuated as the unique person one is; it is to give to the category of difference a universal significance. In respect of A's main preoccupations, what to do with his life and whether or not to marry, it is wrong of A to believe that getting a job and marrying involve a reduction of individuality into something common and undifferentiated or abstract. One who chooses the ethical, says William, 'will not fail to appreciate the importance of the differences'. There is no 'abstract calling', and no 'abstract marriage'. For example, ethics 'tells him merely that he shall marry; it does not tell him with whom'. If he chooses ethics, it will show him how 'difference casts light *on* [*forklarer*, in the sense of 'explains'] the general [or universal] ', while he himself will 'trans-figure [*forklare*, in its secondary sense] difference *in* the general [or universal] '.[22]

We said that the works which concern us here (*Either/Or, Fear and Trembling, Repetition*, and *Stages on Life's Way*) are the result of Kierkegaard's attempt to come to terms with the conflicts surrounding his own failure to 'realize the universal' in respect of marrying Regine, along with the 'civic' side of the universal which Kierkegaard, the academic and ecclesiastical 'drop-out', also failed conspicuously to realize. The terms of reference of these works could be defined in two different ways. The straightforward inter-pretation would construe them as dealing with the difficulties of realizing Judge William's ideal of the coincidence of personal and social virtue on the judge's own premises, that is to say from the point of view from which he himself recommends the universal as a solution to A's conflicts (the ethical 'brings [a person] into harmony with the whole of existence, teaching him to rejoice in this; for as the exception, as the extraordinary, he is in conflict . . .').[23] But they can also be interpreted as demonstrating, by means of these difficulties, the inadequacy of Judge William's premises. And this is indeed how, Kierkegaard makes it clear, they should be interpreted, as first indicated in a final section of *Either/Or*, entitled 'Ultimatum' ('Final Word'), and later in the *Postscript*. *Either/Or* concludes with a sermon by a former student colleague of William's, now a priest in Jutland, and which William thinks might be of assistance to A. The text is the passage in St Luke (xix. 41–8) where Jesus first of all predicts the downfall of Jerusalem and then ejects from the temple the buyers and sellers he finds using it as a market-place, rebuking them for turning a house of prayer into a den of thieves. The point is not, of course, by association, to accuse incumbents of positions of civic and political responsibility of thievery; it is rather, by indicating the opposition, also mentioned in the text quoted, of these ('the chief priests, and the scribes and the chief of the people') to Jesus's taking over the temple to teach the importance of *prayer*, to bring out the incompatibility between civically defined virtue (including the standards set by institutionalized religion) and the notion of a transcendent God as the source and guarantor of personal value or fulfilment. In prayer it is individual conscience that a person places at the centre of morality, not conformity to a set of acknowledged rules of social behaviour. For Kierkegaard this also involves the idea of there being, on the one hand, no determinable limit to what a person might be required to do in pursuance of the good (and of personal fulfilment), and on the other no conclusive grounds for moral condemnation in the event of an evident failure to follow an acknowledged rule. And it even involves the idea, totally alien to William's standpoint, of the individual's natural inability to satisfy the requirements of human fulfilment. In a patent reference (though no doubt not directly intended as such for the reader) to his own situation, Kierkegaard (or William's friend the priest) says:

> Though your only wish were denied you, dear reader, you are joyful nevertheless; you do not say, 'God is always right', for there is no joyfulness in that; you say, 'In the face of God I am always wrong'. Though you yourself were the one who had to deny your dearest wish, you are joyful nevertheless; you do not say, 'God is always right', for there is no exultation in that; you say, 'In the face of God I am always wrong'. Though that which was your desire was what others and you yourself must, in a certain sense, call your duty, though you not only had to deny your wish, but in a way fail in your duty, though you lost not

only your joy but your honour, you are joyful nevertheless; 'In the face of God', you say, 'I am always wrong'. Though you knocked and it was not opened unto you, though you sought and did not find, though you laboured and nothing gained, though you planted and watered and beheld no blessing, though heaven were closed and the witness failed to appear, you are joyful in your work nevertheless; though the punishment which the guilt of the fathers had called down were visited upon you [as in the predicted destruction of the city of Jerusalem], you are joyful nevertheless, for in the face of God we are always wrong.[24]

What William does not appreciate in specifying his ideal of realizing the universal in terms of 'choosing and finding oneself ethically' in 'all [one's] concreteness', is that the self one has to choose is one that is 'in the wrong', i.e. guilty, before God, whatever personal or social goal one sets oneself and may or may not achieve. William assumes that it is enough for his young friend A to 'win himself' that he live through the despair into which the aesthetic life (inevitably) leads him. Kierkegaard gives two different kinds of argument for the error of this assumption. One of them is difficult to formulate clearly enough for its force to be judged. He says that a person 'uses *himself*' to despair, and that although this is consistent with his despairing of everything, it is not consistent with his rescuing himself (i.e. his using himself to rescue himself) from despair. For that he needs *outside* assistance, that is divine assistance (*guddommelig Bistand*), the point being that in order to come out of despair it is necessary to break with the 'immanence' which, as noted in the previous chapter, is characteristic of the ethical (i.e. B's) position.[25] The second argument is more straightforward. It is to the effect that if A is to 'win himself' *in* the ethical, then he must not be, or become, subject to obligations which override the ethical (defined as the system of obligations derivable from the notion of civic virtue).[26] Kierkegaard's point here is that since there are such obligations (as people in A's position soon realize if they turn to the ethical), the simple idea of a coincidence of personal and social virtue has to be rejected.

3 Repetition

Either/Or, a major literary work by any standards, as well as an extraordinarily rich and compelling portrayal of what Climacus in the *Postscript* calls 'the existential relationship between the aesthetic and the ethical within an existing individual', was published in February of 1843. In the following October there appeared on the same day, together with three non-pseudonymous 'edifying discourses', two more 'aesthetic' works, *Fear and Trembling* and *Repetition*. The former was written during a brief visit to Berlin, Kierkegaard's second since breaking off his engagement to Regine two years previously; while the latter, the themes of which we shall now outline, was begun in Berlin (its first section contains a good deal of apparently documentary material from that stay) and finished shortly after Kierkegaard's return to Copenhagen.

Two aspects of Kierkegaard's concept of 'repetition' are important for an understanding of his thought. One is its function in Kierkegaard's own version of a familiar and long-established motif in Western thought: the idea of a triadic progression out of primitive unity, into a dissolution or division into incongruent parts, and then a recombination of these in a 'higher' unity which somehow embraces both the unity of the first phase and the differentiation of the second.[27] The other important aspect of repetition is the notion of silence as incommunicability. The connection between these two aspects can be explained by briefly contrasting Kierkegaard's version of this triadic progression with Hegel's.

In Hegel's *Logic* (*Wissenschaft der Logik*) the primitive unity is called 'being', which Hegel refers to as the 'immediate'. The immediate is an unreflected reality, corresponding to the (Hegel thinks necessarily inadequate, and so problem-posing and thought-generating) notion of being as such. It can perhaps best be thought of as the undifferentiated domain out of which the notion of determinateness, of having these or those qualities, emerges. Its unity is therefore that of lack of boundary or distinction. Reflection, in Hegel's *Logic*, 'mediates' the immediate by, as it were, putting the notion of determinateness into practice and referring the qualitatively empty domain of mere being to an underlying ground, and thus applying the notion of 'essence' to things, which are now no longer seen by themselves as merely being, without being something, i.e. something of a certain sort, etc. But reflection, because it distinguishes *between* things, generates distinction, difference, incompatibility, opposition.[28] We saw, however, in the *Phenomenology*, that what the idea of speculative reason validates is the idea that the very concepts in which distinctions first emerge also overcome these; individual cases of the overcoming of conceptual oppositions (contradictions) are revealed, in the light of the idea of an absolute unity or ground, as advances to more unified levels of understanding. According to this version of the triad, then, the second unity is, in the way we have indicated, a publicly accessible reality. It is a reality of which 'thought-categories' (*Denkbestimmungen*) are part and parcel.[29] And it is therefore one which can, in principle, be communicated directly in those categories.

To Kierkegaard, Hegel's way of explaining reality is essentially Platonic. For all its insistence on world-history as a *developing* process, Hegel's account is really no more than a variant, indeed a paradigm instance, of Plato's doctrine of knowledge as recollection (*anamnesis*). What Hegel's *Logic* purports to give is a key to the completion of a total view of reality. It assumes, therefore, that reality has a determinable, as well as necessary, logical structure. If there is such a key, the development can be no more than the unfolding of what is already there in principle at the beginning. Consequently, what is needed for individual fulfilment is not some creative action on the part of the individual, or of mankind, but an insight that recreates what is already determinably the case. And as far as action itself goes, the properly human goals and purposes will be common and collective ones — as we noted in the previous chapter; they will be projects the motivating interests in which are readily recognizable amongst those who see that fulfilling actions are actions in pursuit of social unity. For the insight that allows them to see this is that social unity is, after all, just an aspect of the all-embracing unity of thought.

That participation in the social whole is necessary for individual fulfilment Kierkegaard does not question; indeed the entire 'aesthetic production' testifies to his conviction that it is. What Kierkegaard claims is that there can be, perhaps even latently always are, *moral* obstacles to participation in the social whole, obstacles which can only be overcome on the basis of new ways of understanding and judging the performances of those who do appear to succeed in realizing the universal, as well as the failures of those who do not. The new ways which Kierkegaard is seeking in the aesthetic works are ones which will enable 'exceptions', whose *guilt* prevents them from realizing the universal, to establish their relationship to it nevertheless. What this requires is a developing insight on the part of the individual into personal guilt and a point of view from which personal fulfilment, or moral failure and restitution, is by no means directly linked to a visible public morality. As the insight deepens, so the aesthetic works indicate, it becomes ever clearer that what is needed to redress such breaches of public morality as Kierkegaard himself found himself involved in is not a greater awareness of the rational connection between private and public ends, or the straightforward removal of what-ever private scruples stand in the way of a realization of the universal, but a new conception of public morality itself, one in which public morality is subordinated to the imperatives of a private conscience in relationship to a transcendent God. Kierkegaard's view is that it is only from the point of view of this 'higher' (or deeper) perspective that realizing the universal can genuinely be an expression of *individual* fulfilment.

Fulfilment on this condition is the 'higher' unity of Kierkegaard's version of the triadic progression. The intermediate phase of separation out of which it emerges (or is brought about) is that of the individual's awareness of being separated from its own nature, involving a loss of spontaneity, and connected with awareness of its guilt. The guilt here cannot be alleviated by a simple absorption into the moral fold, for it needs the idea that the individual *as such* can be an agent of the good; not only independently of, but even in the face of public morality, indeed even, apparently, in the face of personal moral intuition. In other words — and the 'split' here is one we recognize from Hegel's unhappy consciousness — what is needed is the idea of a transcendent source of human value in the face of which, whatever one's public moral status or private moral intuitions, *everyone* is 'always in the wrong'. The primitive unity, which (like Hegel) Kierkegaard calls (sometimes the 'first' as opposed to the second or 'higher') immediacy, out of which this split in turn emerges, is a 'spontaneity', 'certainty' (we might regard it as the moral equivalent of Hegel's 'sense-certainty'), though also 'ignorance' (of the 'difference between good and evil'),[30] in which the individual assumes unreflectively that it is its own moral centre.

The idea of something's being its own centre, or of its having its centre or unity *in* itself, is also Hegelian. In fact, it is Hegel's definition of 'spirit', and spirit, or at any rate self-conscious spirit, is also Hegel's second unity, the notion of spirit as 'self-contained existence' being that of freedom ('for if I am dependent, my being is referred to something else which I am not . . . I am free . . . when my existence depends on myself'),[31] i.e. of human fulfilment. That the formulae for Hegel's first and second unity are identical should be no surprise. The path, for Hegel, proceeds from spirit's sense of being its own centre in sense-certainty to the sense of self-estrangement, generated by reflection, of not being its own centre, and then *in* reflection (or as a reflection on reflection) to the discovery that it is its own centre after all. The operative factor in this discovery — and what Kierkegaard diagnoses as a case of Platonic recollection — is spirit's finding itself at home in the objective, 'external' world. For Kierkegaard, however, for whom there is no such factor, what spirit (in Kierkegaard's case the morally self-conscious individual or 'self') discovers is that the objective, external world is an alien environment for an interest in personal fulfilment. There is, of course, no objective *internal* world to which it can turn in order to find an alternative 'home'; to accept that there was such a world would be to subscribe to Plato's own version of the doctrine of recollection, epitomized in the rationalist belief in reason as an independent source of substantial and (it is usually assumed) ultimately *satisfying* truth. Since there is no *return* to unity that Kierkegaard's divided self can experience, the satisfaction of the unity of the second immediacy has to be achieved within the framework of its dividedness. But from there the ideal of a *self-contained* existence can only be that of a transcendent being, and the second immediacy some kind of participation in that being — though not in thought, for that would again be recollection. In other words, the individual can only conceive its fulfilment as a form of dependence. In a later work Kierkegaard explicitly states that the 'formula' for the integrated (no longer despairing) self is its recognition that it is 'grounded transparently in the Power which posited it',[32] meaning God. (This sounds like a direct denial of Hegelian freedom,[33] though Kierkegaard's description in *Repetition* of the religious individual as one who 'rests in himself' seems to imply that he nevertheless intended individual freedom to have the general Hegelian form.)[34] Arriving at the point of view from which the finite world *as a whole* is reduced to dependency upon a transcendental origin (and source of value) is a case of what Kierkegaard calls 'repetition'. From a new, higher vantage-point one 'repeats' one's earlier experience, giving it a new, and deeper, unity. (An entry from the *Journals* reads: 'The presuppositional basis of consciousness, or, as it were, the [musical] key, is continually being raised, but within each key the same thing is repeated.')[35] Besides differing from Hegel in claiming that each 'key' is applied *to*, and cannot be derived *from*, experience,[36] Kierkegaard thinks that his own repetitional account also differs from Hegel's recollective one in retaining the previous experiences in some sense intact; in Hegel, says Kierkegaard, one vantage-point 'swallows' another but not in the way in which one stage of life swallows another, 'with each still keeping its validity'.[37]

In *Repetition* itself ('An Effort in Experimental Psychology by Constantin Constantius') we meet a young man, evidently a recasting of A from the first part of *Either/Or* though in a simpler mould. Whereas A, as any sampling of the quotable quotes of the opening section of *Either/Or* will confirm, has a good measure of irony bound up in his 'immediacy', the young man in *Repetition*

67

is too closely occupied by the problems of that life to gain an ironic perspective on it. As Kierkegaard notes in his unpublished papers, 'in *Repetition* feeling and irony are kept apart, each in its representative: the young man and Constantin'.[38] The young man is engaged to a girl, with whom he is 'deeply in love',[39] and to whom he feels ethically obligated. But the relationship is one he feels incapable of consummating, as he agrees it should be consummated, in marriage. The immediate reason is his 'melancholy',[40] something which has deprived him of the spontaneity which must *not* be swallowed up in marriage in such a way as to lose its 'validity'. As the author, Constantin, from his more detached perspective, points out, his young friend is 'really finished with the whole relationship'.[41] Constantin, with his capacity for irony, is able to observe that the girl is not in fact the object of the young man's love, but only 'the occasion that has aroused the poetical in him'.[42] He observes in retrospect that 'she made him into a poet and by that very fact signed her own death-warrant'.[43] As his poetic melancholy ('longing')[44] − something that, Constantin knowingly observes, can make him even more attractive in the girl's eyes[45] − becomes compounded by guilt and takes the upper hand, the young man is strengthened in his resolve to sever the relationship.

Constantin Constantius's role is Socratic, fictitiously for the benefit of his friend (though later, because having once confided to him that the girl was a nuisance,[46] his friend can no longer face meeting Constantin, and by omitting to give a return address makes it impossible in any case for Constantin to reply to his letters, which he writes simply to 'vent' himself),[47] but also for the enlightenment of the reader − and no doubt of Kierkegaard himself. He presents the young man with ways of looking at and dealing with his situation, in order for the latter to find out how much he really loves the girl, whether it is his own, or his sense of the girl's, pride that effectively prevents an open break, etc. He also indicates, primarily to the reader, what the young man can and cannot do, in which direction he can and cannot go in order (without self-deception) to solve his ethical dilemma. The principal impossibility is that of returning to spontaneity or immediacy through *philosophy*. The possibility that gradually dawns on him is that of repetition. In his remarks prefatory to the one-way correspondence collected in the second part of *Repetition*, Constantius says:

> The problem he stops short at is nothing more nor less than repetition. He is quite right not to look for enlightenment on

this either in Greek or modern philosophy, for the Greeks make the opposite movement and a Greek would choose to recollect, without his conscience causing him any anxiety; while modern philosophy makes no movement at all, it only makes cancellations [*Ophævelser*, i.e. Hegel's *Aufhebungen*, though Kierkegaard's expression 'den gjør kun Ophævelser' would also suggest to the Danish reader a colloquialism meaning 'making a great fuss about something'] , and whatever movement it does make it always makes within immanence; repetition, on the contrary, is and remains a transcendence.[48]

But there are two further significant impossibilities to note. The first is that of repetition occurring in the young man's case without taking regard to the connection between suffering and *guilt*. The young man compares his own suffering with that of Job, who made the requisite movement to faith, i.e. repetition ('Job is blessed and has got everything *in duplicate* − that is what we call a *repetition*'),[49] but without having to face the problem of guilt ('he knows he is innocent and pure in his inmost heart').[50] The second impossibility is that of Constantius himself 'performing the religious movement'. 'It is', he says, 'against my nature', repetition being also 'transcendent' in the colloquial sense of being 'beyond' him.[51]

With regard to the former impossibility, guilt is the factor which in Kierkegaard's view ultimately destroys Judge William's congenial assumption that the proper, and always in principle possible, solution to the conflicts of an outsider like A is to 'choose himself' *qua* member of the already established ethico-political whole. The idea of guilt was introduced by the Jutland priest as the 'last word' of *Either/Or*, and is pursued in the later *Stages on Life's Way*, in which yet another, still more advanced version of A (but in whom involvement and distance are once more combined), by the name of 'Quidam', extracts the full significance of guilt.[52] Guilt, according to Kierkegaard, prevents public morality from being the dimension in which lost spontaneity can be recaptured and 'transfigured'; but in repentance and faith it offers a platform for ascent to a point of view higher than that of public morality. We return to this in the next section.

Regarding the second impossibility, Constantius's inability to assist his friend into the higher point of view can be seen in two distinct but compatible lights. First, there is the question which must have occupied Kierkegaard himself at the time, namely whether his *writing* could count as a way of realizing the universal. Could his own particular breach with public morality be excused by a service rendered to the universal by the opportunity given him to explain it publicly? Perhaps his failure to do the right thing by Regine could be regarded from some universal point of view *other* than that of public morality as part of a providential opportunity to throw light on public morality's own inherent deficiencies?[53] Could not the conflict and the subsequent breaking-off of the relationship, which had aroused so much of the poet in him, be seen to serve some general human purpose after all? Perhaps it was as the 'poetic exception' that he could conceive his connection with humanity? But Constantius (in a concluding 'letter' to his reader which serves the same baton-changing role in the relay of pseudonyms as the sermon at the end of *Either/Or*) is inclined to reject this possibility on behalf of his friend. Although unable to say specifically what his friend must do to regain a relationship to the universal, in a final parting of his and the young man's ways at the end of *Repetition*, he sketches a framework in which the possibility of a 'religious exception',[54] the theme of *Fear and Trembling*, can be envisaged.

If he had had a deeper religious background, he would not have become a poet. Then everything would have acquired religious significance. The event in which he was entangled would still have had significance for him, but then the repulse [*Anstødet*, also 'obstacle' or 'barrier'] would have come from higher places; but then also he would have had a very different [sort of] authority, even though it were bought by a still more painful suffering; he would . . . have acted quite differently, with an iron consistency and firmness; he would have acquired a fact of consciousness [*Bevidstheds-Faktum*, i.e. some unquestioned assumption which gives consciousness a 'facticity' as distinct from the foundationless 'dialectical elasticity' of the poet's mind] which he could constantly abide by and which would never have become ambiguous to him, but pure seriousness, because it was posited in him by virtue of a God-relationship. The same instant the whole question of finitude would have become indifferent to him; reality properly so called [*den egentlige Virkelighed*, which a poet with 'a religious tone' is nevertheless equipped to 'throw light on'][55] would in a deeper sense be neither here nor there. He would have got religiously to the bottom of all the dreadful consequences contained in [the] event [in question]. Had reality turned out differently, he would not have changed essentially, just as little as, were the worst to transpire, this would have essentially left him in greater dismay than that in which he was already. He would then have understood in fear and trembling, but also with faith and confidence, what he had done from the very beginning, and what in consequence it was his obligation to do later, even though this obligation were to give rise to the oddest behaviour.[56]

Representing, as he does, the *irony* in the original A's make-up, Constantius can accompany A's simpler counterpart (as 'a ministering spirit' [*en tjenende Aand*])[57] only so far. Indeed only as far as the latter's poetic personality can carry him — which nevertheless includes the extra range provided by the 'religious tone' that his suffering has gained for him. For on Kierkegaard's account of irony an ironist, too, lacks the deeper religious background. Irony is negative; it can only conceive the 'positive infinite' abstractly.[58] But it does have an important heuristic role: 'Irony limits, renders finite, defines and thereby yields truth, reality, and content; it chastens and punishes and thereby yields character and consistency.'[59] Constantius's positive contribution has been to give shape and definition to the moral conflict implicit in the 'event', and to prepare us for the new perspective of the pseudonymous author of *Fear and Trembling*.

The second way of looking at Constantius's inability to help his friend further takes us back to the second of the two aspects of repetition mentioned at the beginning of this section: silence as incommunicability. Constantius's remark, just quoted, that the moral behaviour stemming from a God-relationship may be 'odd', may be understood as allowing that the action dictated by the higher point of view need not coincide with conventional moral classifications, may indeed not appear in the conventional way to be moral at all. What the higher point of view allows as a justifiable exception to the public moral code may, from the common point of view which upholds that code (typically as a necessary means to, rather than an expression of, human fulfilment), seem to be no more than a simple failure, or even refusal, to be moral. The point is that as the moral centre is moved from the moral code enshrined in the established ethico-political order to a transcendent source whose direct expression is not the social or political unit but the individual conscience, moral behaviour loses its transparency. A tension arises, a lack of congruency, between the visible surface of action and utterance (what we can be seen to do and heard to say) and their underlying intentions (what we are actually about and what we mean); the former will no longer be a reliable test of the latter. Of the young man, Constantius says that 'as a poet he can never rightly know what he has done', because 'he wants to see what he does in the outward and visible *and* wants not to see it there, or wants to see it [only] in the outward and visible, and so both wants to see it and wants not to see it'.[60] But again, Kierkegaard makes it clear that, as an ironist, not even Constantius himself is someone who could know what he has done. Although irony, in Kierkegaard's use of the term, is the sense of a disparity between the outward and visible ('phenomenon'), on the one hand, and something below the visible surface felt to be more important ('essence') on the other, its focus is still on the former. Even when, as in irony 'in a stricter sense', it is the 'whole of existence' (*Tilværelsens Totale*) that is viewed 'sub specie ironiae',[61] that is, when the finite as such is 'viewed' as something bounded by its opposite, i.e. the infinite or eternal (compare Wittgenstein's remark that viewing the world 'sub specie aeterni' is to view it 'as a whole, a limited whole'),[62] irony does not penetrate the surface. Consequently, irony remains at the level where what we mean is what we can say to others, while repetition requires a level where this is no longer the case.

Because Constantius's ministerings do not allow his friend, or us, to penetrate the surface, the internal or hidden aspect (the 'essence' as opposed to the 'phenomenon') remains abstract. Consequently, any difficulties there may be in connection with it also remain abstract — and therefore remote. Thus it is possible, so far, for the general impression of the inward to be positive. It is not only where any solution to the seemingly intractable problems of guilt *must* lie, it is assumed to be where their solution *can* lie. The difficulties the young man and Constantius focus on are in the finite realm; they are practical obstacles to realizing the universal. With our next pseudonym Johannes *de silentio*, however, the surface is penetrated. Johannes, although like Constantius a poet, as indicated by the subtitle of his work, 'Dialectical Lyric', and in spite of his name just as loquacious, has enough religious background and 'dialectical' ability to bring out the implications of the hoped-for solution. (The fact that he has the religious background excludes a sense in which the dialectical ability which *we* might be willing to call philosophical, could be philosophical in Kierkegaard's sense: it is suggested that a necessary negative condition for Johannes's having the religious background, and one he claims to satisfy, is being 'by no means a philosopher', which is to say that he *will* 'stop at faith', and does not want to 'go further'.)[63] The result is to bring into focus a new obstacle, the experience of that 'repulse' (or barrier) from 'higher places' predicted by Constantius, and what our new author calls the 'shudder of thought' (*Tankens Gysen*).[64]

4 The teleological suspension of the ethical

Johannes remarks that in the 'ethical way of regarding life it is
... the task of the individual to divest himself of the inward
determinants and express them in an outward way'.[65] According
to Judge William in *Either/Or*, 'the beauty of the universal [*det
Almene*] consists precisely in the fact that all [can] understand
it'.[66] As the name *de silentio* implies, the transition to the deeper
perspective involves recognition of the presence of inward determinants that cannot be expressed in an outward way and in
respect of which, for reasons we must try to identify and evaluate,
any universal communication remains silent.

In his journal Kierkegaard writes of secrets he could not tell
Regine and which, by preventing the openness to her which their
marriage would, according to his own and prevailing moral
principles, demand, also prevented the marriage.

> In the marriage ceremony I must take an oath — therefore I
> do not dare conceal anything. On the other hand there are
> things I cannot tell her. The fact that the divine enters into
> marriage is my ruin. If I do not let myself marry her I offend
> her. If an unethical relationship can be justified — then I begin
> tomorrow. She has asked me, and for me that is enough. She
> can depend on me absolutely, but it is an unhappy existence.
> I am dancing upon a volcano and must let her dance along with
> me as long as it can last. This is why it is more humble of me to
> remain silent. That it does humble me I know only too well.[67]

What the secrets were or whether they constituted the only
obstacle to the marriage are not matters of prime importance here.
In an earlier entry Kierkegaard does in fact detail the 'terrible
things' he would have to initiate Regine into were he to explain
himself: 'my relationship to my father, his melancholy, the eternal
night brooding within me, my going astray, my lusts and debauchery'.[68] But apart perhaps from the latter, the importance of
which at least there he appears nevertheless to discount (as due to
'anxiety' and lack of a 'safe stronghold' when that provided by his
father, 'the only man [he] admired for his strength', proved
fallible), these references still effectively conceal the reason for his
scruples. Nor is it possible to say precisely in what way these
matters exclude Kierkegaard from the universal. Is it because to
divulge these things would be a betrayal of a *personal* trust, a
breach of moral principle for which the *Sittlichkeit* cannot provide
any overriding justification? Or is it because others, and particularly
Regine, would not have *understood* them and thus they would fall

outside the scope of the universal as that which 'all can understand'?
Was it perhaps that Kierkegaard saw Regine as an innocent victim
of his own culpably selfish eroticism? Whatever may be the case,
the important point is, first, that in one way or another Kierkegaard found himself unable to comply with an ethical principle
which he himself accepted; and second, that the inability was due
neither to a conflict between that principle and some other, overriding and generally accepted moral principle which he also
accepted, and which in the eyes of conventional morality would
then absolve him; nor to a simple failure to let principle rather than
undirected inclination or desire guide his actions, which would
earn him conventional morality's reproach in a quite straightforward way. As far as his inclinations went these apparently
(and let us just assume) favoured his relationship with Regine; in
marrying her he would simply be following Judge William's advice
to transform a particular wish into the universal.[69] So there is no
basis for the conventional reproach to dereliction of duty, namely
the preference to be swayed by inclination. But in the absence of
any overriding duty it seems that conventional morality will
reproach him all the same. If the ethical is conceived, as Johannes
says, as the 'universal' and therefore as 'valid for everyone [and]
at every instant', then as soon as the individual '[asserts] himself
in his particularity over against the universal he sins, and only by
recognizing this can he again reconcile himself with the universal'.[70]
But is admitting to the proponents of the universal ethic that one
is guilty of a breach of that ethic the only way to reconciliation
with the universal? Is there not, as Constantius asked in his 'letter',
a way open also to 'exceptions'? Or must any justification for
being an exception be at the expense of a split between the
individual and the universal so definitive as to exclude their reconciliation?

In *Fear and Trembling* Johannes *de silentio* raises this complex
of issues under the rubric of 'the teleological suspension of the
ethical'. The theme is one which Kierkegaard first raises in his unpublished papers in connection with the question of whether 'a
great man' should be judged 'according to principles different
from those used for every other man'. There Kierkegaard answers
that, although the question has often been answered in the affirmative, he thinks the right answer is 'No'. For

> a great man is great just because he is a chosen instrument in
> the hands of God. But the moment he fancies that it is he
> himself who acts, that *he* can look out over the future, and on
> that basis he lets the end ennoble the means — then he is small.

Right and duty are valid for everybody, and the great man has
no more excuse for trespassing against them than have
governments, where people nevertheless imagine that politicians
have licence to do wrong. . . .[71]

Later, however, Kierkegaard finds it necessary in connection with
his own 'relationship to the universal' to question this negative
answer. The possibility of a *teleological* suspension of the ethical
is that of there being some *absolute* end (or τέλος) which would
make it possible to construe a case of an inability to realize the
universal as a justified exception to the general (and, in the passage
just quoted, strictly universal) validity of rights and duties.

Johannes distinguishes between two kinds of exception, only
one of which would require the possibility of a teleological suspension of the ethical for its justification. The kind which would
not require this possibility he calls the 'tragic hero', and here he
gives examples from Greek mythology (Agamemnon), the Bible
(Jephthah), and Roman history (Brutus). Common to these is the
ethically required suppression of a natural inclination where the
inclination is backed by an overridden ethical norm. The figures in
question are victims of the fact that their engagement in public
affairs brings them into situations where public (in the sense of
'civic') and private morality conflict. Since private morality is
distinguished from public morality by being, in accordance with
Judge William's ethical view of things, the morality which consists
in the elevating of particular preferences into duties, the distinction corresponds with that between inclination and duty,
except that the inclinations have been 'transfigured' into morally
accepted duties. So when Agamemnon, against his parental inclination *and* duty, sacrifices his daughter in order to win divine favour
for a national enterprise, his responsibility for which, however
much he 'might wish that he were "the lowly man who dares to
weep" ', was an overriding duty; and when the judge Jephthah
does the same to *his* daughter to keep a vow made on behalf of
his nation; and when Brutus 'heroically' ignores the fact that the
man he is duty-bound to put to death is his own son, these exceptions are understood and admired.

The tragic hero still remains within the ethical. He gives one
expression of the ethical a τέλος in a higher expression of
the ethical; he reduces [thereby] the ethical relation between
father and son, or daughter and father, to a sentiment which is
[nevertheless still] dialectically related to the idea of morality.
Here, then, there can be no question of a teleological suspension
of the ethical itself.[72]

In the case of tragic heroism the higher ethical standpoint justifies the suspension of private morality by reducing a moral wish to the status of mere sentiment. The ethical as such, however, is not yet suspended.

To suspend the ethical is to suspend a moral principle without the saving justification that doing so is necessary for conforming to an overriding one. Thus in the absence of a generally accepted moral reason for contravening private morality, a reason which can relativize the moral value of the unfulfilled norms and so bring the contravention within the range of the 'sympathy' and 'admiration' of every 'noble soul',[73] private morality should be accorded its full status as a domain of universally applicable rights and duties. Infractions of it will be totally inexcusable from the universal point of view, and the responsibility for its suspension will rest with the individual alone. Kierkegaard's (Johannes's) main example is Abraham's willingness to sacrifice his son, Isaac, at the command of God.[74] Abraham differs from the tragic hero in having no universal $\tau\acute{\epsilon}\lambda o\varsigma$ to appeal to. There is no question of his 'saving the nation', 'maintaining the idea of the state', or 'appeasing angry deities'. In fact, as Johannes points out, there seems to be no point of contact at all between Abraham's action (proceeding with the preparation for the sacrifice with the full intention of carrying it out) and the universal, other than that he contravened it.[75]

Johannes is careful to pinpoint what for him is the crux of the story. He begins — in an opening section called 'attuning' (Stemning, which also means 'mood' and can be taken here to mean 'setting the mood') — by presenting four versions, all of which contain elements that obscure this crux. In the first (and all of them follow the Genesis account in which God stays Abraham's hand at the last moment) Abraham pretends to Isaac that he wants to kill him, in case Isaac should lose faith at the thought of God's demanding this blatant breach of paternal love. In the second, Abraham resents God's demand and continues living in resentment of it. In the third, he cannot get away from the idea that what God demands of him is a sin, whether he loves his son (which he does) or not: if he loves him he offends his own moral intuition, if he did not he would be offending God by failing to sacrifice his most valued possession. In the fourth version Isaac notices that Abraham is in despair and so loses faith in him. All these versions fail as proofs of Abraham's faith. Faith is belief not just in the existence and authority of God, it requires a wholehearted acceptance that what God enjoins is the right thing to enjoin, which (for Kierkegaard as with Hegel) is coupled with the idea that what is right in the long run is to realize the universal. The second and third versions above have Abraham not fully conceding that what divine authority enjoins is the right thing to enjoin; while the first and fourth portray failure of the participants to let faith cement their personal relationship as one of openness and trust, as realizing the universal requires.

Johannes, in preparing the story for his own use, also deliberately removes all suggestions in the Genesis story that Abraham was motivated by guilt.[76] In doing this he (or Kierkegaard) has made Abraham's situation significantly different from Kierkegaard's own. Kierkegaard himself is seeking a justification for being the exception that his circumstances have already made him, but Abraham *chooses* to make himself an exception. Why? As Johannes says, Abraham is ready to do it '[for] God's sake', 'because God demands this proof of [Abraham's] faith', and by the same token 'for his own sake', because he wanted to 'provide this proof'.[77] But, in providing it, is not Abraham in effect reducing the ethical *as such* (and not simply private morality) to the status of sentiment? Are we not indeed forced to interpret his readiness to sacrifice his son — and it is this, the readiness, which is the proof demanded by God — as the acceptance of a point of view transcending the ethical and separated from it even more comprehensively than public, or civic, ethics was separated from private morality in the case of tragic heroism? In the latter case it was still morally intelligible that private morality should be suspended and thereby reduced to the level of sentiment. In his own suspension of the ethical Abraham seems to be willing to repudiate the ethical altogether. How else are we to construe his willingness to sacrifice his son in order to establish his own 'proper' relationship with God?

But from what Johannes has said earlier it appears that it would be wrong to interpret the example in this way. He has maintained that when the ethical is suspended it is not 'abolished' but preserved at a higher level.[78] The suspension, in other words, is to be construed after the manner of 'Aufhebung' in the Hegelian dialectic. According to this, in suspending the ethical one would not depart from it, but attain a higher point of view from which, on Hegel's version, its nature would be better understood. In Kierkegaard's version, however, attaining that higher point of view is a matter of faith, not a 'movement of thought'. The higher point of view does not stand to the latter as a next stage in a *logical* progression. It therefore does not provide a better *understanding*, it only offers the 'knight of faith' the logical *possibility* that in going 'beyond the ethical and [adopting] a higher τέλος outside it',[79] his 'movement' is indeed to a position which *somehow* validates his suspension of the ethical (as well as, in Abraham's case, his renunciation of his paternal feeling). The hope is not even allied to understanding in the sense that the validation must sanction some outcome which accords with the knight of faith's own moral intuitions. It is true that in the story of Abraham and Isaac, God, satisfied with Abraham's demonstration of his faith, does in fact withdraw the earlier demand and Abraham is allowed to sacrifice a ram instead (though even this defies understanding, the ram is provided); but to be a knight of faith Abraham had to be willing to accept that the outcome would be 'all right' even if God had not relented by producing a result which satisfied his moral intuition and personal preferences; that is, even if the way in which the outcome was 'all right' remained utterly obscure. Thus if Abraham were to proceed with the preparation of the sacrifice only in the belief that God's goodness meant that God would relent at the last minute and reprieve both father and son, his faith would not have been demonstrated. That belief would not have amounted to faith; faith requires that he believe that it would be 'all right' no matter what.

If suspension of the ethical does not imply its abolition, then however radical the breach of the higher point of view with intuition and understanding, it seems clear that the hope attached to that point of view is that it justifies an exception to the ethical (or universal) *without* at the same time forcing abandonment of morality altogether. And perhaps even without abandoning the essentials of the repertoire of moral judgments shared by those for whom the ethical has its τέλος 'in itself'.[80] For the latter, of course, the idea of a *teleological* suspension of the ethical is contradictory.[81] But not for the knight of faith, since by adopting a τέλος outside the ethical he is not putting himself above morality so much as extending morality's universe; and although he places himself outside the self-sufficient universalist ethics, he still feels the contrary pull of that ethics, as well as of his own preferences, the latter the more so that he no longer has the benefit of any overriding universalist principles on his side to supply moral support for his personal sacrifice. In allowing that universal morality 'is reduced to a position of relativity',[82] he is not accepting that the value ordinarily attributed to conventional moral practice may be revoked at any time by non-moral divine imperative. He is accepting, in order to disprove the suggestion that his assumption of a moral point of view which justifies his suspension of ordinary morality is just an *excuse*, that the 'odd' actions which (as Constantius warned) morality may require may well be actions which not only depart radically from those ordinarily taken to comprise moral duties,[83] but also fly in the face of the moral agent's personal preference and own moral intuition. Johannes, by purposely confining the Abraham and Isaac story to the matter of faith and its proof, uncomplicated by the real-life situation in which failure to realize the universal arises from problems in one's earlier self, 'accentuates'[84] the principle involved in the idea that there can be *morally* motivated exceptions to the rule that ethical norms apply universally. Or, in the idea that, corresponding to the suspension of private morality in deference to overriding civic obligations, there can be a suspension of both private and public morality in deference to an authority which imposes moral obligations directly upon the individual. Or in short, in the idea, which is totally alien to *Sittlichkeit* ethics, that, ethically speaking, 'the individual as the individual is higher than the universal',[85] and so need not 'express himself constantly in it [or] abolish his particularity in order to become [it]'.[86] Since Abraham's case is free of background difficulties of the kind to which an 'act of faith' might be suspected of being a strategic solution, his act is the more convincing as a demonstration of faith in a transcendent moral authority.

It may be objected that this is all a naïve ideological ruse just the same. In order to justify an inability to comply with accepted moral standards, Kierkegaard has simply projected the myth of superordinate values (furthermore, absolute ones) into his moral universe, and then with maximum arbitrariness assumed that the values stemming from this supposedly autonomous source will be the ones he needs.

There are three considerations which weigh against regarding Kierkegaard's appeal to an absolute moral authority in this light. In the first place, the inability which concerns him is not due to a simple disinclination to comply with accepted moral standards: the appeal to an absolute τέλος which 'relativizes' these standards is based on a *moral* experience: it is a moral scruple which prevents Kierkegaard from realizing the universal. In *Fear and Trembling* Johannes also recounts the legend of Agnete and the Merman,[87] again in a version modified to bring out the crucial points. The legend illustrates the 'logic' of Kierkegaard's own special situation with regard to the universal, as he saw it, in respect of his relationship with Regine. The merman (or water-sprite), a mythical seducer, is so touched by the (in Johannes's specially adapted version) innocence and trustingness of his would-be victim that he not only leaves her unmolested, but finds he cannot return to his 'immediate', spontaneous activities as a seducer. Guilt has interposed itself between him and his 'nature'; or, as Johannes puts it, his 'native element [has proved] unfaithful

79

to him'.[88] Similarly with Kierkegaard, the moral scruple which prevented him from realizing *his* 'universal-human' nature was guilt. In order to extend the analogy between the legend and Kierkegaard's own case, Johannes endows the merman with a human consciousness and a past ('in the consequences of which his life is entangled').[89] This suggests that in the human case the salacious activities, which in the unedited version of the legend come *naturally* to the merman, are the results of (not necessarily untypical) complications in human life, e.g. anxiety and loss of confidence in others, for example one's father.

Second, it appears that the appeal to the absolute is not, as the objection implies, a way of alleviating guilt. Kierkegaard does not mean it to provide a means of excusing the pain one has caused others, nor therefore of alleviating whatever pain one feels oneself on that account. Indeed, not only does the postulating of an absolute τέλος *preserve* guilt as a moral scruple based in the (universal) ethic, it compounds it, because from the higher point of view one takes responsibility for the circumstances which led to the pain. So in addition to the guilt one feels because of some particular breach of another's legitimate ethical expectations, one may now also feel guilty for having provided such expectations in the first place.

Third, the postulating of an absolute τέλος is not meant as a way of *legitimating* the breach with the universal; on the contrary, Johannes says it is a way, indeed the only way, of *repairing* that breach.

> . . . when the individual by his guilt has gone outside the universal he can return to it only by virtue of having come as the individual into an absolute relationship with the absolute.[90]

Johannes attributes to the merman three options once his relationship to his 'nature' has been disrupted by guilt. Since the point of amending the story by giving the merman a history of human hardship is to indicate that seduction is not his optimal activity, the merman's case can be generalized to that of the individual human being confronted with the possibility of realizing the universal. One option, not mentioned by Johannes, might be to try to return to the kind of existence from which guilt has removed one, i.e. immediacy. But this is in fact already accounted for in his amended version of the legend. The merman's activities are depicted as being due to the earlier hardships, as a necessarily unsuccessful attempt to solve the problems arising from them *by* a return to immediacy (*vide* Kierkegaard's explanation of his 'lust and debauchery'). The three possibilities Johannes actually lists are:

First, one may remain 'hidden' and '[initiate oneself] into all the torments of repentance', which involves becoming a 'demon' (Kierkegaard's name for one who 'fears the good') and as such being 'annihilated'.[91] This amounts to succumbing to the temptation to believe that the breach with the universal is justified by the self-inflicted pain incurred in cutting off the relation to it. This pain may not be simply the thought of loss (by both parties) of satisfaction available in the relation, it might include the additional pain of trying, in an exercise of well-meaning demonic 'shrewdness' aimed at alleviating the other party's pain, to get the latter to believe that one never really seriously entertained the possibility of entering properly into the relationship, that one was a despicable person, best forgotten, an incorrigible seducer by nature, etc. The attempt, apart from being well-intentioned, might (as Johannes adds in a 'psychological observation') even succeed; it may promote the other party's greater strength of character. But since it is nevertheless motivated by fear of the good it remains a 'demonic' possibility. Even if the demonic individual believes he has 'the proof that his silence is justified' because of the pain it brings him, and wants to be 'the individual who is higher than the universal', his position is not that of the knight of faith: 'he can still talk'; that is, he can in principle explain his situation to others in a way that would command sympathy and thus make himself a tragic hero, the thought of which can in turn provide him with further demonic justification for the breach with the universal.[92]

Second, one can repent properly, that is, not in *fear* of the good. In this case there are two alternatives. Either one remains 'concealed' but, no longer relying on shrewdness, 'finds repose in the counterparadox that the deity will save [the other party] ';[93] or — the third possibility listed by Johannes — one becomes 'saved' through (*ved*), i.e. in relation to, the other party. In the former case one remains cloistered, 'lost for this world', and thus fails to realize the universal; in the latter one becomes 'revealed', thereby realizing the universal and becoming the 'greatest man' Johannes can imagine.[94] Being 'revealed' means here disclosing a social nature, making and fulfilling social and personal commitments, in short participating actively in the private and public affairs of life in the way recommended by Judge William in *Either/ Or*.

This does not mean, however, that William's ideal and Johannes's conception of the greatest man are identical. Indeed in the later *Stages on Life's Way* William's position is presented as being no longer the 'highest'.[95] Not, however, because the ideal proves to be either inadequate or unnecessary; what the later work brings out are difficulties in realizing the ideal which William is unable to envisage. Although William acknowledges the need to '[choose] oneself in one's eternal validity' in order to be confirmed in one's selfhood, and claims that this is the only thing that can be chosen absolutely, since everything else is finite and finite things cannot be chosen absolutely,[96] his ideal of a stable personality in 'Equilibrium' is based on an inadequate grasp of what an absolute choice of one's self amounts to. As we saw, he assumes it is possible to reconcile the aesthetic and the ethical life-views. In admonishing A for mistakenly supposing that the universal and the particular are incompatible, William assumes that all that is necessary in order to realize the universal is that 'particular' personal inclinations be given continuity, i.e. time and direction, by the superimposition of the 'universal' in the form of personal and social commitment. He assumes that the aesthete's 'concealment' (in his case the more or less wilful lack of a stable social personality) can give way to 'revelation' (the presence of such a personality) just by choice. The point of raising the possibility of a teleological suspension of the ethical, however, is that the choice may be prevented not by indecision, but by guilt, a moral consideration. If a dereliction of social and personal duty is occasioned *by* guilt, and the guilt is not (in a way the common moral consciousness would readily understand) incurred by such dereliction, say by giving in to personal inclination, then expiation cannot be sought by an act of repentance directed at the common moral consciousness. If repentance is possible it must be through a 'private undertaking' with the absolute,[97] an undertaking which implies that the particular individual is prior to the universal.

In order to achieve the ideal of revelation a person must make two 'movements'. The first is the 'infinite movement of repentance' (for Abraham simply of 'resignation') in which, as mentioned above, responsibility is taken not just for the suffering caused (which, after all, may well be compensated — or at least forgiven — if the person really does manage to realize the universal), but (something that does not apply to Abraham) also for the nature of the past out of which the suffering arose. This involves a refusal to make excuses (as it seems Kierkegaard was earlier disposed to do) by appealing to personal difficulties in the past. Kierkegaard must be thinking here not of society's but of God's forgiveness. He is saying that in order to make the first movement one cannot excuse oneself in the eyes of God by pointing to 'extenuating' circumstances claimed to be the effective antecedents of one's defaulting actions or inactions — or at least sufficiently contributory to absolve one from *moral* (as distinct from *de facto*) responsibility for them. Ordinarily, and as this suggests, it is in connection with excuses protecting an agent from moral blame that one draws attention to such circumstances, and not — as here seems to be Kierkegaard's main concern — with finding some basis for continuing to call actions in contravention of common morality moral. Withholding blame and bestowing praise for a given action are, of course, logically different notions: although the latter implies the former (a person can praise me for something only if he does not blame me for it), the converse does not hold (he can withhold moral reproach without bestowing moral approval). Consequently, it might seem difficult at first glance to place this 'infinite movement of repentance' in Kierkegaard's general argument: why can one *not* excuse oneself in this way? Surely all that is needed to establish the religious exception is God's absolving the individual of *moral* responsibility, divine love and understanding doing what the common morality, on account of its particular limitations, cannot do, i.e. preserve the exception for 'humanity'? But then you might think that an enlightened common morality, too, could forgive exceptions for the same reasons, pointing, say, to unequal background circumstances which exclude the individual from the normal conditions of moral accountability. In either case all that is needed is to withhold blame, not bestow praise.

To forgive, however, is not the same as to excuse. Or rather, to forgive someone is to excuse them for doing something under conditions which *do* make them morally accountable; whereas the extenuating circumstances referred to are precisely those said to make a person morally *unaccountable* and so not in need of forgiveness. And it is clear that Kierkegaard is not at all interested in being *excused*. Far from wanting to appear a *victim* of special circumstances, he wants there to be a point of view from which the circumstances can be accepted as having a special *moral* relevance. He wants his ruptured relationship with Regine to be part of a project of realizing the universal that is deeper and more difficult than that envisaged by Judge William, a project whose depth and difficulty he, Kierkegaard, precisely *by virtue* of his special circumstances, has been privileged to grasp; and also in a practical sense as a problem which can still be solved, whose solution is the re-establishing (or 'repeating') of the relationship on a higher basis. The assumption is that the common morality cannot *forgive* (though it might excuse) the secrets and sacrifices involved in the rupture, because forgiveness is, after all, one side of a bilateral *moral* undertaking and (it is also assumed) the common morality must have some overriding communal goal in its repertoire to give it the necessary power of negotiation. Since in this case (it is again assumed) it has no such overriding goal, the sacrificer (Regine being the offering, though Kierkegaard also saw himself, his own happy future, as going to the flames)[98] has therefore no recourse but to go beyond the common morality and appeal directly to higher authority.

It seems that faith, in the context of the 'aesthetic production', is the belief that there is such an authority which is the foundation for this deeper and more difficult moral task. In *repenting* of the aesthetic life-style that gave rise to the need for secrecy and to the subsequent sacrifices, instead of excusing it as a reaction to hardship, with the secrets and sacrifices as excusable consequences, Kierkegaard is clearing the way for the forgiveness (from the only quarter from which in a *Sittlichkeit* ethics he could hope to receive it) that will make it possible for his aesthetic past to count as something for which, as a necessary part of the deeper task, he can make some kind of moral restitution. This, of course, involves a radical repudiation of Judge William's belief that the aesthetic can form a basis for the individual's realization of the universal. Repentance, as Climacus says later, requires 'dying away from the life of immediacy while still remaining in the finite'.[99] But it also means that the individual must now conceive the problem of realizing the universal as a matter of returning to the universal from what Johannes *de silentio* calls the 'absurd' position of the priority of the individual over the universal. It is this return to the universal that constitutes the second movement — also 'by virtue of the absurd'.[100] (Johannes says the first movement consumes *all* one's strength so that the second, returning and grasping reality, calls for outside help.) It requires faith that the moral scruples that force the separation from the universal can nevertheless be accommodated in a form of reconciliation *with* the universal, though not necessarily the form one normally expects. Thus the pseudonymous works that follow *Either/Or* stress the *separation* of universal and particular, and make it clear that the harmonious reconciliation prescribed by William becomes possible only through an act of faith.

5 The unsayable

At the beginning of this chapter, I said it was an important matter of interpretation whether, and if so in what sense, Kierkegaard claimed that human fulfilment involves something that cannot be 'content'. I suggested that this question had to do with Kierkegaard's rejection of the Hegelian principle that human fulfilment is essentially linked to knowledge and mutual understanding. And I also pointed to the knight of faith as someone whose position in this respect was the diametrical opposite of Hegel's. It is time, in conclusion, to vindicate these claims and suggestions by drawing some threads together.

The discussion meanwhile has centred on a fair range of Kierke-gaardian concepts, and the weight of exposition (some of it no doubt controversial) that it has had to bear may have obscured the immediate relevance of these for the required clarification. But at least two main threads can be discerned. First, fulfilment, reached at the higher point of view in repetition, rather than recollection, is, as was said earlier, a matter of faith, not thought. And second, faith means accepting the idea that 'the individual as the individual [den Enkelte] is higher than the universal [det Almene]'. Add then to this Johannes de silentio's claim that this idea 'is and remains in all eternity a paradox, inaccessible to thought',[101] and we have some idea of the intended connection between fulfilment and lack of content. If we then gloss this in accordance with a later remark to the effect that 'faith cannot be mediated into the universal' and that therefore in faith 'the individual is absolutely unable to make himself intelligible to anyone',[102] we can trace the connection further to the notion of some barrier to mutual understanding.

However, the cash-value of these promissory notes remains unclear. What is the paradox? Why should the idea that the particular takes precedence over the universal be unthinkable? And why should subscribing to a paradoxical belief, as opposed to the paradoxical content of the belief itself, be something that cannot be made intelligible to anyone?

The answers which it is not unreasonable to suppose that Kierkegaard himself might have given to these questions may perhaps be gleaned from some remarks of Hegel's in the Phenom-enology. There Hegel says that when we try to pick out some particular experience of our own with a demonstrative expression like 'this', we 'directly refute what we mean to say'. He says that what the expression actually conveys — what we in effect though unintentionally say — is 'being in general'. Now Hegel does not deny that there is something, in this case some 'sensuous content' (the content of sense-certainty), that we mean. What he claims is that since 'the true [content] of sense-certainty [is] the universal' it is language, what the words we use actually convey, which is 'the more truthful'.[103] Sensuous content as such is not what is essential. Now Fear and Trembling is littered with remarks, such as 'As soon as I speak I express the universal', and 'The relief of speech is that it translates me into the universal',[104] which seem clearly to express allegiance to the same view of what language can and cannot express. The allegiance, it should be noted, need not be Kierkegaard's own. Not, as some would be (I think, too) quick to point out, because the pseudonymous Johannes, whose expressions these are, is just one of his 'productions'; but rather because the fact of the view's currency at the time — as part of the Hegelian orthodoxy — would make it natural for Kierkegaard to adopt it in any case as a common basis on which to air his differences with the orthodoxy. The differences concern essentiality and truth, not language; it is easy to see how Kierkegaard could usefully exploit the current view, that the descriptive component of a pure demonstrative expression is 'more truthful' than the deictic component, by assuming to grant its terms of reference and presenting his own view as being (on the granted linguistic premise) the direct opposite: that is, as the view that more truth is to be found in the deictic component.

But what is the paradox in that? The sentential clause in which the view has just been phrased seems well enough formed, and nothing on the surface suggests that what it purports to convey is 'inaccessible to thought'. A possible answer might be to invoke a general view of language which denies that particulars can be referred to as such at all, on the grounds that the meanings of linguistic expressions are exclusively concepts, so that language systematically 'refracts' the world of particulars into an alien medium. This would entail, not that there *were* no particulars, but that no meaningful linguistic form could be used to describe, or even refer to, a particular in respect merely of its particularity. To regard oneself, or anyone, or indeed any thing, in one's own, or their, or its, 'concrete' particularity would then be to do something which could not be put into words. But if the knight of faith is to explain *why* he acts as he does, he must put something into words; he must say that in acting as he does he is regarding himself as a concrete particular in relation to another, presumably in some sense concrete, particular, namely God. But according to the view of language in question the particularity of these references cannot be represented linguistically. The same applies to the particularity of the relation between them.

That answer depends on a thesis about the limits of language as such.[105] However, it may be that what Johannes *de silentio* has in mind is a thesis, not about the limits of language, but about the limits of the language of ethics, or even more narrowly, the limits of the language of a particular theory of ethics, a universalist ethics of the *Sittlichkeit* variety. A word that Johannes constantly uses in connection with the universal is 'mediation'. This, as we saw in the section on 'repetition', is linked in Hegel's philosophy with the notion of making things determinate in respect of an underlying ground, or source of their essence. In this respect it could be said that mediation has only secondarily to do with communication; its primary application is in the context of conceptualizability or intelligibility. 'Mediation' derives from 'middle term', in the sense of a term which unifies or links two further terms which appear to be logically distinct, even incompatible generally and not just in respect of their coinstantiation in a given particular. Providing a middle term amounts to explaining the other two. Thus Johannes says that Abraham's action cannot be mediated, and that Abraham himself cannot be mediated.[106] What he means is that there is no middle term. It is lacking because faith itself 'has lost the middle term', i.e. the universal that could provide an explanation. It is the absence of this universal in the case of faith that makes faith paradoxical.[107] An alternative answer might then go as follows. The problem is how to render Abraham's action intelligible as one grounded in his 'human essence', i.e. to grasp how this apparently grossly inhuman action could be nevertheless a human one. Our two apparently incompatible terms are 'human action' and 'Abraham's action'. Suppose now that we postulate two things: (1) that a necessary condition of calling an action a human action is that it either expresses or designedly contributes to, let us call it, the developed state of being human, so that any losses resulting from the action in this respect must be outweighed by gains in the same respect, taking humanity as a whole as the measure; (2) that a universal is not only a shared characteristic 'valid for everyone [and] at every instant',[108] but also one that is mutually recognizable in its instances as either expressing or contributing to the developed state of being human. On these postulates it is clear that Abraham's intention to sacrifice his son is irretrievably inhuman (not even just non-human, since the terms here are not just distinct but incompatible). To 'mediate' the action and Abraham would require what it is possible to do in the case of the tragic hero, namely appeal to an overriding universal. But this is just what Kierkegaard's version of the Abraham and Isaac story is designed to exclude.

There are two points of view from which the situation can be regarded as paradoxical in these terms, radically so from the one point of view though perhaps only provisionally so from the other. The first point of view is that of the Hegelian understanding of what it is to become properly human. Thus the Abraham story can be read as illustrating a situation in which a person's humanity cannot be analysed in the sense of (2). That is, the story allows that it is possible for a person to qualify as essentially human independently of any specifications that may be given, or arrived at, of what, in the context of intention and action, is properly human *in general*. To Hegelians this would be unthinkable in a strong sense; for they would assume as a matter of principle that there is an inseparable link between becoming human, that is to say, acquiring the status of a developed human being, and conforming ever more successfully to, and convergently upon, some generally accepted 'human' specification. The paradox for Hegelians here would not be that Abraham's action fails to be human in the sense of (1), that is, by virtue of the fact that the human losses are not here outweighed by human gains, or even by an attempt to secure gains at all. What Hegelians would not understand is that even where there is a 'revealed' balance of human gain, it is not this that counts for the action's being human. The paradox here is in the very idea that a person can be said to become human — that is, acquire or appropriate his or her human essence — in a private, subjective relationship to the absolute. Another way of putting it would be to say that the account implies that people can be properly human prior to the expression of their humanity in the universal, so that the universal itself becomes an expression of a humanity pre-established, as it were, at the level of the particular and no longer the category *in which* humanity is established.

The second point of view is that of Johannes *de silentio*. We recall that in his preface he has made it clear that he is not a Hegelian. This might lead one to suppose that what is unthinkable in the above respect for Hegelians is not so for Johannes. This is not strictly speaking so. Of course, as the presenter of purported counter-examples to the Hegelian principle, he is willing to envisage, and in that sense 'think of', alternatives. But we must bear in mind that what makes it true to say that he is philosophically not a Hegelian is precisely his willingness to *stop* at faith, and not 'go further' in the sense of trying to incorporate faith itself within the system. Johannes can envisage in principle the possibility that at least in the human case essence is grounded in something logically analogous to Hegel's 'sensuous content' — in that it cannot be 'said' — and also that it is not in what *can* be said that the greater truth lies. However, since he accepts Hegel's view of *language*, he must accept, particularly as a poetic writer whose special talent is to throw light on external reality in words, that the notion of faith upon which the envisaged possibility is based contains a principle (the priority of the particular over the universal) that renders the notion inaccessible to language. In Johannes's case this means that the notion is also unintelligible, for the only kind of explanation he envisages is that by mediation in the third, or middle, term, i.e. a universal. Since it is his recognition that faith cannot be explained in that way which makes him a non-Hegelian, his project, like that of Constantius before him, faces a barrier. In spite of his ability as a poet to provide imaginative settings for the ideas which occupy him, first among them faith, and of his ability as a dialectician to put them in an illuminatingly discursive order, as far as explanation is concerned he has had to remain silent about faith itself. As silent in explanation as Abraham himself 'remains'.[109] Hence his tag 'de silentio'.

Now although Johannes says he himself does not understand Abraham,[110] he implies that Abraham *can* be understood: he says that what his portrayal shows is 'the necessity of a new category' for understanding him.[111] He does not say what this category is, but it is not implausible to guess that it is *faith*, the central topic of the next main work in the corpus, *Philosophical Fragments*. If so, the understanding Johannes refers to is not, even here, one that allows us to see anything ethical in Abraham's action. Nor one that allows us to 'go further' by incorporating faith in a systematic understanding of the world. What we are to understand is faith as the end of understanding. The author of *Philosophical Fragments*, Johannes Climacus, is a more professionally 'dialectical' author than his namesake, and takes his reader further than the latter has done, just as the latter has taken him further than was possible for the constructive ironist Constantius. Not further in the same direction, if by that is meant over and beyond the limits of what can be said. As we shall see, Climacus in fact leads us back from this brink in order to give us a wider philosophical perspective. His project could be called conceptual clarification. His topic is once again the position from which the essential is what cannot be said. His purpose is to outline its ontology and epistemology in order to contrast these as sharply as possible with those of the position Kierkegaard rejects: that from which what *can* be said is 'the more truthful'.

IV

The Dialectic of Faith

Dialectic is really a benevolent ministering power,
which discovers and helps to find where the absolute
object of worship is. . . . [It] does not itself see the
absolute, but it leads the individual as it were up to
it.[1]

1 The dialectical works

According to *The Point of View*, the aim of the aesthetic works
has been to loosen the grip on their readers of a false picture of
fulfilment. People professing Christian goals see them falsely
through the eyes of immediacy. Since, as Kierkegaard says, to take
someone somewhere you must begin where they are, he has joined
them within the aesthetic, in order to lead them out of it. We are
asked to look at the 'whole pseudonymous aesthetic production'
as a 'description of the path one must follow to become a Christian:
back from the aesthetic'.[2]

The undisguisedly autobiographical nature of these works makes
it prima facie unlikely that the development they trace is as
strategically arranged as this assumes. In the retrospective *Point of
View* Kierkegaard is evidently concerned with 'revealing' himself
to posterity as one who has served the universal as an *author*,[3]
moreover as a *religious* author, that is from the point of view
which the aesthetic works make it clear is the one from which it
must be served if it is genuinely to be served at all. The claim that
he was serving the universal even before he was aware of doing so
is clearly coloured by what has become an essential part of his

own faith at the later stage: namely that he had been guided divinely from the very beginning.

Nevertheless, whatever inaccuracies the retrospective account contains as a report of the author's earlier intentions, there is no real reason to doubt the accuracy of its explanation of the functions served by the end result. Faith is indeed the category in which the aesthetic works culminate. If the focus is shifted from the young friends to the ascending series of their authors and advisors, and if the problems raised by (rather than explicitly in) the works are seen as conceptual rather than practical, the idea that their main function is to bring the reader to an adequate understanding of that category makes sense. In this chapter we are interested in finding out what the 'dialectical' works are intended to contribute in this regard. So, with these qualifications and partial reassurances in mind, let us now preface the chapter with Kierkegaard's own, again retrospective, conception of the role of the 'dialectical' works, which he maintains are designed to add *further* to the description of the path one must follow to become a Christian.

Kierkegaard says that whereas the aesthetic works describe the way 'back' from the aesthetic, the dialectical works describe the way 'back from the System, speculation, etc.'.[4] By analogy with his grounds for calling the former works 'aesthetic', one would suppose that he might have called the dialectical works 'systematic' or 'speculative'. That would certainly sound strange, but why in that case and not, if indeed not, in the other?

We have seen how in the aesthetic works Kierkegaard does indeed begin *with* the aesthetic, he begins with it in the sense that his accounts, of the young men bound up in their various degrees of immediacy and of their problems, are sympathetic and full of insight. The irony in which their perspective is enlarged and whose 'corrosive' influence is designed to encourage them to lift themselves out of immediacy seems almost to be an integral part of their lives of immediacy, at least a natural and healthy development within it. With the 'System', however, Kierkegaard seems to see no such natural progression. So the dialectical production does not begin 'with' the systematic and speculative, but 'against' it. Speculative philosophy is a blind alley for the human spirit, an object of misplaced seriousness, and irony and humour are weapons to be used against it from the very start.

Philosophical Fragments opens by distinguishing between two epistemological positions. One is described as Socratic, while the other goes 'indisputably further than Socrates'.[5] They are contrasted under the headings 'A' and 'B', but are not related to the positions represented by the authors A and B in *Either/Or*. They correspond to the two forms of religiousness outlined in Chapter II. There we noted that the distinction turned on acceptance and rejection of the belief in the human being's innate capacity to acquire essential knowledge. Religiousness A is the 'immanent' position according to which 'annihilation' of the self in the pursuit of temporal goals re-establishes a person's harmony with existence. Religiousness B, on the other hand, is the 'paradox' religiousness in which the individual accepts that no exercise of human faculty, or forms of activity, can perform that function unaided. Religiousness A, we saw, places the 'contradiction' within existence, which is conceived as being, as a whole, 'borne' by eternity; while in religiousness B the contradiction is placed *between* existence as a whole and eternity. Now the sense in which Kierkegaard describes his position B as going further than Socrates is that in which he thinks that Socrates was nevertheless going in the right direction, and the respect in which Socrates was going in the right direction is what can be roughly characterized by saying that he was an 'existential' thinker. In a criticism directed at the philosophical style of his contemporaries, Kierkegaard has Climacus say:

> If thought in our time had not become something queer, something one learns parrot-fashion [*noget Tillært*], thinkers would make a quite different impression upon people, as was the case in Greece, where a thinker was also someone whose thinking inspired him to a passionate interest in his own existence; and as was also once the case in Christendom, where a thinker was someone whose faith inspired him to try to understand himself in the existence of [one who has] faith.[6]

The respect in which Kierkegaard thought Socrates had not gone far enough was that, at least in Plato's version,[7] he continued to assume that essential truth lay within the scope of human cognitive and practical capacity. Kierkegaard's 'advance' on Socrates is his rejection of this assumption. It was precisely the philosophical tradition's acceptance of it which made the culmination of that tradition in Hegel's 'System' a colossal diversion. Ideally, Kierkegaard's own philosophical project should have been that of showing the path out of Greek philosophy (paganism, religiousness A), via Socrates (existential thought and irony), and into the anti-philosophical, non-humanist position where the only saving truths are paradoxes (religiousness B). But the philosophical tradition and its off-shoot, organized religion, formed an obstacle; Kierkegaard had to contend with an ideology which offered easy ways out of the hard truths of his advanced position; which encouraged people to believe there were readily available ways of being borne along by the eternal, not least by also helping to bear *it* along, which it was assumed could be done, even, as the ironical Climacus says, just by being baptized into the Danish State Church.[8] These obstacles to spiritual progress are the targets of the dialectical works. In them Kierkegaard appears, in the guise of Johannes Climacus, as a latter-day Socrates demolishing the fabric of illusions that prevent people from posing the problem of their fulfilment as a personal problem, a problem their reflection on which could inspire them to a passionate interest in their own existence.

Although pseudonymous, these works are published under the 'editorship' of Kierkegaard. In his 'First and Final Explanation' he says of this that, because of the 'absolute importance of the subject in relation to reality', he felt it necessary to 'name some-one responsible for accepting whatever reality might offer'.[9] This points to another important difference between the aesthetic and the dialectical works. The former do not pretend to describe reality independently of the various conceptions of it which they portray. Their primary category is, in Kierkegaard's Aristotelian terminology, that of poetic *possibility*. (The Danish term here translated 'reality' is 'Virkelighed' which, like its German counter-part 'Wirklichkeit', is often rendered in philosophical contexts as 'actuality', in contrast to 'possibility'.) In the dialectical works Kierkegaard made categorical pronouncements on reality/actuality, and apparently felt bound to put his name to them. One good reason for doing so would be to prevent the impression that the dialectical works were to be read as the expression of just another poetic possibility to be superseded by another later.

The *Fragments* has both an ostensible and a covert theme. Ostensibly it sketches (in the form of a 'thought project', i.e. no more than an interesting hypothesis) a possible alternative to Platonic idealism, an alternative which preserves a Socratic element but dispenses with the idealist one. The Socratic element is the method of refutation, the so-called elenctic method, which proceeds not by establishing any thesis constructively but by destroying initial assumptions. The idealist element is the principle that the process of eliminating falsity is tantamount to laying bare the truth, as if falsehood and illogicality were merely impediments to a pre-established capacity to grasp the ultimate nature of things. The latter element is archetypal immanentism, and as such is Kierkegaard's most general target. More or less implicitly, however, the subject of the *Fragments* is the relation of philosophy to Christianity, and its immediate target the specifically Hegelian understanding of this relation.[10] We have already seen what that is. According to Hegel religious truths are in the end philosophical. In the introduction to the 'Smaller Logic', Hegel says that philosophy and religion have 'virtually' (*zunächst*) the same subject-matter, namely truth.[11] Philosophy is that special mode of thought in which 'thinking becomes knowledge',[12] and the philosopher, 'in dealing with the objects of religion, and with truth as a whole', has the special task of 'showing that philosophy is capable of apprehending them from its own resources . . .'.[13]

Kierkegaard was clearly occupied by what he saw as the pernicious influence of the local prophets of Hegelian philosophy, a concern reinforced by his belief that the essential point of Christianity is lost when this particular religion is taken over by (or up into) Hegelian philosophy. A key figure here is Hans Lassen Martensen (1808—84), formerly Kierkegaard's university tutor and later Bishop Primate of the Danish State Church.[14] In 1849 Kierkegaard wrote in his journal:

> It is now getting on for ten years since Professor Martensen
> returned from a trip abroad, bringing with him the latest
> German philosophy, and aroused such a tremendous sensation
> with this novelty — Martensen who has really been more of a
> reporter and correspondent than an original thinker. It was the
> 'standpoints' philosophy — the pernicious side of such surveys
> — which fascinated the youth and gave them the idea they
> could swallow everything in half a year. He is having a huge
> success and young students are even taking the opportunity of
> informing the public in print that with Martensen a new era,
> epoch, or era and epoch, etc. is beginning.[15]

The *Postscript* elaborates on the question of 'standpoints':

> It is . . . a fundamental confusion in the new science [i.e. the
> Hegelian 'System'] to mistake, without further ado, the
> abstract consideration of standpoints for existence, so that in
> acquainting oneself with this or that standpoint one thinks that
> that is what it is to exist [in it] ; whereas any *existing* individual
> must, just because he exists, take sides to some extent. From an
> abstract point of view there is in fact no decisive conflict
> between the standpoints, because the abstraction is precisely
> from that in which the decision has to take place, namely *the
> existing subject.*[16]

And the *Fragments* ends with a statement of the special relevance of Christianity for the deciding subject's real interests:

> As is well known, Christianity is the only historical phenomenon

which in spite of the historical, or rather precisely by way of [it] , has wanted to be the point of departure for the individual's eternal consciousness. . . . No philosophy (since it is only for thought), no mythology (since it is only for imagination), no historical knowledge (which is for memory) has come by this idea, about which one may say in this connection, with all due ambiguity, that it has not entered [*opkom* — lit. 'come up' (Greek — ανέβη)] into the heart of man [a reference to I Corinthians ii.9] . This latter, however, is something I have tried partly to forget, and making use of the unlimited freedom of a hypothesis I have assumed that the whole idea was a curious invention of my own, one which I wouldn't give up before I had thought it through.[17]

The author adds, as a reason for offering his hypothesis in isolation from others' discussions of its topic (or in the style of Aristotle and Hegel as the proper successor of these previous 'standpoints'), that 'if in speaking of the relation between Christianity and philosophy one began first to recount what others have said', one would never begin, let alone finish, since history 'continues to grow'.[18]

Philosophical Fragments or a Fragment of Philosophy (1844) is a short work of under one hundred pages. Its Danish title, *Philosophiske smuler*, more accurately translated 'philosophical crumbs',[19] or perhaps better 'remnants' or 'scraps', suggests a modesty not only of physical format but also of philosophical pretension. This, however, is misleading, as is also the suggestion, particularly emphasized by the translation 'fragments', that the work does not comprise a systematic whole. It does. In fact, the *Fragments* is possibly the most closely argued and perfectly rounded of all Kierkegaard's writings. As for philosophical pretensions, the size of the work's topic emerges from the list of questions displayed prominently on the title-page:

Is an historical point of departure possible for an eternal consciousness; how can such a point of departure have any other than a merely historical interest; is it possible to base an eternal happiness upon historical knowledge?

Not what the modern philosopher would consider a standard set of questions, certainly. And Kierkegaard's posing them without raising prior questions of the status of the notion of an eternal consciousness, or of its correlates, eternal truth and happiness, will seem to many to involve begging fundamental issues. But given the assumptions that Kierkegaard shared with the tradition he criticizes, together with the fact that the proper interpretation of religion, particularly Christianity, was a central and wide-ranging philosophical topic in his time, the questions would seem fundamental enough to his contemporaries. And though the subject of eternal happiness engages few philosophers today, in posing and answering questions about the possibility of such a thing Kierkegaard does in fact raise very general, fundamental, and far from dead issues about the nature of human ideals, existence, and the sources of human satisfaction and fulfilment.

Why, then, 'crumbs'? First of all, surely, because of the author's serious wish to resist the insistent embrace of a totalitarian philosophy which claimed to have synthesized into its own version or 'standpoint' everything of lasting intellectual and spiritual value, and particularly one which, in the version imported by Martensen into Denmark, held out to its devotees, Kierkegaard's readers, the prospect of 'swallowing everything in half a year'. Had Kierkegaard claimed to be contributing to the public philosophical debate, something the pseudonymous Climacus, like Johannes de silentio before him, carefully disclaims at the outset,[20] his attempted critique of the Hegelian philosophy would have been swiftly disposed of as a reactionary move rooted in a stage of spiritual growth now, according to that philosophy, left definitively behind. It is little wonder that Kierkegaard should try, amongst other things by choosing a conspicuously unpretentious title, to prevent his own philosophical works from being taken as serious contributions to a discussion whose very premises they were intended to undermine. His fears are summarized in the motto facing the Preface of the Fragments: 'Better well hanged than ill wed',[21] and in the Postscript Climacus says, of the reception given to the Fragments, 'undisturbed, and in compliance with its own motto: "Better well hanged than ill wed", the hanged, yes well hanged author was left hanging. . . . [But] better well hanged than brought through an unhappy marriage into systematic affinity with the whole world'.[22]

Besides the serious reason, however, there is certainly also a deliberate irony in the contrast between the exaggerated modesty of the title and the pretensions of the Hegelians. To Kierkegaard's contemporaries, for whom 'philosophy' was synonymous with 'system', there would have been an immediate and provocative incongruity in the juxtaposition of the notions of philosophy and randomness or lack of system. The irony is compounded by what seems undoubtedly an allusion to the beggar, Lazarus, who ate the crumbs that fell from the rich man's table. Contemptible fare, perhaps, for those who have gorged themselves at the feast of speculative thought, but palatable enough to those whose taste for clarity about truth and happiness has not yet been blunted by superfluity.[23]

2 Faith and the condition

The five chapters of the *Fragments* divide into two parts separated by an 'Interlude' which introduces some basic tenets of a non-idealist ontology and epistemology. The first part (comprising four chapters, one with appendix) considers in general the assumptions that must be made by someone wishing to acquire essential truth from the point of view of one who professes not to be in latent possession of that truth, that is, from the B-position. The Interlude introduces the notions of coming into being, history, and knowledge of the past, which are then applied, in the single chapter of the last part, to the question of whether there is any essential difference, either advantage or disadvantage, between the situation of a B-proponent contemporary with the teacher of essential truth and one for whom, as in Kierkegaard's and our own time, the teacher is a distant historical phenomenon. The teacher is Jesus, though never named as such but only as 'God in time', and the subtitles of the first three chapters ('thought project', 'imaginative experiment', and 'a metaphysical fancy') emphasize that the religious component here is being presented hypothetically rather than dogmatically. It is clear, however, that Kierkegaard's discussion as a whole is directed at what was, in his view, an unholy alliance between two main contemporary currents in religious thought: one a renewed interest in the historical Jesus as the source of true human value, in distinction from the traditional interpretation of Christianity in which this value is derived (as in the unhappy consciousness) from a relationship to a transcendent source;[24] and the other the Hegelian belief that significant historical events occur with a retrospectively discernible necessity. The combination of these two leads to the belief that the central doctrine of Christianity, that of the Incarnation, can be established as (necessarily) true and that, because it *can* be established, its truth implies a special kind of cognitive advance for humanity as a whole. It is with this prevailing belief in mind that Kierkegaard asks whether 'an historical point of departure is possible for an eternal consciousness', how such a point of departure 'can have any other than *merely* historical interest', and whether it is 'possible to base an eternal happiness upon historical knowledge'.

The *Postscript* contains a rather profuse acknowledgment of Kierkegaard's debt to Lessing, and, amongst other quotations from that author, cites his statement that 'the accidental truths of history can never become the proof of necessary truths of reason'.[25] This is the basis of the familiar notion of the 'leap' (of faith) (*Springet*), which Kierkegaard actually derives from Lessing.[26] The leap is the logical distance between any accumulation of true empirical, or 'historical', statements and the necessary or eternal truths of reason. To say that there is a leap is, first of all, to claim concerning any (even infinite) set of statements of one logical class that they cannot provide an adequate logical ground for statements of another. The leap is, in this sense, what is often referred to as a logical 'gap'. For Lessing (influenced as he was by Leibniz, to whom this sharp dichotomy between necessary and contingent statements, or propositions, is due) the truths at the other side of the gap are 'truths of reason', i.e. mathematically certain truths known *a priori*. But for Lessing, as with Kierkegaard, 'truth' here means primarily 'religious truth'. The logical gap is that between the contingency of all that history can tell us and the absolute or unconditional certainty required by religious faith.

In Kierkegaard, as in Lessing, the gap is construed as the (logical) fact that statements (or 'truths) of the one kind at best render statements of the other kind probable, or, as Kierkegaard frequently puts it, as the fact that the former can only 'approximate' to, never entail, certify, or prove the latter. The metaphor of approximation can be misleading. It sounds as if more statements of the former kind can at least help; and that seems to imply that if lent enough support they *could* conceivably be enough. But the idea of a logical gap is that of the impossibility of there ever being enough, so that given even (*per impossibile*) every possible true statement of the one class, the possibility remains not only that any particular statement in the other class is false, but even that there are no true referring statements in that class. Since the distance is an absolute one, 'approximation' in this context cannot imply any closing of the gap. It can only mean an increase on this side of the gap of the kind of truths which incline one to accept a statement about something on the other side. If, as Kierkegaard (unlike Lessing) consistently insists, the human mind is limited to contingent, empirical knowledge, and has no access to timeless propositional truths, it follows that acceptance of such a statement involves a decision, a leap in another, and practical, sense 'over' the logical gap. Kierkegaard applies this principle of Lessing's in order to stress that anyone interested in the truth of those timeless propositions which would guarantee religious satisfaction must make a personal decision, a leap of faith. He stresses the existence of the gap 'between an historical truth and an eternal decision', and the consequent need for the leap, because of the tendency in his time, as he says, 'to let the eternal become historical without further ado'.[27]

Some brief comments on the leap of faith can provide a framework within which to clarify and assess the main topics of the *Fragments*:

Faith is usually defined as acceptance of truth on some other basis than reason; but sometimes just as acceptance of the truth of a proposition in the absence of sufficient reason; and the latter definition might even be offered where the notion of sufficient reason is to be interpreted in a strict way as that of proof. In cases like the latter the question of what the 'other' basis is may seem redundant: normally some 'pragmatic' justification falling short of proof can be provided, for instance that the belief is justified by events. But where faith is associated, as it commonly is, with *religious* belief, the question of an alternative basis does intrude. It is certainly less appropriate in the case of a religious belief to give the Humean answer to the question, Why do you believe that?, that one cannot *help* doing so, than in the kinds of case Hume himself was thinking of, such as the supposedly rationally unjustifiable belief in the existence of the physical world or in continuing physical identities. In general one *can* help having religious beliefs, even if there are often strong pressures on people to maintain them. Indeed the full spectrum of religious belief tends in a direction which is the opposite of that exemplified in the progression above. That is to say, religious belief is not only faith *qua* acceptance of what one has insufficient reason to believe; it can be faith *qua* acceptance of what one has no reason to believe, and even of what one has sufficient reason *not* to believe. The basis sought is not a supplement to reason, but a functional alternative.

What can it be? Religious belief is often said to be supported by revelation, whether the believer's own or that of some acknowledged authority, sometimes one on whose alleged testimony a whole institution has been erected. The presence of such institutions can confuse the issue of the basis of religious belief. Given their influence, a person might 'believe' simply through fear of the consequences of not doing so, where the fear would be the same whatever the content of the doctrine subscribed to; or through mistakenly taking the existence of the institution as itself a good reason, in which case the doctrine has not been identified as specifically religious. It seems essential, when looking for the motivation and support for religious belief, that these be seen to attach to the content of the belief itself; that is, that the belief represent some state of affairs which the believer would like to obtain, or to be presently obtaining; and that the support be understood as working independently of whatever evidential basis there is for believing that it does or that it does not obtain. Religious belief, then, might be said to be acceptance of a preferred conclusion on some basis other than whatever rational (including observational) grounds there are for preferring it.

It might be thought that the only other basis needed was the believer's actual preference. But it could be argued that this conflicts with an idea central to rationality, and even essential to the very notion of belief itself, that the beliefs one holds should be determined by what one's experience of the world *gives* one to believe, and not by how one wants the world to be. The argument can be put in the following form.[28] First, assume that a belief is a state of mind. Second, then, it cannot coherently be the case that a person intends to have a belief where the explanation of his having it would be, as he presently acknowledges (and whatever he may come later to admit under the effects of hypnosis, drugs, etc., or as a result of whatever other means he adopts to obtain this goal), that at this time he wanted it to be true. The reason is that the state of mind of belief is one which, for the believer, must be thought of as stemming in some way from the world. To hold a belief, on this picture, is standing with an assessment of how the world (or a relevant sector of it) impresses itself upon one as being.

The picture applies most convincingly, of course, in the case of empirical, as distinct from religious and moral, belief. In the empirical case we would certainly require a person's 'decisions' as to what to believe to be grounded in information accessible through normally functioning perceptual channels, channels which the believer in principle keeps constantly open so as to allow his beliefs to be modified in the light of new information. As such, however, they are not decisions so much to *acquire* as to *acquiesce* in a state of belief — typically after some critical reflection on the ancillary beliefs which support the belief in question. It is true, of course, that where there is more or less strong but still significantly inconclusive evidence for something — as, for example, in connection with a crucial future outcome — people often have to decide, for economical reasons, in favour of one rather than another set of expectancies. But these decisions are not decisions to *have* the belief that what seems most likely *will* occur and that what now appears less likely will not; they are assumptions made in full consciousness of the possibility that the assumption may prove wrong. It is true, too, that, apart from reporting one's present states of belief, or ceremoniously affirming them, statements

100

prefixed by 'I believe' are sometimes used to express a kind of qualified belief ('I *believe* he's coming, but I'm not certain'), in the sense that the expression 'believe' is used to disclaim the certainty or authority conveyed by the unprefixed assertion. Indeed, a belief in the sense of what one takes on the evidence to be true, is perhaps what would be most straightforwardly conveyed by the *un*prefixed assertion: the statement that something or other is or will be or will prove to be or to have been the case. But, in any case, it is with regard to belief in this latter sense that the charge of irrationality is made. What is irrational or incoherent, to repeat, is that I should be willing to accept that the explanation of my subsequently believing rather than disbelieving something should not be some further information to which I have had access, but simply my having wished to have that belief. Also, a person who decides to produce in himself an impression of how the world is, rather than allowing his impression to be produced by it, is deciding to be (in some way bring it about that he is) in a state of mind in which an integral part of his belief is that the resulting impression is due *not* to his having decided to have it, but to the world's being such as to convey it independently of his will. So apart from the irrationality of assuming that wanting a belief can be the explanation of one's having it, the project also involves self-deception.[29]

Assuming the above argument is substantially correct in regard to empirical belief, the question to bear in mind in what follows is whether, or how far, Kierkegaard's notion of *religious* belief, or faith, is subject to the same charges of irrationality, incoherence, and self-deception.

(1) Kierkegaard mentions two different senses of the term 'belief' or 'faith' (*Tro*, which means either). One is belief in a general sense, which he discusses in connection with knowledge of the past. The other is belief in what, following scholastic usage, he calls an 'eminent' sense, and which applies to religious belief.

To begin with the former sense. Here Kierkegaard is arguing against the Hegelian doctrine that historical events occur with a retrospectively discernible necessity.[30] To this he opposes the postulate that every event is brought about by a cause, none by a *logical* ground, and that every cause 'points definitively back to a freely effecting cause'.[31] Ground and cause belong to mutually exclusive categories, as therefore also do their cognates, necessity and change. The kind of change Kierkegaard refers to here is not that undergone by something already existing (for example, in a change of position or configuration), but that in which something hitherto merely possible is translated into reality (actuality), that is, the change of coming *into* existence, or, as Kierkegaard also says, the change from not-being to being. 'Everything which comes into existence', he says, 'proves precisely by coming into existence that it is not necessary'; and since 'the necessary *is*', necessity is indeed 'the only thing that cannot *come* into existence'.[32] Since nothing that comes *into* existence does so necessarily, no event which counts as a change of the kind in question can be considered the only possible outcome; the actual outcome is therefore said to occur 'with freedom'.[33] That some thing or event has come into existence, says Kierkegaard, suffices for it to count as historical.[34] But then the freedom with which this transition from not-being to being occurs means that it cannot be fully determined by obtaining relevant observational information — the kind of information (derived from what Kierkegaard calls 'immediate sensation and cognition [*Erkjenden*]') which 'cannot deceive'.[35] Since the knowledge the historian aims to acquire is precisely of such transitions, for it is after all the explanation of some event's having occurred (come into being) that the historian tries to give, and not just a record of contingently assembled facts, or of changes of location and configuration, it follows that historical knowledge is constitutionally uncertain. The uncertainty, it should be noted, is not due to the temporal distance between the historian and the facts he is out to explain; it is due to the outcome's being only one of a set of possibilities and to the observational indeterminacy of the transition to the actual outcome. Thus even 'a contemporary does not perceive the necessity of what comes into existence'.[36] Nor does the fact that 'the essentially historical is always the past' *bestow* necessity upon the outcome, even if the lapse of time may create an illusion of necessity. In general, the past does not *become* necessary through someone's apprehension of it, for 'apprehension like knowledge has nothing to give'.[37] Consequently, however close to or far from his facts, the historian can never overcome an inherent elusiveness (*Svigagtighed*) in that aspect of the facts that interests him.[38] His knowledge of the past is therefore (as well as for familiar epistemological reasons with which Kierkegaard is not occupied) uncertain. The attitude of the historian to the past, then, according to Kierkegaard, should be that of someone 'moved by that passion which is the passionate sense for coming into existence: namely wonder'.[39] The *cognitive* attitude corresponding to wonder is belief. But 'belief' here is used in a sense which lays as much stress on the epistemological *un*certainty of what the historian believes as on the psychological certainty with which he believes it. Thus, when the perceiver [*den Sandsende*] sees a star, the star becomes an object of doubt for him the moment he wants to become aware of its having come into existence. It is as though reflection took the star away from perception. So much then is clear, that the organ for the historical must have a structure analogous to the historical itself, must have in it something corresponding to the way in which, in its certainty, it continuously negates [*ophæver*] that uncertainty which corresponds to the uncertainty of coming into existence; a two-fold uncertainty, embracing both the nothingness of the not-being and the annihilated possibility which is at the same time the annihilation of every other possibility. Now belief [*Tro*, i.e belief or faith interchangeably] has the required character; for in the certainty of belief there is always present the negated uncertainty which in every way corresponds to that of coming into existence. Thus belief believes what it does not see; it does not believe that the star exists, for that is something seen, but it believes that the star has come into existence. Similarly with an event. What has happened can be immediately apprehended, but certainly not *that* it has happened, nor that it is happening, even when it happens, as one says, right before your nose. The elusiveness of what has happened is that it has happened, in which fact lies the transition from nothing, from not-being, and from the manifold possible 'how'. Immediate sensation [*Sandsing*] and cognition have no notion of the uncertainty with which belief approaches its object, but neither have they any notion of the certainty which emerges out of this uncertainty.[40]

Whatever unclarities afflict Kicrkegaard's highly abstract account here, as in the rest of the Interlude (and it should be remembered that his aim here is not to give a positive account of freedom, but to state a general anti-Hegelian principle),[41] it is clear that his concept of belief stresses two things which our earlier account of belief, as what someone takes on the evidence to be true, failed to feature. One is the extent to which (both self- *and* other-) attributions of belief carry the suggestion that the believer may be wrong. And the other, connected with this, is that a central case of believing — one might call it actively believing — involves deciding about the facts where the facts themselves are systematically under-determined by all possible information. If a person has done all that can be expected, is aware of this, and yet the knowledge he seeks escapes him, it would be left to him to *decide* how the facts would appear if it *were* possible to determine them. His decision

103

would not, of course, make it true that the facts were so, nor
would it defeat the inherent uncertainty about what the facts are;
but by taking a chance on their being so, and adopting a kind of
decisiveness to this which it would not be inappropriate to call a
state of mind of certainty with regard to their being so, he can
quit *himself* of their inherent uncertainty. This certainty (the kind
which 'emerges out of [the] uncertainty') *is*, as Kierkegaard here
hints, rather special. In deciding how things are, a person as it were
takes the facts into his own hands, and so long as the decision
holds, is not disposed to revise his opinion. Now although this
could (in some cases) be wishful thinking, it could not be self-
deception; for the systematic absence of the sort of information
needed to acquire the impression that such a revision was needed
means that any state of mind corresponding to the facts being so
or not so *has* to originate in the subject rather than the object. In
this case, therefore, that the explanation of one's subsequently
believing something should be that one had chosen to do so is not
an irrational thought, nor the corresponding project of deciding to
believe an incoherent one. On the contrary, it is a requirement of
one very central kind of belief, the kind most naturally associated
with faith as acceptance of the truth of a proposition in the
absence of sufficient reason.

It is worth noting that the second of these two features of belief
indicates a diversity of criteria for attributing the qualification
mentioned as the first feature. Even if an attribution of belief
typically carries the suggestion that the believer may be wrong,
there are at least two quite different ways in which it can carry it.
To say of someone that he (only) believes something may be a
way of pointing to a culpable lack of justification for the certainty
he evinces and expresses. But where the attributer knows that the
person in question fully acknowledges the inadequacy of the
evidence, and that the certainty therefore cannot be of the kind
that stems from the weight of the facts themselves, the point of
the attribution is precisely to convey that the certainty evinced
and expressed by the believer is due to his having decided about
the facts in spite of the possibility, which he recognizes, that he
might be wrong. Generally, it will only be in those cases where it
is assumed that experience can *prove* the believer wrong, that is to
say where the beliefs are empirical, that attributions of belief as
insufficiently supported certainty will imply criticism. In the case
of moral and religious beliefs, as these are often understood, and
with which it is natural to link the second kind of attribution,
there would be no *such* criticism, though, of course, there can be
others.

It is also important to bear in mind that, because of the systematic elusiveness of the historian's target, Kierkegaard places historical belief in the same bracket as moral and religious belief; it is analogous to these in requiring a decision or choice. '[Historical] belief', he says, 'is not a case of cognition [*Erkjendelse*] but an act of freedom, an expression of the will',[42] though we shall see in a moment that in the case of religious belief (belief in the 'eminent' sense) an essential condition for describing this latter as an act of will is said to be absent. We can note, too, though without attaching too much significance to the fact, that despite this denial that historical belief is a case of cognition, Kierkegaard is still willing to refer to historical belief as both cognition and knowledge.[43] He could presumably say, if pressed, that such belief was knowledge (and cognition in an achievement sense) when the decision was the right one, though whether it was the right one is not something that could strictly be known. In other words he would have to say that in such a case it is possible to know without knowing that one knows.

(2) If we turn now to what Kierkegaard says about religious belief, the importance of this discussion of historical belief will be apparent. According to the hypothetical B-position there is no knowledge of the eternal. It is its denial of the possibility of this knowledge that distinguishes it from the A-position, i.e. from the 'Socratic' view. On the latter view, as we saw in Chapter II, man is assumed to be in possession of an 'eternal determinant', something (e.g. reason) which gives him access to essential truth (and value) in 'recollection'. The view assumes not only that such truth can be grasped, but that it can be grasped independently of historical knowledge, and indeed that essential truth embraces the historical and thereby also the (necessarily both temporal and temporary) existence of the individual. Or as the *Postscript* puts it: 'In A, the fact of existing, my existence, is a moment [*Moment*] within my eternal consciousness. . . .'[44] According to the B-position, however, there is no eternal determinant. The knowledge available to the existing individual is exclusively historical (empirical, contingent, and approximate). Confined within the limits of merely empirical knowledge, the individual's only connection with a putative eternal realm could be via the historical. Hence the questions of the *Fragments*: 'Is an historical point of departure possible for an eternal consciousness; how can such a point of departure have any other than a merely historical interest; is it possible to base an eternal happiness upon historical knowledge?' Now one might unreflectively think that these questions address

the issues affecting the choice between positions A and B; that is, that they directly concern the distinction which is the ostensible as opposed to the covert theme of the *Fragments*. But on reflection it is clear that this cannot be so. In the first place, Kierkegaard is not occupied in the *Fragments* with the question of which of these two positions is valid, or indeed with whether either of them is valid. He is simply presenting B as a hypothesis and spelling out its consequences. Second, the questions cannot in any case be addressing the issue of A or B, because according to A the question of the possibility of an historical point of departure is superfluous; the point of departure lies in man's eternal consciousness, and the historical functions only as 'an occasion'. By this Kierkegaard means that the role of a *teacher* in relation to someone intent on learning essential truth is the Socratic one of prompting rather than instructing the learner. As noted earlier, the A-position assumes that the process of eliminating falsity is tantamount to clearing the way to recollection, as if falsehood and illogicality were merely impediments to a pre-established capacity to view the ultimate nature of things. 'On the Socratic view every human being is his own centre, and the whole world is centred only on him, because his knowledge of himself is knowledge of God.'[45] Thus, 'looked at Socratically, every point of departure in time is *eo ipso* accidental, a vanishing [transition], an occasion'.[46] The questions are, in fact, addressed to Hegelians. The point is that Hegelians accept the idea of an historical point of departure. They accept 'the pleasant illusion', as the *Postscript* has it, that there can be such a thing as an 'eternal historical fact',[47] or, in an Hegelian formula cited in the Interlude, that necessity is a 'synthesis [*Eenhed*] of possibility and actuality'.[48] In other words, they assume that the eternal becomes historical 'without further ado'. The Interlude's discussion of historical knowledge takes up the covert theme of the *Fragments*, the relation of philosophy to Christianity, and is intended to undermine the basis of this assumption. Therefore, the question Kierkegaard raises is whether, as is required of an eternal happiness by the B-position, it really *is* possible for the historical to become eternal, and if so with what consequences, not least for our conceptions of rationality.

The inescapable fact Kierkegaard says anybody wishing to base an eternal happiness on something historical must face is that it is contradictory to talk of an eternal historical fact. It implies that the eternal, which belongs to the category of the necessary, has come into being, something which proves, according to the statement quoted earlier, that it is *not* necessary, since everything that comes into being does so 'with freedom'. The historical events or event which Kierkegaard has in mind, and which are part and parcel of the B-position, are, of course, those identified in Christian doctrine as the Incarnation. The doctrine that 'the deity [*Guden*] has been in human form'[49] implies in philosophical terms that 'the eternal truth has come into being in time'.[50] This 'paradox' is exclusive to Christianity and picks out that religion as (the only extant case of) religiousness B. (As we recall, religiousness B is the 'paradox-religiousness' in which the individual 'related himself in time to the eternal-in-time', as opposed to religiousness A, or the form of religious consciousness in which the individual 'relates itself in time to the eternal'.)[51]

From the account just given of the contradiction, the paradox appears as the contradictory claim that the necessary (eternal) has demonstrated, by coming — necessarily freely — into existence, that it is at the same time not necessary. This makes it look as though the paradox were simply a direct entailment of the initial statement defining logical ground and cause as mutually exclusive categories. But this is by no means the whole of the paradox. A better indication of its scope is given in the remark that the doctrine of the Incarnation is that God 'has been' in human form; in other words, the doctrine assumes that it makes sense to describe the eternal in a language employing tenses, a point Kierkegaard again stresses when he remarks earlier that the assumption of his 'hypothesis' is that 'the deity *has been*'.[52] Here the paradox presents itself as a direct breach of the general logical principle that nothing can simultaneously have and lack the same property. The property in question can be named 'possessing spatio-temporal boundaries', or 'having either or both a beginning and/or end', and it is ascribed to the eternal, which by definition has no duration and therefore lacks both a beginning and an end. I am assuming that the concept of eternity here is not that of infinite succession or everlasting existence, i.e. 'sempiternity' which is a limiting case of duration, but that of the eternal in contrast to time, i.e. time-lessness (as Plato's αἰώνιος or Parmenides' τὸ ἕν).[53] In other words, I assume we are to think of the eternal here as that in which all temporal distinctions vanish or are illusory. That this is a correct assumption is confirmed by, amongst other things, Kierkegaard's insistence in the *Postscript* on the 'absolute' difference between God and man, noted in the previous chapter.[54] In the *Fragments* the difference is interpreted epistemologically as that between the unknowable and the knowable. The contrast between the unknowable deity and what is accessible to human understanding is so complete that the former can be defined only negatively as lying beyond the limits of intelligibility. Kierkegaard says here (and we should bear in mind that it is a view attributed to his pseudonym) that the term 'the deity' merely conveys that it *is* unknown, and that as the 'absolutely different . . . it can have no identifying characteristic'.[55] So, besides the contradictions of the necessary's having come into existence, of the eternal's having had duration, and — now one can add — of the unknowable's identity, by virtue of its 'existence' in human form, with the knowable, the paradox contains as one of its terms — independently of its paradoxical juxtaposition with the other — an empty idea. Kierkegaard calls it the 'limit' (*Grændsen*) and the 'unknown' (*det Ubekjendte*).[56]

This has two consequences: first, in spite of coming up against its own limits, the understanding (*Forstanden*, sometimes translated 'reason', but in that case in a wide, non-technical sense of a faculty for discerning content or structure) persists in trying to come to grips with the paradox, that is to say, with the unknown (and in any scientific sense unknowable). In doing so — and it is in the nature of human understanding that it should — it has to formulate such content or structure as that its own relationship to the unknown is one of absolute difference. But since the understanding cannot 'negate' or 'go beyond' itself 'absolutely', it can only 'conceive such superiority over itself as it conceives by means of itself'.[57] Similarly in formulating the proposition, underlying the paradox, that God and man are absolutely different; despite its inability 'even to conceive [*tænke*] an absolute difference', the understanding must postulate at least one similarity between them, namely that each is unlike the other.[58] So the very formulation of the paradox, which is the only way we have of representing the notion of the deity in time, involves a misrepresentation of the actual paradoxical situation. The unknown, or the deity, is in terms of the distinction between time and eternity no more than the idea of a limit. The self-deception by which the understanding presumes to bring the deity 'as close as possible' makes the deity itself 'the most appalling deceiver', because in fact it is 'still as remote as ever'.[59]

The second consequence concerns what Kierkegaard calls 'the absolute paradox'. Here the scope of the paradox is widened further to embrace the ethico-religious idea of redemption, which is the form taken on Kierkegaard's view by the goal of religious satisfaction. The notion of an absolute difference in epistemological terms is that between having and not having eternal knowledge. Assuming, as one does from the point of view of position B, that there are essential eternal truths, though beyond the scope of human reason, this is expressed by saying that man is not merely ignorant of the eternal, but that he is in 'untruth' (*Usandhed*, sometimes translated 'error').[60] In this practical context, however, the absolute difference is to be understood as that between not being and being in sin. Now religious satisfaction in these terms requires the constitution of a 'kinship', i.e. some essential similarity, with the eternal. But if man himself has no 'eternal determinant', or, in the words of the *Postscript* quoted earlier, 'no fundamental kinship with the eternal', the only chance lies in the possibility mentioned in that same passage, that 'the eternal has entered time and wants to constitute the kinship there'.[61] This possibility requires us, on the one hand, to believe that God wants to teach man the absolute difference as regards sin (according to the B-position men are incapable of teaching each other consciousness of sin, since their confinement to time deprives them of the ability to form an adequate conception of the precise nature or extent of what they lack).[62] On the other hand, it requires us to believe that God wants to show man the way to redemption, i.e. to ethical kinship with God. So we have to accept that God 'has wanted to make himself like the individual man so that the latter could fully understand him'.[63] In a related passage in his journals Kierkegaard refers to this latter idea as the highest *ethical* paradox; it is that 'God's son entered into the *whole* of reality, became a *part* of it, bowed himself under all its pettiness ... [in order to] carry on a polemic against existence [*Tilværelsen*]'.[64] The original paradox, then, 'becomes even more appalling': it not only claims, negatively, to 'reveal sin's absolute difference', it also, positively, 'wants to overcome this absolute difference in absolute similarity'.[65] (The word 'absolute' here presumably cannot mean that to escape sin man must become identical with God; the idea must be that what has to be overcome is the difference as regards sin, a difference which Kierkegaard says in the *Fragments* can only be due to man himself, and not to what he owes to God, since the latter must be something in which they *are* 'akin' [*beslægtet*].)[66] It is this twofold paradox which Kierkegaard calls the 'absolute paradox'.

(3) How, then, does the desire for religious satisfaction fare when this formidable and complex illogicality arises in its path?[67] Normally, if confronted with even a moderate balance of evidence against the likelihood of an outcome, a person who continues to use it as a background for expectation and planning will be suspected of verging on irrationality. But a person who continues to envisage an outcome in the knowledge that the proper description of it, or of a necessary means to it, is incoherent, will surely be

convicted of irrationality out of hand, for here the outcome is not just unlikely but inconceivable. Accordingly, a rational person who wants religious satisfaction, but is led to conclude that the only means to this satisfaction are transparently paradoxical, will give up this goal. He might still entertain it indirectly, in the sense that he wishes it were not paradoxical; but he cannot rationally continue to believe that it is both paradoxical and possible, and he certainly cannot assign it any degree of likelihood.

Yet Kierkegaard says that such a person can not only continue to entertain the means and the outcome, but believe that the means are actually at hand; that is, accept that it is unreservedly true that the paradoxical state of affairs exists. How can this be rational? To prepare the way to a possible answer, let us first take note of two related concepts employed by Kierkegaard. One is the concept of an 'affront' to reason; the second is that of the 'instant'.

First, the affront (*Forargelse*, the state of being scandalized or offended). According to Kierkegaard there are two ways in which a person aiming at religious satisfaction can react to the confrontation with the absolute paradox (henceforth simply 'paradox'). One is to come to terms with it. This 'happy' outcome involves, he says, the 'passion of faith', and is the alternative the question of whose rationality we are preparing the way to discuss. The other involves a failure to come to this 'mutual understanding', and Kierkegaard calls this 'being affronted' or 'taking offence'. This is a fundamentally passive state of mind in which a person, critically or uncritically accepting human reason as the highest court of appeal, feels compelled to condemn the paradox as an absurdity.[68] It is passive even if, instead of giving in to the paradox in dumb suffering, the affronted individual is emboldened to pour scorn on it. Whether the affront takes away 'the last crumb of comfort and joy' or makes one 'strong', the result is still a surrender to the superior strength of the paradox.[69]

Why, we might ask, should the paradox have the upper hand, and not reason? The answer could be that, on Kierkegaard's assumptions, the desire for religious satisfaction is at least as basic as the reliance on human reason, and the discovery of the paradox is therefore *necessarily* a cause of suffering, however one reacts to it. If it necessarily appears as an obstacle, the decision to abide by human reason is, in terms of the desire, necessarily a defeat. In the Appendix to Chapter 3 of the *Fragments*, Kierkegaard describes as 'an acoustic illusion' the manner in which a person who takes this decision typically expresses himself. In insisting that the victory is on the side of reason he will point, for example, to the 'absurdity' of the paradox. But then, he claims, there are only two possibilities:

either the terms employed on behalf of reason here are constructed by reason itself 'in isolation', in order to express in its own way whatever falls outside its limits, in which case they are constructed independently of the specific encounter with the paradox, and thus are not genuinely expressions of the situation in which the paradox is experienced as a direct affront to reason; *or* they are the expressions of that affront and therefore indirect expressions of respect for the paradox — Kierkegaard even suggests they are indirect expressions of an acceptance of the 'rightness' of the paradox (*Paradoxets rigtighed*).[70] Thus the affronted person does not speak from his own resources (*af sit Eget*), he speaks with those of the paradox: 'just as one person mocking another doesn't invent anything new but simply turns the situation around by mimicking the latter'.[71]

Second, the instant (*Øieblikket*, often also translated 'the moment'). In a parenthetical paragraph Kierkegaard remarks that, psychologically, the 'more active and more passive forms' of the affront will display a 'high variety of nuances'. The details of these, he says, are not his concern in the *Fragments* (they are in fact the topic of *The Concept of Anxiety*, published in June 1844 only five days later than the *Fragments*, and to be discussed in the next chapter), but we are to bear in mind that all such affront is essentially a misunderstanding of the instant; this because the instant *is* the paradox 'in its most abbreviated form'.[72] By 'the instant' Kierkegaard here refers to what is assumed in the paradox, namely a moment in time at which there came into existence not something merely historical, but something historical which was *also* eternal. Unlike that elusive instant in which *anything* historical comes freely into being, this instant (*the* instant) is elusive also in the radical sense of defying understanding. Because it is also the hypothesized, and paradoxical, instant at which the eternal came into time, the belief that has this instant as its object is directed at a fact which is historical, and therefore past, *and* 'absolute', though Kierkegaard observes that because the word 'fact' has its home in the historical it is not strictly correct to talk of an absolute fact.[73] As an absolute 'fact' it is not past, for the absolute cannot be described in a language that uses tenses. Kierkegaard says that in order to believe this special historical fact, it is necessary to receive the *condition*, and to receive it in time from the deity (or the absolute) itself.[74] Since the deity, as absolute, is essentially timeless, the accident of the believer's placement in time — i.e. whether as a contemporary of the fact or living, say, 2,000 years later — is irrelevant.[75] The condition can only be received now, *in the present*, from the deity. This 'now' in which the condition is received Kierkegaard also calls the instant. Thus in respect of an historical fact that is also absolute, belief has as its condition something which puts a contemporary and his successor on an equal epistemological footing. It can only be received from the absolute itself, to which every believer is contemporary in the instant.[76]

(4) What, then, is the condition? After some deliberate beating about the bush, Kierkegaard confusingly tells us it is faith, the passion in which the understanding and the paradox 'encounter one another happily in the instant'.[77] He says the name is not all that important. Still, since at least in its normal sense it would be incoherent to talk of *receiving* faith, its appropriateness seems at least initially questionable. It might be all right to say, as Kierkegaard also does, that what the condition, and therefore faith, conditions is an understanding of the eternal truth (though clearly in some sense the decision to do something *presupposes* the ability to describe what counts as having done it),[78] an understanding which he says occurs in 'the passion of the instant'.[79] But what sense can be given to the notion of *receiving* faith in that instant? Where, for example, does the will come in as a part of faith, as Kierkegaard insists it does (in the *Postscript* he says faith is taking risks, 'the more risk the more faith'),[80] even if, according to the *Fragments*, religious belief or faith, unlike historical belief, is *not* properly called an act of will (*because* the condition for understanding has to be received, and the human will 'is efficacious [*formaaende*] [in this respect] only within the condition').[81] The conceptual confusion is compounded by the understanding being said to *consist* in that 'happy passion' Kierkegaard finally identifies as faith.[82] Yet another problem is that we are told that the condition of understanding the eternal (or here God's 'divinity' which Kierkegaard stresses is not a perceptual, or 'immediate', property, i.e. 'given' in the different sense of being directly cognizable) is 'the sense of sin . . . [that] deepest reflection which the teacher must first develop in the learner'.[83] But how can the sense of sin be identical with the happy passion of faith, particularly when in another context we are told that faith is the opposite of sin?[84]

From this confusion what sense can be salvaged for a notion of a condition for the understanding of the eternal which must be *given* by the deity in (the instant in) time? And if there is sense in it, how can the notion of the condition's being *given* apply to religious belief?

First of all, Kierkegaard says that the learner is 'aware' of receiving the 'eternal' condition in the instant.[85] But surely the gift cannot be anything that is *recognized* as such. Any way in which one tries to interpret the gift as known to be given will conflict with a principle of Kierkegaard's B-hypothesis. It could not be recognized in itself, because the ability to identify it would presuppose prior possession of an eternal determinant, i.e. an ability to grasp eternal truth; indeed, the whole idea of the condition's having to be *given* is that there is no such ability, and this must include the ability to recognize anything that originates *in* the eternal, at least in the sense of recognizing *that* it originates there, as the proposal would require. Perhaps it could be recognized by inference? Suppose, for the sake of argument, that I have a grasp of something which I infer cannot have been acquired by the exercise of purely native abilities, say the ability to predict Derby winners more often than not. Could one not then call this capacity a *gift*? There is an objection to this. Even if the ability to recognize the gift in this indirect way employs purely native talents, conceived as an effective means of *recognition* of what has been given from elsewhere, it still implies a capacity to determine eternal truth — the truth that the eternal gives — and this implies that one has still not 'broken with immanence', as the B-position requires.

Perhaps, then, what is provided in the condition is the *ability* to recognize eternal truth when one sees it; so that, given the condition, a person is *then* in a cognitive position in which he previously was not: namely in the position to identify the circumstances which make it true that the historical phenomenon is the one which the paradoxical claim says it is. But this is clearly not what Kierkegaard means by the 'condition'. He explicitly denies that faith is a form of knowledge (*Erkjendelse*).[86] Whatever faith may make possible in the realm of understanding (and we have to bear in mind a reference by Kierkegaard, at the end of the *Fragments*, to faith as a 'new organ'),[87] and whatever certainty resides in a belief that the eternal has entered time in order to effect a reconciliation between time and eternity, the possibility remains (there is the 'risk') that the eternal has not done this, and indeed that there is no eternal.

If not the ability to grasp the claim's truth, then perhaps what is given in faith is a proper grasp of the claim's content? This seems a more promising track. But what could be meant by this 'proper' grasp? Now there is a sense in which a person who accepts, perhaps at first uncritically, the possibility of religious satisfaction 'understands' well enough what he believes. If he did not he would not be hoping for (perhaps even expecting) the satisfaction, and typically it is his expressions of doing so that are our criteria for ascribing to him a belief in its possibility and *a fortiori* some understanding of it. What is required here is simply that he believe that any sentences in which he might formulate the future satisfaction are or can be true, a condition which can be satisfied even if he has no fixed or concrete idea of the form the satisfaction might take, or of the circumstances upon which it depends. His understanding here might be called 'intellectual'; similarly if he subsequently becomes convinced, by force of his own or someone else's 'dialectical' arguments, that his expectation rests on a contradiction. Of course, he might be 'affronted' by the discovery and feel compelled to give up his hope of expectation on that account. But he might equally decide to retain his belief. This he could do simply by appending to it another, namely that what is contradictory can nevertheless be true, and by implication that reason or understanding are not the last word. Here too, however, strictly speaking, all that is needed is that he accept that whatever sentences he might formulate to express these subsidiary satisfactions are or can be true: there need be no fixed or concrete idea of the form these latter satisfactions might take.

There is, however, another way of believing something, and *a fortiori* of understanding what is believed, in which a fixed or concrete idea of the object of belief does play a necessary part. As distinct from merely believing abstractly and indeterminately that *p*, or from there being a mere abstract sense of *p*'s being true, let us talk of there being 'a sense of its being the case that *p*'. The state of mind which this expression is meant to distinguish is a 'cognitive' one, in which it can be said that 'that *p*' is 'exhibited' in experience, though not necessarily by virtue of the *truth conditions* of '*p*' being determinably present. We might call it the cognitive state of mind in which the 'truth-*seeming*' conditions of '*p*' are present. It seems natural to associate this notion of a *more* than merely intellectual understanding with, amongst whatever other varieties, the kind of belief with which we began, namely belief as what a person takes on the *evidence* to be true. For where someone accepts that something is the case in this way, it is typically because the course of experience, backed by dispositions generated by previous experience, leads to some determinate and concrete expectation, for example that a friend is about to pay a visit, or to a determinate impression of what is presently the case, for example that the friend is on the way. However, the presence of determinate expectations of how things will be, or of impressions of how things are, need not be confined to 'passive' belief; I can just as well form such fixed and concrete ideas by *deciding* that this is how things will be or are. Indeed, it seems clear that the acquisition of some kind of settled sense of how things will be or

114

are (or were) is an important element in just those forms of 'active' belief in which self-deception can, but need not, occur; that is, where they are formed more or less consciously to provide the satisfaction of things seeming to be as one wants them to be.

Let us assume that it is in this latter sense of understanding that Kierkegaard means an understanding of the eternal to be first acquired in faith. 'The object of faith', the *Postscript* tells us, 'is God's [or the teacher's] reality in existence' or 'the reality of another'.[88] How, then, can a belief with this object be said to be a condition of the more than merely intellectual understanding of the eternal? Well, like any belief, this belief, too, can take an abstract and indeterminate form, so it might be claimed that *faith* as merely intellectual assent is a prior condition of the understanding that accompanies faith in a fuller sense. This would give us one interpretation of the claim that faith is a condition of the proper grasp of the content of the belief that has God's reality in existence as its object. And to the question, Why *is* it a condition?, one might plausibly answer that without the initial belief a person cannot have the expectancies which are part of that settled sense of how things are which is necessary for the 'proper grasp' of the content of faith. Where a belief is such that the sense of how things are which form its content cannot be derived from the world itself, that sense has to be brought about by a decision to 'have' the world as though it can be derived from it. Certainly, the world itself will not impart a sense of an 'absolute difference' between it, the world, and something 'other' than the (intelligible) world, or of that other-than-the-world's being *part* of the world, and of its being that having, in addition, the sense of the possibility of establishing a 'kinship' with what is absolutely different. In order to have a sense of all this one must first be *disposed* to accept that reality has these characteristics even if they are absolutely paradoxical. The point is not, of course, that the belief in question is connected *analytically* with the ideas of sin and redemption, which is of course true, but which anyone can understand, whether or not they accept the paradoxical nature of reality. It is rather that unless a person acquiesces in the idea that reality is paradoxical in the ways in question, the idea will remain merely abstract.

A difficulty with this interpretation arises, however, when we try to account for Kierkegaard's claim that the condition, which is faith, is *given*. For it is surely much more plausible to attach the idea of something's being 'given' to the understanding which is the result of an initial acquiescence in the paradoxical nature of reality, than to that prior condition itself. It seems, then, that we shall

115

have to look for another possibility. Let us fasten now on the consideration just mentioned, that faith's sense of the paradox's being true cannot be such that the facts themselves could ever impress themselves upon the mind of the believer in this way. Now if that is so, surely any objective basis this content may have, i.e. any grounding in reality, must be transhistorical, thus transcendent, and so 'given' in the form of a necessary, though essentially inconceivable, presupposition. We should note that Kierkegaard's requirement is not that one 'understands the paradox', only that one understands that it *is* the paradox.[89] Faith has as its content not the real basis of the paradox, but only the paradoxically conjoined ideas (some, such as that of the 'unknown', no doubt merely abstract), together with intellectual acquiescence in the claim *that* they are paradoxically conjoined. But none of this is of any value as belief (as a settled sense of how things are) unless the world really is as one has induced oneself to grasp it as being. Besides the settled sense of the paradox's being true, there has to be its truth. It would be as if the believer said: 'This state of certainty I am in with regard to the paradox's truth only makes sense so long as I assume the transhistorical basis that counts as its being true. If that basis happens not to be provided, my certainty and faith are cognitively vacuous, while if the assumption is correct then what makes it so is given.'

A similar, and surely more compelling, interpretation might focus on the historical rather than the transhistorical. One could point to the phenomenon which according to the paradoxical account is the teacher, and for the believer signifies a revelation of the eternal's reconciliatory intention, as also a demonstration of the form of the reconciliation itself. Now although this phenomenal content, too, is formally unintelligible, the historical reference does form a presentational aspect accessible to the understanding. Suppose this aspect extends to a content answering to a description of the kind 'appearing genuine or trustworthy in respect of its claim to signify and demonstrate the [aforementioned] paradoxical purposes'. Normally, of course, contradictory states of affairs do not make claims on their own behalf: there are no circles professing to be round squares, or solids claiming to be dimensionless points on excursion in space—time. The question of *their* veracity, therefore, does not arise. But in this case the contradiction is located in an historical person whose utterances, behaviour, and life-style *can* be interpreted as constituting a contradictory claim, in respect of which the question of veracity therefore can arise. The content here too, of course, requires grounding in a transhistorical reality if belief in the truth of the claim is not to be cognitively vacuous. But where in the first argument the faith-sustaining 'given' remains abstract, in the second what is given has the form of a crucially significant and educative historical event. Someone willing, in spite of the contradiction, to risk the inference from the claim's apparent sincerity to its truth, will see the historical event as God's giving the condition of understanding the eternal via the claim itself. And in so far as the believer acknowledges that his certainty is cognitively vacuous if the event happens to be *merely* historical, but that if the claim is true then its being made with the intention of being that kind of event is the giving of what is conveyed, the faith which is that state of certainty, but also the state in which alone the benefit can be realized, might itself, again by extension, be said to be given.

Assuming that in one or another, or in some combination, of the ideas (i) of an objective basis validating the contradictory interpretation of an historical phenomenon, (ii) of the special role assigned to the phenomenon in the contradictory interpretation, and (iii) of faith as some kind of hermeneutic presupposition of the understanding of this interpretation, we have captured the main elements of Kierkegaard's idea of the condition that must be given by the deity, and in a way in which the learner is somehow aware of this, in the instant of time, let us now in conclusion raise the question of the rationality of Kierkegaardian faith.

There were, we recall, two kinds of objection to willed belief, one to the very notion of a belief that is willed, the other to the implication of self-deception in the notion. The first said that it was irrational to assume, as one does in setting about deciding to believe what one wants to believe, that having wanted to believe something will be a satisfactory explanation of one's subsequently believing it. The other said in effect that since, where a person believes something out of choice, it is typically because holding the belief in question is more comforting than accepting what (it is more or less consciously admitted) an unimpeded access to the facts would force upon one, this is letting satisfaction override good sense, a form of irrationalism which is also dishonesty.

If we confront Kierkegaardian faith with the first objection — assuming for the moment that it is one — it might at first glance seem that it is protected precisely by this notion of the condition. For is not the idea, contained in the two latter interpretations, of a kind of necessary concurrence between believer and believed, precisely that of the believer's *not* being in the position of having to say that the explanation of his being in the present state of mind of acceptance is only that he wanted to be in it? A nice proposal, perhaps, but on reflection unsatisfactory. The way in which the concurrence is a necessary part of the belief is that of being essentially contained in *what* is believed, not of supplementing the will to believe with something necessary for it to have *believing* as a result. According to our two subsequent interpretations the condition is an objective ground needed to validate a contradictory interpretation of an historical phenomenon as a revelation of the nature of the eternal. But this is given in precisely the same way as the objective basis of any kind of belief, even my belief that there is a piece of paper before me on which I am now writing, something which I clearly can believe unaided. The difference with Kierkegaardian faith is simply that what is given is not what presents itself to a perceiver, but something not presented which (if it *is* given) warrants the contradictory *interpretation* of something presented.

But why should it be incoherent to admit that the reason why one believes what one does is that one has chosen to believe it? The reason offered earlier was that, in a basic sense of the term, 'belief' refers to a passive state of mind caused by facts to which it is freely exposed. This, in practical and empirical contexts, is what one would call its rational basis. What makes a willed belief anomalous here is also what would make one want to call it arbitrary. Not that the choice itself lacks an explanation (it might have a very good, and even a rational explanation) and is arbitrary on that account, but simply that a choice is the wrong kind of cause. But whatever force the argument may have it clearly applies only to empirical belief, that is to beliefs which further or fuller exposure to the facts *can* cause to be revised (though even in the case of empirical belief there might well be room for belief as a state of qualified certainty *caused* by a choice of expectations — a choice that need not be at all arbitrary). Although experience might undermine the Kierkegaardian believer's belief in the historical phenomenon — in its having occurred at all, or in its having had the characteristics of a genuine-seeming claim to be the paradox — on which his faith rests, it could not undermine that part of his belief which is his taking the claim to be true. And it is this part which is the faith that has the *reality* of the deity in time, or the paradox, as its object.

It may be objected that the very conditions claimed here to render a willed belief coherent — namely the immunity of the belief to empirical restraints — deprive it at the same time of any content. That is a valid objection if the content it is said to lack is empirical, and the objection is useful in making it clear that it is not whatever empirical facts the belief concerns that make it

118

Kierkegaardian faith. The faith has as its object something impenetrable to human understanding but which would validate the paradox's claim to be a true account of reality. But since that there is such an objective reality is what Kierkegaardian faith accepts, this *is* its content, albeit an abstract one.

In another respect, however, the belief's immunity to empirical restraints does seem to deprive it of something essential, and that is any objective source of grounds (or as we said at the beginning, 'other basis') for inclining one to accept rather than reject it. The only grounds seem to be, first, the apparent genuineness of the claim made on its own behalf by the paradox, and second, the desire for religious satisfaction which inclines one to infer from the apparent genuineness of the claim to its truth. Since, again, it is the legitimacy of this latter inference that is at issue, the manner in which the claim is made cannot, without circumstantial support which in the nature of the case is unavailable on pain of begging the question, be a relevant objective ground, and the mere wanting it to be true is obviously a subjective ground.

There is nevertheless a precedent for regarding subjective grounds as capable of providing an independent basis for the rationality of religious belief: Pascal's well-known 'wager'. Although the basis is independent of reason in a sense of 'reason' in which this term is associated with empirical belief, Pascal's argument is indeed an appeal to reason in a more abstract, though still pragmatic, sense. Pascal argued that where (1) you cannot know whether or not God exists, and (2) *belief* in God's existence is a necessary condition of the acquisition of religious satisfaction, it is rational to believe in God's existence. The reason is that if you do not believe in God's existence and God exists, you are denying yourself the opportunity of acquiring that satisfaction; while if you do believe in God's existence you lose nothing by God's not existing.[90] Generalized to cover the present discussion the argument can be put as follows: given (1) the idea of a certain satisfaction (say a highest good), (2) an empirically indifferent choice between believing and disbelieving something (God's reality in existence, or the truth of the paradox),[91] where (3) believing it is itself a necessary condition of acquiring the satisfaction in the event of the belief's being true, it is more reasonable to believe than to disbelieve, since where the belief is true, not to believe will be to deny oneself the chance of acquiring the satisfaction, while to believe where the belief is false will not be to lose or deny oneself anything. In brief, the proposal can now be that the advantage uniquely offered by the paradox's being believed to be true outweighs the consideration that its being a paradox counts as much as anything ever could against its being true; consequently there is this 'other' basis for believing that it is true.[92]

There seems little doubt that much of what Kierkegaard says about faith can be put into a form similar to that of Pascal's argument. According to Kierkegaard it is only if we believe the paradox that we understand it, and understanding the paradox is a necessary condition of deriving the benefits which are in store if the paradox is true, so that disbelieving that it is true is to risk losing the benefits which accrue if it is true. Nevertheless, Kierkegaard would surely oppose any suggestion that whatever rationality a Pascalian argument bestowed upon religious belief provided an *objective* ground for accepting the truth of its 'object' – a ground stemming as though from the facts themselves, via whatever forms of ratiocination. The argument relies on purely *subjective* considerations of the strategy of belief, of the kind that even in a state of total ignorance one knows what one risks losing. That it is strategically justified to believe rather than disbelieve the truth of the paradox in no way diminishes the affront presented by the paradox to reason. Rather the reverse: the strategical considerations are really no more than a rational reinforcement of the desire to persist in the hope of religious satisfaction; but then the more strongly one is motivated to believe that the paradox is true, the greater the conflict generated by the objective consideration that what one is motivated to believe rests on a contradiction. So, although a Pascalian argument provides a basis other than empirical justification for having a belief in what cannot be decided empirically, the basis it provides is not an alternative to empirical justification for believing that what the belief says is true.

Is Kierkegaardian faith a form of self-deception? Kierkegaard himself would definitely deny that it was. He maintains, on the contrary, that self-deception in this context is either to abandon one's interest in an eternal happiness (or, rather, to *pretend* to oneself and others that one no longer has it), or to drag the goal down to a level at which there is no problem of reaching it (implicitly returning to the A-position). Here, too, at least from the B-point of view, he would appear to be justified. The allegation was that where a person believes something out of choice, it is typically because holding the belief in question is more comforting than accepting what, more or less admittedly, unimpeded access to the facts would force him to acknowledge. That Kierkegaardian faith is not typical in this respect can be argued as follows: if we distinguish between, on the one hand, the future satisfaction or comfort implicit in having attained the goal of eternal happiness, and on the other, the present satisfaction or comfort involved in expecting it, it is no doubt the latter which provides the immediate motivation for any self-deceptive belief in the prospect of the future one. But in the case of Kierkegaardian faith, the prospect of the future satisfaction entails present and continuing discomforts which can easily outweigh any present satisfaction to be derived from the prospect itself: namely those connected with becoming 'eternal' or 'a different individual' (as the *Postscript* says)[93] — something which actually involves rejecting present satisfactions, or even the prospect of future ones, as motives for one's choices — and in general the constraints of the 'life of spirit'. Moreover, since the very idea of an eternal happiness as that of a reconciliation of eternity and time is contradictory, it cannot (when this fact is realized) form a concrete goal which could then provide a present satisfaction at its prospect. (This will be elaborated in Chapter VI.) Finally, apart from having to admit that, in the event of there being no such happiness in store (either because what cannot be understood cannot exist, or because, even if it can, the required cosmological theory happens to be false — there is no God), the renunciation of all that one has hitherto prized will have been in vain, a person who accepts the possibility of the prospect — or in one fell swoop the prospect itself — must also admit that he is risking everything on something that is absolutely unintelligible. (As the *Postscript* says, the 'everything' that he risks includes his 'thought'.)[94] So there are two reasons why Kierkegaardian faith cannot be explained by the chosen belief's being more comforting than the beliefs which the facts themselves would dictate. First, it is not more comforting, and second, the facts are indeed faced. They are faced but not allowed to dictate; the believer here dictates his own preferences in full consciousness of the discomforts and risks involved. The interest in eternal happiness is retained in open defiance of its unintelligibility — of what reason would say amounts to its unattainability. This is done, moreover, without supposing that one has risen *above* reason. (The *Postscript* also says: 'Because [he] gives up his understanding in faith and believes against understanding, he should not think meanly of the understanding.')[95] Deliberately, and without any false support from the assumption that he has risen to a higher level of understanding (which is, after all, 'still an understanding'), the Kierkegaardian believer sets himself squarely against the pressing reason the unintelligibility of his goal gives him for not retaining his interest in it (in contrast to the nympholept for whom the unattainability of the goal would automatically intensify an interest in it;[96] and unlike the wishful thinker or self-deceiver whose wish to retain the interest would make him try to conceal from himself the fact that the idea of the goal is unintelligible; and yet again — a case Kierkegaard mentions only in passing — unlike the person who remains bound by the criteria of reason, in frank defiance of a genuine interest in an eternal happiness, *and* without self-deception, lets his interest die, so to speak, a rational death).[97] To Pascal's point that, if you do not believe, you will be losing your only opportunity of an eternal happiness should the belief be true, while if you do believe you will lose nothing, Kierkegaard would no doubt reply, first, that if you do believe, you will have risked and lost everything if the belief is false, and second, that whatever reasons there are for preferring belief to disbelief, there is absolutely no reason to suppose that what is believed is not false.

3 Subjectivity and truth

The *Postscript* — or to quote the title-page, 'Concluding Unscientific Postscript to the Philosophical Fragments: A Mimic-Pathetic-Dialectic Compilation: An Existential Contribution, published [*udgitt* — lit. 'given out', and in *that* sense 'edited'] by S. Kierkegaard' — is a 'next section' mentioned tentatively (since to promise such a thing would be an affectation of seriousness unbefitting a mere 'pamphleteer') at the close of the *Fragments*.[98] It is a work of some 520 pages, nearly six times the length of the *Fragments*, much more prolix, though also with a clear argumentational structure. The writing is more expansive, allusive, anecdotal, witty, and often downright funny, though the main text is interspersed with passages in a terser, more direct style, usually in footnotes and annotational comments (*Anmærkninger*), which generally serve an expository purpose similar to that of the Interlude in the *Fragments*.

The two chapters of Part One discuss the possibility of objective knowledge of Christianity. The discussion is preparatory to the later definition of faith as the 'contradiction' between the 'infinite passion of inwardness' and the 'objective uncertainty' of that truth on which eternal happiness depends.[99] The opening chapters reject current denials of Lessing's dictum, quoted earlier, that the 'accidental truths of history can never become the proof of necessary truths of reason' (in this case religious or 'saving' truths).[100] The first section of Part Two opens with two chapters on Lessing in which Kierkegaard (Climacus) introduces the main elements of the 'subjective problem', or the 'subject's relationship to Christianity, or becoming a Christian'. And the main section of Part Two proceeds with what is a main problem of the *Postscript*, a heuristic problem: namely, what is required of subjectivity 'in order for it to see the [above] problem'. The central issue is Kierkegaard's doctrine that *truth* is subjectivity. This doctrine is a conceptual successor of the notion put forward in the *Fragments* that faith is an 'organ'. For, as it will appear, the definition just given of 'faith' – as the contradiction between an infinite passion of inwardness and objective uncertainty – is also Kierkegaard's definition of truth.

But let us return to the beginning and to the second of these aspects of faith. The first chapter considers the historical approach to knowledge of Christianity. Here the questions both of the truth and of the content of Christian doctrine are assumed to be matters to be decided by a 'critical consideration of the various sources of information, etc.',[101] just as any other historical truth. But historical knowledge is at best an 'approximation' and so not sufficient for 'a researching subject . . . infinitely interested in his relationship to this truth'.[102] Kierkegaard says he does not scorn 'erudite critical theology' as such, but opposes a more or less latent duplicity in it: the suggestion that the investigation is not just historical but will eventually turn up something critical for faith.[103] This it cannot do in any case, but the opposite assumption falsely presupposes two things: first, that the proper attitude to the question of the truth (and content) of Christianity is one of outward anticipation of some publicly accredited evidence for the correctness of Christian belief; and second, that the material investigated contains something ('a word, a proposition, a book, a man, a community, or what you will') not subject to the 'dialectic' of doubt and personal decision.[104] Suppose it *was* possible to authenticate certain writings as belonging to the canon, even to say that it was 'as if every letter were inspired'; it would still be impossible by any 'quantitative approximation' to settle the question of whether they were in fact inspired.[105] Whether the supposed source of truth is scripture or the living church, or even the simple survival of Christianity ('the proof of the centuries of [its] truth'),[106] once these dialectical considerations are taken into account it becomes clear that it is only those who 'know not what they do' who can resort to the historical approach to convince people of the truth of Christianity, or for that matter to argue its falsity.[107]

The second chapter briefly considers the speculative approach, or the attempt to determine the 'philosophical truth' of Christianity. Here Christianity's truth and content are conceived as questions to be decided by discovering whether, and in what terms, Christianity can be brought into conceptual relation with eternal truth. This inquiry, says Kierkegaard, takes as its data the accredited results of the historical investigation.[108] But it does not presuppose, as does the historical approach, that something essential is immune to the dialectic of doubt. Indeed, the supposed advantage of the speculative approach is that it makes no presuppositions at all: 'It begins with nothing, assumes nothing as given, begins with nothing it may have to give back' (*begynder ikke 'bittweise'*; the German term is one used by Hegel in his *Logic*).[109] And yet, says Kierkegaard, it does make assumptions. Although it does not assume anything beyond the accredited historical facts, it assumes that the historical facts themselves occur with a necessity which can be grasped in thought, so that Christianity as a whole can be regarded as 'given', as something that occurs as a matter of historical course.[110] Again (though not quite credibly), Kierkegaard says it would be wrong to think that he opposes speculative philosophy as such: 'All honour to speculation, all praise to everyone who occupies himself with it in a true spirit [*i Sandhed*].' Anyone who, like Kierkegaard himself, admires Greek philosophy and is familiar with Aristotle's view which 'identifies the highest happiness with the joys of thought' must have a sense for 'the fearless enthusiasm of the philosophical scholar . . . [in] his persistent devotion to the service of the Idea'.[111] But the basis of Aristotle's view, the idea of the 'blessed gods', who are also the speculative philosopher's 'great prototypes', leaves no room for *concern* about an eternal happiness. The view is pagan, and the crucial point about Christianity is that it is not a pagan religion. So the speculative philosopher who *is* troubled about an eternal happiness will not find what he wants in his philosophy. 'Speculative happiness', as a passage we have already quoted says, is an 'illusion'. 'For the speculating [philosopher] the question of his personal eternal happiness cannot present itself, just because his task consists in getting more and more away from himself and becoming objective.' The speculative philosopher 'vanishes' from himself and becomes the 'contemplative power of philosophy itself'.[112] The second chapter ends with an illustration of the 'contradiction' between 'the infinitely and passionately interested subject' and 'the speculation which is supposed to assist him' in this respect.

> In sawing wood it is important not to press too hard on the
> saw; the lighter the pressure, the better the saw operates.
> If one presses down with all one's strength, one won't be able
> to saw at all. In the same way the philosopher has to make
> himself *objectively* light; but anyone who is in passion
> infinitely interested in his eternal happiness makes himself as

subjectively heavy as possible. . . . [If] Christianity requires this interest in the individual subject (as is assumed, since this is what the problem turns on), it is easy to see that it is impossible for him to find what he seeks in speculation. This can also be expressed by saying that speculative philosophy doesn't allow the problem to arise at all; so that its whole answer is only a mystification.[113]

Since the missing certainty here is not of a kind which could *ever* satisfy a concern for an eternal happiness, and it is the concern which motivates faith, it seems that it is not *speculative* uncertainty that Kierkegaard has in mind in calling faith 'the contradiction between the infinite passion of inwardness and the objective uncertainty [*Uvished*]'. The uncertainty must therefore be historical. Does Kierkegaard, then, mean by 'the objective uncertainty' the inability conclusively to authenticate the facts on which Christian belief is based? Or does he mean rather the inability to authenticate (however well authenticated) facts as being facts of the kind assumed by theology? The observations that 'the greatest certainty with respect to the historical is after all merely an *approximation*', and that 'an approximation is too little to base an eternal happiness on',[114] seem to support the former interpretation. The point would be that in faith the believer, in accepting the theological interpretation of the facts, is prevented for traditional epistemological reasons from grasping them in the way needed for absolute certainty. But clearly Kierkegaard does not mean this. Following Lessing's dictum, the disparity we are to focus on is not that between one historical claim with its theological interpretation taken for granted (the conclusion) and other historical claims (the evidence), but between a claim about the eternal (conclusion) and historical claims (evidence) in general, no accumulation of which could ever provide more than psychological reinforcement of a believer's inclination to accept the former. As the *Postscript* says, 'I look at nature in order to discover God, and I do indeed see omnipotence and wisdom; but I also see much that alarms and upsets me. The long and short of it is the objective uncertainty . . .'.[115] That is to say, the uncertainty confronting faith, and which faith must overcome, is whether the theological interpretation is *ever* the right one. Its being the right one is precisely what, in the absence of any evidence *at all* that historical phenomena, or nature itself, are manifestations of divinity, he must *choose* to believe. This, then, is the uncertainty of which Kierkegaard speaks and of which he goes on to say that, in faith, it is 'embraced' by 'inwardness' with 'all the passion of the infinite'.

As for the inwardness itself, this is clearly a mental state involving, as the term 'contradiction' indicates, some form of conflict. Indeed Kierkegaard says that it is the 'tension of the conflict form' (*Modsætningens-Formens Spændstighed*) that is the measure of the *strength* of inwardness,[116] and not any direct 'outpouring' (*Udgydelse*).

A wide range of mental states can be characterized as states of conflict or tension. Indeed, probably no mental state cannot be so characterized in some respect. Thus although the examples which may come most immediately to mind are conflicts of decision where a person must choose between two or more incompatible courses of action (conflicts of duty, or of inclination, or of duty versus inclination), or tensions of frustration in which the incompatibility is between a wish on the one hand and presumed present lack of capability on the other, any mental state at all directed at a future situation significantly different from a present one, or from an envisaged situation which a present action seeks to avoid, involves a kind of mental tension, however attenuated and unacute, corresponding to the logical 'conflict' between incompatible descriptions of reality. Now there is a clear sense in which Kierkegaardian faith involves the tension of frustration, and because Kierkegaard's concept of inwardness is also clearly that of a characteristically acute form of mental tension, it might be natural to link it with that. But although Kierkegaard does indeed describe faith as the 'suffering' of the understanding's 'despairing' inability to establish (or even envisage) the soul's highest wish, its 'happiness',[117] it is not *this* conflict that gives inwardness its special stamp. In spite of faith's being a form of suffering, the *inwardness* of faith is an active rather than a passive component, and the conflict a tension created *by* the believer rather than inflicted *upon* him. Kierkegaard compares the inwardness of faith to that of the 'lover, the enthusiast, or the thinker'. Like these, the believer fastens on to what he wants, in spite of the uncertainty that he will get it. But *'faith [det at troe]* differs in kind from all other appropriation and inwardness'. It 'holds fast' to the 'objective uncertainty due to [lit. 'with'] the repulsion of the absurd' with the 'passion of inwardness', which in this case is therefore the 'phenomenon [*Forhold*] of inwardness intensified to the utmost degree'.[118] The translation of 'Inderlighed' as 'inwardness' is misleading if it suggests a direction inwards;[119] 'Inderlighed' refers rather to the inner form or quality of a person's *outward*-looking engagement. Indeed the word suggests what is sometimes actually meant by 'engagement', that is an active, personal involvement. ('Inderlig' is a very commonly used adverb meaning 'heartily',

though without the convivial overtones, and its range of application would cover roughly what is meant in English by 'in a
heartfelt way', 'fervently' or even just 'sincerely', though this, like
the American 'cordially', has a ritual use more or less unconnected
with inwardness.) *Inderlighed* is therefore not to be confused with,
say, self-absorption, introversion, or withdrawal *into* the self (cf.
the discussion in the following chapter of *Indesluttethed* — or
closed-inness — as a pathological state). More importantly, the fact
that inwardness is an active component, and associated therefore
with positive frames of mind, means that the conflict of inwardness
is not that of frustration. It is not the conflict between what a
person wants and all that he believes he can achieve, it is the
conflict between what he believes he can achieve and the (in the
case of Kierkegaardian faith total) absence of any warrant for his
believing that he can achieve it. The former conflict is the conflict
of despair, which as a matter of fact we are told elsewhere is the
'opposite' of faith.[120] Despair, in Kierkegaard's sense, is remaining
uncertain *because* of the objective uncertainty; its conflict is that
what is wanted is certainty concerning an eternal happiness. Faith
is being certain *in spite* of the objective uncertainty — indeed in
defiance of it; its conflict is that it has no reason at all to believe
(indeed has every reason not to believe) that the happiness is
available. Clearly this is a conflict that does *not* occur in despair,
which is precisely the frame of mind of one who withholds belief
where there is no reason to believe (or every reason not to believe)
what he wants more than anything to believe. In describing faith
as the 'contradiction' (*Modsigelsen*) between the 'infinite passion
of inwardness' and the 'objective uncertainty', Kierkegaard is
referring to the conflict between the subjective, or personal,
certainty one seeks, and has found, on the one hand, and the
objective uncertainty, on the other, which has made the finding of
the former depend on a strenuous personal choice. The passion of
inwardness is the active passion of someone who has decided upon
a risky course of action and knows that the determination with
which he pursues it would give way to despair were he to fall back
on the impersonal authority of reason. The objective uncertainty
is neither replaced nor obscured by the subjective certainty, rather
it is a necessary condition of the latter.

> If I can grasp God objectively, I do not believe, but just because
> I can't do that I have to believe; and if I am to keep myself in
> faith I must take constant care to insist on the objective
> uncertainty, to bear in mind that in [this] objective uncertainty
> I am 'upon those waters seventy thousand fathoms deep' and
> still believe.[121]

(It may be recalled that in another context it was *despair* (or sin) that was described as a contradiction, and faith (or health) as a 'matter of resolving contradictions'. The contradiction of despair took either of two forms: that of knowing oneself as merely finite while wanting also to be infinite, and that of knowing oneself as also infinite while wanting to be merely finite. Faith resolved the conflict by virtue of exemplifying the form 'knowing oneself as being also infinite and wanting to be so'. In the present case we are looking at the same contrast (faith versus despair), but from another perspective. What we saw earlier as the conforming of the will to what is 'known' to be right, we now see as the setting up of the will in opposition to what there is reason to believe it can attain. Thus the contradiction said now to be *present* in faith, but *absent* in despair, is between being subjectively certain but objectively uncertain of an eternal happiness, while despair is there being both objective *and* subjective uncertainty — though in despair the former contradiction might be said to linger residually in the optative mood in the form of the opposition between what the despairer would like but dares not aspire to and the good reasons he has for not aspiring.)[122]

The concept of inwardness is an important, indeed the central, element in Kierkegaard's answer to the question of what is required of subjectivity for it to grasp 'the' problem of the *Postscript*: the subject's relationship to Christianity. The idea is that without inwardness with regard to this topic a person does not yet see the problem. The title of the second section of the *Postscript*'s Part Two reads: 'The Subjective Problem, or How Subjectivity Must be for the Problem to Appear for it'.[123] The importance here of the adverbial modifier 'how' is reflected in Kierkegaard's constant use of a distinction between the 'how' of an utterance (etc.) and its 'what'. Inwardness is a mode of the 'how', and it would be a logical extension of the idea in the *Fragments*, that faith is a condition of the understanding of the eternal, to say that it was the 'how' of the inwardness, specifically, of *faith* that tells us what subjectivity needs for it to grasp the problem of the subject's relation to Christianity. This leaves us, however, with the puzzle of grasping how faith can be both the solution to the problem and a condition for grasping it. But it is clear enough, at least, that by the 'subjective problem' Kierkegaard still means the problem of this relationship, now considered as a subjective problem, given both that as an objective one it cannot be answered except 'approximately' (and that is not enough for the kind of certainty needed), and that, properly understood, it is not an objective problem in any case (and so the solution cannot be legitimately put off just because there can be no adequate proof).

The how/what distinction has a clear polemical import. Kierkegaard uses it *both* to make an important and *accepted* distinction *and* to reverse the accepted ranking of the disjoint terms. The accepted distinction is, as Kierkegaard puts it, that 'the objective accent falls on *what* is said, the subjective accent on *how* it is said'.[124] The revolutionary proposal, outrageous to an Hegelian audience, is that the notion of truth belongs to the 'how' rather than to the 'what'. We noted earlier that the Hegelian ideal of truth was that of a common vision, though we stressed at the same time that the knowledge gained in this vision is conceptual, not empirical, and that it is knowledge of the *self* in respect of its fulfilling activities and goals, not knowledge of an objective reality 'outside' the self or subject, to which the latter stands opposed. Kierkegaard's target, then, is the idealist doctrine that there can be knowledge of ultimate human goals; or that, in the terminology of Hegel's *Phenomenology*, it is in the 'idea of reason' that the individual can acquire a consciousness of its action and being as being action and being 'in themselves'.[125] It is worth noting that, given this practical frame of reference, Kierkegaard's proposal would seem neither revolutionary nor outrageous to a Kantian. The idea that it is a feature of the individual's interest that gives an action issuing from that interest its intrinsic value clearly mirrors Kant's doctrine that an action's intrinsic worth derives from the nature of the will that intends the result, rather than from any measurable benefits of the (actual or intended) results themselves. In fact, as Kierkegaard states the distinction, his reversal of the Hegelian ordering might seem merely to express a commonplace. He identifies the 'what' (*det Hvad*) with 'the categories of thought' (*Tankebestemmelserne*), roughly whatever can be represented in conceptual form; and the 'how' (*det Hvorledes*) which he opposes to this is, he says, not 'demeanour, tone of voice, diction, etc.', but the degree and nature of the utterer's own concern with what he says or thinks, or, in Kierkegaard's own words, 'the relationship of the existing individual, in his own existence, to what is asserted'.[126] In other words, the everyday distinction between what may or may not be true, on the one hand, and what its being or not being true means for the actively engaged subject, on the other. From an 'existential' as opposed to, say, a scientific point of view, the latter might well be said to be, in some fairly obvious way, more fundamental than the former. So in practical contexts, and it *is* these that Kierkegaard focuses upon, the reversal of the how/what ranking as found in Hegel might seem perverse only to Hegelians.

The real difficulties arise over Kierkegaard's reinterpretation of the notion of truth. Hegel's ideal of truth is that of a conceptual geography, which can be universally shared, in relation to which subjectivity plays a merely parasitic role. 'How' stands to 'what' as accident of perspective and partial vision to a total and unimpeded view of the whole; or as non-cognitive 'heart' to cognitive 'head'. On this view the 'how' is a psychological domain of feelings, longings, attitudes, etc., which, with whatever justification they can be said to be ways of 'possessing their object', are at best a 'movement towards thinking', 'musical' thinking, as Hegel calls it, not thinking itself, because they are 'not yet in conceptual form'.[127] Kierkegaard claims that with reference to essential truth (or 'the truth that is essentially related to existence')[128] the situation is the reverse. Essential truth is to be identified with a 'how' rather than a 'what'. 'The "how" of the truth is precisely the truth'.[129] 'Subjectivity, inwardness is the truth.'[130] In fact, as we anticipated at the beginning of this section, Kierkegaard claims that faith and truth are essentially the same notions. In his proposed definition of 'subjective truth' ('the highest truth there is for one who exists') as 'an objective uncertainty held fast in an appropriation of the most passionate inwardness' we are given, as he himself puts it, an 'alternative expression [*Omskrivning*] for faith'.[131]

There has been much dispute over the doctrine that truth is subjectivity, some of it confused by failing to take account of its intended scope, and all of it complicated by difficulties of interpretation. We shall tackle the issues here by raising three questions: first, What *is* the precise scope intended for the doctrine?; second, What are the constituents of the state of inwardness said to amount to the possession of subjective truth?; and third, Is the definition intended to provide a criterion of objectivity after all?

(1) 'The reader will bear in mind', says Kierkegaard, 'that it is a question here of the essential truth.'[132] By this he means, as just noted, 'the truth that is essentially related to existence'. That is to say, the individual's existence. In a different context, and in a loose sense of the term, this could sound as though the truth in question concerned such concrete and crucial 'essentials' to human existence as the material and social conditions of life, before, and on some views even to the deliberate exclusion of, say, metaphysical truth. But for Kierkegaard it is the reverse. In its connection with the term 'truth' he uses 'essential' interchangeably with 'eternal', and so essential truth has to do with the 'unchangeable'. It is a presupposition on Kierkegaard's part (or, more specifically, on that of his pseudonymous author) that individuals (or, perhaps even more specifically, this particular pseudonymous author's

readers — people who have not opted for an eternal *un*happiness) are interested more than anything (at any rate in the long run) in grasping themselves as being (in their actions) manifestations of an unchangeable order. This is also a presupposition of Hegel's, except that Hegelian philosophy allows that individuals can grasp themselves in this way in *thought*. Kierkegaard denies this possibility, but not that there is some way in which, in some sense of the term, they can 'grasp' themselves in this aspect nevertheless; moreover — as he claims is excluded on the Hegelian 'solution' — grasp themselves in it as the particular individuals they are, and not simply as replaceable instruments of a collective spiritual advance. In the *Postscript* the requirements of this possibility are spelt out. They are said to be found in the form of the individual's relationship to something asserted, in the 'how' rather than the 'what'.

(2) What are the characteristics of the 'how' of *faith* which are said to be tantamount to the individual's grasping itself (in some sense) as a manifestation of an unchangeable order?

The neat answer, on the basis of the foregoing, would be that the characteristics of the 'how' are those (however else we should describe them) of the state of mind of one who, specifically in respect of the absolute paradox, is convinced *both* that what is desired is obtainable (that the conditions making this possible already obtain) *and* that there are nevertheless no good grounds for believing that it is obtainable (or every good ground for believing that it is not).

In what sense, however, could an individual satisfying this condition of 'inwardness' be said to 'grasp' itself in its eternal aspect?

One answer might be: given that the assertion that a certain historical phenomenon is the absolute paradox is true (i.e. allowing that the truth conditions of the content of the 'what' of faith are satisfied although not known to be), the individual is in fact — though not in knowledge — in a state of mind appropriate to the truth. By 'appropriate to the truth' one could mean something like 'having a mental state (dispositions, expectations, and the like)' which is in fact matched by the actual state of affairs. And to allow for the notion that the individual grasps itself as *having* an eternal aspect, where the initial assumption is that it has no such aspect, one could add that the aforesaid state of inwardness (the state of faith) is essential to being a manifestation of the eternal order — of actually *having* an eternal aspect. In none of this would there be any implication of *knowledge* of essential truth or of the individual's *knowing* itself as having its eternal aspect.

131

Unfortunately, however, or apparently so, for this interpretation, Kierkegaard allows that the 'how' may be the 'how' of truth *even when the assertion corresponding to the 'what' is false*. He says: 'So long as this relationship's "how" is in the truth the individual is in the truth, even if it relates itself in this way to what is untrue.'[133] What we might expect Kierkegaard to be saying is: the 'how' is the 'how' of truth if, in addition to its having the characteristics of the 'how' of Kierkegaardian faith, the claim about the historical phenomenon's being the paradox also happens to be true. We could then understand the idea of 'how' of truth on the analogy, say, of a very badly grounded but consistently sustained optimism. In the rationally unexpected even of its later vindication, one would be able to say that the optimism nevertheless now proves to *have been* correct all along, though not implying by this that there really *was*, after all, a rational warrant for the optimism. And although in the case of Kierkegaardian faith no such event could be envisaged, let alone be rationally expected, this need not destroy the significance of the analogy. What we could say is that the 'how' of faith is the 'how' of truth so long as the assertion is true. In the context this would not be the trivial statement it seems to be. The point of saying it would be to stress that, if there is to be anything at all answering the notion of having, or 'being in', essential truth — and granting for the sake of argument that there is such a thing — it can only be via a 'how' of the kind described. On this interpretation, however, the truth of the assertion (though not its verification) *is* a necessary condition of the 'how' of faith's being the 'how' of truth. But Kierkegaard seems to deny that it is a necessary condition. In a much-quoted passage we read:

> When one asks objectively about the truth, reflection is directed
> objectively on truth as an object to which the knowing [subject]
> relates himself. Reflection is not directed at the relation, but
> on its being the truth [*Sandheden*], on the truth [*det Sande*]
> he is related to. So long as what he relates himself to is the truth,
> the actual state of affairs [*det Sande*], then the subject is in
> the truth. When one asks subjectively about the truth, reflection
> is directed subjectively at the individual's relationship [to the
> state of affairs]. So long as this relationship's 'how' is in the
> truth the individual is in the truth, even if it relates itself in this
> way to what is untrue [*Usandheden*].[134]

In other words, Kierkegaard allows that the individual is in, or has in some way hit upon or 'grasped', the truth even if the actual state of affairs is not the one it believes itself to be in relation to. Thus our believer can be 'in the truth' even if the event he believes is the absolute paradox is not the absolute paradox at all, but just another historical phenomenon.

The above passage has led commentators to distinguish two different sorts of claim in Kierkegaard's text and to charge him with conflating them. One is that being subjectively in the truth is a way of arriving at, or grasping, the truth itself; the other, in order to accommodate the possibility here envisaged that one can be 'in the truth' even when the thought-content of one's belief is simply false, is that being subjectively in the truth is simply a criterion of a way of being true to oneself, of maintaining one's 'true' aspirations in the face of reason and natural inclination. Consider, for example, the following:

A proper evaluation of Kierkegaard's doctrine that truth is subjectivity and his use of it as a means of defending Christianity is impossible unless it is realized that what he offers us is not a single theory but an amalgamation of two quite distinct positions. . . . [A]lthough much of the time Kierkegaard appears to tell us that we should forget about the objective questions except as a means of heightening the tension of inwardness, he does revert to these issues and as a Christian he must do so. Putting it in different words, Kierkegaard reverts and must revert, from the new sense of 'true' in which to say that a belief is true means no more than that it is held sincerely and without reservations, to the old sense in which it means that it is in accordance with the facts or with reality.[135]

It is not clear, however, that Kierkegaard employs a sense of 'true' confined to the manner or 'how' of the believer's believing, and which takes no account of what, for the Christian, must be objectively the case if his belief is to have the significance in reality he supposes it has. If we look at the text immediately following the passage quoted, we find that Kierkegaard contrasts two situations. One is where the question of essential truth is treated as an objective one and the conclusion drawn that the historical phenomenon was indeed 'the true God',[136] and the other is where a person fastens on the *wrong* temporal object ('an image of an idol'), but does so 'with all the passion of the infinite'.[137] Kierkegaard raises the question of in which of these two situations 'most truth' lies.[138] Naturally, he thinks it beyond doubt that there is more truth in the latter.[139] There is no suggestion, however, that this would be so even if there were nothing that was the true God, that is, if there were no historical phenomenon that was the eternal in time. In saying that a person who

133

fastens on the wrong object in the right way is closer to the truth than one who fastens on the right object in the wrong way, Kierkegaard (Climacus) is obviously still thinking in terms of the B-hypothesis, and pointing out what is needed if essential truth has to be grasped on *its* assumptions. What is not enough on these assumptions can be clarified by combining two earlier distinctions (one ours, the other Kierkegaard's). A person who believes in an abstract way in the truth of the teachings constituting the 'what' of Christianity, without any accompanying sense of what it would be like (in practice and for oneself) for them to be true — that is, a person who simply acquiesces in them intellectually, saying yes to the relevant propositions, however decisively — has not acquired that relationship to the doctrine that is the 'how' of the Christian. The fact that the propositions acquiesced in happen to be true will not be *enough* for the acceptance to amount to the beliefs of a believer who is 'in the truth'. Now although in the passage in question Kierkegaard seems to be saying that it is not necessary either, this is not entailed by what he actually says. First of all, with regard to the original passage where Kierkegaard says that the believer can be in the truth even if he relates himself 'to what is untrue', it is evident that this latter situation, being in relation to what is untrue, is exemplifiable in a number of logically different ways. One is where there is no God at all, in which case the 'object' to which the believer believes he is related does not exist. Another is where what is believed to be God is not that, though something else is, in which case there is still an essential part of his belief, indeed that fundamental part of it that makes his belief specifically a Christian belief, which *is* objectively true, namely that there is some historical phenomenon that is in fact the eternal in time. Or finally, even if the believer has fastened on the right historical phenomenon, a number of the peripheral theological details of his *overall* belief may be false, in which case the situation as a whole is not as he believes it to be, but the essential core of true belief is there. Second, however, Kierkegaard's reference to an image of an idol in the passage following could indicate that it is the case of a pagan believer he has in mind, someone who believes that God is directly manifested in time. Lacking *conclusive* evidence that the image in question is indeed the image of God, the pagan believer can still generate some inwardness (and there are, of course, other grounds for uncertainty, namely positive evidence for the non-existence of a benevolent deity, that can add to it); so that such a believer could well be said to be nearer the truth than one who simply acquiesces intellectually in the propositions of Christian doctrine, provided again that the fundamental tenet of Christian doctrine is true. Assuming that the fundamental tenet is true (and Climacus — *qua* dialectician and humorist — tells his reader repeatedly that it is not part of *his* project to decide that it is), a believer can be 'in the truth' even if the propositions he believes are not *the* true ones. In other words, what is necessary is, first, that there is at least one true proposition of Christian teaching, namely that 'an eternal happiness is decided in time through the relationship to something historical' — a proposition which Climacus later says is the only one that matters, since all the others are 'contained in this one and can be consistently derived from it',[140] and second, that the idol-fixated believer believes with the passion of inwardness that he is related *qua* temporal being to something that decides his eternal happiness. His inwardness may not be that of the paradox-believer, an inwardness which 'steeps the passion of the infinite in uncertainty' to an absolute degree;[141] but it is a truer way of believing what is (assumed to be) true than accepting the principles of paradox-religiousness in a merely intellectual way. In short, then, what is not necessary is that, being true, these principles and not some others be acquiesced in. The others must, of course, pertain to the same goals and believing them to be true must involve inwardness. It is in this sense that Kierkegaard would say that if one has the 'how' of the Christian, the 'what' of Christianity can in principle be dispensed with. But this will have to be qualified. The standpoint of a person whose 'how' is that of the Christian-in-truth must in any case be that of the B-hypothesis.

(3) An entry in the *Journals* reads:

> there is a 'how' which has this quality, that if *it* is truly given, the 'what' is also given; and that is the 'how' of faith.[142]

This makes the 'how' of faith look like what philosophers nowadays call a 'criterion', that is a guarantee or sufficient indication of the presence of something, in this case of the 'what'. Assuming, as we surely can, that the 'what' guaranteed by the 'how' of faith is the 'what' of faith, we might be satisfied with interpreting this latter as the *content* of the fundamental principles of Christianity (or the basic propositions from which they all 'derive', i.e. that some historical event is such that the individual's relationship to it is decisive for the latter's eternal happiness). But we might not be satisfied with that. We might insist on interpreting it as a presentation in some way of its truth-conditions, of the actual circumstances making the principles or the propositions true. In that case, the proposition must represent the truth-conditions constituting the actual historical event, since it is not possible for any

other truth-conditions to be the 'what' that *verifies* the fundamental proposition of Christianity. In short, what we would then
have in Kierkegaard's theory of truth as subjectivity is an attempt
to show that Christian doctrine is true, and that subjectivity, or
inwardness, provides the necessary cognitive vantage-point.

There is admittedly a certain amount in Kierkegaard that can be
read in isolation as supporting this interpretation. For instance,
the continuation of the above passage says that 'inwardness at its
maximum proves to be objectivity'. Second, Climacus says in the
Postscript that there is a still 'more inward expression of truth'
than 'subjectivity is the truth', namely one that conjoins this latter
expression with the contrary 'saying' that 'subjectivity is untruth'
(though not, he points out, in the way that 'speculative philosophy'
also subscribes to the latter).[143] Third, there is a remark by
Climacus towards the end of the *Postscript* to the effect that,
unlike the immanentist religiousness A which, according to a
'dialectic' that confines it to the deepening of inwardness (*Inder-
liggjørelsens Dialektik*), does not conceive the individual's relationship to an eternal happiness as depending on 'a definite something'
outside, i.e. some historical phenomenon which 'defines the
eternal happiness more closely', religiousness B does not conceive
it as depending on such a something. Perhaps the strongest support
comes, fourth, from what Climacus says in regard to proof in
'essential' matters. Thus, commenting on the 'incredible pains the
System takes to prove immortality', which he points out is effort
wasted anyway since it is only in someone's 'willing to become
subjective' that 'the question can properly emerge', Climacus says:

> Systematically immortality cannot . . . be proved [*lader sig
> ikke bevise*] . The fault doesn't lie in the proofs, but in its not
> being understood that from a systematic point of view the
> whole question [of immortality] is nonsense, so that instead of
> looking for further proofs [*yderligere Beviser*] , one should
> rather try to be a little subjective. Immortality is subjectivity's
> most passionate interest; precisely in the interest lies the
> proof.[144]

And in a similar vein we find, in the *Journals*, the claim that 'there
is only one proof of the truth of Christianity, the inner proof,
argumentum Spiritus Sancti'.[145] And finally, in *Fear and Trembling*
we read that 'the conclusions of the passion [of faith] are the only
reliable ones, that is the only convincing conclusions'.[146]

There is, however, an overwhelming objection to the interpretation. As a sequel to the *Fragments*, the *Postscript* explicitly
continues, in the latter's experimental vein, to treat the question

of Christianity's truth or falsity as a hypothesis. Among his repeated reminders to this effect we find Climacus recalling, in the very middle of his account of truth as subjectivity, that the project is to find a 'thought-content' which 'really goes further [than Socrates]', but that 'whether [this content] is true or not, it is no concern of mine, since I am simply experimenting'.[147] It would be very odd if, in spite of such clear disclaimers, Kierkegaard were after all really proposing some alternative method of validating the claims of Christianity — an inward appropriation by some intuitive apprehension of their truth-conditions as an effective substitute for the inadequate objective procedures. To suppose that he were it would be necessary first to be sure that the above remarks and formulations did not lend themselves to interpretations that are consistent with the disclaimer. Or else show that on any alternative interpretation the experiment becomes trivial in some way that Kierkegaard in his confusion has failed to see.

That there are plausible alternative interpretations which, even if the experiment presupposes the truth of Christianity, do not drain the notion of truth of all significance in this context, is certainly not out of the question. Thus, taking the apparently anomalous remarks in the same order: (i) the 'what' that comes with the 'how' of faith can just as readily be identified with the content of which Climacus, as just noted, says he is not concerned to determine its truth, as with the circumstances which amount to its being true; while the 'objectivity' that inwardness at its maximum is said to prove to be could correspond to the claim that eternal truth, or its source, lies *outside* existence as a whole, an idea which we earlier saw was said to be first constituted in consciousness through religiousness B's 'break with immanence', i.e. its break with religiousness A's idea that the relation to an eternal happiness is established without essential reference to a 'teacher' in time and simply by an intensification of subjectivity. Inwardness might 'prove' to be objectivity only in the sense that this is the content (not the truth) of the belief of one who adopts the paradoxical form of religiousness as against one who believes, as it were, that enough subjectivity is enough.

The same basis could surely underlie the statement (ii) that, in the final instance, subjectivity (alone) is untruth (i.e. not sufficient in itself to establish a relationship to an eternal happiness), as well as actually amounting to the claim (iii) that for religiousness B the passionate, but (or because) objectively uncertain, relationship to an eternal happiness is a relationship to a 'definite something'. None of this, if we ignore for the moment the implications of the word 'proves', suggests that Kierkegaard is giving an account of how the truth of Christianity can be ascertained. All we have are various ways of formulating an ingredient in the position already elaborated, Climacus's hypothetical position B, according to which essential truth can only be appropriated as a gift in time from a source which human understanding can never conceive as being in the position (in time) to give it. As far as the 'thought-experiment' is concerned, that there *is* an essential truth is obviously part of the experimental set-up, not what is being tested. The object of the experiment is to see what happens conceptually when one brings this truth into 'dialectical' contact with the epistemology of the B-position, given what Climacus calls the *conditio sine qua non* of the individual's 'infinite interest in its eternal happiness'.[148] The 'thought-content' that enables Climacus to 'go beyond Socrates' emerges from this contact by reason of the B-position's idea of the individual's having *no* natural access to eternal truth. Hence the conceptual apparatus of 'faith', 'sin-consciousness' (the awareness of a natural lack of an eternal determinant), the 'instant', and the 'deity in time', with which Climacus says, in a concluding 'moral' to the *Fragments*, he has amended the Socratic view, although disclaiming there, too, to have maintained that the amended version is 'more true' than the Socratic doctrine just because it 'indisputably goes beyond' it.[149] It would contradict this clear statement to suppose that inwardness or subjectivity was some kind of substitute for systematic proof, as though it were another avenue to the same destination (certainty). Kierkegaard cannot, at least in the guise of Climacus, consistently argue that passion does what dispassionate systematic proof cannot do. He could consistently claim, however, that it is only in a certain subjective state that a person can acquire an adequate grasp of the *content* of the thought that enables him to go beyond Socrates.

As for the use of the term 'proof' (and its cognates), this raises difficulties only if one is determined to be officious in one's treatment of its comparatively rare occurrences in Kierkegaard. A warrantedly officious solution would be to say that he should not have used it at all, since whatever he means to convey by it is mis-leadingly represented in this term as proof in some technical sense, analogous to that of logical or mathematical proof, a proof which one seeks and may find and which establishes *objective* truth, but here by a subjective procedure. It would be unwarranted and arbitrary, as well as officious, to assume without further ado that the term *is* used in such a technical sense. It would be more reasonable to conjecture, for example, that Kierkegaard associates the word 'proof' with psychological rather than factual or logical certainty, i.e. with conviction, or certitude, without in any way confusing the former with the latter. Thus a remark of Wittgenstein's:

> Queer as it sounds: The historical accounts in the Gospels might, historically speaking, be demonstrably false and yet belief would lose nothing by this: *not*, however, because it concerns 'universal truths of reason'! Rather, because historical proof (the historical proof-game) is irrelevant to belief. This message (the Gospels) is seized on by men believingly (i.e. lovingly). *That* is the certainty characterizing this particular acceptance-as-true, not something *else*.[150]

Following this suggestion, which may stem from Wittgenstein's own reading of Kierkegaard, we might even suppose that Kierkegaard considered some states of mind, for example those fortified by a life-view, in particular by a religious life-view, to be self-confirming in the sense of providing their own form of justification, and not only not in need of further justification, but as belonging to a 'proof-game' for which any other kind of confirmation, e.g. empirical proof, or disproof, is irrelevant. A dangerous notion, perhaps, if the different senses of 'proof' are confused, but there is no prima facie evidence that Kierkegaard himself confuses them. And an acceptable motivation for his using traditional terminology in an extended sense could be his wish to draw attention to what he sees as its widespread misapplication in connection with 'essential matters', these being conceived inappropriately as objective problems. Certainly Kierkegaard wants the traditional projects of philosophy to be transferred to the subjective domain, and there, of course, the traditional terminology for stating them will acquire a different meaning; or else, where there is no basis for this, it will or should be dropped. If, in stressing that the certainty a person seeks in religion must be something he chooses, rather than waits for in the form of some conclusive argument or unassailable evidence still to come, the idea that the certainty itself is a kind of proof is misleading, because it suggests more than the negative point that what was liable to be left to due process is in fact a matter for instant personal decision, then it would no doubt be better to drop the notion of proof altogether in this connection, and make do with conviction or certitude (*Vished*).

4   The problem of existence

In the previous chapter, in connection with the alleged unintelligibility of faith, we referred to Hegel's remark in the *Phenomenology* that whenever we try to pick out something 'immediate', some particular experience of our own (the object of what Hegel calls 'sense-certainty') with demonstrative expressions like 'this', we 'directly refute what we *mean* to say'. Notwithstanding our intention to pick out the experience itself, what the word 'this' actually conveys is 'being in general'. 'It is just not possible', says Hegel, 'for us ever to say, or express in words, a sensuous being that we *mean*.'[151] In the 'Smaller Logic' he makes parallel remarks on 'I'. This is also an expression of a universal, 'in which everything peculiar or marked is renounced and buried out of sight'; but it is also 'as it were the ultimate and unanalysable point of consciousness'. Although Hegel allows 'I' a meaning of sorts — since '[e]very man is a whole world of conceptions, that lie buried in the night of the "Ego" . . . [the 'Ego'] is not a mere universality and nothing more, but the universality which includes in it everything' — the way in which the Ego is 'the vacuum or receptacle for anything and everything' is, he says, one in which 'we *leave aside* all that is particular'.[152]

What Kierkegaard first and foremost attacks is this systematic concentration on the universal instantiated at the expense of the particular circumstances of its instantiation. Where the circumstances are those of the individual human being's existence the universality of thought does not capture what is essential. In this regard the individual's relation to a thought counts at least as much as the (assertable, directly communicable) thought itself. Truth here is not, in Kierkegaard's expression, 'like a circular on which signatures are collected', but 'the intrinsic value of inwardness',[153] inwardness being 'when the thing said belongs to the recipient as if it were his own — and now . . . is his own'.[154] So far as human existence is concerned, Kierkegaard would say, it is incorrect to say, as Hegel does, that when what the language we use *allows* us to say refutes what we *mean*, it is the language that is the more truthful.

The language we use when our own relation to what is asserted is not what we mean to convey is the language of 'positive' knowledge, of science, the topics of 'objective' thinking, the thinking that can very well issue in truths printed on circulars to which one merely attaches one's signature. Kierkegaard does not disparage science itself as the investigation of nature. In the *Journals* he does, however, express familiar reservations about its scope and influence:

Almost everything that nowadays flourishes most conspicuously under the name of science (especially as natural science) is not really science but curiosity. (In the end all corruption will come about as a consequence of the natural sciences.) . . . But such a scienticity becomes especially dangerous and pernicious when it would encroach also upon the sphere of spirit. Let it deal with plants and animals and stars in that way; but similarly to deal with the human spirit is blasphemy, which only weakens ethical and religious passion. Even the act of eating is more reasonable than speculating microscopically over the function of digestion. . . . Oh! what dreadful sophistry spreads microscopically and telescopically into folios, and yet in the end produces nothing, qualitatively understood, though it does indeed cheat people out of the simple, profound, and passionate wonder which gives impetus to the ethical.[155]

That in his own age people had 'forgotten what it means to *exist* and what *inwardness* signifies' Kierkegaard puts down, in the *Postscript*, to the 'great increase of knowledge'. But the real source of the *malaise* is not science in the ordinary sense; behind it lies the all-pervading influence of the 'System' of speculative philosophy, that is to say *Hegelian* science.

Each age has its [immorality]. Ours is perhaps not pleasure, indulgence, and sensuality, but rather a pantheistically dis- solute contempt for individual persons. In the midst of all the jubilation over our age and the nineteenth century one hears an undercurrent of concealed contempt for . . . and despair at being a human being. . . . Maybe this is why so many, even of those who have seen the anomalies in his philosophy, cling to Hegel. They fear that if they were to become particular existing human beings they would disappear without trace, so that even the daily paper couldn't catch a glimpse of them, let alone literary reviews, or the speculative thinkers of world-history.[156]

If the alternatives were as Hegel suggests — between the visibility of an, in principle, directly communicable nature and the total abstraction of bare particularity — they would indeed vanish. But Kierkegaard's notion of a 'how' is that of a *quality* of the individual's experience or thought; a quality essentially linked to its being the experience or thought of that particular individual; something that language cannot represent; and a source of identity more important than the public one that can be so represented. The 'dialectic of world-history' has no room for this notion, or for that of the problems facing the 'subjective thinker'. In the dialectic of world-history 'individuals fade into humanity'; there it is 'impossible for you and me, for any individually existing human being, to be detected whatever new magnifying glasses for the concrete are invented'.[157] As for the *essential* problems facing the individual, it misrepresents these by lifting them out of their — what from the subjective viewpoint is the properly 'concrete' —[158] context.

> In the language of abstraction the difficulty of existence and of the exister never comes to light.[159] . . . Thus abstract thought helps me with my immortality by [first] killing me off as a particular existing individual . . . helping me much as the doctor in Holberg [Ludvig Holberg's comedy *The Lying-in Room*] who killed the patient with his medicine — but also got rid of the fever.[160]

The eclipse of the individual and this raising of the problems to an abstract level are not only backed by Hegelian philosophy but also, thinks Kierkegaard, preferred for psychological reasons; they absolve individuals of personal responsibility for the solutions; these can be left to history, necessity, reason, logic. But here again, although 'abstract thought talks of contradiction, and of the immanent propulsive power of contradiction', it 'removes the difficulty *and the contradiction* by disregarding existence and existing'. The individual is thus relieved of the 'task of understanding itself in existence'.[161]

Kierkegaard describes this task as that of 'understanding the greatest opposition . . . and oneself as existing in it'.[162] The opposition emerges in its clearest form in the contradictions of the absolute paradox. But the absolute paradox represents the B-position (in which, it will be recalled, the 'contradiction' is between eternity and existence as a whole) which is in effect the culmination of an increasingly strenuous 'existential' progression involving three distinct — though not always clearly distinguished — polarities which Kierkegaard uses as a framework in which to describe both the existing individual *and existence itself*.[163] These polarities are infinitude/finitude, possibility/necessity, and eternity/temporality. The task of the individual is to 'synthesize' these opposites which are juxtaposed in existence. It is a task, because the latter element in each opposition represents a felt limitation. Traditionally, *finitude* is the limitation of distinctness, and is a logical consequence simply of being something of a certain sort; *necessity* is the logical property of being what one is by virtue of some logical grounds; while *temporality*, implying succession, is susceptibility to change. Broadly, the aspects of the Kierkegaardian individual corresponding to these are, being just a particular, being constrained by environment and endowment, and lacking a stable centre or essence. The most crucial departure here from the tradition is the use of 'necessity' in connection with situational rather than logical constraint. But since, as we saw, Kierkegaard denies that anything comes into being by necessity, one could say that in the absence of its traditional function as a determinant of action, it is natural enough that he should apply the term by analogical extension to factors that limit free choice. The individual's interest in the eternal is assumed; for Kierkegaard the 'real' individual is in this sense a 'compound of infinite and finite',[164] and the problems of existence ('existential problems') are those involved in keeping these opposites deliberately and consciously in full view of one another (existential problems being thereby 'passionate problems').[165] The contradiction that abstract thought removes (by not genuinely holding the opposites up against one another) is generally said to be that between the infinite and the finite. In the type(s) of understanding that conform to the A-position, the eternal is conceived as pre-established, and the individual's assumed possession of an 'eternal determinant' as a means of reconstituting it, first of all, in thought and then in action — as if essential action was the implementing of a prepared plan. But in the B-position, with its rejection of the idea of an eternal determinant, there is no plan which can be reconstructed, and the only way in which the eternal can enter is in the 'passionate decision'. Here the eternal can only be related 'to the future', to 'what is in process of becoming'. And 'when I put eternity and becoming together I get no rest. . .'.[166]

In a *Journals* entry Kierkegaard remarks:

It's quite true what philosophy says, that life must be understood backwards. But one then forgets the other principle, that it must be lived forwards. A principle which, the more one thinks it through, precisely leads to the conclusion that life in time can never properly be understood, just because no moment can acquire the complete stillness [*fuldelig Ro*] needed to orient oneself backwards.[167]

'It is no doubt for this reason', says Climacus, 'that Christianity has preached eternity as the future life.'[168] Apart from the task of coping with a 'restless' existence in which the eternal is now something that has to be chosen (hence Christianity's assumption of the 'absolute', i.e. irreducible, 'either/or'),[169] and not recognized or recollected, the existing individual is also faced with the problem of 'uniting the phases of life in simultaneity', of the 'ennobling of the successive in the simultaneous'.[170] Criticizing his own age for being not so much 'one-sided' as 'all-sided' (a one-sided person 'rejects, clearly and decisively, what he does not want to include', but an 'abstractly' all-sided person 'wants to have everything in the one-sidedness of thought'),[171] Kierkegaard says:

> The subjective thinker is not a scientist, he is an artist. Existing is an art. The subjective thinker is aesthetic enough to give his life aesthetic [immediate, sensuous] content, ethical enough to regulate it, and dialectical enough to master it in thought.[172]

His task, says Kierkegaard a little later, is to 'transform himself into an instrument that clearly and decisively expresses in existence what is human'.[173]

Speculative philosophy, in its attempt to bring Kant's 'the thing-in-itself' in, as it were, from the cognitive cold, fails to see that 'the only *An-sich* [in-itself] which cannot be thought is to exist'.[174] It considers thought in abstraction (to the notion of which Kierkegaard also attaches the connotation of 'absent-mindedness', of which he frequently accuses the speculative philosophers); its abstract thought is 'thought with no thinker', i.e. thought unrelated to 'any definite (individual) object of thought' or to 'time and place'.[175] (Kierkegaard says that if only Hegel had published his *Logic* anonymously under the title 'Pure Thought', and without giving any inkling of the circumstances of its composition, this would have been 'to act in the way of the Greeks', who because they assumed possession of an 'eternal determinant' had no idea of having to proceed to the eternal by way of the contingencies of existence. As it is, reading the *Logic* with its 'foreword, notes, didactic self-contradictions and confusing explanations of matters that are really self-explanatory', is like being given a letter purportedly from heaven (*et Himmelbrev*) but with the blotting paper still inside 'revealing all too clearly its earthly origin'.)[176]

'Existence', says Kierkegaard, 'cannot be conceived without movement.' He refers to as 'humbug' (*Spilfægteri*) Hegel's claim that logic can mirror the movement of life once the notions of 'contradiction, movement, and transition, etc.' have been incorporated into the discipline.[177] The dialectical triad of thesis, antithesis, and synthesis (the 'systematic *ein, zwei, drei*' of Hegelian philosophy)[178] is wholly inappropriate where, as in the individual's existence, the 'goal of movement is decision and repetition'.[179] Earlier in the *Postscript*, in the section (two chapters) of Part Two devoted to the sources of Kierkegaard's philosophical point of view in Lessing, Kierkegaard argues that although it is possible to construct a logical system, an 'existential' system is out of the question. His reason is that the notion of a system implies finality, or lack of open-endedness. The idea of an all-embracing system is that of the identity of thought and being; but in the individual's actual experience the only finality corresponding to this idea is that of the past (we remember from the Interlude in the *Fragments* that the finality of the past does not imply necessity). As far as the existing individual's confrontation in the *present* with the open future is concerned, thought and being are separate, and the illusion that they are not is due either to sheer absent-mindedness or to assuming mistakenly that experience of the past provides the basis for a phenomenology of the present.[180] Whatever the reasons, in Hegelian practice it means that the system aims to *include* individual existence, so that, to be completed in all its consistency, 'no existing remainder can be left out, not even such a tiny little appendage [*Dingeldangel*] as the existing Herr Professor who writes the system'.[181]

Kierkegaard rejects Hegel's claim to have founded his system on an absolute beginning. His argument is in effect a restatement of the position that thought and being are separate in existence, except for the insistence that Hegel's system be classified as a thought-product, i.e. as Hegel's own conception, and not as a kind of natural expression of the unrolling of reality itself. Kierkegaard points out, as indeed Hegel would agree, that to begin something is always the result of a process of reflection. So, too, with beginning the 'System'. But how to *end* the reflection that must precede it? Reflection is, says Kierkegaard, 'infinite', which at least means it has no natural conclusion.[182] Here, however, Hegelians say they find one in an 'absolutely exhaustive' abstraction which enables them to say that they begin the system with 'nothing' — or, and it is equivalent, with 'being', i.e. the idea of pure thought without the thought of any thing that is. Thus, they say, the system, in a way, begins by itself. But, argues Kierkegaard, if the abstraction were truly exhaustive, it would abstract from the abstracter's own existence, the domain in which he makes choices and does things. There would then be no possibility of his *doing* what is required to begin the system.[183] Again, he argues, the system cannot begin with immediacy 'immediately'. If the system is intended to 'conform to existence' (*at være efter Tilværelsen*), then clearly the system does not come first; it cannot, therefore, be said to begin immediately with the same immediacy with which existence begins. (Though Kierkegaard observes that, strictly speaking, not even existence begins immediately with immediacy, since existence includes thought — not vice versa — and its immediacy is transcended by being, as it necessarily is for a conscious human being, the object of thought. This, too, we note as Kierkegaard does not, is something Hegel would agree with, though for him the 'mediation' of the immediate in thought is the beginning of the process of becoming conscious of all reality, while for Kierkegaard it is the first step away from a reality which by its very nature cannot 'be thought'.)[184]

At the end of the first chapter ('Becoming Subjective') of the second section of Part Two of the *Postscript*, Kierkegaard offers 'in all brevity' some examples of 'how with perseverance the simplest problem can be turned into the most difficult'.[185] (In another context he says that 'existence makes the understanding of the simplest truth for the common man in existential transparency very difficult and strenuous'.)[186] The examples are: 'what it means to die', 'what it means to be immortal', 'what it means to have to thank God for the benefits he bestows on me', 'what it means to get married'.[187] By turning a simple problem into a difficult one, Kierkegaard does not mean that it ceases to be simple and becomes sophisticated and complicated instead. In fact the opposite. He means that by seeing them as uncomplicated questions the subjective thinker appreciates the issues involved in answering them in his own case. Even just raising them becomes a kind of action, a 'deed' (*Handeln*). Thinking about 'death in general' does not amount to an 'action' (*Handling*) for in that case there is no specifically personal engagement. The topic 'is only a something in general, and what something is in general is very hard to say'.

> [I]f the task is to become subjective, then the thought of death is *not* the thought of something in general, but an action, for precisely in it lies the development of [the subject's] subjectivity which consists in his activity working over himself in his thinking concerning his own existence, so that he really thinks the thought by making it a reality. . . .[188]

The expression 'by making it a reality' does not, of course, refer here to the bringing about of some reality, as where a person has in mind a goal and sets about achieving it, translating a thought, as it were, *into* reality. What Kierkegaard means is the thinker's making the thought a real one for himself, i.e. applying it squarely to his own case, and not making the issue a general one so that the subject's own particular fears, hopes, etc., are lost to view.

5 The problem of communication

There is a link in Kierkegaard's mind between the inability of a philosophical system to capture the open-endedness of human existence and the impossibility of conveying descriptively the quality of a thought 'made real' in the above sense. It is not apparent what precisely that link is, but clearly the latter is a more general inability than the former. If the quality of the subjective thinker's thought defies direct description, it does so independently of whether any attempted description of it occurs as part of a philosophical system. It is also clear that the general problem of communicating subjective thought occupies Kierkegaard just as much as the specific inability of the philosophical system to capture existence. So even if a philosophical system might conceivably embrace the open-endedness — the eternal becoming — of human existence in Kierkegaard's sense, the main issue would remain unaffected, namely whether the reality that is the subjective thinker's view of his own situation is directly describable. (It should also be said that, even if a philosophical system could be, or perhaps has been, devised that embraces the inherent open-endedness of human existence in some sense, so long as the adoption of a philosophical system implies acceptance of the possibility in principle of satisfactory answers to the questions which concern the individual as such most deeply, such a system could not embrace the precise aspect of the open-endedness of human existence which Kierkegaard wants us to take into account.)

Corresponding to his how/what distinction, Kierkegaard defines two sides of what he calls 'double reflection':

> When the thought has got its correct expression in the word, which is the result of its first reflection, there comes the second reflection which concerns the relation between the communication and the communicator, and reflects the existing communicator's own relation to the idea.[189]

In a long footnote at the beginning of the second of the two chapters on Lessing, Kierkegaard says:

> The double reflection is implicit in the very idea of communication, [for] communication [implies a] subjectivity existing in the inwardness of isolation [who] wants to make himself known, i.e. to maintain his thinking at the level of the inwardness of his subjective existence and at the same time communicate it, a situation that cannot possibly find expression in a direct form.[190]

The reasons Kierkegaard gives for this impossibility have nothing to do, as one might suppose, with privacy *per se*; they are in fact the same as those he gives for the impossibility of a system's embracing the category of existence. Thus when someone in love wants, as we 'well understand', to communicate the quality of his inwardness, the reason that he cannot adopt a direct form of expression (or that if he did it would necessarily be inadequate) is not that the quality is concealed from public gaze, but that in his inwardness, 'being essentially concerned with the constant renewal of love's inwardness', he has 'no result and is never finished'.[191] Still, you would think that the notion of 'an existing communicator's own relation to [an] idea' covered more than is conveyed by the notion of lack of finality, at any rate that this latter did not give an adequate general characterization of what makes an aspect of thought fall under the 'how' rather than the 'what'. The defining characteristic or characteristics one is after must surely mark something like the traditional opposition of subjective and objective, of what belongs to the subject's attitude to some content and the 'objectively' conceivable content itself. Which is what Kierkegaard himself implies. That in ordinary communication the inherent two-sidedness goes undetected, so that 'when one person says something and the other acknowledges the same, word for word, it is assumed they are agreed and have understood one another', he says is due to the fact that people in general 'exist in immediacy'.[192] This means that their *thinking* (not just their saying what they are thinking) lacks the aspect corresponding to the second side of double reflection; it is not doubly reflected thinking, but 'objective thinking', and as such 'wholly indifferent to subjectivity [and] inwardness'.[193]

There are doubtless several ways of interpreting the subjective/objective distinction here. I shall suggest two only, both of which, however, would give substance to the suggestion made earlier that Kierkegaard be understood as opposing Hegel's view that it is the universal content we convey in language, not the particular experience we may want to try to convey in it, that is 'the more truthful'. The first interpretation makes the distinction a relative one, the second absolute. I suspect that in attributing either interpretation, or even perhaps both of them, to Kierkegaard we are going beyond what he would have felt bound to commit himself upon.

The first interpretation fastens on inwardness as a kind of response, though a 'positive' one, of the individual to the realization that the solution to a fundamental problem is not to be found (either in 'sociality and fellowship' — these, as Kierkegaard, or Climacus, points out, being themselves fundamental problems — or in scientific knowledge or speculative reason, or in mysticism or romanticism, for that matter).[194] Any solution, then, must be due to a special decision, or fundamental choice, of the individual's own. Now, intuitively, it seems correct to say that the less a problem can be solved for you, and the more you are left to your own resources in solving it, the greater will be the extent of the relevance of your own specific circumstances and situation to a specification of the problem itself, as well as of its solution. The greater, too, in that case, the disparity between the universal content of your thought and utterance in this regard, on the one hand, and the meaning actually invested in these by yourself, in thought and word, on the other. And, in respect of what is important from the subjective thinker's point of view, there is in such a case surely more 'truth' in what *you* mean by what you say than in what you manage directly to convey to others in the words that you utter.

The second interpretation links Kierkegaard, speculatively, with the early Wittgenstein. The connection is to be found in certain passages dealing with what Kierkegaard calls 'life-views' or 'world-views'. Explaining it allows us to introduce some interesting details of Kierkegaard's thought not hitherto touched on here.

That Kierkegaard conceived his own position in terms of the notions of life-view and world-view we saw earlier with regard to his recognition of his role as a religious author. In the thought involved in that role, that he was concerned with the individual rather than the public, 'is concentrated', he says, 'a whole life-view and world-view'.[195] Kierkegaard was early drawn to the idea of a life-view. Many early entries in the *Journals* indicate a systematic attempt to arrive at a satisfactory philosophical anthropology, to achieve which Kierkegaard seems to have seen the need to look for principles according to which various cultural perspectives have been organized, and which could also be used to distinguish them — an Hegelian enterprise which he later developed into the anti-Hegelian account of the three spheres of life. A life-view, for Kierkegaard, imparts a certain order upon experience, functioning in the individual's subjective sphere in much the same way as Hegel's 'ideas' are supposed to do in relation to the objective world in general. His interest in life-views was also personal; Kierkegaard sought a principle that could organize his own life and experience, not a view of nature or a cosmology but an ethical principle.[196] In his first book, *From the Papers of One Still Living* (1838), he published an attack on his contemporary, Hans Christian Andersen, criticizing his novels for their *lack* of a life-view. On what a life-view is, he says:

> [It] is more than a totality [*Indbegrep*] or a sum of positions, maintained in its abstract impersonality [*Hverkenhed*] ; it is more than experience, which as such is always atomistic; it is in

fact the transubstantiation of experience, it is an unshakeable certainty [*Sikkerhed*] in oneself won from all experience [*Empirie*]. . . . If we are asked how such a view of life comes to be acquired, we answer that for him who does not allow his life to fritter away completely but as far as possible seeks to turn its individual expressions inwards again, there must of necessity come a moment in which a strange illumination spreads over life — without his needing in even the remotest manner to understand all possible particulars — for the subsequent understanding of which he now has the key; there must, I say, come a moment when, as Daub observes, life is understood backwards through the idea.[197]

Thus besides being a key to understanding further details within its own frame, a life-view also throws light on the past. As an organizing principle, a life-view is imposed upon, not imparted by, experience. In this it is analogous both to a first principle and to an inductively inferred law — parallels which Kierkegaard himself draws.[198] A life-view is a 'principle' or 'law' that cannot be justified by appeal to further principles or laws. It involves a 'leap'. In this respect it is also analogous to a Popperian 'conjecture': a life-view is a kind of conjectural stab at a personally satisfactory organization of experience, though lacking the benefit of either objective proof or refutation. As Popper intends with his conjectures, Kierkegaardian life-views can also be arranged in a progressive series. In a continuation of the passage quoted, Kierkegaard mentions two life-views which could give depth and direction to a novelist's work, and certitude to anyone who holds them: 'a merely human point of view, Stoicism for example . . . which', he says '[nevertheless] remains out of touch with a deeper experiential basis [*Empirie*]', and the 'religious' view, founded upon that deeper basis and identified as 'the fully Christian conviction [*Forvisning*]'.[199] The latter is higher than the former. There is some form of continuity between stages, for Kierkegaard wants to allow that the same experience (*types* of experiences, not particular experiences or tokens of the type) can be subjected to different depths of illumination, or (following the quotation) be made to form an 'experiential basis' of less or greater depth (we saw that it was part of Kierkegaard's concept of 'repetition' that the same experiences can be repeated and experienced from successively higher levels). And the stages are also bound together as steps in a unified but progressively modified enterprise. But just as significant is a fundamental lack of continuity: the principle underlying the internal consistency of one life-view is incompatible with that of another. So, however internally consistent two life-views may be, they are mutually exclusive. In a sense now familiar to students of the theory of scientific change, they represent distinct paradigms; or, as Kierkegaard says, each view has its 'qualitatively different dialectic'.[200] Just as there is no logical transition from experience to principle, so there is no logical transition from one principle to another. It cannot even be said, as is claimed for scientific paradigms, that one view embraces another, or 'explains', a wider range of experiences than another; each Kierkegaardian 'life-view' covers exactly the same range. Any greater adequacy of one viewpoint in relation to another has to be understood, therefore, in terms other than its superior ability to 'save' the phenomena. Presumably it has something to do with experiential depth and conviction.

The relevance of this account of the role and 'logic' of life-views to what can and what cannot be 'said' is one with which readers of Wittgenstein's *Tractatus* will already be familiar. Towards the end of the *Tractatus* are a number of remarks on the topics which are central themes in Kierkegaard's writings, namely God, Fate, ethics, life's problems and meaning. Readers of the *Postscript* will be struck not only by the parallel in topic but also by a noticeable similarity in formulation (struck, but perhaps not surprised on learning that Wittgenstein was one of their number). Compare, for example, the *Tractatus* entry, 'God does not reveal himself in the world', with Climacus's 'God cannot reveal himself . . . the totality of created things is the work of God [and] yet God is not there'.[201] Nor is the parallel confined to topic and formulation. Wittgenstein's treatment of these ultimate topics involves, roughly, a twofold claim: first, that they concern the world as a whole, not any particular things (or states of affairs) in it — ethics, for instance, is 'transcendental',[202] God is 'how everything stands',[203] the sense of the world, the existence of any genuine value, and of necessity, 'must lie outside the world';[204] and second, that language, the medium in which we formulate questions and answers, *can only represent states of affairs*. Since the topics in question do not belong in this domain, because in a manner of speaking they embrace it, there is nothing that can be said (in a representational way) about them. Once this is clear, says Wittgenstein, the problems vanish. And *that* is their solution.[205] This sounds like the orthodox positivist way with ultimate questions. But strictly, since Wittgenstein does give transcendental roles to these notions, he does not let *them* vanish; they merely recede from their spurious position as topics of questions to which it is meaningful to offer answers. It might not be inconsistent with what seems to be the gist of Wittgenstein's remarks, therefore, to see in them a parallel to

Kierkegaard's view that there are qualities of life-views but that these are not communicable qualities, and that a life-view gives unity and depth to experience from, as it were, outside experience. One notes that the way in which Wittgenstein allows these ultimate notions or categories to embrace the world (for Wittgenstein a world of 'states of affairs' rather than 'experiences') is also one in which he allows that they can infect or invade it. Thus the world of the happy man 'is a different one from that of the unhappy man'.[206] The incommunicability of what distinguishes these worlds, of the ethical, and the rest, is due to their not consisting of any states of affairs which can be envisaged. They are, as it were, something about, some subjective quality of, states of affairs, and not either themselves states of affairs or having any basis in such. In Kierkegaard's case, since his theory of language, such as it is, is closer to Hegel's than to the (disputed) sources of Wittgenstein's Tractarian theory, the incommunicability of the distinguishing properties of life-views should no doubt be seen accordingly as their inexpressibility in the common currency of the 'idea', in which on Hegel's view objective reality reveals itself to consciousness as *its* reality. But in whatever specific theory one dresses the distinction Kierkegaard is making, his main point is that the subjective aspect both is *not* directly communicable (in the way that anything that can be *represented* in language is directly communicable, and in the way that, on Hegel's theory, anything that can be given conceptual form is without further ado an, in principle, common conceptual possession) and *is* the essential aspect.

There is some evidence that Wittgenstein would agree with Kierkegaard on the latter also. There is his letter to a would-be publisher of the *Tractatus* summarizing the work's content.

> My work consists of two parts: the one presented here plus all that I have *not* written. And it is precisely this second part that is the important one. My book draws limits to the sphere of the ethical from the inside as it were. . . . I believe that . . . I have managed in my book to put everything firmly into place by being silent about it.[207]

But whatever the extent of the parallels here, they should not be allowed to conceal a notable contrast between Kierkegaard's and the early Wittgenstein's conceptions of *reality* and the *world*. Wittgenstein's world is 'all that is the case', and he says of it that it is 'independent of my will'.[208] Kierkegaard's reality is also independent of the will, but is not, like Wittgenstein's, the object of *thought*; for what Kierkegaard calls 'reality' is *ethical* or *subjective* reality. Towards the end of the *Postscript* Climacus says that the 'object of faith' is 'that something occurred', in other words a *reality*, something that is the case, actual. This, he goes on to say, 'surely can't be any person's . . . *thought*', and the reason he gives for this surprising claim is that 'thought is at most *possibility*'. To say that the object of faith is something that is thought is therefore to say that it is *not* a reality. Possibility is thus the form of understanding 'in which the backwards step is taken of giving up one's faith'.[209] The background for these remarks is to be found in a section, just prior to his return to the problem of the *Fragments*, where Climacus offers an inverted Hegelian ontology adapted to the concerns of the subjective thinker. What is real, on this ontology, is not the objective, universal reality of the directly assertable contents of thought, but the 'ethical reality of the individual'. This is 'the only reality'.[210] What Hegelians call real is therefore, from this perspective, mere possibility. For the subjective thinker all that is believed or known to be the case is *possible*,[211] in the sense not of 'may be true' but of 'may be done'. Consequently, what is thought is not what is the case and independent of the will, but what may be made the case by an act of will. The subjective thinker is an agent and his world, therefore, all that he may make the case. Kierkegaard says that

> if there is to be any distinction at all between thought and action, the former must be assigned to possibility, indifference, the objective, and the latter to subjectivity. However, it seems clear that there is a boundary zone. When I think I will do this or that, this thought is not yet an action, and in all eternity it is qualitatively different from action, but it is still a possibility in which the interest of reality and action are already reflected. The indifference and objectivity are in the process of being destroyed, because reality and responsibility want to take hold of it.[212]

The knower, says Kierkegaard, 'cannot know an historical reality before it has been dissolved into a possibility'.[213] Action is 'putting an end to mere possibility' and 'identifying [oneself] with what is thought in order to exist in it'.[214] 'Between the action as it is envisaged and its reality − between the possibility and the reality − there may be no difference at all as far as content is concerned', but

> in regard to form the difference is essential. Reality is the interest in existing in the thought . . . and not to be confused, [as] so often, with all kinds of images, intentions, attempts at conclusions, anticipatory moods, and the like.[215]

As with Frege and his 'thought', Climacus is anxious to distinguish 'reality' as thought about what to do from its psychological accompaniments.

Kierkegaard's category of the possible is a capacious one, and includes the ethical realities of individuals other than oneself as conceived by oneself. Being mere possibilities they are *not* realities for anyone but themselves.[216] Kierkegaard says that our only access to the *reality* of another is in thought, and that does not give us the other's reality as we have our own or as the other has his. From this he says it follows that 'one human being cannot judge another ethically'; or 'when someone takes it upon himself to judge another, the measure of his impotence is that he is really only judging himself'.[217]

The equation of understanding and possibility is not intended, as it were, to bestow on possibility the *benefit* of cognizability; rather it is to give the cognizable the unsettled status of 'mere' possibility. It is to reduce it from what *is* the case to what might be (or be left being) the case, and to place it always in the context of what it is in one's power to *make* (or leave as) the case. In respect of the crucial reality which is the object of faith, to accept or believe in it is therefore to surpass understanding *in any case*, quite apart from the complications of the paradox upon which this reality is premised (assuming that Kierkegaard means here reality in the sense of the reality of another). But presumably these latter complications must be taken to deprive us of the ability to understand this particular reality even as a possibility.

Nevertheless, the conclusions Kierkegaard draws in the section from which these quotations are taken concern communication between (human) realities that can at least understand each other as 'possibilities'. The fact that they can *only* understand one another as possibilities, however, has consequences for the form of their communication. Since 'existential reality cannot be communicated, and the subjective thinker has his own reality in his own ethical existence', if this reality is to be grasped by another it can only be as a possibility in relation to the latter's reality, in *his* thought. So the former 'must be careful to give his existence-communication, precisely in order to make it relate to existence, the form of possibility'. Giving it this form brings 'the recipient as close as is possible between man and man to existing in it'.

> The subjective thinker's form, his form of communication, is his style. His form is as manifold as the oppositions he holds together. The systematic *ein, zwei, drei* is an abstract form, and must therefore fall short whenever applied to the concrete. In

the same degree that the subjective thinker is himself concrete [as the objective thinker is not] , his form will also be concretely dialectical . . . [employing the categories] of poetry, ethics, dialectic, and religion.[218]

This, Climacus, lets us know, is the form employed by the pseudonyms preceding him. The chapter on truth as subjectivity, which follows the one on becoming subjective, ends with the author's recounting how he had once planned, as a corrective to the age's forgetfulness about what it means to exist and about what inwardness means, to publish works that would remind them. The first task, 'to begin at the ground floor', would be to 'exhibit the existential relationship between the aesthetic and the ethical within an existing individual'.[219] But then, in an extensive appendix ('A Glance at a Contemporary Effort in Danish Literature') to the chapter, he describes how the pseudonymous works, beginning with *Either/Or* (which exhibits just that relationship), began to appear, anticipating his own intentions at every step. This literary device appears to serve a twofold purpose. On the one hand, it marks a discontinuity between Climacus's 'dialectical' writings and the works of the 'aesthetic' pseudonyms (showing that Climacus is not to be identified as just another in the series). But, on the other hand, it implies that Climacus understands what is going on in the aesthetic works, and the direction in which they are going. We have already noted that Johannes Climacus, the author of the *Fragments* and the *Postscript*, calls himself a humorist. 'Humour' and 'irony' have a special significance for Kierkegaard. Climacus himself succinctly places them:

> There are three spheres of existence: the aesthetic, the ethical, and the religious. To these there correspond two boundaries [*Confinier*] : irony is the boundary between the aesthetic and the ethical; humour the boundary between the ethical and the religious.[220]

As to the roles of irony and humour, these can be grasped, first of all, by observing that for Kierkegaard the transition from one stage to the next is not, as in Hegelian philosophy, a rational or logical one. Thus, in the *Journals*, we read that 'the [transition] between aesthetic and ethical . . . [is] pathetic, not dialectical; [it marks the beginning of] a qualitatively *different* dialectic'.[221] In the case of the transition from the aesthetic to the ethical the 'pathos' involves some form of synoptic reflection affording insight into the limitations or worthlessness of a life dedicated to immediacy. This is the domain of *irony*. In the case of the transition to religion from ethics, *humour* affords a corresponding insight into the limitations of the finite, including the limitations of human reason. In the *Journals* Kierkegaard writes that

> the humorist can never actually become a systematizer . . . for he regards every system as a renewed attempt to explode the world with a single syllogism . . . . whereas the humorist himself has come alive to the incommensurable which the philosopher can never make sense of [*beregne* — lit. 'compute'], and therefore must despise. He lives in the fullness of things [*i Fylden*] and is therefore sensitive to how much is always left over, even if he has expressed himself with all felicity. . . . The systematizer believes that he can say everything and that whatever cannot be said is erroneous and secondary.[222]

The humorist (because of *his* synoptic reflection) is both elevated and limited. Elevated by virtue of his theoretical grasp of the individual's development from immediacy to religion (as we noted, sometimes referred to as the 'second' immediacy); but limited because what is needed actually to enter the religious stage is faith, commitment, and 'seriousness'. In the former respect Johannes Climacus (named after the author in antiquity of a work, *Scala paradisi*, which described the virtuous path to heaven) is so called precisely because of the name's connotation of 'ascent'.[223] But like Wittgenstein's ladder, Climacus and his dialectic are to be thrown away once used. In the *Postscript* Climacus himself describes 'dialectic' as

> in its truth a benevolent ministering power, which discovers and helps to find where the absolute object of faith and worship is — there, namely, where the difference between knowledge and ignorance collapses in ignorance's absolute worship, there where the resistance of the objective uncertainty tortures forth the passionate certainty of faith, there where the conflict of right and wrong collapses in absolute worship with absolute subjection. Dialectic itself does not see the absolute, but it leads the individual as it were up to it, and says: 'Here it must be, that I guarantee; when you worship here, you worship God.'[224]

It is a clear enough statement that the Kierkegaardian dialectic is to be interpreted *not* as a method for laying hold of essential truth, but rather as a method for ensuring that, if there is such a truth, one has an adequate grasp of what it is (as of what it cannot be), from an unclouded and undistorted conception of the human situation. For one who successfully scales Climacus's ladder, there still remains the leap of faith.

V

Pathology of the Self

The greatest danger, that of losing one's self, may
pass off in the world as if it was nothing; every other
loss, an arm, leg, five dollars, a wife, etc. is bound to
be noticed.[1]

1   The psychological works

The Concept of Anxiety (1844) (under the pseudonym Vigilius
Haufniensis, lit. 'watchman of Copenhagen') and *The Sickness
unto Death* (1849) (under the pseudonym Anti-Climacus, but, like
the dialectical works, 'edited' by Kierkegaard) are aptly enough
called Kierkegaard's psychological works. True, *Repetition* (1843)
is called an exercise in 'experimental psychology' and could also
be included, as also a section ('Guilty? Not Guilty') in *Stages on
Life's Way* described as a 'psychological experiment'. But these
works differ from the former. Only the latter, 'aesthetic' works
conform to Climacus's requirement that a subjective thinker's
existence communication be in the 'form of possibility'. Thus,
whereas the author of *Repetition*, despite the irony that places
him at the outer boundary of the aesthetic sphere, can only gesture
towards the religious viewpoint which he sees as the solution to his
young friend's difficulties, the pseudonymous authors of *Anxiety*
and *Sickness* firmly base their writings in the reality of that viewpoint. In fact, these are not 'existence communications' at all.
They are direct communications offering general descriptions of
conscious states. Not, nevertheless, from the specialized and
experimental point of view of modern psychology. If we are to
apply an established use of the word 'psychology' to these two
works, it must be that of Hegel, for whom psychology is part of an

157

all-embracing science of man as emerging self-conscious spirit. In fact Hegel classified psychology, along with (also in his senses of these terms) phenomenology and anthropology, as a science of 'subjective spirit', a topic comprising, roughly, the dynamics and events of spiritual emergence from the point of view of consciousness — in opposition to 'objective spirit', by which Hegel meant the public manifestations and historical forms of this emergence, including legal institutions and social morality, but also the socially significant aspects of individual conscience. Hegel, of course, intended his science of spirit to be literally all-embracing in the sense that no aspect of human life — not even, as we have just noted, individual and social morality — lay beyond its grasp.

But Hegel's science of spirit is precisely that System whose impossibility Kierkegaard seeks every opportunity to expose, not least its claim to embrace a scientific grasp of moral principles and concepts. So what role can Hegelian psychology play in Kierkegaard's own philosophy of emergent spirit? The question presses the more insistently when we find that *Anxiety* is subtitled 'a simple deliberation in the form of psychological observations directed towards the dogmatic problem of original sin', and *Sickness* 'a Christian psychological exposition for edification and awakening'. Given Kierkegaard's view of the autonomy of ethics, what can scientific deliberations and expositions have to do with the ethico-spiritual themes of sin and edification?

In Kierkegaard's context the autonomy of ethics has two sides corresponding, one might say, to an upper and a lower limit. On the one hand, ethical principles and concepts are not mere expressions of a surpassable stage in spiritual development; they contain specifications of irreducible, and in that sense ultimate or absolute, *desiderata*. In this sense, to say that ethics is autonomous is to say that one *cannot* go beyond ethics, for ethics forms an upper limit. It is also, in some sense, a proper goal which any pre-ethical understanding of human existence fails to apprehend. But ethics is, on the other hand, also autonomous in the sense that it envelops, rather than arises out of, the conditions of human existence; neither ethical principles and concepts themselves nor the individual's understanding of them are a natural, logical, or 'dialectical' product of elements already found in a pre-ethical stage. Ethics in this respect lies beyond the self and its world, that is, beyond time. It belongs to, indeed *is*, the eternal. In order to become an ethical subject the self has therefore to make a radical conceptual readjustment. It has to acquire a concept of itself as a being 'really' placed in a transcendent context, a conception for which, on Kierkegaard's assumptions (those of the B-hypothesis), it has no speculative or scientific support, that being part of what is meant by calling the context 'transcendent'. In this respect one can say that although the ethical forms an unsurpassable upper limit from the moral agent's or the moral describer's point of view, its own lower limit nevertheless lies beyond nature, time, and history.

This latter aspect of the autonomy of ethics has two aspects in its turn. In the first place, assuming that the self is motivated to achieve self-fulfilment, and therefore has some notion of a 'true self' which it admits that it falls short of, the notion it has of a true self — or more generally, of its relationship to the external — itself undergoes development. In *Anxiety* Kierkegaard describes the self's development from a stage in which it locates the source of its value animistically in time and nature, to one in which it separates the notion of its value *from* time and nature but without yet grasping where this value is located, until it eventually realizes that its only possible location is in its own active, individual *relationship* to a transcendent goal. This development clearly conforms with that already outlined, from a state of immediacy, through the 'ethical' and immanently religious stages, to the paradoxical religiousness. Second, since the comprehensive conceptual readjustment the transition to this latter stage requires is no mere intellectual affair, the aspiring individual is faced with the need for a radical break with the whole gamut of criteria of identity and achievement bound up with a merely temporal existence, and for their replacement by an unfamiliar and inherently unattractive criterion whose only initial specification is the negative one that all that was thought to count in these respects no longer does.

Let us focus first on this latter aspect. Because the process (though, in view of the centrality here of will and choice, we should be careful with this word) of becoming spirit is personally strenuous, it must obviously have a psychological side. If the goal of human fulfilment goes against what we call human nature, human nature 'naturally' responds with anxiety and reluctance. Here, however, we must understand 'human nature' in a narrow sense. Kierkegaard would not want to imply that what the individual brings to its given human nature is something which it superimposes from without; for the 'addition' is part of a specifically *human* potential and also the means to the fulfilment of a specifically human longing or need; and in a wider, ethical sense human nature is to be conceived from the very beginning in the categories of selfhood and individuality in which the strenuous transformation of the given nature is to be brought about. In a wider sense it is indeed human nature to strive for spiritual fulfilment, even when that project is seen to require the changing of

159

human nature in the narrower sense. Furthermore, in denying that spiritual emergence is natural, Kierkegaard would not want to imply that spiritual growth is a matter of extinguishing natural instincts in favour of a hard-won asceticism; he wants to describe his spiritual person as one who has *changed* his or her given nature, not stamped it out.[2]

To talk (as Kierkegaard does not) of human nature in a wider sense may provoke misleading analogies with other things, e.g. seeds and caterpillars, whose nature also is to grow. Human, that is to say personal, growth differs essentially, however, from that of plants, whose development consists in a 'natural', and in this sense 'necessary' (not *strictly* inevitable, in so far as other 'necessary' developments may prevent it), unfolding of an already implicit potentiality.[3] What distinguishes a person from a plant is, among other things, the person's consciousness of an 'infinite' disparity between familiar finite nature and the unspecified infinite aspiration. Psychology, in Kierkegaard's version of this Hegelian discipline, describes consciousness in its relationship to the infinite. If man is conceived as a being whose ethical task is to become spiritually developed,[4] in the sense of conforming his temporal existence to the radically unfamiliar, then psychology describes the various temporal (natural) states of man that correspond to his growing inability to understand himself in natural categories, and his developing response to the demand which he acknowledges that this makes for his living within his 'eternal qualification', that is, for the possibility of his genuinely possessing that qualification.

Since Kierkegaard denies that there is a higher state from which the ethical can be seen to be the mere expression of a surpassable stage in spiritual development, his psychology must accept ethical principles and concepts at their (properly understood) face value. But then as a psychology of the individual who is interested in the fulfilment traditionally linked to ethical values and practice, it cannot describe human states and conditions in departmental abstraction from these. That would be impossible where the states and conditions are the psychosomatic entity's developing responses to the truly ethical notions of good and evil. So Kierkegaard's psychology flatly acknowledges the reality of ethics and attempts no scientific explanation of it. This is how we should understand the paradoxical assertion, near the beginning of *Anxiety*, that although Haufniensis's psychological treatment of anxiety takes account of sin, it does so 'only tacitly'.[5] This is paradoxical because there is scarcely a page in the book where sin is not mentioned, and the word appears in four of the five chapter headings. Indeed the very first chapter opens with a 'dogmatic' discussion of the meaning of original sin. By taking account of sin only tacitly, Kierkegaard clearly means that he is simply assuming the reality of sin and not trying to explain it.

So science must take account of ethics. But why must, indeed on Kierkegaard's anti-Hegelian assumptions, how *can*, there be the converse involvement? If scientific explanation cannot extend to non-temporal, ethical phenomena, what part can psychological deliberations or expositions play in the individual's choice of and subjection to ethical categories?

Kierkegaard's main concern in *Anxiety* within the category of the spiritual is, as indicated, with sin. In saying why psychology cannot explain sin he also points to something it can explain *about* sin, namely, how human nature can (and if it is to clothe itself in ethical categories at all, *must*) become predisposed to the consciousness of sin. Psychology, he says, can only describe states and since sin is not a state,[6] but 'something restless that is either constantly producing itself or is repressed',[7] it cannot describe that. But, he says,

> the abiding state [*det Blivende*], that out of which sin
> constantly arises [*vorder* — lit. 'becomes'], not by necessity,
> for arising by necessity is simply a state of being (just as, for
> example, the entire history of the plant is a state), but by
> freedom — this abiding state, the predisposing assumption,
> the real possibility of sin, is an object of psychological interest.[8]

Though the psychologist cannot explain sin because it is an ethical not a natural category, he can explain, as Kierkegaard also says, 'the still life of its possibility'.[9] This is a limited explanation, but a necessary one. Psychology cannot explain why there is such a thing as sin in the first place, but 'how sin can come into [the individual's] existence' is something it can explain. The assumption is that for sin to occur in existence — and sin is nothing if it does not do that — then its 'ideal' possibility (explained by theology in terms of original sin) has to be complemented by a psychological state which is its 'real' possibility.[10] Psychology interests itself in this 'predisposing' state of the psychosomatic organism, 'in what psychologically might be called the psychological attitudes which freedom assumes towards sin, or the psychological, approximating states'.[11]

Kierkegaard's reference to freedom and necessity is easily misconstrued. He might be taken as saying that certain psychosomatic conditions necessarily precede the consciousness of sin as its causal antecedents, but that once the consciousness of sin is there it is no longer possible to talk of psychosomatic *states*, because the restless spirit has, so to speak, entered in and freedom now pervades the self, putting it beyond the scope of scientific explanation. This misconstrual can take two forms depending on how 'freedom' is interpreted here. If by 'freedom' one understands free will or freedom of choice, the role of psychology might be incorrectly identified as that of describing the deterministic states of man prior to the acquisition of freedom in the 'leap'. However, as noted earlier, Kierkegaard's whole world-view and procedure presuppose the presence of freedom in *this* sense, even if minimally in the power to pay attention to and to be swayed by this rather than that, at every stage of personal development, and not just subsequently to the recognition of the distinction between (genuine) good and evil. So even when states of the self are open to psychological description they must be regarded as free in this sense.

The alternative misinterpretation can arise from taking 'freedom' in the sense of 'individual autonomy', that is as designating a condition in which the self's actions and responses are by and large to be explained in terms of its own autonomous initiatives, part of what Kierkegaard means by being spiritually developed. What this might amount to more precisely we could say, for the sake of argument but without putting too fine a point on it, is a condition in which free choices in the narrower sense are free also in the wider sense that the having of the goals, or the employing of the maxims governing the self's responses to contingent environmental circumstances, is not itself part of those (or perhaps even of any longer-term or previously established) responses. However, although a psychosomatic entity dominated by freedom in this wider sense looks very like Kierkegaard's paradigmatic individual, or 'whole person' — the ideal of an integrated personality controlling its transactions with its environment in accordance with a freely chosen transenvironmental, or selfless goal[12] — it does not represent the situation in which a person actually develops spirituality in the workaday world. Ordinarily such freedom is indeed an ideal rather than a fact. What this interpretation does is push the freedom/necessity distinction too far back. Kierkegaardian psychology is concerned, at least in the first instance, with psychosomatic states prior, not just to the fulfilment of the ideal of freedom, but even to the very entertaining of that ideal. The qualitative leap at which science stops short comes where sin emerges as an obstacle to freedom, not where freedom is achieved by the overcoming of that obstacle. The 'finite spirit', says Kierkegaard in a *Journals* entry, 'is, as it were, a unity of necessity and freedom . . . of the product and the striving'.[13] So although 'freedom' and 'spirit' are used interchangeably in *Anxiety*, there is a distance — embracing the *spielraum* of ethics — between the advent (or 'positing') of spirit and the acquisition of freedom in the sense of individual autonomy. In fact, we have to distinguish on Kierkegaard's behalf between freedom as reality and freedom as possibility and say that it is the latter which is 'posited' along with spirit. Positing freedom is not the same as being free. Nor is positing spirit the same as being spiritual. If the necessity which Haufniensis attributes to psychological states is to be opposed to freedom in the wider sense, it is to the condition in which freedom and spirit are *posited*, rather than both posited and realized, that it is to be opposed.

In what then does the necessity of a predisposing state consist? Part of what Kierkegaard seems to be saying is that a person not yet envisaging the ideal of freedom in its true guise cannot see beyond the temporal horizon and is therefore 'determined' by contingent temporal goals; not necessarily deterministically, but such a person's activity might be said to be adequately explainable in purely naturalistic terms. The assumption could then be that this is not so once, subsequent to the leap, the genuine ethical categories have emerged in a person's consciousness.

However, this does not strictly accord with Kierkegaard's terminology. He sometimes refers to post-leap conditions of the psychosomatic synthesis as if they, too, were 'states' and therefore as if there was a necessity even after the leap. In *Anxiety* certain psychological *states* are even referred to as sinful, i.e. in ethical terms,[14] while in *Sickness* sin, or despair, comes close to being the human condition itself, the 'state' of man. Kierkegaard might be interpreted as follows. Psychologically, sin *is* a psychosomatic state, namely that state in which the individual has not yet chosen the idea of the eternal qualification as the source of initiatives. Ethically, however, it is not proper to call it a state, because from that point of view the self is not simply a psychosomatic entity but one in which spirit is assumed to be competing for control. Spirit is not a scientific category but psychological descriptions can include a spiritual reference, e.g. to freedom. Even when the spirit is dominant, i.e. freedom is attained, there must still be psychological states. But in that case they would no longer provide an adequate explanatory basis for the actions of the individual; the latter would be expressing freedom in the form of independence of merely temporal goals. In what Kierkegaard calls the 'bondage of sin',[15] however, to some extent they still do provide such a basis; for in sin a person positively affirms a willingness to be 'determined' by temporal goals. Such a person is 'unfree in relation to the good',[16] and so in a state, psychologically speaking, because now the only spiritual reference in the description of consciousness is to a spiritual goal from which the sinful person shrinks. In sin the spiritual fails to emerge properly from its psychosomatic matrix. One might say, though perhaps one should not take Kierkegaard's passing analogy of the 'abiding state' of the plant's history too literally, that in states which, from a psychological point of view, can be called states of sin, as in the states predisposing to sin, persons' actions come closer to this model of necessity than when, in terms of the interplay of body, mind, and spirit, the latter no longer interacts passively, or competitively with, but dominates (Haufniensis says 'sustains'),[17] the synthesis of the former.

In the everyday context the ideal of autonomy is not, on Kierkegaard's view, or at any rate not at first, a conscious goal. It is a growing sense of the inability of temporal categories to provide criteria of personal identity and humanly fulfilling achievement. This is the birth of anxiety, a psychological state which varies according to the adequacy with which the self grasps the total and irreducible disparity between finite and infinite, temporal and eternal; and varies also according to the kind of response the self makes to the discovery of the nature of its 'eternal qualification'. An adequate grasp of the distinction implies, as noted, that the only possible location for the infinite in human existence is in a personal, i.e. direct, relationship to an absolute and inconceivable goal — direct in the sense of unmediated by anything in time (history and nature). Affirming this amounts to 'positing spirit' and, as we have said, also involves a threshold insight into the nature of the value afforded by the infinite — into the nature of good and evil. Kierkegaard envisages two alternative attitudes to the threshold insight, or rather to sin, which is this insight's natural initial form (natural in view of the human predisposition to remain anchored in the psychosomatic). The first attitude, the natural one, involves refusing to adopt the ethical, retaining and even reaffirming one's grasp of the familiar, temporal and psychosomatic. If the ethical continues to be denied or repressed, the development is negative and follows a predictable pattern, or 'dialectic', which culminates in the extreme of despair, the conscious rejection of the very idea of the identification of personal value with an eternal qualification. The other attitude, which becomes progressively harder to adopt, involves forcing oneself out of the initially natural negative development by affirming this source of personal value. By choosing the ethical, one then frees oneself from the domination of the familiar, temporal, and psychosomatic. If this positive choice is sustained, still in the face of anxiety, the development is positive and healthy, and culminates in the elimination of despair. In that case, as we shall see later, although there are still obstacles to achieving the ideal of freedom and individuality, they are of an essentially different nature.

The scientific topics of the two psychological works can now be summarized as follows. In both, Kierkegaard systematically describes the psychosomatic states or psychological attitudes of the self in its relationship to an ideal of individuality or freedom which requires the rejection of any temporal concept of selfhood. Anxiety, the topic of the first, is a person's apprehensive and basically defensive attitude in the face of the ideal. In this sense anxiety is in general, as Kierkegaard says, 'an expression of the perfection of human nature'.[18] There are, however, two qualifications. First, anxiety is a state which varies according to the adequacy of the grasp of the finite/infinite distinction, and there can be cases of the state in which the ideal is not properly envisaged at all, and therefore states of anxiety which cannot have the ideal and its unknown possibilities as their *conscious* target. Second, although in such cases they cannot be the conscious target of such states, Kierkegaard frequently writes (to use a distinction of Wittgenstein's) as if they could nevertheless be their cause. That is, he writes as though the possibility envisaged at the stage at which spirit is posited exerts a disquieting influence upon the self even before the self has reached that stage.[19] This accords with a general tendency on Kierkegaard's part to describe spiritual growth as if it *were* nevertheless natural ('Every human life is religiously organized'),[20] and as if spirit pursued its end (rather like in Hegel's notion of the cunning of reason) even without the individual's conscious participation. But here we have to note that Kierkegaard does also give 'target' descriptions of these states, and the reader is free to prefer these as being the more literal ones, treating the reifying talk of spirit, for example, 'dreaming', of its being 'excluded', and a 'creditor' from whom one cannot 'slip away' as metaphorical.[21] Kierkegaard says that the state of anxiety which is the 'predisposing assumption of sin' has as its target not the possibility of freedom, of 'being able', but the possibility of that possibility.[22] There is also an earlier stage where freedom's possibility takes the even more diffuse form of the fanciful and mysterious, though he also says that this embryonic spiritual condition of fascination with the unknown does not amount to genuine anxiety;[23] for that the fascination with the unknown has to be combined or tempered with *fear* of the unknown, an apprehensive dread of 'the enormous nothing of ignorance'.[24] He also characterizes the targets of these two stages as, 'a nothing that becomes, as it were, more and more a something'.[25] The two-way pull characteristic of anxiety proper is referred to as a 'sympathetic antipathy and an antipathetic sympathy'.[26] Kierkegaard says that this ambiguity is characteristic of psychology; by this he surely means that it is a, or the, characteristic of the conditions (states) of human consciousness which makes them of interest to psychology. The qualitative leap, however, is 'outside all ambiguity',[27] so with the leap this 'dialectical ambiguity' disappears.[28] But not after all, it appears, either anxiety itself or the relevance of psychology as a science of anxiety. For anxiety now enters its second main form with the reality of sin as its unambiguously *to be feared* object; sympathetic antipathy and antipathetic sympathy give way, in the first instance, to fear of evil, that is of the possibility of sinking further into it,[29] and then – what is really an expression of the realization of this latter fear – to fear and eventual rejection of the very idea of the good.[30] In the face of these clearly defined targets, the self is no longer enclosed in a temporal world from which it merely has an 'anticipatory presentiment' of its freedom;[31] it now conceives its freedom as a form of separation from the temporal world. Psychological ambiguousness is replaced by the 'ingenious sophistry' with which the self tries to minimize, ignore, or reject the identification of itself *as* separate from the temporal world.[32] *Anxiety* ends with an account of the unique educative possibilities of anxiety for those willing to seize them by passing through, instead of shrinking from, this threshold to the spiritual.

The topic of the second, and significantly later, work is despair, otherwise characterized as sin and sickness. Despair is the inherently morbid and, to the enlightened observer, predictably unstable condition (or set of conditions) in which the self fails to exploit the unique educative possibilities offered by anxiety. It could be called the active, self-accommodating side of shrinking from the threshold. It is a form of adjustment; Kierkegaard (now Anti-Climacus) says that despair is an action, not just 'suffering',[33] though this is only the case in despair proper, which requires a conception of the self as having 'something eternal in it'.[34] In fact, the topic of *Sickness* is the subject's difficulty in constituting itself as just such a self. The forms of despair, which are the psychological expressions of this difficulty, correspond in broad outline to those of anxiety. *Sickness* focuses, however, on the notion of a self (mentioned in *Anxiety* only in terms of the need for the 'real' self to be 'posited by the qualitative leap' for attributions of selfishness to be appropriate),[35] and on the difficulties themselves. In other words, it concentrates on the individual's response to insight into the nature of good and evil, rather than on the conditions 'predisposing' to that insight. Anti-Climacus represents the ethical ideal and speaks from that point of view, one which it is worth noting that Kierkegaard said he himself did not adequately represent.[36] (Anti-Climacus is also the author of *Practice in Christianity* which together with *Sickness*, its companion piece, forms Kierkegaard's last major work.) *Sickness* is therefore concerned more with the sophistry and subterfuge of fallen man than with the psychological ambivalence of the predisposing state of innocence and the approximations to sin. It takes 'despair about the eternal and over oneself',[37] in *Anxiety*'s terms a post-leap characterization, as the formula for all despair and proceeds to apply it to a range, or rather succession, of personality structures in which the eternal is no longer genuinely expected or hoped for, despair being, first of all, the loss of the hope of the genuine possession of an eternal qualification. The object of despair is, as noted, the self, a self first constituted in awareness of itself as 'something essentially different from the environment',[38] and not a product of unmediated responses to contingent environmental circumstances. But once the subject has this conception of itself it 'stumbles on difficulties' which lead to despair and loss of the eternal.[39] The loss of the eternal is a matter of despair because in losing it the self is giving up the project of being the self it knows it should be. The impression left by *Sickness* is that in order to exploit the educative possibilities of anxiety one must plunge deeply into despair. In this respect despair is proper to human nature in the wide as well as the narrow sense of human nature mentioned earlier. The breakthrough of spirit is correspondingly difficult and strenuous. It is therefore not surprising that 'very few . . . live even passably in the category of the spirit . . . [or] even . . . make an attempt at this life'.[40]

Both anxiety and despair, then, are psychological phenomena in the sense that they are describable and predictable states of the mind/body synthesis in confrontation with the individual's growing awareness that *qua* this synthesis it is not (is 'infinitely' less than) the full or true or real self. And the negative development, which the individual undergoes when it fails to respond positively to anxiety, thereby denying itself its new-found possibility of freedom, and clings to the familiar, to nature, is itself in a manner of speaking a determinable state, in so far as it is allowed to unfold in its predictable way. The analogue for 'state' here is any determinable development, such as that of the healthy plant — or even an unhealthy plant, given the conditions of its morbidity. However, note that in the case of persons a determinable development is for Kierkegaard invariably a *morbid* one, a failure of the self to subject itself to the infinite and transcendent source of (its own) value.

167

Kierkegaard also describes such a development as a *succession* of states,[41] where the transitions involve repetitions of the fall into sin. The point is that sin is, ethically — and therefore really — speaking, not a state or condition which a person acquires by virtue (or vice) of a particular act. It is a continual default, a succession of constantly reiterated choices of the easier but negative options.

There is a difficulty of interpretation in this connection: how can these choices genuinely be repetitions of the original when the original lapse is simultaneously the positing of spirit and thus of the ethical as such, as Haufniensis suggests it is? The repetitions cannot, presumably, be repeated positings of spirit, but negative choices against the background of an acknowledgement of the positive spiritual option. The interpretational difficulty really goes back to the qualitative leap and what it means to say that sin 'comes into being . . . not by necessity . . . but by freedom'. That could sound as if sin came into being by a free choice. But perhaps Kierkegaard is really only saying once again that the category of the spiritual, and therefore ethics and therefore sin, is autonomous and the transition into it inexplicable. This is compatible with consciousness being thrust into the category of the spirit without the opportunity of choosing it. Indeed Haufniensis's account of the states that predispose a person to consciousness of sin strongly suggests that it is not only the self's progression to the threshold of the spiritual that is inevitable, but also the self's actually crossing the threshold. If so, should it, then, not be impossible to choose sin? And if it was indeed impossible to choose sin, it would be plausible to argue that sin, too, was impossible, at least as an ethical concept implying a state of imperfection for whose continuation the ethical subject is responsible. But the difficulty might be resolved by distinguishing between the emergence in consciousness of the ethical as such, and with it an awareness of the imperfection of the natural man (Kierkegaard does not appear to contemplate an intermediate stage in which ethical language is constituted but where the self refuses to admit its genuinely referential status), and the failure to respond positively to this awareness. Clearly the qualitative leap cannot be interpreted as requiring a *choice* of the ethical, for in order to choose the ethical the ethical option must already be at hand,[42] and the ethical therefore already 'constituted' in consciousness, which is precisely what it is not prior to the leap. Nor, and for the same as well as other reasons, can the emergence of the *consciousness* of sin be a matter of choice. But the failure to overcome sin, or even to want to overcome it, can be; and it is presumably this that is common to the original lapse into sin and its subsequent repetitions.

We said that Kierkegaard's psychological descriptions are of states of the mind/body synthesis. But it is important to note that the descriptions are not always in exclusively mind/body terms. Often the two pseudonymous authors, and particularly Anti-Climacus, characterize psychosomatic states from 'the point of view of spirit'. The fact that the psychological works include descriptions from the spiritual point of view is obviously connected with one of their main functions, namely to give ethically correct reconstructions or diagnoses of the familiar phenomena of anxiety and despair; though it must be added that part of Kierkegaard's reconstructive purpose is to present certain everyday conditions not normally classified in these psychological terms as indeed expressions of a deep and pervasive unease. The diagnoses will, of course, only be accepted by those who accept the ethico-spiritual vocabulary, the qualitative leap, the eternal qualification, and the rest of it. The psychological works cannot, therefore, be interpreted as attempts to argue for acceptance of the ethical vocabulary by appealing to the authority of science; this 'science' is only authority to those who already accept the vocabulary. The diagnoses *also* cover the 'case' postulated by the science, however, of one who rejects the vocabulary, so it is perhaps intended that their awakening and edifying function should extend even to the sceptic.

Otherwise, one must look for the justification of the psychological works in a consideration of the ethical point of view in two diametrically opposed but important ways. They show, especially *Sickness*, just how strenuous is the ideal of the life of spirit. From the opposite vantage-point they make it clear that the challenge of ethics is concrete and particular, a point encapsulated in Kierkegaard's observation in the *Journals* that the Christian (ethical) way of life remains 'seriously deficient' without 'adequate knowledge of human life, and sympathy for its interests'.[43] Unless ethics takes account of the psychological background against which people actually encounter their ideals and have to come to terms with them, it remains an abstract discipline, unrelated to life. Ethics must include an account of circumstances that not only make it difficult to realize ethical goals, but actually lead people to turn their backs on them. In general we might say that the purpose of the psychological works is to offer an account of human life and its interests in which even the apparently most rational denials of a transcendent source of personal value are to be interpreted as expressions of a deep-seated dread, a fear of the very notion itself.

Still, Kierkegaard obviously does not believe that a sympathetic knowledge of human affairs can by itself induce people to face their ideal — or this particular ideal — anew. If it were thought that it could do so, the main problem of ethics, namely sin, would have been transformed into some form of puzzle which only requires persistent scrutiny — the 'dauntlessness of the spy' — for its solution.[44] A purely scientific approach (even in the guise of Hegelian psychology) to sin distorts it, since the mood of such an approach is inappropriate to the topic. The scientist evinces a kind of fascination for his material,[45] which in the case of sin is quite out of place. He surveys sin with 'antipathetic curiosity' and subjects it to an 'unessential reflective refraction'.[46] Sin is to be recognized, opposed, and overcome, not gazed at in fascination or horror as some kind of abnormality. (As noted, Anti-Climacus does describe despair, or sin, as a sickness, but not as an abnormality and not even as a normal sickness since it is contracted 'continually'.[47] Similarly with 'aesthetic' and 'metaphysical' approaches. To contemplate the 'contradiction' of sin aesthetically is to enter either into a frivolous or into a melancholic mood, as opposed to the seriousness proper to it;[48] while to 'think' it metaphysically is to adopt a mood of 'dialectical indifference' in which the contradiction or intransigence of sin, instead of being a practical problem, appears as a theoretical one — the problem of finding a place for the concept — thus implying that there might even be no place for it.[49] This, incidentally, is Kierkegaard's objection to traditional ethics; that it finds no real place for sin;[50] it assumes that persons are naturally capable of realizing whatever ideals reason dictates, and fails to appreciate that the significance of sin is its denial of this assumption. Traditional ethics talks of human perfectibility in terms of the perfection rather than of the alteration of human nature. A realistic ethics has to accept the reality of sin and get to work on changing human nature, by 'accusing, judging, acting',[51] so that sin (despair) *can* be overcome. In Kierkegaard's view even theology ('dogmatics') has the advantage over traditional ethics that it accepts the reality of sin and sees clearly that it is an obstacle to the fulfilment of ethical ideals — in other words that ethical ideals do not correspond to perfections of human *nature*. But even theology can only unfold the content of the concept of sin, or explain its 'ideal' possibility in the myth of Adam's fall,[52] it cannot explain the origin of sin itself. Nor, of course, any more than science, can it do anything to overcome sin. That is an ethical task — *the* ethical task.

2 Sin and human imperfection

But why is sin essential, and central, to ethics? Why must the true ethical view contrast the good with sin and not with such more immediately recognizable evils as, for example, brutality, injustice, or unnecessary suffering and pain?

As noted, *Anxiety* opens with a discussion of the meaning of *original* sin. Whatever else it is, the concept of original sin is at least that of an imperfection introduced by some historical event which is often construed as the imperfection's cause and the imperfection itself as thenceforth innate to human nature. Until, that is, by dint of divine sacrifice, human effort, and the grace of God the imperfection is removed. The transition from innocence through sin to redemption is conceived as a kind of progress; in particular redemption is attended with a knowledge not available in the state of innocence, which is therefore also one of ignorance, specifically of good and evil. The point of Kierkegaard's discussion is to stress, first, that Adam's fall from innocence is not itself to be explained as the consequence of, or a development out of, any state or act of innocence, e.g. savouring the forbidden fruit — and that the only 'dialectically consistent' account, however elusive to the understanding,[53] is the Genesis one that sin came into the world *by* sin — that is, in 'knowing' that he should not eat of the tree of knowledge of good and evil and yet wanting to do so, Adam was already in the state of sin; and second, that mankind's subsequent imperfection is to be understood not as causally consequent upon, but as repetitions or exemplifications of Adam's fall, the only difference being that, subsequent to Adam, the fall into sin occurs in a world in which sin has acquired both a history and institutions — corresponding to what Kierkegaard calls 'objective anxiety' ('objective' in the sense of the Hegelian distinction mentioned earlier between 'subjective' and 'objective' spirit). The important point here is that mankind in Adam's form does not of itself produce sin, but falls into it. And that is, of course, another way of saying that the ethical concepts in question are autonomous and irreducible, and therefore, amongst other things, that when we describe a person as sinning we adopt a terminology in which we accept that persons are more than natural beings.

The notion of a progress from innocence through knowledge to redemption suggests a dialectical advance parallel to that of the Hegelian development from immediacy, via the unhappy consciousness, to absolute self-consciousness, and it is tempting to ask whether the 'necessity' of sin can be explained as a consequence of, on the one hand, Kierkegaard's acceptance of the formal structure of the Hegelian triadic motif together with, on the other, his rejection of the Hegelian dialectic's terms of reference. So let us return to the theme of the unhappy consciousness.

We recall from Chapter II that the unhappy consciousness has progressed beyond the ultimately self-defeating 'Stoic' attempt to find its fulfilment or identity in pure universal thought at the expense of particular existence, and also the subsequently futile 'sceptical' attempt to engage in a *merely* particular existence to the total exclusion of universality. It has, so to speak, recognized that its identity is inescapably bound up with both elements but is unable to reconcile particular existence with pure thought in its *own* existence. Hence the unhappiness. The unhappy consciousness knows itself as finite, and can even think of an infinite existence that *is* particular (God), but it cannot think of *itself* in that light. Accordingly it projects the notion of the possibility of its own perfectibility into that of a transcendent God from whom all human value is then thought to stem. The problem for the unhappy consciousness is that it is unable to convert what it sees as its virtual possession of infinite characteristics, in its capacity for — or rather, in Hegelian terms, in its capacity *as* — pure thought into a genuine possession of those characteristics. It 'has not yet risen to that thinking where consciousness as a particular individuality is reconciled with pure thought itself'.[54] Hegel's doctrine is, of course, that it can reach that level: the harmonious reconciliation is brought about by the further advance of consciousness to Reason, that 'certainty of consciousness that it is all reality'.[55] Having developed Reason, consciousness no longer needs to project the source of its value into a transcendent bestower of value and grace. It now knows *itself* as both an infinite and a particular existence, and human nature in the form of thought or mind (*Geist*) has therefore demonstrated its ability to overcome the 'imperfection' by its own resources.

Thus Hegelian Reason obviates the need for redemption. For Kierkegaard, however, Hegelian Reason is an academic myth; the idea of 'human nature in the form of thought' is simply an 'absent-minded' abstraction from the individual's particular existence. Human reality, its particularity, cannot be understood in the categories of pure thought, and so the imperfection remains as a real imperfection and not a contradiction like any other to be resolved, if at all, in a mood of 'dialectical indifference'. Nor is the subject of particular existence a legless and pervasive *Geist* with a built-in instinct for certainty and infinitude. The would-be reconciler is a solitary self ineradicably rooted in infinite reality, increasingly conscious of the inability of Mind to establish, or in any way amount to, human infinitude, and as a result even more personally and passionately interested in achieving it.

In the field of knowledge or objective understanding, moreover, there can be no substitute for Mind as Thought. Now we did note in the previous chapter that Kierkegaard (Climacus) says that, because Christianity is a matter of inwardness and therefore not an objective truth to be appropriated in thought, but nevertheless (if true) is a truth to be appropriated somehow, then it must be appropriated in feeling; and that he seems sometimes to represent intensity of commitment in neo-Platonic fashion as a superior, direct form of knowledge. But this, we argued, is not what Kierkegaard means. For him any 'certainty' afforded by feeling depends on, and in no way renders superfluous, a prior choice. So, in terms of the traditional tripartite Mind, it is to Will, and not to either Thought or Feeling, that Kierkegaard looks for his harmonious reconciliation. But if neither dialectical indifference nor ecstatic union with God can repair the 'contradiction' between finite and infinite, what power of reconciliation rests in the idea of willing? There is no speculative equivalent of wishful thinking, no such thing as Voluntaristic Idealism, or merely *willing* truth into existence. The most that willing can achieve is belief in something for which the evidence is inconclusive. But in order to have a content, and thus to be a belief at all, a belief must represent a possible state of affairs, and it is precisely an inability to be represented in understanding that constitutes the elusiveness of the desired reconciliation to thought. Now one could perhaps assign to the will the second-order prerogative of choosing to believe that this inability is only contingent, not absolute, and that might be one way of willing the reconciliation. But it would not be a way in which a person could hope to achieve it personally. In fact, the situation here would be no different in effect from that of unhappy consciousness itself, in which the ideal of reconciliation is entrusted to that other transcendent custodian of not-impossibilities, God. The solitary individual's goal of a personal certainty would remain a mere abstract possibility unrelated to any contribution in thought or action on the part of the individual itself.

If reconciliation is to be a project of the individual will, lack of human perfection in this sense cannot be excused by appealing to the immaturity of the prevailing *Geist*, any more than its achievement can be left to that *Geist*'s future coming-of-age. Human imperfection must be a matter of individual responsibility. But again, if the state of perfection cannot even be envisaged, no amount of personal effort can ever guarantee it. The doctrines of

173

salvation and grace correspond formally to a denial of the assumption that human faculty is sufficient to achieve the harmonious reconciliation of particular and infinite in the individual person. They amount to the propositions that the form of the effort required for the reconciliation, or of its representation in practice, has to be given by transcendent authority; and that even if the effort conforms to the requirement, the actual achievement of the reconciliation still depends on a certification 'on the other side' for which there can be no proof.

Suppose that the notion of sin can be analysed accordingly into the following three ideas: first, that human nature as such is imperfect; second, that the imperfection can be remedied in part by personal effort; and third, that because the unhappy consciousness's account of human value is the right one (that is, the conversion of virtual possession of infinite characteristics — in Kierkegaard's case, if one may so put it, by virtue of virtual virtue — into genuine possession of them is an act of God and not of man), no particular individual effort guarantees perfection. If this were supposable, then it would be by no means implausible to claim that Kierkegaard's ethics of sin and redemption follows from this personalization of the Hegelian dialectic of spiritual emergence, together with his denial of the ability of thought to bring off the harmonious reconciliation.

Even if this is granted, however, the burden of our question, Why the centrality of sin?, is now simply transferred to that of justifying the Hegelian framework with its accommodation of the project of reconciliation in the first place. This is obviously a vast philosophical question and here we must be content with some provisional observations which may help to present Kierkegaard's psychological themes from a perspective which reveals some of the special assumptions underlying his handling of them.

As our key we can take Kierkegaard's philosophical relationship to Feuerbach. As we have already mentioned, Feuerbach attacked Hegel for personifying human characteristics and capacities, as if they themselves were capable of reactions, plans, and initiatives. Hegel's *Geist*, for example, is a personification of the human capacity for thought. Feuerbach (a Ryle of his time) proposed that the terms referring to these characteristics and capacities be treated not as substantives referring to mythical universal agents but as predicates qualifying the activities of particular persons. At least in this respect Kierkegaard is clearly Feuerbachian. It is individual persons who think, feel, and act, and not thought, feeling, and action which express themselves in persons. Abstract thought, says Climacus, is thought without a thinker.

174

But Feuerbach tackles the problem of reconciliation differently. He considers the religious conception corresponding to Hegel's unhappy consciousness to be an alienated expression of the true view which locates human value in the natural (but adequately socialized) human species itself — an influential view among Left Hegelians and requiring only a short step to the Marxist and Freudian analyses of religious categories (guilt, sin, redemption) as, respectively, ideological instruments and the internalization of external conditions of authority and repression. The step was not one which Feuerbach himself took, for although he saw the unhappy consciousness as an expression of avoidable alienation, he did not see the religious conception of man itself in the same light. In this respect one may even think of Feuerbach and Kierkegaard as co-defenders of the faith in the face not only of Marx's but also of Hegel's doctrines of the transitional status of religious consciousness. But in their understanding of religious consciousness Feuerbach and Kierkegaard are totally at odds. Feuerbach reduces the transcendent to an expression of the value and perfectibility of human nature; Kierkegaard regards it as the very source of human value to which human nature must subject itself in order to acquire that value and achieve whatever perfection it can.

Is it Kierkegaard or Feuerbach whose insight remains the more obscured by philosophical myth and speculation in this respect? Much of what Kierkegaard writes in the psychological works, though not only there, suggests a speculative conception of an autonomous spirit. As we noted, he talks as if the human capacity for spiritual development were capable of sustaining itself independently of the conscious aspirations of the as yet incompletely spiritual human being. Indeed, Kierkegaard's constant references to 'spirit' as some sort of entity bent upon its own self-development even invite a Spinozistic interpretation; a conservative reading of Kierkegaard would see him as holding a conative or teleological view of spiritual emergence which differs from Hegel's only in specifying the individual will as the locus of the drive to spirituality. Although his descriptions of anxiety and despair can indeed often be construed phenomenologically, they are nevertheless liberally supplemented by descriptions specifying or hinting at a divine destiny, as if the abyss of ignorance into which freedom of spirit inexorably draws the self were the gateway to a goal whose nature has been fixed in advance of an analysis of the situation of individual existence. Why, then, might not we, or the self, choose, for instance, like Feuerbach, to find divinity in the 'complete' man — that is, in the perfection of the *human* being

(Feuerbach specifies the human perfections as reason, love, and force of will)[56] — and to interpret the notion of a transcendent God as 'nothing else than the realised idea, the fulfilled law of morality, the moral nature of man posited as the absolute being'?[57] The fulfilment of the moral law in that case would not require acting out some kind of token representation of the reconciliation of finite and transcendent infinite, by divine command, in hope of salvation and from fear of damnation, but the actual effecting of a reconciliation between 'the perfect and the imperfect, the sinless and sinful being, the universal and the individual, the divine and the human'.[58] Feuerbach himself says the reconciliation is achieved in love, not 'immaterial' but 'flesh and blood' love, which he calls the 'middle term' (for Kierkegaard's opposite view, see Chapter VII below). Here there would be no need for the alienated and repressive view which 'sets man's own nature before him as a separate nature, and moreover as a personal being, who hates and curses sinners, and excludes them from his grace, the source of all salvation and happiness'.[59]

But will such a reconciliation satisfy the individual's longing for eternal happiness? Or, to anticipate the rejoinder, must any longing that *cannot* be satisfied by this or any other reconciliation which is possible within nature and history be the disguised expression of humanly remediable alienation? Kierkegaard would say no. For him the longing for eternal happiness is an expression of a form of alienation that is endemic to human nature or the human situation itself, and it can only be requited by belief in a personal God. The crucial question is whether, by framing the distinction between imperfect and perfect human nature in terms of a logical opposition between finite and infinite, which not only gives perfection the form of a 'separate' nature but also in effect makes that perfection a divine dispensation, Kierkegaard is merely giving expression to his own inability to achieve a humanly achievable satisfaction, or perhaps that of his historical epoch, or the inability of the cultural tradition in which he lived to see what earthly forms that satisfaction can take; or whether he has simply probed more deeply than others into the human psyche and given a more adequate account of what would be needed to requite true human longing. Defenders of a 'progressive' Kierkegaard might argue, for instance, that it is only by subterfuge and evasion that earthly perfection can appease the fear of finitude and (not necessarily just one's own) death; that Feuerbach's reduction of theology to anthropology,[60] however well intentioned (he wanted to make 'the friends of God into friends of man, . . . candidates for the other world into students of this . . . , and Christians, who, on their own confession are half-animal and half-angel, into men — whole men'),[61] is really no more than a vainly Promethean attempt to retroject eternal values onto a temporal domain that cannot support them;[62] and that a fully progressive Feuerbachian would accept the consequences and construe the divinity of man as the exclusively finite individual's forlorn expression of a longing for eternal happiness. Whether they would be right to deny that this is how Kierkegaard's own philosophy of spiritual emergence should be construed is another matter. Kierkegaard himself would certainly add, however, that to become a whole man it is necessary to *become* a Christian; and furthermore (as we shall see in Chapter VII) that, unless love of man has *God* as its 'middle term', that love is morally worthless. If this means that, with Feuerbach, we must classify Kierkegaard as a candidate for the other world rather than a student of this, what might Kierkegaard's rejoinder be? Apart from observing that we had failed to understand what it is to be a Christian (for instance, that its *practical* content is altogether this-worldly), he might claim that in respect of the thoroughly this-worldly topic of human existence he, not Feuerbach, was the better qualified student. And as far as being a candidate for the next world was concerned, he would probably protest that his own personal preoccupations had been his shortcomings as a candidate for this one. In considering Kierkegaard's account of the this-worldly topics of anxiety and despair it may be useful to keep in mind the question whether it bears witness more to an exceptional psychological situation than to an exceptional psychological insight.

3   Pre- and post-threshold anxiety

Kierkegaard (Haufniensis) calls *The Concept of Anxiety* a 'simple' psychological deliberation. There is no everyday sense of 'simple' which would make this a fitting description. What Haufniensis seems to mean emerges, however, in his Preface where he says that he prefers to be regarded as a 'layman'.[63] And it is true that, whatever its thematic complexities, the work is written with a certain linguistic informality. Indeed, *Anxiety*'s terminology is often metaphorical rather than technical. Anxiety itself, for instance, is described as

> the dizziness of freedom which arises when the spirit would posit the synthesis, and freedom now looks down into its own possibility, and then lays hold of the finite to steady itself.[64]

Obviously, however, the author presupposes some acquaintance with current philosophical jargon, in particular with the notion that a person is a 'synthesis of the temporal and eternal' (Haufniensis says that he realizes that in saying this he is saying nothing new, but that it is his business and pleasure to think about things which '*seem* quite simple').[65]

What is this conception of a synthesis with which Kierkegaard assumes his readers are familiar? The natural answer would be that it is a synthesis in the Hegelian sense, that is to say a combination of two initially opposed terms by virtue of the 'mediating' offices of a third term. But it is not that simple. The idea of the synthesis of eternity and temporality (which in *Sickness* we find related to the two other polarities referred to in the previous chapter, namely infinitude/finitude and possibility/necessity) is that of the goal of their reconciliation, but also, by extension, that of the situation in which the problem of their reconciliation first emerges. There are, in *Anxiety*, two 'syntheses'. One is the initial and in itself unproblematic fusion or combination of mind (or soul) and body. Such a synthesis is unproblematic so long as spirit is not 'posited'. But positing spirit is the same as spirit's positing the 'second' synthesis, that of time and eternity, as an 'expression' of the 'first' synthesis.[66]

The point is that, prior to the positing of the second synthesis, the two terms, mind (or soul) and body, are understood from the point of view of immediacy as forming a synthesis on their own, as if naturally combined, in the way in which they are in the case of psychophysical organisms lacking a 'spiritual' possibility. This is the situation before spiritual consciousness emerges in the human individual, a situation in which one can talk metaphorically of the spirit, the third term, as an outsider. But the emergence of spiritual consciousness *is* the idea that what appears initially to be a combination of soul and body is really a juxtaposition of opposites. Phenomenologically, that realization is what Kierkegaard *means* by the emergence of spiritual consciousness; for spiritual consciousness, or 'the positing of spirit', is recognizing an identity apart from and overordinate to the finite mentality belonging to the first synthesis. Haufniensis says that it is not necessary for his purpose to enter into any 'pompous' philosophizing about the soul/body relation (though he says enough to let us know that he could do so if he wanted); it suffices to say that 'the body is [the] organ of the soul and thus, in turn, of the spirit'.[67] Transforming the soul/body synthesis into a spirit/body synthesis (or, rather, a (spirit)/(soul/body) synthesis) is the task which first appears with the positing of the (second) synthesis. The 'synthesis' is thus the framework in which Haufniensis (and Climacus and Anti-

Climacus) describes the goal of fulfilment, also the framework in which the *problems* and *failures* of fulfilment are described. It is on the latter that the psychological works focus attention.

Theoretically, however, we need to know what the 'third term' is which achieves the resolution of the opposition of time and eternity. Haufniensis poses the question himself, and answers it in a crucial but complex passage which introduces the notion of the *instant* as the moment of eternity in time.

His answer is to the effect that the ordinary spatialized conception of time as a succession, or continuum, with the past extending backwards from the present and the future stretching forwards, contains the instant only as a limiting concept, or an abstract discrimination (as with a geometrical point in relation to the means of defining it). By acquiring a sense of the instant as a 'now' that is not abstracted from a spatialized continuum, but itself (as we would now say, intentionally) contains both past and future, we synthesize the temporal and the eternal by incorporating the former in the latter. The eternal is then no longer 'the future' (as it is to 'innocence'), nor 'the past' (as it was to the Ancient Greeks),[68] but the present. It is the instant (Danish, '*Øieblik*' — lit. 'glance of the eye'), that 'ambiguity in which time and eternity touch one another'.[69] The instant defines the present *as* a present, and not as a vanishing time-slice cut out of a time-continuum. Instead of being defined in relation *to* past and future, the present becomes (in some sense) identical *with* past and future.[70] Since nature and the sensuous life belong essentially to time and history, they have to be defined in relation to past and future; they 'have' a past and future. This is their 'imperfection':[71] they can have no eternal qualification in which their past and future can be incorporated in a 'now'. It is only by positing the instant that the past and the future (*Tilkommende* — lit. 'forthcoming') can be grasped as they are — as dimensions of the individual's existence — instead of as mere extensions of, respectively, the future and the present. Haufniensis also notes that if the past and future are grasped in the latter way, the central Christian concepts of conversion, atonement, and redemption (in respect of the past), and of resurrection and judgment (in respect of the future) are lost sight of since they become merely dimensions of individual and world-historical evolution.[72] The instant is not really an atom of time, but of eternity; it is the 'first reflection of eternity in time, its first attempt as it were at bringing time to a stop'.[73] (Further, and more deliberate, efforts in this direction will be encountered in the next two chapters.) Positing the instant is positing the synthesis of time and eternity, or positing the combination of body and soul as

179

a compatible combination if, and only if, sustained by spirit.[74]

But this talk of spirit as some kind of an outsider intruding upon the initial soul/body pair, making this latter 'synthesis' increasingly conscious of its being no synthesis at all but a juxtaposition of opposites, and then offering its good offices as the 'third term' to effect a reconciliation — all this is highly abstract and presumably metaphorical. What more concrete and literal ways of expressing these operations of the emergence from innocence to the predisposition to sin does Haufniensis provide?

The vertigo metaphor says that when the spirit 'would posit' the synthesis it shrinks from doing so, grasping onto the finite to keep its balance. Why should it need to do that? Because it stands before itself as a *nothing*. If the 'it' here were the (embodied) subject of consciousness, the 'nothing' would be this subject's as yet empty idea of its possible true nature. But Haufniensis makes 'spirit' the subject term and the nothing corresponds to the absence of any specification of spiritual identity. Spirit's vertigo is due to its so far lacking any bearings with regard to its own true nature. All it has is the *possibility* of itself, an undifferentiated conception of a possible true nature, founded on the more or less dim awareness that its existence is more than a bodily existence. The talk of spirit dreaming and 'as immediate', but 'disturbing' the body/soul partnership,[75] and being 'left out' when ignored,[76] are again very 'simple' descriptions despite their being couched in the current Hegelian argot. The literal descriptions are phenomenological, that is to say those in which Kierkegaard says that the object of anxiety prior to the consciousness of sin is this 'nothing'. This term denotes the, so far, phenomenologically empty spiritual category — a fact which distinguishes anxiety from 'fear and similar concepts that refer to something definite'.[77] Thus the state of innocence, or of dreaming spirit, is also described as one in which spirit 'projects its own reality', but where, because it has no idea of what this reality is, in doing this it projects 'nothing'; not, however, in a way which entails that there is no projecting, for 'innocence constantly sees this nothing outside itself'.[78] A still more literal interpretation of 'dreaming spirit' would construe it as saying that the embodied subject has a premonition that it is potentially something more than a consciousness confined to a body, but has as yet no idea as to what this 'more' could amount to, and in the 'dreaming' state perhaps does not even explicitly entertain the possibility that it could be something more. Here the premonition, or anxiety, takes the form of 'a seeking after adventure, a thirst for the prodigious, the mysterious'.[79] In the 'later individual', who is 'more self-conscious', the object of anxiety crystallizes to a degree, it becomes 'more and more a something', though not as yet sin. For the 'nothing' in the face of which the subject is anxious is still only 'a complex of presentiments',[80] something that can be described without yet drawing on the ethico-religious vocabulary which is (or turns out later to be) needed in order to specify anxiety's object.

This then is freedom's looking down into its own possibility. But what of its grasping at finiteness to steady itself? This suggests a more or less conscious reflex in which the subject-to-be-spirit redirects attention back upon familiar sources of identification and achievement. But who or what is the subject of this defensive reflex, what form does it take, and what is there about it that leads 'spirit' and 'freedom', as the metaphor continues, to 'succumb . . . in this dizziness', thus reaching that moment, the 'leap', where freedom 'raises itself again' and 'sees that it is guilty'? In other words, what is the psychology of the fall — or Fall —[81] out of which 'springs' knowledge of good and evil?

The fall occurs, says Haufniensis, 'in impotence'.[82] That is why it is better described as a reflex rather than, say, an initiative. In falling, the subject is subject *to* the pressures of its psychosomatic nature. But in anxiety there is also an active or at least optative element, 'possibility's selfish infinity', something which 'does not tempt like a choice, but captivates in the unease it brings with its sweet anxiousness'.[83] Here we have the 'dialectical ambiguity' mentioned earlier. The idea is that the attitude associated with the sense of having a not merely bodily existence is not only a reflex in the direction of immediacy. (The project of such a return would, in any case, be impossible: innocence cannot be a perfection since 'as soon as one wishes for it, it is lost';[84] the state of consciousness in which one has a sense of a more than bodily existence cannot have as one of *its* satisfactions a state in which that consciousness does not exist.) There is also the forward-looking fascination with the prospect of a fulfilment of this sense of being more than a finite being. But alarm at the direction in which that fulfilment lies, away from the familiar, establishes a more or less settled tendency to try to revert to the former state all the same. And, of course, once innocence is lost the attempt must always be in vain.

But it may not always seem to be in vain. Haufniensis describes a state of apparent happiness, or complacency, in which anxiety does not, or does not seem to, occur. Consistently with the view that anxiety is a manifestation of spiritual emergence, he calls it a state of 'spiritlessness'. A spiritless person has a concept of spirit in the sense that he can talk about it. Indeed he talks a great deal about this as about everything, but mechanically.[85] His talk of spirit is empty, formal, a caricature; it is something he has learnt by heart. In fact, his whole condition points away from spirit and represents stagnation rather than development. Although he is not consciously anxious, anxiety is nevertheless there. To the observer the excessive chatter can be seen as a defence against any form of reflection. The spiritless person's condition is an attempt to avoid spiritual reflection. But the spirit will not be denied. 'One can imagine that a debtor succeeds in slipping away from his creditor, and in holding him off with [mere] talk, but there's one creditor who never comes off worst, and that is the spirit'[86] — not because the spirit always breaks through, but because even if it does not it is still able to exact the price of its exclusion.

Haufniensis describes other forms of anxiety a common feature of which is that the subject either locates its spiritual possibilities in something finite or conceives the infinite in space—time terms. He comments on two forms of religion, paganism and Judaism. Both are, of course, directed towards spirit, but nevertheless represent incomplete forms of spiritual emergence, the first more so than the second. Paganism's limitation is that it is concerned with fate, the form now taken by the 'nothing' which the pagan anxiously confronts. For Judaism it is guilt. The pagan lacks the 'deeper reflection' needed to acquire a sense of guilt, and his world appears to him to be the result of operations beyond his control. Although his wish to come to terms with fate is an expression of spirituality, the relationship to spirit is 'external',[87] and his concern is vitiated by the impossibility of coming to terms with what is 'at one moment necessity, the next moment chance'.[88] His anxious concern is manifested in the need to consult oracles, and Haufniensis says that the tragic element in paganism is not the ambiguity of the message which the pagan receives from the oracle, but the inherent 'sympathetic antipathy', or ambiguity, of his own attitude to the oracle. Although Judaism's sense of guilt represents a closer approximation to the spirit (and, in fact, exemplifies Climacus's concept of religiousness A), it is left with a similar ambiguity: 'to the oracle of paganism corresponds the sacrifice of Judaism'; to cope with his dread of guilt 'the Jew has recourse to the sacrifice'. But that is of no avail, for the sacrifice does not give him what he really needs, which is not the elimination of guilt but the elimination of anxiety in the face of guilt.[89] So 'the sacrifice becomes ambiguous, a fact which is expressed in its repetition, a further consequence of which would be a pure scepticism with respect to the act of sacrifice itself'.

Haufniensis also describes two kinds of 'genius'. A genius differs from ordinary persons in an ability to recapture the essentials of human development from the beginning:

> Within his historical presupposition, he consciously begins just as originally as Adam. Every time a genius is born, existence is as it were put to the test; for he rehearses and experiences all the past until he catches up with himself. The genius's knowledge of the past is therefore quite different from that which is offered by surveys of universal history.[90]

The first kind of genius is the 'immediate' genius. He differs from the pagan in being genuinely capable of the deeper reflection of guilt, but, in a way like the spiritless person, he avoids it. Unlike the spiritless person, however, the immediate genius does not just talk; he acts in a grand, ostensibly constructive manner. He is set upon worldly achievement. Consequently he, too, is concerned with fate, the propitious turn in events, the tides of fortune which he believes himself somehow specially equipped to detect and exploit. Yet, whatever his success, he 'never becomes great in his own eyes. . . . All his activity is outwardly directed, but what one might call the planetary nucleus from which it all radiates does not come into existence'. He cannot master, and in the end founders upon, fate. The example of Talleyrand is given, a man who avoided what was so evidently a capacity for a 'far deeper reflection upon life'. 'If such a genius had disdained the temporal as immediate, had turned towards himself and towards the divine, what a religious genius might have come out of it!'[91]

The second kind of genius, the 'religious' genius, represents the closest consciousness can come to the ethico-spiritual threshold without crossing it. Not being content, as the immediate genius, to 'stop with his immediacy', he turns (as one now expects) 'towards himself and *eo ipso* towards the divine'. Accordingly, the tasks he undertakes are not worldly ones. Fate is therefore of no concern to him, nor the possession or cultivation of talents which might give him worldly success.[92] In turning towards himself he discovers freedom, not as the power to do things in the world, but as the capacity to see himself as not being bounded by the temporal, as able to act beyond or outside the temporal. But this freedom brings with it the idea of guilt and so guilt replaces fate as the object (still a 'nothing') of this genius's anxiety. Significantly, since he has turned *away* from the outer world, guilt is the only thing he fears. But what he fears is not that he may already be guilty; the idea of 'positing' his own guilt has not occurred to him; but that the freedom he has found brings with it the danger of his *becoming* guilty. It is this possibility of becoming guilty that he

183

sees as endangering the 'bliss' (*Salighed*) of his new-found freedom.[93] What still escapes him is the threshold insight that he is already guilty. Not seeing that he *is* guilty, he still has a forward-looking fascination for guilt: 'freedom cannot help staring at guilt and this staring is the ambiguity of anxiety'.[94]

There is a problem of interpretation. These descriptions might be read as if the pagan, the Jew of Judaism, the immediate genius, and the religious genius all represent abortive attempts to locate the true identity of the more-than-temporal self. Common to all four would then be that they see this identity as resting partly in powers beyond their control, while all but the religious genius make the added mistake of supposing that temporal events, activities, or achievements themselves either are or symbolize modes of more-than-bodily fulfilment. Their mistake, in general, would be to assume fulfilment to be possible *if only* an alien infinite does not intervene. The abortiveness of the attempts would rest in the fact that the means chosen for fulfilment are incapable of achieving it, precisely because the intervention of the alien infinite cannot be excluded.

But the vertigo metaphor suggests something different; namely that the resort to means which fall short of the goal is a psychological consequence of the true goal having been glimpsed but recoiled from. It suggests that these attitudes represent more or less deliberate rejections of the true goal, an instinctive, self-preserving grab at finiteness in order to regain balance following the disorienting insight into the true nature or at least location of the infinite; not that they confine themselves to the means adopted simply because that insight has not yet been gained.

This question of interpretation is important, for on it turns the question of whether the anxiety inherent in these attitudes is a result of inadequate identification of the goal or conversely. A literal interpretation of the vertigo metaphor applied to the attitudes described prescribes the latter, that is that the wrong identifications are (more or less) deliberately adhered to, even though they are admitted to be wrong, because the truth is too hard to bear. But although the spiritless person and perhaps also the immediate genius might, may with some plausibility, be described as persons who have been to the brink and stepped back from it (thus the immediate genius is one who is capable of the deeper reflection of guilt but avoids it), it would be much less plausible to say of the supposedly spiritually more advanced religious genius that his failure was, in fact, a refusal to accept a truth that he had already glimpsed. Having turned away from the world, he has no 'finiteness' to grab hold of. In general one might prefer to treat the vertigo metaphor as even more of a metaphor than we have so far assumed. It is, after all, an abstract subject, the spirit, not the embodied subject of consciousness, of which it is said that it 'would posit the synthesis' but then lays hold of finiteness to steady itself; and we could interpret the reference to the spirit here as an indirect way of referring to the embodied subject's growing inability to associate itself exclusively with 'external' reality. The pre-threshold stages could be understood not as recoilings from the threshold insight, but as more or less approximating premonitions of where the dissociation with the external is leading. The corresponding anxieties would then, as in the former interpretation, be due to the inadequate ways of grasping the true relationship to the more-than-bodily source of identity, and not the converse.

There are two further points. First, anxiety is not a contradictory state of mind, only an ambivalent one. Haufniensis describes it as being 'dialectically determined' by something outside it (fate, guilt, or the elusive object of bashfulness).[95] It is only from the higher post-threshold point of view of spirit that the states in question are said to be contradictory. Thus it is only from this point of view that the sexual can be called 'that monstrous contradiction that the immortal spirit is characterized as sexual difference [*genus*]', a contradiction which Haufniensis says is *expressed* in the pre-threshold erotic consciousness, and also in the 'deep shame which *conceals* this [contradiction] and does not dare to understand it'.[96] A person's first glimpse of this contradiction, incidentally, is said to be the first 'positing of the synthesis' (of temporal and eternal) and thus the beginning of man's true ethical history.[97] The general point here is that characterizations of pre-threshold states of anxiety as contradictions are not phenomenological but diagnostic. What the phenomenological descriptions express is, on the contrary, an apparent or attempted unity of really incompatible terms. The inadequacy of the pagan's 'fate' is its 'unifying' of the two incompatible terms 'necessity and chance'.[98] From the inadequate erotic point of view, beauty is 'the unity of the physical and the corporeal',[99] while the spiritual description is that it is 'at once beauty and the comical', for from this higher vantage-point the psychical and corporeal are no longer compatible. In order to become so they must now be 'sustained by spirit'. Still, all these descriptions of pre-threshold anxiety do indeed assume that the higher point of view represents the position towards which the subject's striving tends, and there is some basis for calling the tendency in the fashionable sense a 'dialectical one'. Just as in the historical materialist account of social evolution, according to which the emergence of an authentic social reality is preceded by a stage in which necessary components in that reality, e.g. the socialization of the work force, emerge, but not yet in their authentic context, so here the allegedly authentic ethical reality is preceded by a stage in which a necessary part of that reality, guilt, emerges but not yet in its proper context; and is itself preceded by a stage in which, though guilt is incomprehensible — you cannot become guilty by *fate*[100] — the idea of religion is virtually present. The motive force in the tendency, on the other hand, is presumably the urge to 'unify', to bring the bodily and more-than-bodily together, to see some aspect of the former as an 'expression' of the latter, even when these are incapable of being unified except within the category of spirit. It is, furthermore, important to stress that for Kierkegaard the authentic reality is precisely a *unity*; a unity of body and mind 'sustained' or encompassed by spirit. It is not one in which the temporal world, the bodily, and the sexual are put aside in favour of an ascetic ideal. The task, as Haufniensis puts it, is 'to win [the sexual] into conformity with the category of the spirit'.[101] What one leaves behind is not one's human nature, but the various inadequate ways of grasping its relationship to its more-than-natural identity.

The second point again concerns the vertigo metaphor. The spirit is said to recoil after gazing down into its own 'possibility'. Now this latter term, too, has both phenomenological and diagnostic applications. The latter again describe what is true from the higher point of view, that which the subject's actual anxiety merely 'expresses', as when Haufniensis says that anxiety itself is 'an expression of the perfection of human nature'.[102] From the phenomenological point of view 'possibility' is an indeterminate concept definable only in such very general terms as 'corresponding with the future' or 'being able'.[103] But just how wide a concept is it? Is it restricted, for example, to the idea of modes of spiritual growth, of positive development? Or does it include the possibility of *failing* to grow? More fundamentally, does it include the possibility of there being in fact no basis for the idea of spiritual growth at all? No God? No eternal qualification? No spirit, even? In view of the fact that 'possibility' occurs in the definition of 'anxiety', anxiety being the possibility of freedom, or its appearance before itself,[104] the questions can be rephrased: Can the failure to grow spiritually, and even the ultimate illusoriness of the whole notion of spiritual growth, be objects of Kierkegaardian anxiety?

As for the first, if failure to grow means failure to achieve the unity of the corporeal and the psychical, however inadequately grasped and at any stage of development, then the answer must be yes. This is precisely the failure feared by the pagan, the Jew of Judaism, and the two geniuses. If it means specifically *ethical* growth, then this applies to post-threshold anxiety, but only to that, for it is only here that the question of growth takes its properly ethical form. But the second part of the question is not so easily answered. Does Haufniensis allow that one can be anxious in the face of the possibility of there being no basis at all for the notion of human growth in Kierkegaard's quasi-Hegelian sense? No cognitive superiority in the higher point of view? From the stand-point of Kierkegaard's (Climacus's) epistemology this must certainly be reckoned a possibility. But one might think that because Kierkegaard assumes a theory of spiritual emergence in the psychological works, this latter possibility will find no place in his account of anxiety. This, however, would be wrong. In fact, if one reads both on and between the lines, the possibility of man's non-spirituality in the sense of there being no basis for the notion of spiritual emergence seems to play an essential part in the account. Not only in the sense that the account explicitly diagnoses acceptance of the possibility as a form of despair,[105] but also in so far as serious entertainment of the nihilistic possibility seems to be regarded as a necessary preliminary *to* faith and spirituality. This at least is how the final chapter of *Anxiety* on the educative function of anxiety can be read. Anxiety can acquire this function only when the individual 'knows more thoroughly than a child knows its ABC that it can demand absolutely nothing of life, and that horror, perdition, annihilation, live next door to every man'. 'Can' acquire because, in addition to being 'honest towards possibility', one needs faith. The point, however, is that before one can properly be said to have faith, and thus 'become spirit', one must have realized that 'in possibility all things are equally possible'.[106]

Earlier 'possibility' is defined as the active 'being able' (anxiety being that 'intermediate determinant' in the transition from possibility to actuality which logicians do not have to bother with).[107] Here, however, the possibilities must include sufferings, in other words restrictions that may be placed on the subject's (agent's) goals. In this context 'possibility' is broadly conceived in opposition to 'finitude'. These are two 'schools' only the former of which 'educates' in the way necessary.[108] It is tempting to equate 'possibility' here with Heidegger's 'das Nichts'.[109] If correct this would mean that we should understand Kierkegaard as referring to the contrast, genuinely made, between the existence of finite things and the background against which, in a certain mood which Heidegger also calls anxiety, we see 'that they are things and not nothing',[110] a mood which provokes the question, 'How is there anything at all *rather than* nothing?' One notes that just as Heidegger sees this mood of anxiety as resulting in a new apprehension of 'the things that are', an educative apprehension that sets into relief, against the alternative of there being nothing, the usually unquestioned fact that there are things at all, so Haufniensis speaks of the 'pupil of possibility' as one who can reappraise the finite world from the point of view of the infinite.[111] Heidegger (who follows Kierkegaard in distinguishing anxiety from fear)[112] might also accept Haufniensis's account of the educative function of anxiety as that of 'searching out everything and frightening out of [one] the finite and petty',[113] for Heidegger sees human freedom as a 'passionate self-assured, anxious freedom to death',[114] a vision of life as a whole unimpeded by short-term concerns and 'self-forgetfulness'. Haufniensis differs from Heidegger, however, in finding the educative advantage of the experience of anxiety in its propelling the 'pupil' in the direction of faith, in its setting him in the direction of the infinite 'whither he would go'.[115] In fact, it is only 'by the aid of faith' that anxiety is 'absolutely educative, consuming as it does all finite aims and discovering all their deceptions'.[116] For Haufniensis, anxiety's insight is into the status of finite *goals*, not, as with Heidegger, things. And the insight has an ethical significance only if the pupil selects the contrasting background where everything is possible, the equivalent of the Heideggerian nothing, as the focus of his ethical attention, in other words as the realm of his specifically *developmental* possibilities.

But what now about post-threshold anxiety? So far we have only followed anxiety to the door of the ethical, not followed it into the ethical. But does Kierkegaardian psychology allow us to do that? Let us read the vertigo metaphor in full: anxiety, it says, is

the dizziness of freedom which arises when the spirit would posit the synthesis, and freedom now looks down into its own possibility, and then lays hold of the finite to steady itself. In this vertigo freedom succumbs. *Further than this psychology cannot and will not go*. In that very moment everything is changed, and when freedom raises itself again it sees that it is guilty. Between these two moments lies the leap, which no science has explained or can explain.[117]

But even if science cannot explain the leap, Kierkegaard's book goes on quite explicitly to describe states of anxiety which occur after the leap. How can that be so, given the claim italicized above? Recall also the claim that with the leap there vanishes that ambiguity which makes anxiety a suitable topic for psychology. And then again, Haufniensis's clear definition of anxiety as 'freedom's appearance before itself in *possibility*';[118] since that possibility has now presumably been replaced by the actuality, the 'intermediate determinant', anxiety itself, should thus have slipped into the subject's past.

Haufniensis's not very laymanlike explanation of why his simple psychological deliberation should continue past the threshold stage is hard to grasp. On the one hand, he seems to be saying that, since the reality which has emerged is sin, it is not really real because sin has in its turn to be 'annulled' and this constitutes a further possibility;[119] while on the other, he writes as though once sin is there, the subject is not *in* a state of sin but repeatedly enters into it, so that this old possibility is still part of a state 'predisposing' to sin and thus amenable to psychological description. But whatever the technicalities, the conscious subject is understandably still prone to anxiety — indeed to two kinds of anxiety: anxiety in the face of evil and anxiety in the face of good, the latter condition also bearing the name 'the demonic'.[120] Haufniensis's descriptions largely anticipate the later account by Anti-Climacus in *Sickness*, and are in fact descriptions of the conditions Anti-Climacus calls 'despair' — various ways, tricks of sophistry and self-deception, by which the subject contrives to shun its freedom. For instance, it flirts with sin instead of seriously trying to get rid of it, making do with remorse, which merely 'delays' the action 'ethics requires', and becomes itself an object of remorse![121] These manoeuvres represent anxiety in the face of evil and as such, from a higher point of view, represent the individual as being 'in the good' In the demonic configuration, on the other hand, the subject is 'in evil' and is anxious in the face of good. This inherently complex condition (Haufniensis describes it as 'ambiguous' but presumably not in the way of pre-threshold anxiety)[122] involves all three terms in the synthesis: body, soul, and spirit. The demonic subject puts up defences against the good, protecting his evil identity with a brittle barrier that shuts out the good, thus making his sin into a personal strength, and inventing the 'sin' of being or doing or welcoming good. Haufniensis concludes his chapter on post-threshold anxiety with a typology and specification of the ways in which the subject who is anxious in the face of the good 'loses' its freedom: by procrastination, indolence, shiftless curiosity, joining the bandwagon, self-deception, affectation, superciliousness, and so on;[123] in short, attitudes that protect the subject from the certitude (*Vished*) (requiring choice) and inwardness the combination of which forms the proper attitude to ethics, namely 'seriousness' (*Alvor*); though Haufniensis characteristically warns that already in trying to *define* this notion one is entering into the triviality of abstraction.[124]

4 Despair and its cure

In a rare reference in *Anxiety* to the 'self' Haufniensis says that the genuine (*egentlige*) self is first posited by the qualitative leap. His point is to deny that there could be such a thing prior to the threshold insight into the nature of good and evil.[125] But Haufniensis does not tie the notion of a self in with the concepts which form the framework of his discussion, in particular that of the 'synthesis'. Anti-Climacus, the pseudonymous author of *The Sickness unto Death* does just that. In an opening passage, sometimes regarded as a deliberate parody of the Hegelian style but in effect a neat, though spare, definition of the place of 'self' in the synthesis (now enlarged to comprise all three of the main polarities), we read:

> The human being is a synthesis of infinity and finitude, of
> temporality and eternity, of freedom and necessity. . . .
> A synthesis is a relation between two [factors] . Considered
> in this way the human being is not yet a self. . . . In the
> relation between two [factors] the relation [itself] is the
> third [factor] as a negative entity [*Eenhed*] , and the
> [other] two relate themselves to the relation, and in
> the relation to the relation; this is the way in which the
> relation between soul and body is a relation when soul is
> the determining category [*under Bestemmelsen Sjel*] . If,
> on the other hand, the relation relates itself to itself, then
> this relation is the positive third [factor] , and this is the self.[126]

In *Anxiety* we were told that the synthesis is achieved in the 'instant' (the instant is eternity in time); and that the synthesis is first 'posited' by spirit when spirit posits itself. Spirit is now said to be the self ('Man is spirit. But what is spirit? Spirit is the self'); and the ideal of reconciliation against which Anti-Climacus matches failure to become a self, in other words despair, is one in which the self is a fact about a relation *in* the synthesis ('The self is a relation which relates itself to its own self, or it is that in the relation [which accounts for its being the case] that the relation relates itself to its own self; the self is not the relation but [consists in the fact] that the relation relates itself to its own self').[127] In order for there to be a self the relation between finite and infinite must exemplify a 'positive unity' in which 'the relation [between them] relates itself to its own self', and not the 'negative unity' of body and soul in which each of the two terms relates itself to the relation, which *is* then the third term. In plainer language, the Kierkegaardian self is not to be identified with the relation between soul and body; for then the self would be a merely dependent factor, mirroring the interplay of the other two with each other and with the environment. Kierkegaard's self is a controlling rather than a controlled or controllable factor, this being the respect in which it is said properly to belong to the category of spirit.

But 'a relation which relates itself to its own self (that is to say, a self) must either have constituted itself or have been constituted by another'. To continue:

It is true that, if this relation which relates itself to its own
self is constituted by another, the relation is the third
[factor], but this relation, the third [factor], is in turn a
relation relating itself to that which constituted the whole
relation. . . . Such a *derived, constituted*, relation is the
human self, a relation which relates itself to its own self,
and in relating itself to its own self relates itself to *another*.[128]

If this were not so there would be only one form of despair properly so called, namely 'not willing to be one's own self . . . willing to get rid of oneself'. It would not be possible for there to be a second kind of despair which is willing to be oneself, or as this second kind is more perspicuously defined, 'wanting to be constituted in and by oneself'. The formula, 'the self is constituted by another', is

the expression of the fact that the self cannot of itself
attain and remain in equilibrium and rest by itself, but only
by relating itself to that power which constituted the
whole relation.[129]

The second form of despair is either open defiance of that power or the denial of its existence.[130] The defiance is open because this form of despair is only possible for a subject that has come so far as to conceive itself as an infinite self. Instead of relating this infinitely conceived self to the power in which both it and the 'necessity and limitations' of its 'perfectly definite' concrete self are rooted, the subject exploits its consciousness of being an infinite self, i.e. a self not bound by temporal criteria of identity and achievement, to 'refashion the whole thing, in order to get out of it in this way a self such as [it] wants to have'.[131] The extreme form of this despair is the devil's defiance, for the devil is 'sheer spirit' and so 'absolute consciousness and transparency'. In the devil there is 'no obscurity which might serve as a mitigating excuse, so his despair is the most absolute defiance' — the 'maximum of despair'.[132]

Why should it be despair or defiance on the part of the self to refuse to acknowledge a power over it? Is it because it knows the power exists all the same? Or is it because it recognizes that the very existence of such a power is a prerequisite of equilibrium and rest? In other words is Anti-Climacus merely telling believers in a transcendent God that they will despair if ever they gainsay that God, or is he saying something of quite general significance: namely that, in approaching the transparency of sheer spirit, consciousness realizes that the unity it has sought ever since it emerged from immediacy and first sensed its separation from the world can only be achieved by acknowledging its dependence upon a transcendent being? In saying that the self can only achieve equilibrium and rest by relating itself to 'that power', and not in general to *a* power, Anti-Climacus seems clearly to be advancing the more parochial thesis which already assumes the power's existence. But then Anti-Climacus is a representative of the higher point of view, in fact a Christian in the Kierkegaardian sense; if he was to make the general point one might well *expect* him to express it as a believer would. It would, furthermore, be radically inconsistent with Kierkegaard's view and attitude to have anyone, let alone Anti-Climacus, imply that one should become a Christian *in order to* avoid despair. That would make belief in God a remedy for a preconstituted disequilibrium, whereas the whole of Kierkegaard's work presupposes a preconstituted *assumption* of a 'highest good' or unity, to which despair only gradually becomes an accompaniment as, with consciousness's increasing transparency, this assumption's implications and difficulties become increasingly evident. Kierkegaard's subject begins as a naïve believer in 'that power' which constitutes it. It is only later, at the end of a dialectical development, that the subject finds it has to choose between that strenuous version of its constitution and the easier but despairing one. In effect, then, the wider thesis is presupposed. Only one who can refer to 'that power', i.e. a believer, is in a position to establish the unity, or harmony, or equilibrium, or rest, the absence of which is despair. In other words the transparent consciousness whose options Anti-Climacus lays before it is Hegel's unhappy consciousness.

It is illuminating, plausible, and I believe correct, to read *Sickness* as Kierkegaard's account of the emergence of a self out of the opacity of immediacy into the clear and merciless transparency of the unhappy consciousness where nothing can save consciousness from despair at its mere particularity but surrender to God. The crucial transition, the break with immanence that occurs in advancing from the A- to the B-position, presupposes the individual's interest in an eternal happiness, and in his analysis of the transition Climacus has assumed that there is an objective basis for this interest, even though the analysis denies that it can be understood or known (in Hegelian philosophy being understood would be in principle synonymous with being known). Faced with this impossibility the individual either follows reason and is unhappy, or believes against reason, and thus becomes happy. Normally the former alternative would count as a form of despair, provided the interest is retained and strong enough. But neither of Anti-Climacus's two main classes of despair coincide with the unhappy choice of the rationalist. In both of them the interest is not only retained but in one or another way assumed to be fulfilled. In one form of despair the individual gives its essentially trivial undertakings in the (finite) world the 'infinite interest and importance' that they must really derive from a transcendent source; in the other the individual assumes the capacity to create its own (eternal) nature.

Despair is described in *Sickness* as 'the incongruity [*Misforhold*] in the relation comprising a synthesis'.[133] The incongruity, it should be noted, is not the fact that the terms in the synthesis stand opposed to one another; that they do so is a given fact of existence once spirit is posited. And in any case, it is 'not up to the existing [individual] to make existence out of finitude and infinity [by putting them together], but being himself composed of [these] to *become, qua* existing, one of them [namely infinite] ....'.[134] Furthermore, '[if] the synthesis [itself] were the incongruity, despair would not exist, for despair would then be something inherent in human nature as such . . . something that happened to man, something he suffered, like a sickness . . . or death'.[135] It is essential to Kierkegaard's view that there be an alternative to despair, that despair — unlike a normal sickness — is an option that the individual chooses, or at least remains in by default. So the incongruity is a feature not of the framework, of the synthesis, but of the *self*. More exactly, it is that whereby this 'third factor' fails to establish itself, or be 'posited' as a self, fails to 'relate itself to itself', and thus to become the 'positive' third factor in the synthesis. As Anti-Climacus puts it in conclusion of the opening section:

> The incongruity of despair is not a simple incongruity
> but an incongruity in a relation which relates itself to its
> own self and is constituted by another, so that the incongruity

in that self-relation reflects itself infinitely in the relation to
the power which constituted it.

Anti-Climacus caps this with his formula for the cure for despair —
for the condition in which it is 'completely eradicated': 'by relating
itself to its self and by willing to be itself the self is grounded
transparently in the power which posited it'.[136]

Sickness is in two parts, one devoted to despair as sickness, a
pervasive or general sickness, and the other to despair as sin. The
first part contains a catalogue and classification of forms of despair
under two main aspects, one in which only the factors of the
synthesis are taken into account, that is finitude and infinitude,
possibility and necessity, but not consciousness itself, and the
other in which despair is looked at specifically with regard to and
from the point of view of consciousness. We shall confine our
brief survey to the latter aspect, under which again despair is
classified into two main types: first, despair at not willing to be
oneself, the despair of weakness,[137] and second, the despair of
defiance which we have already noted, the despair of willing
despairingly to be oneself (one's *own* self). The main forms of
despair under these two latter headings correspond to states of
the emergence of consciousness of the self. The crucial expression
is 'infinite consciousness of the self',[138] and the formula for all
despair properly so called is 'despair about the eternal and over
oneself'.[139] The accounts given under the two main headings can
be briefly summarized as follows.

(1)   In despair at not willing to be oneself Anti-Climacus includes
a condition in which there is as yet no infinite consciousness of
self, hence properly speaking no self, and therefore no consciousness of what despair is or of the fact that the condition is one of
despair: i.e. of not willing to be one's self. Here the (to use a neutral
term) subject's identity is fixed by outside circumstances, and
merely reflects the contingent availability of specific threats and
enticements. The subject is in 'immediate' coherence (*Sammen-
heng*) with the other, i.e. whatever thing or person threatens or
entices. There is no third factor mediating between the world and
this passive subject. Its 'dialectic' is accordingly 'the agreeable and
the disagreeable' and its concepts 'good fortune, misfortune,
fate'.[140]

Though this not-yet self despairs, its despair is not despair proper.
For 'to despair is to lose the eternal',[141] and since it does not yet
have the eternal it cannot lose it: 'of this [it] does not speak, does
not dream'. However, despair does in a manner of speaking operate

in such a subject, though it has to be provoked by outward circumstances, as indeed everything must in the case of such a person. What
the subject despairs of is being deprived of its 'immediate being' —
either as a whole or, 'if [one] is at least somewhat reflective, that
part of it to which [one] especially clings'. The shock of deprivation
can be induced by any excess of good or bad fortune, 'for it is a
fact that immediacy as such is immensely fragile, and every *quid
nimis* which calls upon it to reflect brings it to despair'.[142]

However, although he speaks of his despair as loss of the earthly,
this is not what it is. As always it is loss of the eternal. Anti-
Climacus says that this loss can take any of three progressively
'lower' forms: despair at not wanting to be *oneself*, despair at not
wanting to be *a self*, and lowest of all, despair in the form of wanting to be another.[143] 'Despair' is not just another name for the
wanting or not-wanting that has these topics. It is the mood in
which, in view of the topics, such wanting or not-wanting occurs;
a mood of not wanting to proceed where the positive possibility
lies. But in the lowest form there is as yet no consciousness of this
possibility; here the subject wants to be *another* because it has not
yet acquired a notion of itself as the self that it might wish *not* to
be. Nevertheless, wanting to be another is an expression of, or
unspecific awareness of, the fact that there is room for a self
mediating between subject and world. Wanting to fill it with
another person or personality merely indicates that the room is
empty.

(2)   The highest of these three forms of the first kind of despair
corresponds to anxiety in the 'more self-conscious' individual.
Though still a passive form, it can be induced by reflection and
not only by external provocation.[144] This first self-reflection is the
beginning of 'the act of discrimination whereby the self becomes
aware of itself as something essentially different from the environment, from externality and its effect upon it [the self]'.[145] But
now, ready to accept its self, it 'stumbles on difficulties'. The
breach with immediacy is deepened by some traumatic event,
some real or imagined difficulty in connection with the 'composition of the self'. The subject now understands that 'letting the
[genuine] self go is a pretty serious business', that it would be
ludicrous to want to be another,[146] and that one can afford to lose
much in the world, including new self-descriptions, without losing
the self.[147] Whatever the difficulty, it demands a breach with
immediacy as a whole. But for this the subject has as yet too little
self- or ethical reflection; it does not yet have that consciousness
of a self which is

195

gained by the infinite abstraction from everything outward, this — in contrast to the clothed self of immediacy — naked, abstract self which is the first form of the infinite self and the forward impulse in the whole process whereby a self infinitely takes possession of its actual self with all its difficulties and advantages.[148]

The subject here, therefore, succumbs to the difficulties and abandons the consciousness of that self for which the difficulties arise, but retaining 'ownership', or the right to return if the difficulties should vanish or are removed. But if there is no change, it 'swings away completely from the inward direction' and looks for an identity in what is called 'life, the real active life', keeping the self-reflection in the background and eventually forgetting it. The subject has now gone in the opposite direction to that which it 'ought to have followed in order to become truly a self',[149] and the problem of the self in a deeper sense becomes a 'false door' at the back of its mind, false because there is nothing behind it. Such a person 'accepts what in his language he calls a self', e.g. abilities, talents, etc.; he is a 'worthy', a Christian in Christendom, just as in paganism he would be a pagan and in Holland a Dutchman.[150] True, he raises the question of immortality from time to time; but somewhat incongruously in view of the fact that for this self it can have absolutely no relevance. The condition is one of spiritlessness.

This 'despair over the earthly' (and 'ethical stupidity')[151] is the commonest form of despair, since few graduate to the deeper (or 'higher')[152] form in which one lives in 'the category of the spirit'.[153] It is a gross mistake to think of it as the prerogative of youth, something one grows out of. Despair is not sickness unto adulthood; quite the contrary, it is something people grow into as they settle down into spiritually sterile adult complacency.[154] The complacency is sterile because out of this shallow despair, supported by forgetfulness, it is impossible for the 'metamorphosis to occur in which the consciousness of the eternal in the self breaks through so that the battle could begin which either intensifies despair to a higher form or leads to faith'.[155] In order to deepen one's despair, so that at the very depths 'the spirit-life might break through', one must retrace one's steps out of this impasse. However, for further progress there must not only be sufficient depth of despair but also a transition from despair over some particular earthly thing or project to despair of the earthly as such. 'When with infinite passion the self by means of imagination despairs over something earthly, this infinite passion transforms this particular, this something, into the earthly *in toto*, that is to say, the category

196

of totality inheres in and belongs to the despairer.'[156] It belongs to the despairer because it is his *self* that thereby acquires a comprehensive separation from the earthly as such. As soon as the

> distinction (between despairing over the earthly and over something earthly) is essentially affirmed, there is also an essential advance made in the consciousness of the self. This formula, 'to be in despair over the earthly', is a dialectical first expression of the next form of despair.[157]

(3) It is only indirectly that 'despair over the earthly' satisfies the formula for all despair. The formula is: 'despair about the eternal and over oneself'. The grounds for saying that it does satisfy it all the same is that the importance vested in the earthly is borrowed from the eternal for which it therefore serves as a substitute. But in this next form of despair the formula is satisfied directly. The self now grasps that there is indeed something eternal in it.[158] This, however, only deepens the despair. The reason is threefold: first, the self now sees that its investment in the earthly was not only misplaced, but an expression of its own weakness;[159] second, to compensate for this weakness it would have to make a corresponding investment in the eternal, but being aware of its weakness it is more disposed to hate itself than to find the strength to take the demanding steps of humbling itself in faith, as this reinvestment requires; and yet, third, it cannot overcome the problem by escaping from itself, for now there is 'too much [of] a self' for it to be forgotten in spiritlessness.[160] Which also means that the door in the background marked 'self', which for the spiritless person was a 'false door' with nothing behind it, is now a real door and behind it 'sits, as it were, the self occupied or passing the time with not wanting to be itself, and yet enough of a self to love itself'.[161] This self behind the door *loves* itself in so far as it conceives itself as having a quite different value from its worldly precursors. Significantly, now that the self and the earthly are set clearly apart from each other, the self also knows that losing the eternal is losing its self; there is no refuge in an earthly or quasi-earthly self-description.

The loss of the earthly comes like a slap in the face, as if here too despair was provoked by outward circumstance. But in fact this despair is 'not merely suffering';[162] it is the self's active defence against the weakness it recognizes in the earlier form of its passive despair, and now the self more or less deliberately shuns further knowledge of itself. But because it cannot forget its new-found self, the despairing subject acquires a secretive relationship to it.

197

It sees it as something worth treasuring, much superior to mere immediacy (Anti-Climacus says that this form of despair, closed-inness or introversion (*Indesluttethed*), is 'the direct opposite of immediacy'),[163] but only entertains these snobbish thoughts in private; to talk about it or have others talk about it is not to do it justice; indeed it is to cheapen it. The weakness is also admitted privately, but the subject stands sufficiently outside his private admission to take pride in the very admission itself.[164] The combi-nation of weakness and pride lead him into wanting to cultivate his self in private. The locked door now becomes a symbol for the need for solitude. But it does have a positive side; it is an acknow-ledgment that the self is still there to be resorted to.

This form of despair is rare but not for that reason conspicuous. In fact, it is very well concealed. In answer to his own question: Is this introvert to be found amongst us, or is he removed from the world of reality, in the wilderness, the cloister, or the mad-house?, Anti-Climacus says: Yes, of course, he's amongst us, going about just like anyone else, dressed as you or I. Indeed acting like you or I. The introvert's transactions with his or her more than worldly self are so jealously guarded that not even the guarding of them is allowed to manifest itself in the world. One might say that, so long as the self remains a private asylum to be resorted to in secrecy, the despairer is unlikely to attract the attention that might lead to his being pressed into a public one.

There are now three possibilities. There can be a radical revol-ution (*Omvæltning*) that puts the despairer on the road to faith. This first possibility Anti-Climacus does not enlarge upon. Or, second, the despairer can 'mark time'. If marking time continues then suicide is a distinct possibility. But by confiding in someone the despairer may avoid this, although 'there are examples of introverts who are brought to despair precisely because they have acquired a confidant'. Thus the logical solution to the strains of secrecy may conflict with the defensive functions secrecy is supposed to serve. Suicide may be the consequence after all. There are also precedents for eliminating the confidant, and we are even asked to imagine the case of a demonic tyrant 'who [feels] the need of talking to a fellow-man about his torment, and in this way [consumes] successively a whole lot of men; for to be his confidant [is] certain death'.[165] Marking time, however, culminates in the less concrete, third, 'poetic' possibility of the agonizing 'self-contradiction' of the demonic man who needs a confidant but cannot bear having one.

This third possibility can take two forms. Either, the despair 'potentiates itself to a higher form [of introversion]' or else the despairer breaks down the barrier and 'plunges into life' leaving 'only too clear a trace' of his restless spirit in big enterprises or sensual indulgence, even debauchery. The despairer wants desperately to return to immediacy, but cannot because he is burdened with the embarrassing consciousness of his infinite self and knows that sensuality is in open conflict with it.[166] Of these two courses − let us call them the entrepreneurial and the profligate − the former leads to defiance, 'the first expression of which' is 'despair over one's weakness'.[167] Anti-Climacus does not say why the latter does not also lead to defiance, nor what other form of despair the plunge into profligacy takes. This cannot be because the plunge into profligacy constitutes a *successful* return to an earlier stage where defiance is not called for: according to the general view there cannot be any successful return from transparent consciousness to a former, more opaque consciousness; the attempt involves duplicity or self-deceit. Perhaps it is because the profligate life is one from which the choice of the ethico-religious is more to be expected, either because the revolution required involves fewer impedimenta or because the lone profligate is more disposed than the public entrepreneur to undertake radical revolutions. Thus we might identify the profligate with 'A' of *Either/Or*, whose ethical prospects Kierkegaard presumably expects us to take seriously, for 'A' is portrayed as a person in whom the ethical is an, as yet, unrealized possibility.

5   Sin as defiance

The general view of spiritual development and default contained in the psychological works must be seen from the point of view of the later of the two works. The formal condition of spiritual completion is first clearly stated in *Sickness*'s prescription that the self must accept its constitution by a 'power' outside time. The alternative is despair, common to whose variations is the self's unwillingness to satisfy this condition. That is the case both before and after the self realizes that completion cannot be satisfied in temporal categories. In the latter case, the self's unwillingness to satisfy the condition takes the form of exploiting the realization that its own identity cannot be embraced in temporal categories by presuming to fix the criteria of this identity itself; the subject tries to 'refashion the whole thing, in order to get out of it in this way a self such as [it] wants to have'.[168] But it knows this will not provide completeness.

In its most general terms spiritual completion, for Kierkegaard, is the goal of a desire to belong as a temporal and particular being

199

to a not merely temporal order. The desire emerges in its most critical form when the self first realizes that the temporal order itself can manifest nothing but temporality, that it offers none of the consolations (or fears) that in immanentist, or humanist, life-views it is assumed to manifest and offer. It is important that the situation (as Kierkegaard sees it) be put in this way. The desire for completion does not emerge from the idea of belonging to an order *other* than the temporal once the self acquires a sense of not being simply temporal. That would be putting it the wrong way around; the idea, or at least the assumption, of belonging to the world as a whole has always been there, though in the beginning not as an explicit *idea* posed against its negation. For belonging to the world is the 'intentional' description of the subject's general frame of mind in the state of immediacy where it does not yet conceive of the world as a (limited) whole. Belonging becomes an explicit object of desire only when the embodied subject realizes that it cannot understand itself as belonging *ex officio* to the ultimate order of things, that whether there is any belonging is something it has to decide entirely on its own. The alternatives, or what the decision itself amounts to, first become clear in that transparent mode of consciousness in which the now 'naked' self grasps the absolute inability of location or achievement in nature and history to satisfy the longing. In this clear light the task, as Anti-Climacus presents it, is well defined and the options unmistakable: the self has to decide how it is (or is to be) constituted, how to 'relate itself to its own self', and 'a relation which relates itself to its own self . . . must either have constituted itself or have been constituted by another'.

By 'another' Kierkegaard does not, of course, mean another self or other selves, or the self's personal and impersonal environmental relationships, all of which we assume contribute to form personal and characterological identity. He means something outside time and nature. The decision is as to whether the self is to regard itself as the arbiter and creator of its own fundamental nature or whether these functions are to be seen to rest with a transcendent power. According to *Sickness* the former alternative, in its most transparent form, involves defiance. It is called 'absolute' despair. So the only way out of despair is to accept the latter alternative. In Anti-Climacus's theological terms the options correspond to sin and faith, and the claim is that they coincide with the presence and absence of despair.

Accordingly there should, as a matter of psychological fact, never be either despair *with* faith or a lack of despair *without* faith. Of these two correlations the former may seem uncontroversial, though it is surely questionable how completely Kierke-gaardian faith can rid the believer of despair without going over into the kind of self-deception that Kierkegaard would insist is incompatible with genuine faith. But, regarding the latter corre-lation, what would Kierkegaard say in the face of alleged cases of serenity despite outright rejection of the transcendental basis for spiritual completion? He might say that the despair was neverthe-less there, though concealed, repressed, implicit. But then the same might be said in connection with Kierkegaardian faith, and both sides would be exposed to the charge that they were making unfalsifiable assertions. But there is still a certain amount that Kierkegaard might say before exposing himself to that charge. He might say, for instance, that in some cases the serenity could be explained by the fact that the self had not yet divested itself of the comfortable attire of immediacy, had not in fact yet become what he would call a 'self', and so had not achieved that trans-parency of consciousness in which faith and defiance are patently terms in an exhaustive disjunction. He might even argue that, before they can become that, the subject must be in a certain frame of mind. What that frame of mind might be will be discussed in conclusion of this essay. But whatever the conclusions one draws here, it is surely undeniable that, in order for Kierkegaard's account of mental sickness and health to be credible, the notion of faith which the account links with the latter must be that of something from which some crucial advantage ensues, and despair must be grasped (by the despairer experienced) as something whose dis-advantages outweigh whatever strains faith puts on mind and body. It must surely also be the case that, in order to preserve its privi-leged position in the account, Christian belief must be assumed to offer advantages not otherwise available.

In fact, the pseudonym Anti-Climacus maintains that faith is not just an instrumental good, whose value consists in its being the only way out of an unavoidable, and intrinsic, evil; he says it is an intrinsic good, whose value even extends to despair itself, on the grounds that the latter is its necessary antecedent. Raising the question of whether despair is an advantage or a drawback, Anti-Climacus says:

> Regarded in a purely dialectical way, it is both. If one stuck
> to the abstract notion of despair, without thinking of any actual
> despairer, one might say that it is an immense advantage. The
> possibility of this sickness is man's advantage over the beast,
> and this advantage distinguishes him far more essentially than
> the erect posture, for it implies the infinite erectness or lofti-

ness of being spirit. The possibility of this sickness is man's
advantage over the beast; to be aware of this sickness is the
Christian's advantage over the natural man; to be healed of
this sickness is the Christian's bliss.[169]

This calls for some concluding comments. First, the possibility of
despair is man's advantage over the beast only to someone who
assumes that human perfection calls for a kind of growth to which
despair is an inevitable accompaniment. Clearly, despair is not
inherently advantageous, and without the assumption in question
we would surely have to consider the specifically human capacity
for despair disadvantageous and, were other things equal, its
postulated absence in biologically lower animals a decided merit
of their manner of existence. Rather than a sickness, at least in the
sense of a condition of abnormality in respect of a norm of human
health or perfection, it would be more appropriate to consider
despair the normal state of a fully-developed self-consciousness —
supposing, as may be by no means implausible, that a development
in the direction of the state of the self in which Anti-Climacus
describes the self as 'naked' and 'abstract' is natural for human
self-consciousness. Of course, it might be claimed that, though
both natural and normal, despair is nevertheless pathological in the
sense that it is unpleasant and therefore a state one should try to
avoid, irrespective of any ideal of specifically human health or
perfection; that one should try to reverse the development — in
Anti-Climacian terms, have the naked self put on some immediacy
again, or prevent selves from ever putting it off. But in that case
it would be the specifically human form of consciousness itself, its
ability and indeed tendency, to alienate itself from the world, that
we would be regarding as an imperfection, not a particular form of
this consciousness in respect of some healthy possibility inherent
in it. It is clearly this latter that Anti-Climacus has in mind.

So too when, in the second place, he observes that close attention
to the pathology of despair is the Christian's advantage over the
natural man. It is the Christian's acknowledgment of the possibility of a spiritual completion beyond despair that gives him a
perspective from which the self's reluctance to divest itself of
immediacy can be seen as sickness. The natural man has no reason
to give up immediacy, and yet, as the observant Christian is conceptually and psychologically equipped to see, his life in immediacy
is nevertheless a form of despair — a despair that becomes more
apparent, and which the self emerging out of immediacy therefore
becomes more intent on avoiding, the closer consciousness approaches the state of transparency.

Third, regarding the observation that to be healed of this sickness is the Christian's *bliss*, this latter term suggests an exceptional contentment among other contentments. But Anti-Climacus himself seems clearly to suggest that what he calls Christian bliss is the *only* form of contentment possible in the state of transparency where the clear-cut choice between despair as defiance (sin) and a state of harmonious reconciliation (faith) first appears. It is worth adding that the contentment that is to be secured by Kierkegaardian faith is very far from the ineffable peace promised by mystics and others in meditation. To enjoy their kind of bliss the self must become so denuded as to lose even its sense of individuality, its sense of *being* a self. The naked self of which Anti-Climacus speaks cannot go that far. It has to retain a sense of being a self in order to pose and answer the question of its constitution. To go beyond that might even count, in Anti-Climacus's book, as a form of despair. (In *The Concept of Irony* Kierkegaard talks of the Easterner who aims at the vegetative still-life of the plant.)[170]

Fourth, Anti-Climacus surely means what he says when he claims that it is the possibility of despair that is to man's advantage, not necessarily any actual case of despair. It would certainly be anomalous for him to claim that the despair of defiance (sin) was an advantage. But the fact that human beings are liable to sin could be counted an advantage in so far as that liability was a presupposition of the possibility of faith and thus salvation.

Finally, as far as this notion of defiance is concerned, this would be understood in various ways. If one accepts that an interest in human fulfilment, as conceived by Hegel or Kierkegaard, is fundamental to human psychology, the rational denial of its possibility will be a kind of defiance of human nature. In *Sickness*, however, defiance implies something more. It is defiance not of the self's own longing for completion, but of the supposed power in which the possibility of that completion is understood to reside. You cannot defy God without acknowledging God's existence, and the devil's 'absolute' defiance is not the denying but the usurping of the function of God. Similarly, in this extreme of despair a person accepts the terms of reference in which the ideal of spiritual completion is entertained but refuses to bow to the transcendent source of value, claims in fact to be able to operate within the same terms of reference without a 'God-relationship'. But then where would Kierkegaard place, say, a rationalist who rejects the terms of reference? Well, he might see in the rationalist's peace of mind a symptom of superficiality or 'spiritlessness'. In *Anxiety* Haufniensis, commenting on the notion of the educative role of 'possibility', says:

What I am saying here may strike many as obscure and foolish talk, because they pride themselves on never having been in anxiety. To this I would reply that one should certainly not be anxious of men and finite things, but only he who has undergone the anxiety of possibility is educated to have no anxiety, not because he can escape the horrors of life but because these always become weak by comparison with those of possibility. If, on the other hand, the speaker thinks that the great thing with him is that he has never been in anxiety, I will gladly introduce him to my explanation: that it is because he is very spiritless.[171]

Or he might see in the rationalist's peace of mind a Stoical resignation, betokening the deliberate abandonment of a fundamental human interest. In terms of Anti-Climacus's pathology of the self, both diagnoses would come under 'despair'. The former case presents no difficulties for Kierkegaard. On his view the spiritless rationalist's peace of mind is due to failure to appreciate the issue between a fundamental happiness or unhappiness. The framework is not accepted simply because the spiritless rationalist is not fully aware of the kind of need it could satisfy. But the latter case is different. Here the rationalist feels the need but rejects the framework because to accept it would be to countermand the dictates of reason. But then, since he does not accept the framework, he cannot accept the teleological interpretation of his state as that of one denying himself a unique advantage to which his despair is a necessary preliminary. Nor can he accept that his despair, if he admits to it — as he surely should, since the sense of being denied the satisfaction of a fundamental need *is* what is generally meant by a sense of despair — is something that should give way to faith in order for him to secure that supposedly unique advantage. But as we noted at the beginning of the chapter, Kierkegaard places his psychological authors firmly inside the framework. For them the religious viewpoint embraces a reality which offers the despairer not just his only way out, but also his unique and properly human advantage.

VI

Purity of Heart

Isn't despair simply double-mindedness? . . . Every
despairer has two wills, one that he tries in vain
wholly to follow, and one of which he tries wholly
to be quit.[1]

1   The acknowledged works

Kierkegaard has given a detailed, though compressed, account of
the pathology of the self. Nowhere in his writings, however, do we
find any correspondingly explicit account of that condition of the
self in which anxiety and despair are overcome. Superficially this
might seem a philosophically uninteresting fact, due to such contingent psychological circumstances as our author's morbid
fascination with subjective psychology, which has simply eclipsed
in his mind the less engaging topics of health and salvation; or a
pessimistic disbelief in the human ability to develop beyond anxiety
and despair, which has prevented him from seriously entertaining
that possibility as a live option.

If we look in the right place, however, we find that Kierkegaard
devotes considerably more space to the positive possibility than to
the negative. But the treatments of the two differ radically, and to
see why on Kierkegaard's assumptions this must be so is to recognize
that the absence of a similarly detailed account of the positive
condition is not a philosophically uninteresting fact. Pinpointing
the explanation is a crucial preliminary to an examination of
Kierkegaard's ethics: our topic in this and the following chapter.

Earlier, in our 'preview' in Chapter I, we described the psychological works as maps of developing attitudes and personality types
corresponding to consistent and successively unambiguous and

205

conscious renunciations of the choice of the ethical; refusals which are compliances with, and to that extent determined by, the pressures of human nature — or human psychosomatology. We also saw that in Kierkegaard's view it is always possible, however deeply one is subject to these pressures, to release oneself from them by making the ethical commitment. That commitment is a condition of psychological, moral, and personal (that is, individual) integrity. It is at least a necessary condition. Often Kierkegaard writes, however, as if it were also a sufficient condition, as if the choice were itself the end-goal of moral endeavour. This impression is reinforced by the fact that in the pseudonymous works, apart from insisting that the choice must be made, he is concerned almost exclusively with drawing attention to the sheer enormity of the decision and to the intellectual and psychological pressures preventing it.

One might easily suppose, therefore, that all a positive development amounts to is the removal of these obstacles; and consequently that although there is indeed a philosophical explanation for why there is no corresponding account of the positive state, it is a trivial one: beyond overcoming these obstacles there is no further development to account for.

The oddity of the idea of a decision forming the end rather than the beginning of a task should itself render this 'explanation' suspect. True, decisions are often difficult, especially, surely, one so momentous as 'choosing oneself' when this involves risking everything absolutely. And the preliminary agonizings may prove more tortuous than the outcome. But everyday experience tells us that important decisions more often mean agonizing beginnings than happy endings.[2] In fact, the realization of what we are letting ourselves in for can be one main obstacle to making them. And it is not just that common experience tells us that human frailty does not vanish at the touch of a positive decision; nor simply that the kinds of pressure which postpone a decision usually also contrive, once it is made, to delay its consummation. The point can equally be that in making constructive decisions we are often exposing ourselves to whole *new* ranges of problems and pressures.

Take, for example, the professional activity of the contemporary scientist or philosopher — a person who for the sake of argument we may assume to be dedicated to the rational pursuit of an enlightenment. Imagine that it is a pursuit to which, at one time or other, the scientist or philosopher has consciously dedicated himself. Suppose, further, that prior to dedicating himself he had serious misgivings about his ability to engage in such a pursuit, or moments of doubt as to whether some mentally less strenuous activity might not be more rewarding, even times when he was tempted to dismiss the whole project as worthless — perhaps, he subsequently reflects, so as to avoid having to admit to possible incompetence in such a prestigious activity. At least let us assume that the decision, when it came, was itself no mean personal triumph.

But then think of what comes after! Whatever significance one attaches to the eventual commitment, most people would surely say that the true test is still to come, and that the measure of this person's achievement is the degree to which he or she manages in practice to conform with the ideals to which he or she is dedicated. In fact, failing a certain conspicuous degree of conformity, doubt may even be cast on the authenticity of the dedication. But there can be another doubt too, and this is the case we shall concentrate on, namely doubt as to whether the principles in question have been adequately or correctly grasped. Thus, if what satisfies a scientist as a rational hypothesis looks altogether too speculative, or if what he counts as evidence falls consistently below generally accepted empirical standards, we may feel tempted to conclude that he has simply failed to appreciate what the rational and the evident amount to in a scientific context.

For all his preoccupation with the initial ethical commitment, Kierkegaard, too, is conscious both of the need to consummate that commitment and of the pressure working against it. And if we bear the scientific analogy in mind we can begin to appreciate why the positive development is not the subject of a descriptive treatment (as in *Anxiety* and *Sickness*) or a discursive or dialectical one (as in *Fragments* and *Postscript*), but of a critical and cautionary approach. Kierkegaard's ethical writings are in the form of what he calls 'edifying' (*oppbyggende*) and (later) 'Christian' 'discourses' (*Taler*). These can be regarded as similar in spirit to the professional criticism scientists direct at each other's work for falling below accepted scientific standards. This means that Kierkegaard addresses his ethical writings to readers who have already adopted the goal, or the goal as they so far conceive it. He is speaking, one could say, to his ethical colleagues, and not, therefore, for instance, to people who would ask for arguments in support of the ethical ideal itself. That is why the edifying discourses are not pseudonymous. Kierkegaard now addresses himself to his reader as one individual to another (the discourses are dedicated to 'that individual [*hiin Enkelte*]', on the mutually interesting topic of ethics, and in the mood proper to that subject, namely 'seriousness').[3]

Now it is, of course, generally the case that the commitment a person actually makes to something is to that thing as that person conceives it. But since the ordinary limitations of human understanding and the capacity for self-deception, evasion, and illusion can hardly be thought to vanish by virtue of commitment alone, it is reasonable to assume that the committed individual will tend to have a less than adequate conception of the implications of his commitment, and quite natural to suppose that the practice he takes to comply with his commitment falls short of what a literal understanding of it would demand. Not now because of any conscious backsliding on the part of the moral agent: for here Kierkegaard is only concerned with the ethical interpretation of actions and attitudes which the moral agent himself regards as satisfying the ethical ideal; but rather because it is the moral agent's conception of the goal that decides the nature of his avowedly ethical practice. The 'edifying' task which Kierkegaard sets himself is therefore that of bringing to light the distance between the professed moral agent's own grasp of ethical practice and the kind of practice actually demanded by his ideal.

Thus it would be wrong to equate 'edifying' here with 'moralizing' pure and simple. Kierkegaard insists that his discourses are not sermons.[4] He is neither telling his reader authoritatively what is right nor exhorting him to be more attentive to what he already knows to be right.[5] The point is rather that the reader, even though he has in principle accepted the ideal, may still not see its full practical implications. The ethical writer's task might therefore be called conceptual, except that the grasp which Kierkegaard is aiming to elicit is not an abstract, theoretical grasp of the ideal, but a practical grasp, directly expressed in the kind of practice which the moral agent takes to comply with his goals. For Kierkegaard, a person's conception of his life-goals and his moral identity are very closely linked; in *Sickness* Anti-Climacus, talking of the self's 'measure' or 'standard' (*Maalestok*), says that 'that which is qualitatively [the self's] measure is ethically its goal' (*Maal*).[6] (The play on words is lost in translation.)

One way of describing the positive development, then, is to identify it as the progressive increase of the self's own measure of itself corresponding with a progressively adequate grasp of its true moral nature. Anti-Climacus, the pseudonymous expert on these matters, calls this true moral self the 'theological' self, and the scope of the positive development is shown clearly by the fact that the theological self has *God* as its measure.[7] Clearly, there is room for a range of levels of moral consciousness, and thus broad scope for moral improvement, even after the ethical course has been chosen.

Why then should the positive development call for a treatment so different from that given to the negative? A person who fails to make the ethical commitment is by this default a self-made victim of a predictable psychosomatic development, a negative 'dialectical' development the course, as well as the 'moments', of which are psychosomatic 'states'. That is, they include no 'spiritual' activity. Spiritual activity frees one from this psychosomatic development by bringing the determining factors in the development under a supratemporal control. A person who does make the ethico-religious commitment is therefore 'free' of that progression. A decisive factor is knowledge of the difference between good and evil. But once the despairing self has chosen the ideal, that factor – knowledge of good and evil – is no longer external to the person's chosen course; no longer the embarrassment to the self which it was when the anxious self had taken refuge in a psycho-somatic identity to which this knowledge was opposed. In other words, by deciding in favour of what it already knows to be the good, and thereby becoming 'spiritual', the self subordinates the psychosomatic to the absolute.

Our first point was that, in doing so, it nevertheless has a very long way to go. But it is important to grasp Kierkegaard's idea that the progression henceforth is not a psychosomatically determined one. Certainly, psychosomatic pressures are still being exerted, but provided the commitment remains, the main way in which they undermine self-development is by supporting a kind of conceptual complacency, a tendency to make do with a too congenial interpret-ation of the ethical ideal. Increasing clarity about the ideal should therefore be sufficient to lead to further progress. The ethical writer's project, consequently, is neither informative nor, in the ordinary sense, moralistic, but in a practical way conceptual. It is to apprise the reader of his or her moral shortcomings by eliciting a grasp of what is *really* required of the supratemporal goal.

One final point here. Commitment to the ethical ideal is not said to immunize one against anxiety and despair. Just as Kierke-gaard maintains that a saving decision in favour of the ethical is always possible for the despairing self, so also does he allow that, however far one has progressed as a moral agent, it is always possible to relapse *into* despair. Indeed, the depth of the despair one may fall into increases rather than decreases with moral progress. Of the 'theological' self it is said that because at this level the self has a greater consciousness of itself, it is also exposed to a correspondingly 'potentiated' degree of despair.[8] Not only that, since moral progress and greater consciousness of the self go together, and the latter entails greater awareness of the self's cognitive limitations, the moral paragon's commitment has to be correspondingly profounder, and is presumably therefore in greater danger of failing to be renewed. So unless moral progress is accompanied by an increasingly strong commitment, the truly moral self not only stands to fall further than lesser selves when commitment weakens, but is also more liable to such lapses in the first place.

2   The highest good

We recall the principal topic of Climacus's *Postscript*: the individual's relationship to Christianity, or how to become a Christian. In explaining his interest in this topic Climacus writes:

> I, Johannes Climacus, born in this city and now thirty years old, a common ordinary human being like most people, assume that there awaits me, no less than for a servant-girl or a professor, a highest good, which is called an eternal happiness [*Salighed* — lit. 'blessedness'] . I have heard that Christianity contracts to give one this good, and now I ask how I may establish a proper relationship to this doctrine.[9]

The philosophical concept of a highest good (*summum bonum*) stems from Aristotle: roughly it is the concept of the most complete form of humanly attainable satisfaction, and an 'intrinsic' good in the sense that it is good in and of itself, not for or by virtue of some other good.[10] Aristotle himself thought this highest good to be intellectual contemplation, this being for him the most complete and therefore most satisfying fulfilment of the potentialities of human nature. But Climacus's conception of the good as that offered by Christianity comes closer, naturally enough, to the Aquinian adaptation of Aristotle's ideal: the idea of a special kind of contentment bestowed by God, a happiness or heavenly bliss, in the form of a maximally satisfying human participation in the divine; indeed Climacus actually speaks of 'participation' in the blessedness promised by Christianity.[11] Our discussion in the previous chapter reveals an even closer affinity between the Climacian and the Thomist conceptions, as one might expect in view of Climacus's occupation with Christianity. Thomists maintain that a longing for this particular form of contentment has been given to all human beings by their creator, and that to resist it is to pervert true human nature; which looks very like the view underlying Kierkegaard's pathology of the self. But whereas Thomism conceives the tendency as a kind of magnetic force issuing from God, the Climacian view is anthropological rather than theological;

that is to say, even if a concern with this particular form of satisfaction may be natural to man, that there actually is a creator who
can bestow this blessedness, and who has implanted a concern for
it in all human beings, is not something anyone can either know or
find any reason to believe. All that can be said, and here we should
take Climacus the humorist's comment seriously, is that 'common
ordinary human beings' are as a matter of fact concerned with this
highest good.

The notion of a highest good is linked in philosophy with that
of virtue. Generally, it is seen as a satisfaction to be achieved
which requires effort and hardship and in particular self-denial.
The effort and hardship thus become 'virtue', and the problem is
then posed of the relation between virtue and happiness, as well as
of that between these two and the notion of a highest good. (Once
the hardship is conceived as 'virtue', it becomes natural to think of
it not just as a price to be paid for the highest good, but as somehow *part* of that good and not just a means to it.) Kant formulated
and labelled two views as to the nature of this relation, in order to
take exception to both and propose a third. The two were, first,
the 'Stoic' view that happiness is attained in virtuous practice, and
second, the 'Epicurean' view that virtue consists in seeking happiness; or in Kant's more exact terms: the view that 'to be conscious
of one's virtue is happiness', and the view that 'to be conscious
that one's maxims lead to happiness is virtue'.[12] Kant opposed
both views because, although they preserve a conceptual distinction
between virtue and happiness, and also conceive of the highest
good as comprising both elements — assumptions which Kant
shares — they make the two indistinguishable in practice. That is,
for these views, the project of realizing the ultimate satisfaction
is the same as that either of 'willing virtue' or of 'willing happiness'
(to use a characteristically Kantian form of expression also adopted
by Kierkegaard), depending on which of these two notions is
taken as fundamental. In each case, the supposedly distinguishable
complement which establishes the highest good is a logical outcome of the more fundamental notion. Kant, of course, because
he regards virtue, not happiness, as fundamental, would side with
Stoicism.[13] In fact, he wants to regard virtue as an intrinsic good.
But not as the highest good. For Kant the highest good is a *consequence* of virtue but without being that upon which virtue's value
depends; it is related to virtue synthetically ('really'), as he says,
and not analytically. So Kant splits the notion of a highest good
into a supreme good, in the sense of a good not dependent on any
other, identifying virtue with this, and a 'most perfect good' of
which virtue is only a part. He then uses this latter notion, in

which virtue is only a part of the whole good, to explain the notion of a highest good as a goal 'which reason points out to all rational beings as the goal of all their moral wishes'.[14]

That personal morality should have a goal is something Kant accepts; without the idea of something to be achieved by it, moral practice lacks any point. But that moral practice can be motivated by the thought of that goal he altogether rejects; for that would be to subordinate one's respect for the moral law to natural inclination. Thus Kant argues that the idea of a causal connection between being virtuous and achieving happiness is one which *reason* points out to all rational beings. Roughly, because the combination of these two elements into the goal can only be understood by reason and has no basis in experience, it cannot offer a psychological motive for virtue. In fact, on Kant's view the highest good is not an idea which one can have prior to moral experience at all and which could therefore draw one into that experience; it is an idea first generated *in* moral experience as an idea that gives sense to willing the ethical.

Climacus writes as if the notion of a highest good was one he already had before Christianity came with its offer of a way to secure it. In other words, Climacus clearly does regard the idea of the highest good as a motive for following whatever moral injunctions Christianity names as the price of its achievement. And this is confirmed in his introduction where he says that an 'infinite interest in his eternal happiness' is a 'conditio sine qua non' for his presentation of the problem.[15]

We have already noted this 'infinite' interest as a cornerstone of Kierkegaard's philosophy, in the form of a concern on the part of the existentially undeceived human for cosmic satisfaction, a satisfaction we conceived of as having two complementary aspects: on the one hand, a personal conviction that the finite and apparently accidental nature of human life is an illusion; and on the other, a sense of affiliation with an infinite and personal universe. We may suppose that it is this satisfaction that Climacus says that he, like most 'common ordinary human beings', assumes is in store for him. The question is: what is Kierkegaard's view of the relation between this expectation (of happiness) and the individual's concern with the ethical (virtue)?

Kierkegaard appears to accept, with Kant, that moral practice requires a goal in order to 'make sense'. But, unlike Kant, for him the sense it makes must be practical, it must stem from a basic personal longing, not simply from 'reason'. And yet, it becomes obvious that Kierkegaard also agrees with Kant that the thought of the goal cannot provide an incentive to moral practice. How, then, can he have it both ways? What necessary practical role can the longing for happiness play in connection with morals if not as an incentive to moral practice?

There is one possibility with which we may be provisionally content. The expression 'incentive to moral practice' is obviously ambiguous. It can be, and is no doubt ordinarily, understood to mean the motivation for particular moral actions, for example maximizing felicity or minimizing suffering. But it can also mean the motivation underlying an interest in morality as such — what makes one bothered with adding to the general felicity and sub-tracting from the general suffering. In the latter sense one may think of a range of different ways in which the relation of motive to morality is conceived. Thus Climacus's own idea of a highest good, of some benefit which Christian belief or practice will bring him, is to say the least somewhat vague. (We have noted that the problem arises as much with belief as with virtue: to what extent can one believe something because one has an interest in believing it? And could we go so far as to say that no interest in believing what we believe should play a part in our believing in so far as it is genuine believing?) But Kierkegaard obviously presents Climacus as someone who has certain advantages over, say, the servant-girl or the professor in this respect. Where, on the one hand, a servant-girl without prospects of upwards mobility in this life may go no further than dreaming with passion of a place upstairs in the here-after, and a professor, on the other hand, has too little passion to have genuine longings of this kind at all, but merely 'affectations' of a kind that, as Climacus says, can be 'excellently supported by matchstick arguments',[16] Climacus himself is ordinary enough to have the longing and yet theoretical enough to appreciate what an adequate understanding of the relation of virtue to happiness must in the end consist of. At any rate, it soon becomes obvious that Climacus grasps the point that the satisfaction of his longing can-not be a motivation for *doing* good, and that the object of his longing must in the end be conceived as, if not identical with, at least a mode or quality of proper moral practice itself, and there-fore amongst other things as *necessarily* bound to *this* life. As this not altogether ordinary human being says later: 'An eternal happi-ness . . . lies precisely in the diminishing self-feeling of subjectivity, acquired through utmost exertion.'[17] Our comparisons with Kant are necessarily rough. A more detailed assessment might well indicate less disparity between Kant's and Kierkegaard's views. For instance, the interest Kierkegaard talks of, an interest which in its transformation in inwardness must be preserved in defiance of rational standards, in short a very consciously sustained kind of interest, could prove not to be the kind of interest Kant denies can be a motive for moral practice. No doubt there are other debatable points which could fruitfully be examined in another context, not least the whole role of the *summum bonum* in Kant's ethics. Here, however, the important point for what follows is the idea of a transformation of a person's conception of the relationship between virtue and happiness. We have already noted Kierkegaard's equation of a progressive increase in the self's 'measure' with an increasingly adequate grasp of the ethical ideal, where the highest measure of the self is 'God'. 'Ethical ideal' can be understood here as genuine virtue. We could ascribe to Kierkegaard the view that the correspondingly adequate grasp of the notion of happiness is one in which the notions of happiness and virtue are seen to have a common reference, and in which the proper object of longing is recognized as ethical practice itself, not ethical practice for the sake of happiness.

Climacus's initial formulation of his interest in Christian ethics therefore suggests a rather simple-minded grasp of the matter. In the context of a book intended to show what is needed to be genuinely a Christian, that is appropriate enough. One main requirement is to arrive at an adequate understanding of the Christian ideal, a requirement Climacus specifically mentions when he says that it is only in 'the development or transformation of [his] subjectivity' that the individual can achieve, or even acquire a 'real idea of the significance' of the good which 'Christianity proposes to grant the individual'.[18] And a requirement Climacus himself appears to have satisfied when much later in his account he says: 'there is nothing to be said of an eternal happiness except that it is attained by venturing everything absolutely'; and again when he says of 'an eternal happiness as the absolute good', that it has 'the remarkable trait of being *definable solely in terms of the manner of [its] acquisition*', namely by 'absolutely risking everything'. It is interesting to note his reason. Climacus says that any other definition or description of 'the glory of this good is already in effect an attempt to make it possible for there to be several ways of acquiring it, for example an easier and more difficult . . .', which shows, he says, 'that the description does not describe the absolute good but only imagines it does so and essentially talks of relative goods'.[19]

Now even on Kant's account of the relation between virtue and happiness there is only one mode of acquiring happiness, for according to Kant there is, formally, only one way of being virtuous, namely acting according, and solely in deference, to the moral law. So this same scruple might lead a Kantian to make a similar precautionary restriction. However, Kierkegaard is more sensitive than Kant to the forms of illusion that infect ethical ideals, and this gives a special point to his denial that anything can usefully be said of the highest good that is not already expressed in the formulation 'absolutely risking everything'. The crux is that for Kierkegaard the very attempt to say anything more betrays an interest either in some less exacting mode of acquisition which makes it easier to come by, or in some more exacting mode which excuses one for not trying to acquire it. We can interpret him, therefore, not as denying Kant's view that virtue and happiness are distinct, but as reinforcing Kant's point that the happiness which is a constituent of the highest good cannot function as a motive for virtue. For he believes that the alternative descriptions necessarily represent the highest good as the kind of thing that *can* function as a motive, either for aiming at the highest good or for not aiming at it.

3 Double-mindedness

Suppose one does grasp the highest good as a motive. Does that not imply that one has grasped it in temporal terms? Suppose, further, we grant that it does. Then because on Kierkegaard's (as also on Aquinas's and Kant's) conception of the highest good this good is eternal, does this not also mean that to grasp it in this way is in fact impossible? That whatever one has grasped in this way is not the highest good, and in fact something else altogether different? But if so, what would be a proper grasp of the highest good?

The answer suggested just now was that properly grasping the highest good means identifying it in some way with ethical practice itself. Let us try to clarify this answer, and possibly thereby throw some light on the other questions too.

To those who recall the centrality of time in Kierkegaard's ethics, his main idea here will appear paradoxical. Time, or continuity, in the form of duties, roles, responsibilities, clothing oneself in generality, was what marked the transition *into* the ethical and out of the aesthetic stage. And the temporal dimension proved essential in the constitution of a continuing and public identity. But now, for the individual's further moral-conceptual growth Kierkegaard prescribes the suspension of time, or rather of an interest in temporality; just as paradoxically, he also prescribes the elimination of the self, even of that paragon of selfhood, the individual. Obviously, however, this does not mean that in order to proceed further, the good work done in the temporal dimension must now be undone. The point is rather — and we have hinted at this earlier — that in order to reach the 'religious sphere'[20] a self-less and timeless dimension must now be superimposed upon the temporal one. What this amounts to remains to be seen, but we already have a clue. If a person chooses the ethical path because he or she expects some benefit, then that at least could be a reason for saying that a timeless dimension has not yet been superimposed upon the temporal one. For benefits are essentially temporal things, and choosing the ethical path for such a reason surely indicates that one is still firmly situated in time.

To follow up this clue we turn to Kierkegaard's 'Discourses', in the first instance to *Purity of Heart is to Will One Thing* ('A Discourse for an Occasion'), the first of three 'Edifying Discourses in Different Spirits' published in March 1847, the year after the *Postscript*. In this work, 'in search of that "individual", to whom it wholly devotes itself',[21] Kierkegaard (now non-pseudonymously) takes up the notion of 'willing the ethical'; not now in the sense of deciding *upon* the ethical path, for as mentioned earlier, Kierkegaard's acknowledged writings assume this path already to have been chosen. 'Willing the ethical' here means succeeding in making the ethical genuinely the object of one's will. In developing this theme Kierkegaard deals with two aspects of it. First, he enumerates and describes various illusions and evasions by which people deceive themselves into thinking that they 'will the ethical' when they do not. And second, he points out the kinds of hardships that a person genuinely, i.e. successfully, willing the ethical must be willing to undergo. We shall concentrate on the first aspect.

Kierkegaard's procedure is to bring out the ethical shortcomings of purported ethical practice, to show what is wrong when one wills the ethical unsuccessfully. In *Purity of Heart* he has a common label for such willing. He calls it 'double-mindedness', an expression taken from St James's Epistle,

> Draw nigh to God, and he shall draw nigh to you. Cleanse your hands ye sinners, and purify your hearts ye double-minded.[22]

The 'purity of heart' of Kierkegaard's title is therefore the condition in which double-mindedness is avoided. The pure of heart are those who 'will' the ethical successfully; or, in Kierkegaard's alternative expression, they 'will one thing'. To will one thing and successfully to will the ethical (or 'will the good in truth') are the same.[23]

Obviously then, the state of double-mindedness in which people deceive themselves into thinking that they will the ethical is one in which they will not one thing, but two. But what precisely do the

deception and the distinction amount to? And how is the transformation to willing one thing brought about? What, rather, is
willing *one* thing rather than two?

One straightforward answer has to be rejected, though in one
place Kierkegaard himself seems to give it. It is couched in terms
corresponding to those of our earlier distinction between virtue
and happiness, except that these are now designated respectively
'the good' and 'the reward'. A third factor has also been introduced,
namely 'the punishment', which may be thought of provisionally
as denial or deprivation of the reward, but we shall ignore this
aspect for the moment and focus first on the relation between the
good (virtue, or the ethical) and the reward (happiness). 'The good
is one thing', says Kierkegaard, 'the reward is another . . . when [a
person] , then, wills the good for the sake of the reward, he does
not will one thing but two.'[24] Here double-mindedness seems
simply to be willing two things — the good 'for the sake of the
reward'.[25] If so, may we not conclude that willing one thing is to
will one thing without thinking of some other? In this case, to
concentrate single-mindedly upon the path of virtue to the total
exclusion of any benefits in store?

But in that case the conditions of 'willing one thing' could
equally be satisfied by exclusive concentration on the reward
rather than the ethical — an anomalous idea, perhaps, where the
reward in question is the 'highest' good and this notion is linked
inseparably with that of the ethical, but not obviously excluded
in principle by this criterion of willing one thing. However, apart
from any such anomaly, the idea that it is possible really to will
one thing when that thing is a temporal objective is one which we
shall see Kierkegaard wants to say is impossible. So although
Kierkegaard does say that to will one thing is to will the good
without considering the reward aspect,[26] this nevertheless fails to
get to the root of this notion of double-mindedness. It fails to
bring out his idea that double-mindedness involves a fundamental
misconception of the good and of its relation to the reward. Double-
mindedness is not simply having two things in mind, either of
which would have to be ignored in order for the other to be willed
as one thing. It is so conceiving of the relation of the good to the
reward (or punishment) that just such a distinction between them
seems to be possible; that is, a distinction which makes it permiss-
ible to talk of the mind's devotion to the one *rather than* the other.
Of a person with such a conception Kierkegaard says that his 'sight'
is 'confused': 'It is as if a man, instead of naturally using both eyes
to see one thing, should use one eye to see one side and the other
to see the other side.'[27] Such a person is confused because both

his eyes should be focused on one thing. Now in a sense there are indeed two sides to look at — the good and its reward. But the point is that if one thinks of them in such a way that a unified vision can only be secured by ignoring the reward side — so that in order to will one thing we must, as it were, turn a blind eye on the reward (or on the threat of punishment) — the two sides are being conceived as presently incompatible objects. As constituting quite different objectives. And *that* is double-mindedness. 'The double-minded one', says Kierkegaard

> stands at a parting of the ways. Two visions appear: the good and the reward. It is not in his power to bring them into agreement, for [to him] they are fundamentally different from each other.[28]

To secure a unified vision he must bring the two sides into focus as one thing, no longer see them as fundamentally different from each other. Double-mindedness is not just being distracted by the vision of a reward, it is having the kind of conception of the reward which makes it plausible to talk of it as a potential distraction in the first place. Kierkegaard's meaning can be further clarified by adverting to two distinctions, the first of which we have already encountered: between an 'inner' and an 'outer' realm. The second is that between the 'homogeneity' and the 'heterogeneity' of a reward with that for which it is a reward. Let us examine these briefly.

Towards the end of *Purity of Heart* Kierkegaard calls upon his reader to undertake a self-examination. He asks him: Do you truthfully will one thing?, and expects this to be understood as asking not, What goals do you profess?, but What kind of life do you live? He says he is not asking about the externals of his reader's life, but whether the reader lives in such a way, with such an attitude, as to be *capable* of answering the question of whether he wills one thing, whether in fact the question 'truthfully exists' for him.

> Because in order to be able earnestly to answer that serious question, a man must already have made a choice in life, he must have chosen the invisible, chosen that which is *within*.[29]

The distinction between what is 'external' and what 'within' is not one between what is publicly and what is only privately identifiable, e.g. between heads and headaches. As we met it earlier in connection with *The Concept of Anxiety*, it is an application of Kierkegaard's fundamental distinction between the temporal and the eternal. Roughly, the external is the temporal and contingent

218

(including headaches). It is everything that lies 'outside' the self conceived as spirit. The individual acquires a spiritual aspect (or 'true' self) by turning inwards (as the religious genius does, but the immediate genius does not) and discovering the ethical categories of freedom, guilt, and repentance, for which 'external tasks', that is objectives describable in purely temporal terms, lose their potential status as intrinsically valuable goals. That man has this potential relationship to the eternal, and that it is an ethical, not a cognitive relationship is, as we noted earlier, basic to Kierkegaard's thought. Indeed, it is the entire foundation of his Socratic approach (to be distinguished from the Socratic viewpoint beyond which Kierkegaard claims to have advanced). In *Purity of Heart* Kierkegaard makes the Socratic point by quoting from Ecclesiastes: '[God] hath set eternity within man's heart.'[30] The individual's belief that this is the case is the source of the ethical. In practice ethics is, in the first instance, a decision in favour of the eternal as the source of the good; then, second, once the decision is made, it is the task of upholding or consummating it in the face of the temptations of nature, of the temporal or 'external'.

So what Kierkegaard means by what is 'within', or the 'inner',[31] is the eternal as a target or point of orientation for one who accepts that he has a potential relationship with the eternal and conceives the eternal as the source of the good. The external, or 'outer',[32] is the temporal, the natural and the historical. The distinction is one with which we are familiar from the *Postscript*. There Climacus remarks, for instance, that 'the longer life goes on' and

> the more the existing [individual's] activities are woven into existence, the more difficult it is to separate the ethical from the external; and the more readily may the metaphysical principle seem to be confirmed, that the outward is the inward, the inward the outward, the one wholly commensurable with the other.[33]

If the ethical is indeed an 'eternal' category, then to conceive it in temporal terms is a fundamental mistake. And if one first grants that the ethical is an eternal category, to conceive the ethical and the temporal as 'commensurable' is not only a mistake but a confusion. A gross form of this confusion would be where the ethical was itself *identified* with some temporal state of affairs (as in what Kant calls 'heteronomy'). But Kierkegaard is concerned with more subtle and therefore, he thinks, more widespread forms of this confusion. One such is where the ethical is conceived as rewarding. To conceive the ethical as rewarding, even if the ethical is an acknowledged 'eternal' category, is still to treat the ethical as

219

a temporal category. Similarly with punishment, that is, to decide upon the ethical course for *fear* of the punishment, or to see the punishment as, in the long run, a *bad* thing at all.

This might be understood as follows. To think of the ethical as rewarding is to make the promise of some personal benefit ('eternal blessedness' or 'escape from punishment') the motive for one's ethical endeavour. But by making the pursuit of the ethical depend (to *any* degree) upon desires or fears is to reduce the ethical (to *that* degree) to the temporal. Practically speaking, it is still to conceive the ethical as a temporal category.

This is certainly part of what Kierkegaard means. As we shall see below, the sense in which we are to regard the ethical as an eternal category is not just one in which ethical values have to be understood in eternal terms (whatever that may mean), but one in which ethical practice is practice which actually in some way exemplifies the eternal. And the crux of Kierkegaard's position is that no action motivated by the idea of a temporal objective can fulfil that condition. So ethical practice has to be practice the motivation for which excludes any envisaged temporal objective.

Kierkegaard calls the reward an eternal happiness. But does not that definitely exclude any idea of the benefit being a temporal objective? True, but it is still possible, indeed easy, to misconstrue the predicate 'eternal', e.g. as implying that the objective is a benefit in some 'hereafter'. That would still be to conceive the benefit in question in temporal terms, though unintelligibly as being bestowed in some time (however endless) *after* time. Kierkegaard nevertheless does appear to think it possible to conceive of an eternal benefit 'in time'. There are two different ways in which one might conceive of some benefit: either as a state of affairs to be aimed at and secured by whatever appropriate, i.e. effective or dependable, means; or as a state of affairs bestowed by some means outside one's control under certain conditions. Now the reward can be conceived as 'eternal', or 'belonging to the eternal', only if it is thought of in the latter way — specifically as bestowed by God. Kierkegaard says: 'Only that reward which God for all eternity adds to the good in the inner realm . . . is in truth homogeneous with the good.'[34] And this brings us to our second distinction. To conceive the reward and the good 'homogeneously' one must look upon the reward not as some normal benefit or payment for services rendered. That would be thinking of it as a benefit that it is possible, by taking suitable action, to bestow upon oneself, like paying your money and expecting your due, or going out hunting and being disappointed when you come back empty-handed. (Apropos of which, Wittgenstein is quoted as saying, 'I think a religious person regards placidity or peace as a gift from heaven, not as something one ought to hunt after.')[35] Further, one must look upon it as a benefit that may be bestowed upon one in certain qualifying circumstances — which must at least include successfully willing the ethical. Thus we can understand double-mindedness as an inability to see the reward in this light. It is a confusion due to a person's attempt to see the heterogeneous as homogeneous; that is, on the one hand to see the reward for willing the ethical as a state the attainment of which is under his own control while acknowledging, on the other, that the ethical itself — its content and its source — is something over which he exercises no control whatsoever. Double-mindedness is therefore not merely a misconception of the ethical, in so far as it 'reduces' the ethical in practice to a temporal category; it is also a misconception of the nature of the reward, a miscategorization of it.

And yet, surely, however one conceives a promised or even a possible benefit, it *is* necessarily grasped as something desirable. However much the reward or the punishment may properly belong to the 'inner' realm, can they be anything but, as Kierkegaard says, 'temptations'?[36] After all, we mean by a 'reward' precisely something that will encourage us, and by a 'punishment' something that will deter us. Kierkegaard denies, however, that if the reward for virtue is conceived correctly, it can be a temptation: 'the tempting is never the good'. If the reward tempts, then it is 'the world's reward' we are thinking of.[37] So the pursuit of the ethical, as an attempt to introduce timelessness into one's practice, is best undertaken with total lack of consideration of the reward; the individual 'must guard himself even against the reward [which can come from God even in the outer realm] just in order rightly to be able to will the good'. To which Kierkegaard characteristically adds that 'he must not forget that this, even such a desire to guard himself [from consideration of the reward], may once more be a temptation to pride',[38] a point which Kant, who also warns against the temptation to 'take a pride in *meritorious* worth', would have appreciated.[39]

Willing the good for the reward or out of fear of punishment are the obvious examples of double-mindedness — i.e. of referential confusion of the eternal with the temporal. Kierkegaard uses them to outline the nature of the duplicity that lurks in less obvious examples. It is these more elusive cases of double-mindedness that provide the more insidious obstacle to successfully willing the ethical. We can outline Kierkegaard's analyses of the two main types of this more elusive duplicity.

The first is that of 'the man who wills the good and wills its victory out of self-centred wilfulness'. 'He does not will one thing', says Kierkegaard, 'he is double-minded.'[40] In one example of this kind of case the good becomes 'a fruit of conquest' — so that what is willed is the conquest and self-aggrandizement. That is, the good is conceived under the temporal description 'conquest' and its achievement as a conquest that redounds to the self-esteem of the person ostensibly willing the good. The confusion of categories is still fairly obvious here.

But in another example, which Kierkegaard says involves the same form of double-mindedness, but in a 'more disingenuous and concealed' way, one may will the *good's* victory, and not one's own victory through one's promotion of the good. This double-mindedness is 'more presumptuous than [the other] obvious and clearly worldly sort. It is a powerful illusion that seems nearest of all to approach the purity of heart that wills the good in truth'. For Kierkegaard claims that although such a person does not will the good for the sake of the reward, he nevertheless

> wills that the good shall triumph *through* him. . . . The reward
> which he insists upon is a sense of pride and in that very
> demand is his violent double-mindedness. Yes, violent, for
> what else does he wish than to take the good by storm, and by
> force to press himself and his service upon the good!

In his continuation Kierkegaard clearly indicates how the category confusion must be resolved:

> And if he will not give up this last presumptuousness, if he,
> in some way, *does not desire what the good wills*, if he does
> not desire the good's victory *after the fashion that the good
> wills it*: then he is double-minded.[41]

Double-mindedness is failing to will what the good wills as the good wills it. In this case, the good's own (as distinct from the will's) victory must be regarded as taking time (in eternity it has always been victorious),[42] *its* time. We can understand Kierkegaard as saying that the good must not be regarded and hence willed on the analogy of a temporal goal which calls for specifically *our* participation in its achievement. Such a way of looking at it makes the particular moral agent 'important' for its achievement *in time*, just as a person who claims to be devoted to uncovering the truth may prefer that it is *he* who uncovers it rather than that it is simply uncovered. Thus the man who wills the good in truth must abide by the duality of eternal and temporal, remembering he has chosen the former as his Archimedean point. 'Time and eternity cannot rule in the same man.' He must understand the good's 'slowness', and that 'the good can get on without him'.[43]

The section closes with a description of this kind of double-minded person's conception of the good. He takes on the one hand the good, on the other its victory. But 'in eternity', says Kierkegaard, the distinction does not apply: there (for remember, the eternal is the unchangeable) the victory is always achieved. In time, however, they are distinguished, and 'must be kept apart . . . [f]or the good so wills it'. With the eye of his senses the individual 'is not permitted to see the good in victory'; 'it is only with the eye of faith that he can aspire to its eternal triumph'. One kind of double-mindedness dissolves the essential unity of the good by conceiving the reward as something separate; this kind obliterates the essential distinction between the victory of the good and the good itself. The double-minded person sees them as one — in temporal terms, he 'unites what the good in time has set apart'.[44]

The second main kind of case is where the person only wills the good to a certain degree. Although Kierkegaard actually says that all forms of double-mindedness can be called willing the good 'only up to a certain degree',[45] the examples he specifically mentions under this heading are of people who have a 'living feeling' for the good but do not, in the long run, act as the good they have a feeling for requires. Thus one can will the good with an enthusiastic whole-heartedness that is 'a kind of sincerity',[46] but the enthusiasm is not generated by the (correct) idea of the good itself — or, as Climacus in the *Postscript* says it should be, by 'the ethical relationship to God'; instead it is a natural enthusiasm which precedes that relationship and bears it along — for a while. It is as though the ethical rides the wave of an enthusiastic disposition, only to fall into the trough of faint-heartedness once the natural resources on which the disposition feeds run out. Thus, however much one may *feel* unified for the good, in practice one's attitude will show that one does not genuinely will what the good itself wills.[47]

The typical case of this double-mindedness, however, is more protean or 'versatile', as well as more common, than the 'big-minded' form just outlined; and in its variety it infects correspondingly greater parts of daily life. 'It is . . . more rare in daily life', Kierkegaard says, 'just to see someone who wills some perverse thing with any fixed consistency and effort. The transactions of daily life are made in the little things so that double-mindedness is *more diversely compounded* within the individual'.[48] It is the typical obstacle to willing the ethical that confronts those whose

223

activities are 'woven into existence', the complexities of which make it all the more difficult to 'separate the ethical from the external'.

In summary, then, double-mindedness is willing the good in mixed categories. It is willing the good in its proper category only to a certain degree, where the residue is an appetitive element: the person either seeking some good specifically for himself or letting his will for the good be fired by a natural enthusiasm instead of deriving its energy from the idea of the good itself. To be double-minded is to be self-indulgent to *any* degree; to will not the good itself but one's own good. And since willing one's own good is aiming to achieve some goal in time, it is to fail to concentrate on the good in the category proper to it.

Such failure, Kierkegaard seems to concede, is normal. Actually to succeed in willing the ethical requires discipline and clarity. But

in the bustle of life [*i Travlheden*] there is neither *time nor quiet to win the transparency* that is required to understand oneself in willing one thing, or even for a preliminary understanding of oneself in one's confusion.[49]

Presumably, however, a necessary step in the direction of self-understanding and transparency is to become aware of the distance between the ethical proper and one's own avowedly ethical performance. To realize to what extent one's everyday professions of 'faith and hope and love and willing the good [have become] ... only loose words and double-mindedness'.[50]

4   Willing one thing: Kierkegaard and Kant

Earlier we noted that willing the ethical is the state in which double-mindedness is avoided, the state of purity of heart, or of willing one thing. But we still have not grasped what this latter notion amounts to. We are clear, of course, that it is incompatible with having as, or in association with, an ethical goal the satisfaction of any purely personal goal or ambition. And we have also noted the underlying thesis that all goals having exclusively temporal specifications fall into this category and must therefore be excluded. But this gives us no more than a negative characterization of willing one thing. We still want to know what that 'one thing' is — even more urgently now, since without temporal goals the domain of possible candidates seems to be empty. We know also, of course, that we cannot positively identify ethical goals with transcendent states, for the only descriptions *we* can give of such states are in temporal terms and therefore spurious.

An obvious solution to the problem of the empty domain is to treat the term 'one thing' in the phrase 'willing one thing' as qualifying not any object or state of affairs at which the will is directed, but the will itself. In other words, it is to treat Kierkegaard's concept of the ethically good in the light of Kant's well-known view that '[a] good will is good not because of what it performs or effects, not by its aptness for the attainment of some proposed end, but simply by virtue of the volition . . .'.[51] Kant understood this in terms of what he called 'the autonomy of the will', a notion which he presented as 'the supreme [and sole] principle of morality'.[52] Briefly the notion of the autonomy of the will is that of a will which is directed by a law or rule which it gives itself, and not — the only alternative Kant envisages — by a law or rule linking the will directly with any of its objects. The reasoning behind Kant's view closely parallels that implicit in Kierkegaard, and since Kierkegaard's own view represents an interesting variation of Kant's, it will help us to provide a more systematic backcloth for our interpretation of Kierkegaard if we turn briefly to Kant's reasons for his supreme principle.

A moral imperative, in Kant's well-known view, must be categorical. That is, it must be in the form of an absolute law, subject to no conditions, qualifications, or exceptions. Part of what this means is that it must hold for everyone, regardless of particular people's desires and aversions. Now Kant argues that it cannot be such an imperative if the morally good is defined in relation to 'the character of any of [the will's] objects'.[53] The argument, in outline, is as follows. The will, according to Kant, is always determined or governed by a rule. The problem is to grasp how it can govern itself, for otherwise morality, with its implication of responsibility and therefore freedom, cannot exist. Now the rule governing the will in any particular action is expressed in a maxim for the action. Wherever an *object* of the will has to be mentioned in a statement of the rule, then the will is subject to a desire for or an aversion to that object, and so the imperative stated in the rule is only conditional, not categorical. It says merely, '*if* or *because* one wishes for this object, one should act so and so'.[54] In other words, if the good had to be identified as an *object* of the will, morality could no longer be based on an absolute standard or categorical imperative, but would depend on the contingent circumstance that a person sets himself this or that standard. *That* a person sets himself a given standard is an empirical fact, dependent on the *particular constitution of human nature*, or the accidental circumstances in which it is placed'.[55] Nor does it alter the situation if the object identified in a moral preference is selected by reason

225

and understanding instead of by inclination. In both cases 'the will [is determined] by the influence which the foreseen effect of the action has on the will', for the use of understanding and reason, too, are 'by the peculiar constitution of their nature attended with satisfaction'. Kant concludes that then 'the law would be, properly speaking, given by nature', consequently contingent, and therefore 'incapable of being an apodictic practical rule, such as the moral rule must be'.

To avoid this contingency, and thus to permit the imperative stated in the rule to be categorical, Kant appeals to the authority of a formal principle — the principle of the autonomy of the will — which effectively eliminates the 'if' and the 'because' and ensures that the law is given not by nature, or 'a foreign impulse by means of a particular natural constitution of the subject adapted to receive it', but by the will itself, which then prescribes for itself the laws that govern it.

> An absolutely good will, then, the principle of which must be a categorical imperative, will be indeterminate as regards all objects, and will contain merely the *form of volition* generally, and that as autonomy, that is to say, the capability of the maxims of every good will to make themselves a universal law, is itself the only law which the will of every rational being imposes on itself, without needing to assume any spring or interest as a foundation.[56]

Even if a goal of action is arrived at by the most objective and rational procedures, it is still linked to the contingencies of time and circumstance through the fact that it is *satisfying*. So 'in order that practical reason (will) may not be restricted to administering an interest not belonging to it, but may simply show its own commanding authority as the supreme legislation', one must proceed by a purely formal rule which 'abstract[s] from all objects that they shall have no *influence* on the will'.[57] The rule is the well-known prescription that we shall '[a]lways so . . . choose that the same volition shall comprehend the maxims of our choice as a universal law'.[58]

If the good is identified with a certain state of affairs or objective of action, then because that state of affairs must inevitably be regarded, even if in some rather attenuated sense, as 'desirable', the very choice of that objective must be subject to the contingency of nature. So the 'good' here cannot be moral. Kant's conclusion is the same as Kierkegaard's, and the underlying considerations are sufficiently similar to give some, even the same, point to saying that, for both, willing the good must be willing 'one thing'. The expression 'one thing' would refer here not to an object for the will, e.g. the good in some shape or other, but to the form the will must have if it is to be a good will. The view both share is that a good will must be one that is not influenced by the thought of a reward — or, and for both Kant and Kierkegaard it will be the same, by the thought of any object or state of affairs to be achieved or brought about.

But although this may exhaust the connotational possibilities of the expression 'to will one thing' for Kant, the same is not true of Kierkegaard. The point will help us to see the chief differences between these two.

First, it is surely a consequence of Kant's view of morality that the true moral path is available to all rational humans at any time. The key to Kantian morality is something we all possess: the *principle* of the autonomy of the will. Of this principle Kant says that it would

be easy to show how, with this compass in hand, men are well able to distinguish, in every case that occurs, what is good, what bad, conformably to duty or inconsistent with it, if, without in the least teaching them anything new, we only, like Socrates, direct their attention to the principle they themselves employ.[59]

Some of this Kierkegaard would certainly agree with. For instance, that there is no question of 'teaching' the distinction between good and bad, for this comes of itself with the 'positing of spirit'. Kierkegaard would also agree with the letter of Kant's caution that moral laws 'require a judgment sharpened by experience, in order on the one hand to distinguish in what cases they are applicable, and on the other to procure for them access to the will of the man, and effectual influence on conduct'.[60] But not with its spirit. What Kant prescribes against the 'corruption' of morals is, apart from the identification of the 'supreme principle' itself, nothing more than an *intellectual* cultivation of practical reason in the form of a 'thorough critical examination' of the kind he himself provides.[61] For Kierkegaard, however, this omits what he would consider the core of the problem of cultivation: the actual transformation of the will. In order to will one thing conformably with Kierkegaardian ethics it would not be enough to choose to act according to an intellectual principle, a principle which then mechanically guarantees moral performance so long as one holds to it. It is the agent's *direct* grasp of the nature of moral action that is required, and this has as its counterpart the cultivation of a 'proper' moral disposition, a disposition which may indeed conform with Kant's principle, but need not rest consciously upon it.

Kierkegaard's concept of double-mindedness is concerned, as we noted, with the moral agent's ability to choose moral goals for himself without distorting those goals by reducing them to non-moral objectives, either by misrepresenting the goals themselves as appealing to the natural self, or by subordinating them to others which do appeal to the natural self (the acquiring of a reward, the avoidance of punishment). Essential to the cultivation of morals in this sense is the development of a will that concentrates on the eternal source of the ethical. Ethics is self-cultivation in the sense that, according to Kierkegaard (Anti-Climacus), 'every human being is basically planned [anlagt] as a self',[62] and as such destined to (want to) elevate himself above the level of worldly goals, and to find a will, in other words strength and enthusiasm, from the thought of that goal itself;[63] that is, without borrowing whatever strength and enthusiasm he can muster for it from motives of self-esteem or recognition, or any other forms of personal satisfaction, including that of possessing the highest good. Purity of Heart is, as we have also noted, an edifying work. It is designed to help people who are already set upon willing the good, and can define it theoretically, to bring their wills into conformity with their definition; that is, to get their wills to measure up to the absolute distinction made by that definition. Purity of Heart's theme is that it is easy to be wrong about the object's of one's will really conforming to the accepted categorization of the good, and its method is, as we have said, to teach its readers 'how to recognize many errors, disappointments, deceptions, and self-deceptions'.[64] As such, its aim, of course, is not to make moral action easier, but more difficult — this being the special merit of the 'religious address' in Kierkegaard's eyes; the task of such an address being to 'explore all avenues, be familiar with where all the errors lurk, where the moods have their hiding-places, how the passions understand themselves in solitude . . .'.[65] Purity of Heart seeks to 'track down double-mindedness into its hidden ways, and to uncover its secrecy',[66] first by describing the more obvious forms of double-mindedness — willing the good for the reward or for the fear of punishment — and then showing how the same pattern is discernible in cases where, until we learn to see its hidden ways, there is a semblance of its avoidance. It is nevertheless assumed throughout that the reader has a correct theoretical notion of what he aspires to, that is to say, realizes that the source of the ethical is 'the eternal'. Double-mindedness is a failure of ethical practice to conform with ethical intention and theory, but it needs more than 'a judgment sharpened by experience' to bring about the conformity. It needs a growth in understanding, a transformation of experience itself, and thereby also of the will.

Cultivating the will and acquiring an increasingly adequate understanding of the relationship to the highest good are two sides of the same thing. A glance at Climacus's survey of the 'religious sphere' can throw light on the latter aspect. In religiousness A the individual 'annihilates' itself, that is, subordinates its moral projects — as a dutiful citizen, father, etc. — to the good, or God, in the sense of a supratemporal order, though (following the A-position) this is still believed to sustain the whole of existence. A scientist could be said, ideally, to subordinate his scientific practice to the supratemporal ideals of rationality, objectivity, and truth, and just as the scientist becomes the truth's agent, so the moral agent becomes the good's agent — though he must not think there is anything meritorious in that — and in becoming this, he takes a step in the direction of virtue and holiness — though without wanting to be like God by reason of that.[67] The eternal begins then to manifest itself in its proper domain, in the 'inner' or 'subjective'. But in religiousness A (with its 'dialectic of inwardization'),[68] it is still the *relationship to* the eternal rather than the eternal itself that is the focus, and which, by focusing on it, the moral agent from 'within immanence' succeeds in 'defining more closely'.[69] In religiousness B ('paradoxical religiousness'), on the other hand, it is the eternal itself (the eternal happiness) that the moral agent confronts — *as* a paradox — in the realization of the 'absolute contradiction' of existing (in relation to an eternal happiness).[70] According to this distinction the edifying project of *Purity of Heart* belongs to the first of these two ethico-religious stages. It is the reader's *relationship* to the eternal — the good, eternal happiness, the source of moral worth — that is being purified.

The transition from religiousness A to religiousness B also marks a second point of divergence from Kantian ethics. For here we have the idea of a development in the very notion of moral authority — in the first instance of its location. Prior to the ethico-religious stages, the source of value — including reward and blessedness — is conceived as entirely external to the agent — as related to him only impersonally from 'beyond' the temporal, making incursions into it in the form of Fate. But in religiousness A the 'holy resting place of edification' becomes the individual, whose self assumes that it acquires an 'eternal qualification'. Purity of heart, in Kierkegaard's sense, could be said to be the cultivation of this qualification, the acquiring of a sense of virtue (and holiness) uncorrupted by 'external' models or supports. But in religiousness B the authority is once more projected *outside* the individual, because here it dawns upon him how 'infinitely' remote the eternal is in time, and that, after all, is the dimension to which all his eternal qualifications are bound.[71] The result is an intensification of the tension between what the agent wants ('eternal happiness') and what he understands to be possible. In fact, what he wants proves impossible. But then the individual's interest in his eternal happiness is very different here from the way in which Kant portrays it. We have seen that for Kant purity of heart, or goodness or oneness of will, are ensured by the fact that an interest in the highest good can only be 'pointed out' to reason as an abstract goal for the institution of morality as a whole. The only psychological consequence Kant attributes to the successful exercise of virtue is the intellectual bonus of a Stoical serenity or self-contentment,[72] contentment at having secured a certain independence of the incursions of inclination. This is in fact a form of security and independence that Kierkegaard, too, lays some store by, though in slightly different terms, as we shall see; but for Kierkegaard the alternative offered to discontentment due to exposure to inclination is not the calmness of one whose 'beyond' is, as for Kant, a 'super-sensible system of nature' under the 'autonomy of pure practical reason',[73] a world to which as a rational being he claims membership by right; it is the agonizing concern of one whose 'beyond' is a world his membership of which is, to him, totally ungrounded. Kant grounds his ethical theory and his ethics on the 'noble ideal' of citizenship of the 'universal kingdom of . . . rational beings'.[74] To avoid infringing his 'supreme principle' he has to say, in answer to the question, Where does the notion of a highest good come from?, From reason itself. It is what, to a rational being, gives sense to his moral aspirations. For one who stands in Kierkegaard's B-position, the notion of a highest good is what alone, in the face of the paradoxical nature of the only possible evidence he can have for the idea, gives significance to his existence. It is an idea which instead of fading into the intellectual background becomes more and more obtrusive as it becomes more and more problematic.

A third point of divergence from Kantian ethics is the matter of freedom. Unless a choice of a course of action is free, it cannot be judged moral or immoral. But if the choice is for a certain state of affairs, then the will is tied to it in a causal network of preference, interest, and satisfaction. Kant's solution is that to will the good is to will in accordance with the Moral Law. Since the law can be stated without reference to a specific state of affairs, the standard it provides is absolute; and since to choose an action based on the law is to choose the law, and not the state of affairs that the action based on it envisions, the act of choice is free from the net of preference, interest, and satisfaction. Consequently, if it is a moral duty, say, to try to promote the happiness of others, this fact must be arrived at quite independently of the 'contingent' circumstance that the realization of this end 'involve[s] any concern of mine (whether by immediate inclination or by any satisfaction indirectly gained through reason)'; if I ought to try to bring about the happiness of others, it must be, as Kant says, 'simply because a maxim which excludes [its realization] cannot be comprehended as a universal law in one and the same volition'.[75]

For Kierkegaard the problem of freedom does not arise in the same way. It is true that in Kant's sense — that is, in the sense of freedom said to be necessary for the ascription of moral responsibility or accountability — Kierkegaard does also assume freedom; we saw that in the *Fragments* he asserts that nothing comes into being with necessity. But in another sense freedom is not just an assumption, even the assumption of one's membership of a supersensible system; it is a project for the individual. Or rather, the project the individual has of *becoming* an individual, or a self, in the strict sense. Freedom of will in the technical sense is, of course, a necessary presupposition of this project, and in general of Kierkegaard's conception of how human development takes place. ('Spiritual development is self-activity [*Selv-Virksomhed*]'.)[76] The goal of that development, however, is freedom in the Hegelian sense of a form of personal consistency in which the self is not subject to inner conflict. This is what Kierkegaard (Climacus) has in mind when he adds to the statement that ethics concentrates on the individual the comment, that 'ethically it is the task of every individual to become a *whole* man'.[77] As we shall see, this notion of freedom as self-realization turns out to be a rather different notion from that of freedom in Kant's sense. In *Works of Love*, which we shall discuss in the next chapter, it even comes close to a suspiciously self-seeking security, rather than integrity or freedom as such. But here, as in the other two respects, the interesting thing to note is the difference Kierkegaard's consideration makes to his otherwise basically Kantian position.

5   Integrity and truly willing one thing

So far we have taken 'willing one thing' to comprise two separate notions: first, willing the ethical where the ethical is an acknowledged eternal category; and second, homogeneity of such willing, that is to say avoidance of appeal to the temporal self in moral practice. Now this seems to allow for the following possibilities:

that even where the goal is an acknowledged temporal one it is possible to will one thing. Thus if 'willing one thing' is a description of the form of a will that wills the good, why should it not also be the form of a will that wills something other than the good, or than the good as specifically an eternal category? Will we not find examples and ideals of willing one thing wherever there is any sustained, concentrated devotion to a particular goal? If so, will it not be equally correct to acquit such a person of the charge of double-mindedness? And again if so, will Kierkegaard not have to find some other added specification of the form of a will that is a good will?

Clearly Kierkegaard will not allow that 'willing one thing', where the goal is a *temporal* one, is willing the good. But since he takes willing the good and willing one thing to be equivalent, he cannot allow, either, that willing a temporal goal, however single-mindedly, is genuinely willing one thing. In fact, Kierkegaard wants to make a clear distinction between willing a temporal goal 'whole-heartedly' or 'single-mindedly', and willing the good. And he wants to characterize the distinction by saying that the former amounts only to the *appearance* of willing one thing, as against truly willing one thing. Only the good, the eternal, can be truly willed as one thing.

This claim must be carefully interpreted if it is to escape serious objections. Sometimes Kierkegaard seems to be saying no more than that a given instance of the willing of one thing is double-minded because its object does not possess the superior, seamless, and incorruptible unity which is by definition (of 'eternal') the exclusive property of the good. Thus:

> To will one thing . . . cannot mean to will that which only
> appears to be one thing. The fact is that the worldly goal is not
> one thing in its essence because it is the *unessential*.[78]

But then is not the worldly goal's not being one thing derived directly from the metaphysical principle that only the eternal is 'truly' one? Is not the word 'unessential' here no more than a Platonic synonym for 'temporal'? If so, however, why does Kierkegaard, in the same passage, go on to give what he apparently intends to be *empirical* support for the claim that a worldly goal has an unreal unity and cannot be one thing.

> So far is [the worldly goal] from a state of being and
> remaining one thing, that in the next moment it changes
> itself into the opposite. Carried to unlimited excess, what
> is pleasure other than disgust? What is earthly honour at its
> dizzy pinnacle other than contempt for existence? What are

the highest superabundance of riches other than poverty? For all the earth's gold hidden in covetousness amounts to so much, so much infinitely less than the smallest mite hidden in the thrift of the poor! What is worldly omnipotence other than dependence? What slave in chains is as unfree as a tyrant! No, the worldly is not one thing. Diverse as it is, in life it is changed into its opposite, in death into nothing, in eternity into damnation: for the one who has willed *this* one thing.[79]

It is important to identify the status of these claims. First, what they allege is that the temporal projects in question, when carried single-mindedly to excess, in some way and sense turn into their opposites,[80] and that this is inherent in the projects themselves. Second, we have used the word 'empirical', but that word must clearly be used with care in this context. The claims here that certain goals, when pursued to excess, betray the motivations which initially inspired them are not necessarily straightforwardly empirical.

Hegel provides familiar philosophical precedents for arguments that certain intentions lead necessarily to their opposites. The case of the master/slave relationship comes to mind, the more readily in view of Kierkegaard's remark about the unfreedom of the tyrant. Let us therefore look briefly to the master/slave argument in Hegel's own context.

It has two aspects: one 'shallow', the other 'deep'. The shallow aspect can be generalized as follows. Where two concepts cannot be defined independently of one another — let us call them 'correlative concepts' (the criterion is not easy to apply, but let us assume that at least it distinguishes 'master' and 'slave' as correlative concepts from, say, 'fish' and 'chips') — a description in which one of the corresponding concept-terms is used 'analytically' involves an at least concealed parallel use of the other. What this, albeit imprecisely, intends to say is that if there are masters (of slaves) there must also be slaves; further, that if someone wants to be a master (of slaves) he must also want there to be slaves. One could put this by saying that the thought of someone's being a master involves also the thought of someone else's being a slave. There is, of course, nothing contradictory about being, or about wanting to be, a master of slaves. There might be, however, if the being or wanting could be described in terms of some other project, perhaps a more inclusive version of the same project. A contradiction of sorts would in any case be generated if a necessary condition of the first project could be shown to be a sufficient condition for the failure of fulfilment of the second. Now this would be the case if, for example, the other or wider intention was the intention to achieve a form of mastery which permitted release from the kind of dependence involved in having to have slaves. Someone who wants mastery in this sense and goes about trying to achieve it by lording it over other human beings, or, more indirectly, who looks for mastery in ways of life which make him dependent on the services of those who are dependent upon him, fails to see that if he is to enjoy the role of master in *this* way he must also offer someone the role of slave or dependent. In terms of the familiar example, it is as if he thought the intention of buying a cake in order to keep it (in the condition in which the baker sells it to him) could be fulfilled by the intention to buy it in order to have the satisfaction of eating it. Analogous examples of different sorts are to be found in more recent literature.[81]

The 'deeper' aspect is this: that underlying projects of mastery such as the slave-master's is a wider 'spiritual' purpose which the former merely represents. The slave-master must have some inkling of this purpose, but not a clear grasp of it; otherwise he would see immediately that slave-mastery was not a means of achieving it. From within the limitations of his circumstances and point of view, his grasp of the wider purpose is expressed only in his ambitious expectations for the role of master: namely his belief that when he dominates and can exploit others, he will have secured the utmost freedom and autonomy available to anyone. It is only when he first sees the obvious fact that the role of 'master' has to be played opposite that of 'slave' as an actual limitation on his freedom that he realizes that the goal of freedom he is really interested in is incompatible with this dependence he has on the slave — that in respect of his goal, as he now sees it, that dependence 'contradicts' his ambition for independence. Of course, in Hegel's philosophical allegory the master is not actually conceived as an *individual* who assumes the role of master; rather the role of master is seen as itself a character in the development of the plot. It carries the burden of the project of freedom as far as it can, but when it becomes clear (at least to the reader) not only that freedom is a richer concept than that imagined by the 'master', but that the freedom corresponding to this richer concept cannot be his *qua* master, the burden of freedom is passed on to the 'slave'; who then proceeds to pursue the project in terms of its opposite dimension — inward rather than outward mastery — the view Hegel calls Stoicism and which eventually discloses *its* limitations, which consist in its being only freedom in the realm of thought, not of action.

With certain crucial adjustments, it seems that this general account could be exploited as a systematic basis for Kierkegaard's remarks in the quoted passage. The corresponding elements are the following: first, an overt project: the pursuit of pleasure, honour, wealth, or power; second, a covert project represented or indirectly expressed by the former: it could be called the intention to ensure a diachronic stability of will, not just a correspondence between aim and achievement, but a consistency of aim through time — in *this* sense, oneness of will — but more fundamentally it is an ideal of personal autonomy or self-sufficiency present even in the aesthete's project of living in immediacy; and third, there are the outcomes of the overt projects when carried single-mindedly (as is to be expected of an overt intention sustained by a covert intention of this type) to their extremes. These are described as, respectively, disgust, contempt (for the worldly basis of one's honour), poverty, and dependence. These are the opposites of the goals sought in the overt projects, but only when seen from the point of view of the covert project. Then the claim is not a simple empirical one; if it were, the opposites would be identifiable as such from the initial vantage-point, and not only from the new vantage-point of one for whom the external has no inherent value. Only for such a person would these initially valued worldly goals be changed into their opposites. *Anxiety*'s 'immediate' genius, it will be recalled, was described as one who 'never becomes great in his own eyes' and who acted 'big' but was capable of 'deeper reflection', but whose response to anxiety in the face of the depths of his spiritual possibility was in fact to grab securely hold of worldly modes of self-fulfilment. In *Purity of Heart* Kierkegaard's intended readers are those who, although they resemble the immediate genius in finding nothing satisfying in worldly goals, differ from him in no longer being bound by them. They have entered the religious stage and have begun to come to terms with God, guilt, and the good. For such people there would, of course, be little point in reiterating the claim that the good is not to be found in the external: that is assumed. But the implications of the assumption may not be so immediately obvious: for instance, the fact that a will bent even single-mindedly upon worldly achievement lacks unity, that it is an illusion to suppose that it does not, and that only by turning away (inward) from external goals can the kind of unity the ideal of self-fulfilment presupposes be achieved.

That worldly single-mindedness gives only the illusion of unity can no doubt be treated as at least in part a straightforward empirical claim. One could even give it a simple scientific explanation: that to pursue a worldly goal single-mindedly is to expose oneself to the reactive effects of certain self-imposed deprivations which ensue from the single-mindedness itself. A one-sided individual, as Climacus points out, is one who 'rejects, clearly and decisively, what he does not want to include',[82] but what he deliberately excludes can still have the last word. Or the energy he directs upon his chosen goal may fail him. In either case he is at the mercy of the natural self's inherent diversity and proneness to change. The empirical thesis will then be that no amount of dedicated concentration in one area will protect a person from the incursion of conflicting interests in others. In fact, the thesis could be even stronger: that in concentrating upon one element in the diversity to the exclusion of the others, one *generates* disharmony and therefore increases the likelihood of reaction and change.

However, the claim that a one-sided person in this sense lacks real unity is not just empirical. Some standard of unity is presupposed, in Kierkegaard's case a rather special standard. The appeal is not to a standard that could be met, for instance, by producing an Aristotelian harmony-through-moderation in the given diversity, some kind of organic integrity in which the parts are seen to help themselves best by supporting each other. The yardstick Kierkegaard employs is a guarantee of goal constancy, an absolute incorruptibility of the will – a characteristic Aristotle himself would not hope to find outside heaven.

But is this not simply a piece of arbitrary metaphysics? Is not Kierkegaard himself, as a philosopher, imposing a goal of unity on the facts for which there is no psychological, phenomenological, or any other kind of support? Indeed, is not Kierkegaard's 'edifying' conclusion so blatantly obvious once the metaphysics is brought into the open as to be wholly unedifying? For all it amounts to is the claim that given the axiomatic ideal of unity as incorruptibility of the will, it follows logically that the unity in question can only be found, and so must be sought, elsewhere than in the pursuit of temporal objectives.

This, however, entirely misses the Hegelian element. It is not that Kierkegaard must finally admit to a metaphysical prejudice in favour of this kind or degree of unity; it is rather that the individual's developing conception of its own needs of self-sufficiency reaches the point where nothing less than this kind or degree of unity will do. To understand Kierkegaard rightly, I suggest, the three elements – the empirical hypothesis, the concept of an incorruptible unity, and the tautological consequence – should be conceived as elements or factors in a development. The development is one undergone by the idea of self-sufficiency or 'freedom of the individual' itself.[83] Initially, it is the idea of a wholeness or independence unrelated to the notion of the autonomy of the will.

236

Wholeness or independence are sought in time (though in the aesthetic sphere without making time itself essential to wholeness).[84] But — and this is the empirical factor not yet seen in the light of the ideal of unity — temporal objectives have certain outcomes which leave the project of wholeness or independence unsatisfied. The dissatisfaction prompts the perhaps already incipient realization that the ideal is one with which the limitations inherent in such objectives are incompatible — that they are in fact limitations on wholeness or independence. The conclusion that one must turn away from temporal objectives is not a simple intellectual deduction, but the result of a development in the conception of the ideal itself — that development which gives 'wholeness' or 'independence' the sense of 'incorruptible'.

For Kierkegaard the highest good is an ultimate satisfaction a person hopes to achieve when his actions are moral ones. This is one point on which Kierkegaard's notion of the highest good departs significantly from Kant's. For Kant the satisfaction (as what 'reason points out to all rational beings as the goal of all their moral wishes') lacks the kind of content that could make it an inducement to virtue; so that moral wishing has to be done without the attractiveness of the idea of this, as of any other, satisfaction. For Kant, one might say, one wishes morally only because one wishes to be moral. For Kierkegaard, however, the highest good is the idea of a concrete desire. Even in its most developed form it remains a project of the individual's, indeed a fundamental project that somehow encompasses all the others. Relevant here is Kierkegaard's remark, quoted in the previous chapter, that 'psychology is what we need and above all adequate knowledge of human life, and sympathy for its interests', and that without these 'there can be no question of completing a Christian view of life'.[85] In this way Kierkegaardian morality has a more secure basis in human psychology than Kant's.

In respect of their notions of actual moral performance, however, this may seem not to be so. For Kierkegaard, as for Kant, this particular concrete desire, that is, for an ultimate satisfaction, like all motivation for purely *temporal* objectives, has to be inoperative in a case of properly moral willing. In that case, moral activity itself (virtue) is hardly a set of actions and decisions of which it would be true to say that they flowed from projects of the individual, in the sense that they have their psychological origin in the individual's own attitudes and interests. It is precisely the suspension of the *individual's* own attitudes and interests that moral performance (truly willing the good) requires. Because of this, for reasons that, strange though the idea of this particular complicity in error may at first appear, have been offered in criticism of utilitarianism, it might be claimed that Kierkegaardian morality (as well as Kant's) constituted some kind of denial of, or attack upon, personal integrity. The claim would be interesting because Kierkegaard would have us believe that, on the contrary, his own view of morality was essential for the establishing of (true) personal integrity.

In brief, the argument, due to Bernard Williams, is this. Utilitarianism says that the right thing to do is what maximizes the general happiness; so that where what is right according to this principle conflicts with a person's own project, and however deeply engaged in and personally identified with this project the person may be, that project must, on this principle, be thrown into the calculation like any other; but it is impossible for such a person, as a utilitarian, to regard such a project or attitude 'round which he has built his life' simply as one, dispensable, satisfaction among others and

> absurd to demand of such a man . . . that he should just step aside from his own project and decision and acknowledge the decision which utilitarian calculation requires. It is to alienate him in a real sense from his actions and the source of his actions in his own convictions. . . . It is . . . in the most literal sense, an attack on his integrity.[86]

Applied to Kierkegaard, an analogous argument would be that in requiring personal projects in general to be ignored or renounced in favour of an absolute goal, Kierkegaardian (like Kantian) morality forces persons to consider as unimportant the satisfaction envisaged in the pursuit of the projects that in an obvious sense are their *own*, i.e. stem from their individual experience, assessment and convictions. Even more than in utilitarian practice, they are alienated from their actions in the comprehensive sense that they have surrendered their own agency (recall the unhappy consciousness) to a transcendent power, and *a fortiori* forfeited the very possibility of building their lives around their own personal projects and attitudes.

Kierkegaard might point out, in reply, that there is a crucial ambiguity in the mention of a project or attitude around which the agent 'builds his life'. If the life is built around the single-minded pursuit of temporal goals, then the agent lacks integrity to start with; the actions we identify as characteristically his are expressions of an inner conflict. If, on the other hand, his commitment is indeed that of an integrated individual, then it is already the pursuit of a transcendent goal. In that case, being required to step aside from his own projects and decisions in deference to the aims of the good is not so much having to dispense with the satisfactions that can be derived from them, as to locate the true source of satisfaction in having projects and making decisions at all. Furthermore, the utilitarian has a special reason that the Kierkegaardian (and Kantian) does not have for saying that the giving up of personal projects alienates him from his actions and their source in his convictions. The utilitarian imperative is an accidental product of the history of other people's projects. So the utilitarian agent has no influence over the in-put state for a present calculation of utility other than the satisfaction *he* wishes to put into the sum.[87] Whether the result complies with or excludes that satisfaction is therefore, from his own point of view, altogether arbitrary. Morality, like fate, is an alien element over which he exercises no control. In Kierkegaardian self-surrender this is not the case. Here the surrender is not enforced; it is made freely by the agent himself. Nor is it in deference to something 'alien' to the agent's fundamental projects; it is in deference to a highest good that is essentially linked to *human* ideals, the *failure* to surrender to which is what alienates.

Although the rejoinder assumes much that one would wish to debate, it does reveal an important respect in which, even in the question of moral performance, as opposed to the idea of its reward, Kierkegaard's account is sympathetic to the more fundamental, long-term 'interests of human life'. Perhaps it also reveals a respect in which, also in this regard, Kierkegaard's account has more psychological appeal than Kant's. We noted at the beginning that for Kant the *summum bonum* is a whole which contains the intrinsic good of virtue as a part. According to our account in this chapter, the same could be said of Kierkegaard's idea of the *summum bonum*. If truthfully willing the good (virtue) is not just a means to achieving diachronic integrity (happiness), but is in some way identical with, or an aspect of having, that integrity, then virtue and happiness, though different concepts, have a common reference. They have to be different concepts, for otherwise the conditions which satisfy the one would also satisfy the other, and we would be faced with the Stoic and Epicurean alternatives which Kant formulates but neither of which he accepts. Kierkegaard would not accept them either: happiness is bestowed, not earned; i.e. if one has it, then one has to believe that it is being given rather than that one has done what is necessary and sufficient to secure it. It is just that it is only in the context of virtue that one may hope to be given it, though virtue requires that this hope not be conceived as something to whose fulfilment virtue stands as a means. Despite this qualification, however, if Kierkegaard were forced to choose between Kant's Stoic and Epicurean, there is little doubt that, in view of his emphasis on the passionate concern of the individual for happiness, he would favour the latter. That, at least, is one way of marking the difference between Kant's and Kierkegaard's Kantianism.

VII

Love of One's Neighbour

And what is your attitude to others? Are you at one
with everyone — by willing one thing? Or do you
create partisan division? . . . All group solidarity is
partisanship against universal humanity. But to will
one thing, to will the good in truth . . . that is
unity.[1]

1   The happiness of others

We know the general form of a Kierkegaardian ethics — the sort of
restraints Kierkegaard places on a properly ethical frame of mind.
There is a reward which gives ethical endeavour its practical sense,
as well as a punishment for failing in the endeavour, but both the
reward and the punishment must be conceived in the same category
as the ethical itself, and there — on Kierkegaard's view of the
ethical — they cannot assume the form of inducements. But what
about the content of the properly ethical frame of mind? What
fills the heart purged of self-regard, freed from the lure of inducement? The answer is given in *Works of Love* (1847). In two not
necessarily very clear words it is: Christian love. In fact the Christian,
or 'agapeistic', way of life, based on a deliberate or principled
rather than natural or instinctual regard for one's fellows, is for
Kierkegaard the ultimate aim of the positive development. An
ambitious one, too, on Kierkegaard's reading of that way of life.
But also problematic, and in this chapter we shall examine the
problems in some detail.

Philosophically the agapeistic ideal looks distinctly unpromising
Not only can this Christian amendment to a basically Kantian
ethics look suspiciously like a piece of *ad hoc* paste-work dictated

by dogma rather than reason; to many the combination will in any case look like something of a conceptual monstrosity. For despite its high standing in Western culture, the idea of a dutiful love, a love that can be commanded, savours strongly of contradiction, as Kant himself noted.

And yet, whatever personal satisfaction may ensue from ethical practice, ethical practice itself is nothing if not a concern with the happiness or good of others. So when Christ, in endorsing the principle that one must love God with all one's heart, soul and mind,[2] adds that one must also love *one's neighbour as oneself*,[3] he may seem to be doing no more than specifying the conceptual truth that to have a moral intention simply *is* to have a regard for the good of others and not just of oneself. But most philosophers who have examined this principle have concluded, with Kant, that whatever form the *moral* concern of each for the good of others takes it cannot be that of the sympathetic concern individual persons have for one another which we call 'love'; for that kind of concern is by its very nature instinctual; consequently, acts of will are superfluous where such concern exists, and ineffectual and therefore irrelevant where it does not. So those philosophers who, like Kant, are nevertheless interested in upholding the Christian principle must reinterpret it. For Kant this means replacing the impossible duty of *loving* one's neighbour with that of endeavouring to *like* to practise one's duties towards one's neighbour,[4] and interpreting the original commandment in its literal form as an expression of an ideal of free, rational subjects, all allowing for the freedom of each, an ideal community possible only for non-natural beings elevated above the discriminatory network of sympathies and antipathies. Others who do not share Kant's view that moral actions are necessarily dutiful actions may be inclined for the same reason — i.e. that love cannot be commanded — to regard love as a right rather than a duty; as a desirable but discriminatory form of fellowship which as part of the good life people should be maximally free to enjoy; and the specifically moral obligation in this connection as our duty to remove, in ourselves as well as others, obstacles to the free exercise of this form of fellowship.

With all this weight of argument against the view that a universal good will can take the form of a will that loves in obedience to a law, we have some distance to go before offering Kierkegaard's full theory of the positive development for serious philosophical consideration.

2   The non-morality of natural love: three lines of argument

Kierkegaard acknowledges the peculiarity of Christian love, that it 'contains this apparent contradiction, that to love is [a] duty'.[5] And yet he believes such love is possible. If it is, the contradiction must be merely apparent. But he does not make any direct attempt to convince the reader that this is so. The arguments of *Works of Love* are directed mainly at showing that any form of love other than Christian love (neighbour-love) has no moral value, because it is self-love. Others who accept this latter conclusion might be willing to deny that there is a form of love that does have moral value. But Kierkegaard would not be so disposed; love for him has a, indeed *the*, prime value: 'to love one's fellow-humans is the only thing worth living for; without this love you are not really living; and to love one's fellow-humans is also the only blessed consolation'.[6] So obviously we will have to see what kind of case can be built upon Kierkegaard's remarks on neighbour-love in support of the thesis that there is a moral form of love that is not a form of instinctual or natural love.

First, however, we shall examine Kierkegaard's arguments for denying that natural love is a moral form of love. But a repeated word of caution here: *Works of Love* (subtitled 'Some Christian Deliberations in Discourse Form'), like *Purity of Heart*,[7] is addressed to the converted. So whatever arguments we may come across there, we should not expect to find any attempt to justify the Christian way of life as such. In fact, the aim of this work, again like *Purity of Heart*, is not 'discursive' in the philosophical sense at all, but explicatory. This fact obviously bears on the nature as well as the range of its 'arguments'. Kierkegaard is laying bare the anatomy of Christian love in *practice*,[8] confronting the would-be ethical subject with a conceptually adequate picture of his chosen ideal, against which to measure the adequacy of his own actual ethical performance; he is not trying to provide a metaphysics of moral love. Within this frame of reference, however, we do find the outlines of philosophical argument. This is partly because Kierkegaard wants to show that all forms of love which fall short of neighbour-love also fall short of generally accepted minimum requirements of moral behaviour: they are, he claims, forms of selfishness, even of self-love. In this section an argument to this effect will be constructed, based on Kierkegaard's deliberations and with some amendments.

'Love [*Elskov*, i.e. natural love] and friendship', he says, 'are predilection and predilection's passion', something which distinguishes them from Christian love which is 'the love of self-denial'.[9] Let us formulate the first part of this as the claim that,

(1)   All natural love (in practice) is preferential (behaviour).

A little later he says he will show that 'passionate predilection is another form of self-love'.[10] To do this he asks the reader to accept — or see — that in picking out one person rather than another as an object of concern, there is also a reflexive relationship to the bestower of concern, and the latter amounts to self-concern or self-regard. Now it might be that where one person's interest in another takes the form of a loving regard there is a special basis for attributing self-regard to the former. But in order to allow room for this possibility to emerge let us begin by generalizing the claim to,

(2)   *All* preferential behaviour is self-regarding.

From (1) and (2) there follows:

(3)   All natural love is self-regarding.

This conclusion is obviously open to interpretation. In particular it is not clear that the sense in which natural love is said to be self-regarding is one in which we should also accept that it is a form of self-love; and it is clearly in this latter notion that Kierkegaard sees a basis for his assumption that natural love is not moral love. So let us examine our two premises without at first reading this idea into the expression 'self-regarding'. Provisionally it means simply 'having *some* kind of regard for the self'.

First the claim that natural love is preferential.[11] This is surely a simple truism, though one may wonder whether it is a factual commonplace or a tautology. But however one interprets it, a situation in which one person has an affectionate regard or loving sympathy for another surely just *is* a situation in which one person is 'preferred' or picked out from others as an object of such concern. With certain reservations (for example, if a 'love' that borders on sheer sensual gratification could be said to be blind to such differences as determine preference in the case of a *sympathetic* concern, it could not be called preferential so much as, say, opportunistic), it seems reasonable to say that for one person to have a regard — a loving regard — for another implies that the former prefers the latter in the appropriate respect to an indeterminate number of other persons. No new insight is needed to accept that natural love is one form of preference among others.

This truism should not be confused with another. If from any cause, for any reason, or with whatever aim, I currently devote myself to the interests of another individual or group, there must as a matter of *logic* always be some persons currently excluded

244

from that devotion. In this sense my devotion, like any form of attention, is inescapably preferential. In fact if, as Kierkegaard holds, genuine love is a relationship between *individuals* (mediated by God), then even my Christian concern for others will be maximally preferential in this sense, since it involves excluding the rest of mankind from a simultaneous concern. And even if my concern for individuals were analysed dispositionally so that I could be said to be *presently* devoted to all those individuals with whose well-being I am ready actively to concern myself one at a time, a certain 'preference' is unavoidable *in practice* by virtue of the number of available clients. But this 'preference' is, after all, simply a consequence of the limits set on our capacity to attend, and is not itself the result of any partiality or choice between possible subjects of attention. If the claim which Kierkegaard's thesis is to be based on is to have any weight, it must be the claim that natural love indeed involves some kind of choice. And, as we have said, the claim that natural love is in this latter sense selective is uncontroversial.

Now the second premise: the general claim that preferential behaviour is self-regarding. A reasonable interpretation would make this, too, a very weak claim, to the effect that preference in any form at all is *per se* self-regarding, in so far as preferring one person or thing to any other(s) is no more than to pick out that person or thing as, in the circumstances, best suited to satisfying a given need or purpose. If 'need' and 'purpose' are understood widely this premise is really only a tautology. If having a need or a purpose is nothing more specific than wanting to achieve, do, or secure something, and preference is simply part of the indispensably selective process whereby human beings pursue their various interests, any action at all will be self-regarding, in the sense that it will have regard to the interests of the agent. In this case one could only cease to be self-regarding by ceasing to act, that is to pursue one's interests, or to have any, including those interests that come under the heading of 'promoting the interests of others' and amongst which one must presumably look in order to find any that would bear the label 'unselfish'.

As we have interpreted them, premises (1) and (2) are both uncontroversial; so much so that the conclusion to be drawn from them — that all natural love is self-regarding — forms far too weak a basis for the claim that 'to love someone who is in a preferential sense nearer to one than all others is self-love', as Kierkegaard also puts it.[12] To claim that preferential love is in any morally significant, i.e. negative, sense love of self, one would have to show why the self-regard bound up with expressions of interest of any kind becomes in this special case morally reprehensible.

What reasons could one give? There are at least two arguments, which approach the issue, as it were, from opposite ends. The first is an empirical argument which claims that a loving interest introduces a special element of morally reprehensible selfishness additional to the, let us say, morally neutral self-regard common to interest in general. The second argument is conceptual and says that the idea of love is one with which self-regard even in this latter sense is incompatible.

Underlying the former argument might be the following point: that in the case of a loving or sympathetic concern preference is not mediated by a goal which then dictates the selection independently of whatever motives one has for adopting the goal (as in the preference for a hammer over a screwdriver for driving nails into a wall); rather the selection is a direct expression of a sentiment which it is implausible to suppose contains no self-regarding motives, e.g. a desire to have the satisfaction of being the one who helps, or of being the object of that particular person's gratitude. To escape the contamination of this form of personal involvement, concern with the interests of others would have to be mediated by some humanitarian goal, such as minimizing need, which itself selects the objects of benefaction, perhaps in this case those in greatest need. While underlying the latter argument might be something like the idea that, because it purports to be a unidirectional concern with the interests of one or more others, love cannot legitimately contain any element of personal interest at all, and is therefore inconsistent with any kind of selectiveness that might otherwise be warranted by the rational pursuit of such interest. A corollary to this might be that, in its active moods, the verb 'to love' does not designate a legitimate personal interest, since its proper topic is the interest of another.

The corresponding arguments might proceed along the following, respective lines. In the first case, regarding the implausibility of supposing self-regarding motives to be absent in the case of a loving or sympathetic concern, one could argue that, given a commonly accepted distinction between selfish and therefore immoral actions and unselfish and therefore moral actions (a distinction for which we have ready-made paradigms), close attention to the psychology of sympathetic concern will reveal that there is at any rate much less of the latter than we commonly suppose; perhaps so little that even some accepted paradigms of unselfishness should be placed on the other side. The conclusion would be that love brings out an extra degree or dimension of self-regard, enough to count as, or of a type that amounts to, morally significant selfishness.

In the second case it could be claimed that love simply *is* that special kind of interest which purports to be an interest specifically and exclusively in the interests of others. With support in Kant's principle that in moral respects persons must be treated as ends in themselves and never just as means,[13] the point might be stretched to the conclusion that in the case of the pursuit of this kind of interest, its subordination to the satisfaction of any personal interest whatsoever must be considered morally reprehensible. The justification might be that any admixture of the latter is proof that the necessary transfer of interest has not been made.

Both lines of argument have some initial cogency, but hardly enough to win immediate acceptance of the universal claim that

(4)   Natural love lacks positive moral value.

For this requires, in terms of the first argument, that no discriminating actions at all be found to answer to the accepted paradigm of morally unselfish actions; and in terms of the second, that the exercise of love cannot be either itself the pursuit of an interest which those exercising it have or a part of any such pursuit.

Kierkegaard's observations are mainly in the spirit of the former argument. He points to cases of 'love' which fail to take account of the concern or the real interest of the 'loved' one, and where perhaps little insight is needed to disclose not only the involvement but also predominance of the bestower's own interests. We may think of the suffocating protectiveness of a guardian for a dependent, or, the kind of case Kierkegaard is especially concerned with (for reasons we shall return to), the Pygmalion-relationship where the would-be bestower of love approaches the loved one with preconceived ideas as to what form the latter's benefit should take. But these observations are, in the present context, insufficient; even if we agree and accept, we need not be convinced that absolutely all natural affection involves culpable self-interest in one or another form.

Now it might be objected on Kierkegaard's behalf here that the examples are not intended to convince us of the truth of this latter conclusion, since that is a conclusion we, Kierkegaard's readers, are assumed already to have accepted. In fact, in order to reach conclusion (4), that all natural love lacks positive moral value, all that is needed is the insertion of the premise (3¹) that *no self-regarding behaviour has positive moral value*, which is, after all, the view put forward so carefully in *Purity of Heart*.

But this would be unsatisfactory for two connected reasons. First, it would be to treat (3¹) as a metaphysical axiom, a principle imposed upon the facts rather than suggested by deeper insight into them, which is presumably not Kierkegaard's intention.

Second, it would be to assume that we could be satisfied that (3¹) was true independently of arguments about the morality of differ- ent forms of *love*, whereas in view of the centrality of love in Kierkegaard's personal and philosophical thinking he must surely expect an investigation into (4) to *confirm* his (3¹). In which case it would be methodologically self-defeating to deduce the result of such an investigation *from* (3¹).

Natural love, according to our argument, has two directions. It is *self*-regarding and at least *aims* at the other. So far we have con- sidered how the inability of such love to be moral might be established by investigating the former direction. But the latter also offers a possibility; in fact, a possibility that we have already broached in referring to Kant's principle that, morally speaking, persons must be treated as ends and not just as means. Although Kierkegaard does not use the principle, his observations can often be seen as implicit applications of it; and in fact it is in this regard that one should, I think, consider his examples of a 'love' that fails to take account of the concerns or interests of the 'loved' one. So let us now outline a third line of argument for the non-morality of natural (discriminating, and in a wide sense inescapably self- regarding) love.

We suggested that love is an interest in the interests of others. But, of course, it must be more than that. A concern *with* the interests of others may take any number of forms without amount- ing to a loving interest. I might, for example, devote a lifetime to the public good, to benefiting my dependents, or to intermittent and selective philanthropy, without expending a moment of sympathy for the objects of my beneficence. I may be acting simply out of a desire to follow or set a good example, or to pave my way to heaven, or perhaps my beneficence becomes so time- consuming that I lack the opportunity to spare the sympathetic thought I might otherwise have for the recipients of my bene- factions. A loving interest must be at least a felt concern for the other's interest, in the sense that the latter is an ulterior goal, not subservient to the benefactor's own interests. One must want not only to do good to someone, but want that person to be done good to. Furthermore, one must want good to be done to them for no other reason than that this is what the person in question wants or needs. (Complications arising from the possibility that the needs may not always be determined by what the other wants will be discussed below.) All of which might be summed up by saying that, besides being beneficence, love must also be benevol- ence.

A simple formula for a loving interest might therefore be: wanting what another wants (or needs) because the other wants (or needs) it. Or alternatively, though more paternalistically, wanting what would benefit another because the other would be benefited. With two important reservations, these could stand as popular applications of Kant's principle. The reservations are these: first, Kant's principle says in effect that each must treat *all* others (all rational beings, therefore including not only others but also oneself) as ends and not (just as) means, whereas our formula gives only a necessary condition of each person's having a specifically loving interest in *some* other. Second, Kant would not himself accept that the principle could be applied, as we are provisionally applying it, to natural love: not directly on the grounds that natural love is discriminating, but because like Kierkegaard he maintains that only a love which is subject to the will can be moral, and it is characteristic of natural love that it is not, cannot be, willed. In fact, Kant, and in this respect he differs from Kierkegaard, would deny that the principle could be applied to any form of love at all, since for him *natural* love — as we shall see below — is the only form of love properly so called.

Let us nevertheless use Kant's idea that moral actions are directed at others' interests independently of the moral agent's own interests to test the morality of natural love.

Our first premise (1) said that natural love is preferential, that for one person to have a loving regard for another implies that the former prefers the latter in some appropriate respect, prefers the other in this respect to an indeterminate number of other persons. Now it is preferential because (a) it is conditioned upon a certain natural power to appeal and to be appealed to, and (b) this power is variously and unevenly distributed among the human species. To love someone in this conditional way is therefore to love one (not necessarily at first sight; nor necessarily by virtue of physical appeal; it may be the mind that fascinates, pleasurably stimulates, or comfortingly reassures) among that subgroup in which there is a matching of power to appeal and power to be appealed to. However, the power to appeal and to be appealed to, and on which the conditional and preferential aspects are based, may inhere in qualities which are not necessarily part of the loved one's continuing identity. If they are not necessarily part of that identity, then a love conditionally based on them is subject to the restriction that it is compatible with only some of the (let us call them) characterological variations which the loved one may come to exhibit: namely those which include preservation of the qualities in which the aforesaid power inheres. The same applies *mutatis mutandis* to the loving person's power to be appealed to. So apart

249

from being variously and unevenly distributed, the basis of such love is also in principle a biographically temporary condition of any person or persons in whom it exists. Persons loved on such a basis can become unlovable, and a love that fails to embrace the loved one's possible future unlovableness in this respect might aptly be said to fall short of the ostensibly loved one's 'self'; it embraces what may be only a limited biographical phase of the person who is loved and not that person as such. The underlying argument here would be that since the self can be conceived to persist under all such conceivable changes, a love based on any selection of the loved one's possible characterological properties does not have that self as its object. In terms of Kant's principle, it does not address itself to the other as an end. It is therefore not love *of* the other. And if it is an essential feature of love that it does address itself to the other, then it is not love either. Perhaps such an argument underlies Shakespeare's 'Love is not love which alters when it alteration finds',[14] the point being that love ('the marriage of true *minds*' (my emphasis)), in order to be constant, and if it is not that it is not true love, must embrace significant variation in its object.

But this argument, compelling though it may appear at first glance, seems much less so when stretched far enough to be a premise leading to the conclusion that all discriminating love is non-moral. For consider. All that we have so far is the idea that your love would address the other, and thus be morally acceptable love, or even love at all, only if you would continue to evince the same loving concern no matter what changes *that self* could be conceived to undergo. But this would be compatible with there being certain restrictions on the notion of the identical self; certain restrictions on the kinds and degrees of change which the 'same' self could be thought to undergo. These might amount to what is required of a person remaining in some way *recognizably* the same self — not necessarily in appearance, but in character, attitude, responsiveness. Given such restrictions on the self, it would not be a sufficient condition of not having truly addressed one's loving concern to the other if one ceased to love that person (assuming the conditions for identifying a person are wider than those for identifying a self); since it may be that the person in question has ceased to be recognizably the same self. So if we are to use the argument to establish the non-morality of preferential love, we would have to require of love of another self that that self be characterologically a totally unrestricted target. Then in order to love someone morally, you would have to love that person even if he or she ceased to be recognizably the same person, and 'became' any conceivable kind of person at all. Thus, in order for your loving to have as its object something which does not discriminate that object characterologically from anyone else at all, you have to allow that the present object of that love would continue to be loved even if he or she ceased to have any power to attract you, and even acquired the power to repel or disgust you — physically, mentally, or morally.

To stretch the argument's terms of reference that far, however, is to accept this unrestricted notion of the self, and the only reason we seem to have for doing that, so far, is that we want (experimentally) to establish the conclusion that preferential love lacks positive moral value. If that is the conclusion we are trying to establish, the adoption of the notion begs the question. We can equally accept, as perhaps most would in any case be inclined, that if someone ceases to show a loving concern for another because the other has acquired a totally different and, to the formerly interested party, a wholly repulsive character or personality, then the target has simply become *another* self. (Note that the argument in this or the unstretched version does not require us to suppose that the object of moral love is something different from and underlying all these changes, something that puts on or takes off these different guises — a transcendental self. We can just as well think of the object of moral love as something that *undergoes*, and is itself in, all these changes.)

Now the concept of a self employed in the stretched version of our third line of argument corresponds to Kierkegaard's concept of 'neighbour', the object of a dutiful love. When loving a person is a duty, he says, 'there is no limit to love; if the duty is to be fulfilled the love must be unlimited, be unchanged in whatever way the object changes'.[15] The object or self thus conceived is 'the one who is nearer you than all others . . . but not in a predilectory sense'.[16] That is, the neighbour for Kierkegaard is any person with whom one *happens* to be interactively involved, (say) as bystander, partner, negotiator, opponent, or enemy. In this sense your neighbour could just as much be the person you would like to prevent moving in next door as the one who actually lives there. The point is that there be no restrictions on who this nearest person may be. It is only when one loves one's neighbour, in this sense, that one loves morally. For 'to love the one who is preferentially nearer one than all others is self-love'.[17]

Apparently, however, we do not as yet have an argument sufficient to conclude that *such* self-love (i.e. that which is merely a consequence of love's being preferential) morally invalidates a concern for the interests of a selected other. We could even say that a congenial reading of our popular formula (that one person loves another when the former wants what the latter wants, needs, or would be benefited by because the latter wants, needs, or would be benefited by it) would sanction as a genuine example of love a case of such concern even where it is clearly preferential. Even if it were insisted that genuine love must manifest itself in a growth of sympathy, an increase in the power to be appealed to, and thus an increase in the other's ability to appeal, the idea that the growth, etc., should extend to the point at which no cognizance was made of personal distinction or variation at all, would strike most, surely, as most uncongenial. Nor is there, on the congenial reading, any obvious need to call upon the services of the will. Perhaps a love that is a developed response of this kind involves the notion of duty, but the duties could be duties out of love rather than *to* love — duties to do unpleasant things *because* of one's overriding sympathy — not as Kant insists (see below) duties to do good which can have sympathy as a consequence. All in all, our formula seems to express a conventional and *exemplifiable* form of genuine but still discriminating love.

There are two points to make, however, before concluding this section. First, it might be objected that the principle expressed in our popular formula is in fact too weak. It might be claimed, for example, that it does not even amount to being equivalent to our application of Kant's test of morality. Suppose that what the other wants is a short-term, provisional love, whether an affair of heart, body, or mind, still only an 'affair'. Does not a concern with the other that takes account of this want and no other satisfy the formula, but without satisfying the requirement that the other be addressed as another *self*? In that case, it would at least not count as a case of Kantian morality. However, it might be argued that if the reason why the bestower of love enters into a contract of short-term gratification is *really* that the other party wants that, and (whatever the improbabilities) there is no other self-regarding reason for consenting, then the love that is the intention to do what the other wants because the other wants it is already properly addressed to another, namely that other self that has this want among others, and perhaps more fully addressed than the recipient would be content with. (Cf. the poignant affair of Mary Watson and Henry Hickslaughter in Graham Greene's *Cheap in August*, in which consummation with the physically repugnant Henry is possible only because his short-term wants are understood as expressions of longer-term, sympathizable needs.) The case would be different if both recipient *and* bestower entered into the contract for reasons of their own expected gratification. That would not only be plainly self-regarding, there would be *no* adequate reference to the other self — no more than if one wants what the other wants not *just* because the other wants it, but because one hopes to establish or prolong certain opportunities in that way.[18] It seems, therefore, that in general the formula may be adequate for capturing Kant's condition, although no doubt in other respects too simple. For instance, it may have to allow the lover's wanting on behalf of the loved one precisely things the *latter* thinks he or she needs but which the lover may see no point in wanting; and the lover's wanting on behalf of the loved one things that the lover but not the loved one thinks that the latter needs.

The second objection takes us further in the direction of Kierkegaard's own thought. It might be claimed that we have not yet plumbed the moral depths of preferential love; that if we examine the conditions in which preference operates we will see that they place crucial restrictions on the loving concern one person may have for another, *even* when that other is genuinely addressed *as* another self. The restrictions can be (at least) of two kinds. Both correspond to points made in Kierkegaard's 'deliberations'. The first is this: that in the case of preferential love it is a requirement of the lover's that he or she be the one that pursues the happiness of the other. In fact, this is an essential part of the lover's 'interest': not just that this particular lovable person be done good to, but that this particular loving person be the one that does the good. In that case preferential love does not will the good after the manner of the good: the preferring lover prefers that he or she be the benefactor, does not see, or want, that this good 'can get on without him [or her]'.[19] In terms of our formula and the third line of argument, this in effect imposes a kind of restriction on the other self *qua* lovable which might be said to involve an incomplete address to the self. It addresses a self that is one that can only have this good done to it by the addresser personally. Yet can, strictly speaking, a description of *another* self contain such a specification? The second restriction is connected to this one but contains a dimension we have not yet touched upon: the other's own possibilities of self-development. By pressing his preference, the preferential lover is, in fact, denying developmental autonomy to the other self. In these two restrictions, or perhaps they are two aspects of the same restriction, we may see a hint of what we have been looking for: a basis in fact and ordinary judgment for Kierkegaard's apparently abstract and arbitrary assumption that a good will is one purged of self-interest. If acts of love are what the good amounts to in practice, and love is a concern for the good of *others*, then strictly speaking the demand that this good come

253

from a preferred source is not just a superfluous condition, but an incompatible one.

3 The requirements and functions of practical love: Kierkegaard and Kant

Kant distinguishes between 'practical' and 'pathological' love. By the latter he means love based on appeal, or 'tender sympathy'. Such love is not subject to the will. But practical love 'is seated in the will — in principles of action'.[20] Only practical love can be commanded.

Therefore only practical love can have moral worth. There are two aspects to this in Kant's ethics. The first is that if anything at all is to have moral worth this can only be determined by submitting the relevant maxim to the test of universalizability — not, say, by appealing to moral intuition or sensibility. So if it is the case that I ought to try to bring about the happiness of others, as remarked earlier, it must be 'simply because a maxim which excludes [this goal's realization] cannot be comprehended as a universal law in one and the same volition'.[21]

The second aspect is this: that the moral worth of a particular loving act consists in its being done for no other reason than that it has been determined, in the manner prescribed, that it ought to be done. Neither the prescribed manner for determining what ought to be done nor the conditions of the morality of doing it leave any loophole for inclination. Inclinations can be neither objects nor sources of moral evaluation.

This is Kant's case for our thesis (4), that natural love has no positive moral value. It means that 'pathological' love lies outside morality. Love's candidacy to moral status must therefore rest with practical love. But Kant denies that practical love is love properly so called. 'Love', he says in the Preface of the *Metaphysical Elements of Ethics*, 'is a matter of *feeling*, not of will or volition, and I cannot love because I *will* to do so, still less because I *ought*.' Hence 'there is no such thing as a *duty to love*'.[22] Since practical love is 'seated in the will' it cannot be a matter of feeling. But then neither can it be a matter of love.

What then to make of the injunction: 'Love God above everything, and thy neighbour as thyself' (in fact, two distinct commandments of which Christ is reported to have said that on them 'hang all the law and the prophets')?[23] Kant has sufficient regard for scriptural authority to want to reconcile his views with its doctrine. This, with characteristic subtlety, he does as follows. Because God is not an object of the senses, he cannot be loved pathologically; so the pathological element in the commandment must be the *frame of mind in which* one carries out one's duties to God: 'To love God means, in this sense, to like to do His commandments.'[24] Assuming that 'love' is used in the same sense in both commandments, the same formula must apply even where the objects of love are (among other things) objects of sense. So 'to love one's neighbour means to like to practise all duties towards him'. But then since a 'pathological' state cannot be brought about in obedience to a command, even when it involves an activity, the latter commandment cannot be to *have* the relevant disposition or frame of mind, but to try to acquire it. Not, it seems, however, with any expectation of doing so: this law of laws, 'like all the moral precepts of the Gospel', expresses an ideal of holiness unattainable 'by any creature, but yet . . . the pattern which we should strive to approach, and in an uninterrupted but infinite progress become like to'.[25] In the *Metaphysical Elements of Ethics* Kant talks of this disposition as 'the love of men . . . as a settled habit of inclination to beneficence',[26] noting that the instruction to love one's neighbour cannot be an instruction to feel sympathy and then to act out of that sympathy, but rather to do good (dutifully) to one's neighbour and then the inclination will follow. But though Kant refers in one place to the disposition as 'moral',[27] it is clear that in doing good out of this disposition, however much it may be acquired by effort and practice, one is not, on Kant's principles, acting morally.

> I cannot have respect for inclination, whether my own or another's. . . . It is only what is connected with my will as a principle, by no means as an effect [e.g. of inclination] . . . in other words, simply the law of itself, which can be an object of respect.[28]

For moral purposes inclination and will are, in Kant, essentially opposed. Doing good to others 'first acquire[s] its true moral worth' when done from duty. So a loving will, and for Kant this can be exemplified either in tender sympathy or, where that does not exist, in an inclination to perform duties of benefaction, is not a *morally* good will. In fact, on Kant's view, acting out of an inclination to do something generally admired, even where what is admired *conforms* with moral law, has no more value than failing to stifle an inclination to do something generally deplored. 'It is a very beautiful thing to do good to men from love of them and from sympathetic good will, or to be just from love of order', but

> this is not yet the true moral maxim of our conduct which is suitable to our position amongst rational beings as *men*, when

we pretend with fanciful pride to set ourselves above the thought of duty, like volunteers, and, as if we were independent on the command, to want to do of our own good pleasure what we think we need no command to do.[29]

Kant strains consistency at two points. He interprets the moral commandment to love one's neighbour as an injunction to try to acquire a form of will — a duty-loving disposition. But if one succeeded in acquiring it, on Kant's own premise that moral action belongs to an earthly context in which moral will and disposition are in opposition to one another, this would mean that one's actions were no longer moral. Kant mends this crack by defining success in such a way that no earthly creature could *completely* succeed, for complete success 'would mean that there does not exist in him *even the possibility* of a desire that would tempt him to deviate from [moral law]'.[30] The second point is related to this one. Successfully to cultivate the inclination to love one's duties to others would surely be to decrease the opportunities for a rational consciousness of one's membership of a 'supersensible system of nature under the autonomy of practical reason'; for it would be to encourage people to act as if they had a *more* than merely rational consciousness of that membership. And that, in the circumstances of human existence, would be, on Kant's assumptions, to have a *less* than rational consciousness of it. In both respects Kant's reading of the Scripture produces an inner tension when combined with the principles of his ethical theory.

Now, whatever inconsistencies threaten Kierkegaard's account, on these two particular points the theory unfolded in *Works of Love* departs crucially from Kant's. I shall briefly outline the relevant aspects of the theory (as I read it), and then discuss the consequences.

In Chapter 5 Kierkegaard talks of acquiring a 'loving attitude'; and he also talks of the effects of adopting this attitude to our neighbour. The idea seems to be that we can adopt it deliberately, and that since these effects are desirable, we should adopt it, or at least try to. What is this attitude? Of the person who succeeds in adopting it he says that he or she ignores evil in other persons just as the child does so naturally,[31] and even refrains from taking steps to understand it. To try to understand evil, says Kierkegaard, is always to try to come to some kind of terms with it,[32] thus as it were giving it diplomatic recognition; moreover, an eye trained to detect evil finds it everywhere and eventually sees nothing else.[33] In trying to understand evil (and here Kierkegaard would almost certainly include investigations into the environmental or hereditary causes of evil actions) one actually becomes blind to the good. Kierkegaard attributes to a loving attitude two positive effects. First, this epistemological one: by ignoring evil it enables the other-wise undetected good in people to be discovered.[34] Second, a practical effect: by being willing to look for, and by offering, extenuating (*formildende*) explanations of evil, as well as by being forgiving,[35] it can actually prevent the emergence of evil by removing the occasions for it. Love is a lubricant which smoothes the jagged edges on which evil thrives. By cultivating a consistently loving attitude, not only will differences and antipathies come to dominate one's personal relationships less, not least because they will be deprived of many of the occasions on which they depend in order to do so, but previously unnoticed virtues will come into view. Love, for Kierkegaard, has a unique practical function. Since he spells out the effects in such detail it seems clear that he means us to regard them as having moral and not, say, merely some form of aesthetic value.

The second point at which Kierkegaard departs crucially from Kant is this: for Kant, the intrinsic value of virtue or moral practice consists in its representation in the form of the practitioner's will of an ideal of rational freedom that belongs only to a super-sensible world. Moral practice is a mundane being's *conformity* with the supermundane ideal, a conformity that is found exclus-ively in dutiful action; it is not a way of introducing the ideal *into* mundane reality. But in Kierkegaard we have the idea that the sensible world can itself come to bear the imprint of an ideal, even though the 'source' of that ideal remains ineradicably transcendent. It does so when, by virtue of a practice that is the expression of a unified will, we give room to the infinite qualities of unity, perfec-tion, and incorruptibility — in the first instance, by making the will the kind of 'room' that can accommodate them, a will that is formally unified by directing itself upon an absolute goal (as Climacus says); a will purged, as in *Purity of Heart*, of all personal goals. But by extension they might also be said to be qualities of the world in which such a will operates. For Kierkegaard as well as Kant the ideal of freedom is mutual as well as personal: that is, it is a freedom in which the freedoms of individuals are compatible. In *Purity of Heart* he seems to assume that unity of will is linked closely with the idea of the unity of mankind: the love of each for all. He says that 'all group solidarity [*Sammenhold*] is partisanship against universal humanity', while 'to will one thing . . . is unity [*Samdrægtighed*] '.[36] In practical terms the link is no doubt to be found in the effects of the loving attitude just mentioned, that attitude being, one might say, a specification of the will that genuinely wills one thing, in that it contains no admixture of selfishness. Mankind becomes the object of a person's actions, for Kierkegaard, only when that person is not himself the object of his actions.

If the interpretation is correct on both points, Kierkegaard's view is that a properly good will is a universally loving will, and that cultivating such a will is a moral project. But then, how can he retain the principle which he apparently shares with Kant, but which would force Kant to deny that cultivating a loving will is a moral project: namely that moral love is love in obedience to an externally given commandment? How can moral love be both disposition *and* duty? Either you force yourself to do something in the absence of an inclination to do it, perhaps in the face of a disinclination to do it, or you do as you are inclined. You cannot do both simultaneously, and only the first two can be acting from duty. Furthermore, how can there be any kind of *love* for someone when, as Kant says, I am 'repelled by a natural and unconquerable aversion',[37] which is what the principle of universal love requires?

Let us take both points and try, in an appropriate spirit, to find 'extenuating' interpretations of them.

First, the matter of duty versus disposition. The crux here for both Kierkegaard and Kant is freedom of the will — the will's autonomy — as the basis of morality. But it is not altogether clear, without Kant's special reasons, that this freedom can only be established by the will's acting dutifully in accordance with preference-excluding laws that it prescribes to itself. Why should not the will continue to be free when it acquires the habit of, even a taste for, acting in accordance with such laws? If the laws exclude preference, then habits regulated by them should also exclude preference, and if the exclusion of preference is what guarantees freedom, a dispositional self-sufficiency should be as good a demonstration of the will's autonomy as any self-imposed law-enforcement. In fact, it may be a better demonstration. In *The Spirit of Christianity* Hegel writes:

> the Sermon [on the Mount] does not teach reverence for the laws; on the contrary, it exhibits that which fulfils the law but annuls it as law and so is something higher than obedience to law and makes law superfluous.[38]

and

> Jesus makes a general demand on his hearers to surrender their rights, to lift themselves above the whole sphere of justice

or injustice by love, for in love there vanish not only rights but also the feeling of inequality and the hatred of enemies which this feeling's imperative demand for equality implies.[39]

Hegel describes a movement to a higher level where duty, law, and the constraints of conventional morality are no longer felt as constraints. In Kantian terms it is in effect an un-Kantian movement in the direction of the Holy Will, where respect for the duty to love is transformed into the will to love. Hegel obviously sees it as a movement towards a greater freedom, a freedom *unconstrained* by a sense of duty. Perhaps what Hegel sees as a world-historical possibility for the species, Kierkegaard would see as a possibility for the individual? Certainly the aesthetic production contains passages to this effect. Thus Judge William says, 'When with all his energy a person has felt the intensity of duty he is then ethically mature, and *in him duty will emerge of itself*'.[40] Johannes *de silentio* says that 'the task of most men in life is precisely to remain within their duty and by their enthusiasm to transform it into their wish';[41] and, in extolling the example of the Apostle John, though cautioning the reader not to forget that the example of this 'Apostle of Love' is special, Kierkegaard allows that a person may become so 'conversant' (*fortrolig*) with the commandment to love one's neighbour as to become as though 'one' with it, and to 'love it' (cf. Kant's interpretation of the commandment as 'like to do your duty to your neighbour'). But the comparison with Hegel should not be overworked. The limit of the analogy is indicated by Kierkegaard's observation that this latter transformation of duty into wish implies no change at all in the status and content of the commandment. For Hegel the development in consciousness reveals the actual superfluity of the law, not just its redundancy as a guide to action. As we saw earlier, unlike the Hegel of the *Phenomenology*, for Kierkegaard there can be no appropriation of the role of law-giver. *We* do not 'approach' God in love, God has to approach us. As the Apostle of Love himself puts it: 'If we love one another, God dwelleth in us, and his love is perfected in *us*.'[42] Nevertheless, this does involve a development at least of the will, into something which does not bear the mark of 'duty's rigor'; nor, none the less, of the 'heat of the poet's passion or of inclination';[43] in order to remain moral, the disposition to love must not degenerate into heat and heroics, or for that matter into sentimental bonhomie and glassy-eyed indulgence.[44] Of the apostle's words, 'let us love one another', Kierkegaard says there is something 'transfigured [*Forklaret*] and blessed' in them, 'but also a sadness which is affected by life and alleviated by the eternal'.[45]

But now to our second point. Whether dutiful or dispositional, a loving will (logically) needs something to love. But outside the conditions in which preference operates, what could possibly function as love's object? Obviously it could not be anything analogous to the complex of qualities that comprises a particular person's character; not, for example, some hidden beauty beneath a possibly repellent exterior. For that would be to plunge anew into the conditions of preferential constraint. Nor an abstract idea, for example the collective notion of 'humanity' (Climacus comments that 'humanity' is something 'infinitely large and also nothing at all').[46] Kierkegaard does not mean that, in dealing with a noisome neighbour, we should find in the mere thought that he is after all a human being ('one of us') some basis for a loving attitude towards him.

What other avenues are then open to Kierkegaard? One suggestion may be found in Kant's principle that 'every rational nature is an end in itself'. As Kant himself insists, this 'supreme limiting condition of every man's freedom of action . . . *is not borrowed from experience*'; both because it applies universally to all rational beings and 'experience is not capable of determining anything about them', and, for us more importantly, because it 'does not present humanity as an end to man' − that is, it does not represent any goal which could *naturally* commend itself to us. Kant says that the idea of humanity in this sense as a goal stems from pure reason.[47] Consequently, that persons are ends in themselves is a property that has to be actively *attributed* to them; it is not something they can be found to possess. So whatever value inheres in the property is actually assigned to a person by the moral agent, furthermore by virtue of the latter's satisfaction of a necessary condition of being a moral agent − though Kant believes the attribution is backed by objective reason. And it is bestowed indiscriminately upon all rational beings. Why then should not a similar attribution, backed by faith rather than reason, be made by a Kierkegaardian moral agent, and the corresponding value bestowed indiscriminately upon all 'neighbours'?

This would not yet be satisfactory. Neighbour-love is supposed to have flesh-and-blood people as its objects, and Kierkegaard specifically insists that it 'loves every man according to [i.e. not in spite or regardless of] his peculiarity'.[48] Unless this invisible mark of humanity attributable indifferently to all persons can somehow be linked to personal or characterological diversity, it will not represent the 'other' in the way required.

Kierkegaard distinguishes, however, between two kinds of peculiarity, or ways of being 'oneself': one that is valuable and one that is not. The latter can be brought under the heading of 'pettiness' (*Smaalighed*). Pettiness is not worthy of love because it is a trait which the person himself acquires, 'the created being's own impoverished invention', in defiance of what he knows to be his own better nature.

> The petty-minded person has seized hold of a quite definite guise and form which he calls his own. It is only this that he seeks, only this he can love. If [he] comes upon it he loves. In this way pettiness cleaves to pettiness, [and] this petty solidarity is then prized as the highest form of love, as true friendship, as the truly faithful, honest form of unity [*Samdrægtighed*] . . . . [It] is equally petty in both directions; just as petty in idolizing . . . one of pettiness's 'own' . . . as in wanting to suppress everything else. Precisely because pettiness is an acquired nature, and thus false, [and] precisely because it has not, in its inmost depths and never openheartedly, had anything to do with God, but has crippled itself and falsified God, precisely for that reason it has a bad conscience. For him who has [his own] peculiarity, no foreign peculiarity is a disconfirmation; rather it is a confirmation, or one more proof; since what he believes, that each has his peculiarity, proves to be the case it cannot disturb him. But for pettiness every peculiarity is disconfirmation; it therefore experiences a clammy, uncomfortable anxiety at the sight of an alien peculiarity, and nothing is more important for it than to get rid of it.[49]

The opposite of pettiness is therefore openness to peculiarity. In interpersonal relationships it amounts to an optimistic willingness to accept human diversity as an intrinsic (divine) good. To acquire it a person must give up all personal projects which put constraints upon an openminded regard for others. The latter must be allowed to flourish independently of any expectations one entertains on one's own behalf. Such expectations are constraints on diversity, and having these, too, is a symptom of pettiness; though the inflexibility and unamenability of pettiness can also take domineering, imperialistic forms — and these are, in fact, the ones upon which Kierkegaard concentrates. Pettiness in all its forms 'seeks its own' and not 'the other's own'.[50]

Clearly, the message here is that a loving attitude is itself a form of openness rather than of pettiness. By destroying one's preconceptions and expectations with regard to others, the latters' own peculiarities will be allowed to confirm the value of diversity. But this diversity has no moral value by virtue of its power to *attract* the attribution of value: it is no more 'borrowed from experience' than Kant's limiting condition. The principle that individual peculiarity is of value must have some other basis. It seems reasonable to interpret Kierkegaard as regarding this other basis as each person's possibility of becoming an integrated and independent individual — the 'whole man' which Climacus says it is everyone's ethical task to become, and whose activities are manifestations of the good (the eternal). To become this is, amongst other things but also crucially, to overcome pettiness and embark upon a career of optimistic openness. In the possibility of this task's fulfilment, therefore, we may see a not impossible, non-discriminating object of neighbour-love.

However, it may be objected that we still have not quite succeeded in providing neighbour-love with its object. After all, one's noisome neighbour is one thing and his possible future another, and although his future integrity may call for a loving attitude in the sense that such an attitude is a means to its realization, there is nothing in the neighbour at present that calls for such an attitude. So we are really still in Kant's position: namely that, when one is 'repelled by a natural and unconquerable aversion', one's love can only take the form of liking to carry out one's duty to the neighbour — a duty that cannot be the duty to *love* him. Here it is not what the neighbour is, but what he can *become* that one likes.

Kierkegaard's position nevertheless appears to give dutiful love a better chance than Kant's. If openmindedness is a way of *conquering* initial aversions, then in recognizing in another person the possibility of the fulfilment of the ethical ideal of individuality-in-peculiarity are we not actually attributing the required value to the other? In freely attributing such a possibility to a person are we not already demonstrating openness towards that person — perhaps even demonstrating a form of love? If so, not, however, a love that is strictly dutiful. Once the value is attributed, and assuming that the proper response to it *is* love, then the love is dispositional in form. The object is *grasped* as essentially lovable. But since the lovable characteristic is neither presented nor discriminatory, the love is not what Kant would call 'pathological'. It rests on a decision upon how we should look upon humanity, and not upon how such an end *naturally* commends itself to us.[51]

4 Is practical love humane?

We have looked for support in Kierkegaard's own views for his assumption that there can be a willed and universal love — arguments for the practicability of 'practical' love. But what about its morality? Here, too, is something we need to be convinced of. But let us be careful to distinguish this question from another.

Whatever sense can be made of a 'practical' love (here applied specifically to Kierkegaard's views), to many the conclusion that no natural forms of love have ethical value will be morally repugnant. From a conventional moral standpoint the distinction between ethically valuable and ethically valueless love is made *within* the realm of natural love, and not by distinguishing that realm as a whole from some dubiously ethereal alternative. Many will find in the non-humanistic nature of Kierkegaard's view a compelling reason for rejecting one or other of whatever premises it is based upon. The obvious candidate here will surely be the general ethical position of which this, after all, is but a special case. To those who find Kierkegaard's conclusion on love repugnant, the claim that self-regarding activities in *general* are devoid of ethical value must seem even more so.

But this is not an issue we have room to argue here. Instead, I want to raise the question of whether, or to what extent, the 'ethereal' alternative itself offends normal beliefs and attitudes, in other words, whether or to what extent practical love is humane. There are, it seems to me, three points on which doubts in this respect can be raised. The main reason for raising them here is to deepen our insight into the implications of Kierkegaard's own views on the morality of love — a necessary preliminary to any useful discussion of the wider issue.

The first doubt concerns mutuality. Love is generally thought of as mutual, and its value as stemming in part from this fact. But in the case of practical love mutuality seems to be simply a toe-to-heel/heel-to-toe affair, an inessential symmetry involving no more than the fortuitous coincidence of two instances of the same basically unilateral tie. Practical love is expending oneself on the other — though not a preferred other.

Second, preference itself. We suggested earlier that conventional morality distinguishes itself from Kierkegaardian morality by condoning preference as a feature of moral love. In fact, many would argue that this is no mere concession to human frailty on the part of conventional morality; on the contrary, they would argue that preference in some forms is an indispensable condition of precisely those features of love on which what many will consider its real moral value rests. They would point to (favourable examples of) parental and other familial ties, and maintain that the preference shown the child by its parents or those close to it is not only necessary for the child's sense of security, but also, in view of that for its later ability to return love inside the family circle anc eventually to bestow it outside. More generally, it can be maintained that in favourable circumstances intimate familial ties, or intimate relationships generally, provide a paradigm of sympathetic and understanding love, this being the kind most deserving of the title 'moral'. Granting, of course, that parental preference often takes destructive forms, it certainly seems not implausible to propose that some preferential ties play a highly important part in the actual promotion of moral love.

Our third doubt concerns what Kant calls 'tender sympathy', also generally considered among the essential and valuable features of love. Conventional morality distinguishes self-gratificatory, or erotic, forms of love from the more stable but less palpitating ties of friendship, and lets the burden of morality rest upon the latter. But Kierkegaard distinguishes both these from neighbour-love, which on his view can alone support that burden.[52] The three forms of love are ranged in ascending order of 'spiritual determination' and, correspondingly, descending order of psychosomatic involvement. Recall that 'psychic' refers to a world-directed, or world-bound consciousness, and we should note that Kierkegaard sees the spiritual present in embryo even in erotic (and romantic) love: 'it isn't *yet* the eternal', says Kierkegaard, 'it is eternity's beautiful daze',[53] perhaps the positive equivalent of the vertigo of anxiety with which one approaches spiritual freedom. Friendship lies in the middle, freed of the bodily determination but still shackled to its psychic determination. 'Only in love of one's neighbour', says Kierkegaard, 'is the self who loves a purely spiritual category.'[54] But if this means that in undergoing the transition from *eros* to *agapè* one has to drop not only the bonds of sensory gratification but also ties of friendly sympathy, conventional morality will surely be outraged. Surely one should allow that 'neighbours' *can* also be friends, perhaps even loved ones, even erotically loved ones. That the ideal of universality which Kierkegaard has built into the notion of 'neighbour' can only be achieved by relinquishing both friendship and passion is a totally inhuman suggestion.

I offer some brief and partially remedial comments on these three questions.

First, regarding mutuality. It is, of course, a convention that the unit of love proper comprises two persons who knowingly love each other. But unrequited love, or parental love which is not, indeed cannot be, returned as such, are familiar phenomena, so no one could reasonably assert that mutuality was necessary for love. Indeed, the suggestion that you could only love another if the other loved you — in whatever way — implies a contractualism or conditionality that is surely incompatible with a genuine concern for the other (see the third line of argument in Section 2), and therefore incompatible with a necessary condition of unilateral love. Love, even if it can be discriminating, cannot be conditional in the sense that one loves another only on condition of being loved *by* the other. But then, if mutuality cannot be a necessary condition of genuine love, because making it so would be a sufficient condition of there being no such love, the fact that practical love is inherently unilateral is no argument against it.

It is a different question whether one should say that practical love and an interest in a reciprocation of love are inconsistent with one another — that is, whether the absence of such an interest is a necessary condition of love's being practical. That would be an inhuman thing to have to say. But it is unclear that Kierkegaard is committed to the position. So long as such a reciprocation of love is treated as the result of an overriding interest in the other's benefit, and not as a condition of that interest, it does not appear to be precluded by the ideal of neighbour-love.

Second, preference. The objection was that practical love, by excluding preferential concern, finds no place for those close bonds of selective sympathy and understanding which are arguably not only beneficial in general but even morally valuable in cultivating the very moral attitude which Kierkegaard calls practical love. There are a number of points here. First, it can be replied that what is inconsistent with practical love is not, primarily, that one or more persons be selected as objects or purveyors of affection and concern, but that the selection itself be due to a self- rather than an other-serving interest. It is not inconceivable that what is in the loved one's interest is that the love be bestowed by this person or these, rather than that person or those. Given the backgrounds of the special ties of dependency and sympathy defining the child/parent context, it might very well be the case, for instance, that a child's proper benefits and best interests are purveyor-selective in this way. But then a person may in principle select himself or herself as the purveyor from an interest in bestowing those benefits, and not at all because he or she prefers to be the particular benefactor. It is no doubt true that such ties do, in fact, express themselves in unjust preference where equal treatment is expected, but there seems no reason to assume that they must; nepotism, for instance, is not a necessary consequence of parental devotion and understanding. Second, it is important to note that the origin of such ties is not always preferential. A mother's preference for her child is in the first instance not an expression of choice or selection, however much she may come to prefer her child to others. And her continuing devotion may not be conditional on its object being *her* child, or any other discriminatingly identified child. A mother may, after all, be the one most qualified to judge how much attention is called for in the case of concern for others, and thus to appreciate how 'discriminating' she is forced to be in a morally harmless sense.

Finally, the question of sympathy. The problem here was how to avoid, or at least defend, the consequence that neighbours can also be at any rate friends. The first point here is that Kierkegaard himself seems to want to say that they can; in fact, that they can *as neighbours* even enjoy a sexual life. Recall the passage in *Anxiety* where he (or Haufniensis) says that once the sexual has been brought to mind it is no use trying — like the church — to ignore it; the task is rather to 'win [the sexual] into conformity with the category of the spirit'.[55] There was also Climacus's stress on the requirement of the 'simultaneity' of the three stages, as against the passing *from* a previous stage into the new one.[56] In other words, the spiritual goal is not an ascetic ideal, but the spirit's appropriation of a natural function. Or, from the opposite end, 'neighbour' is a dimension added to love and friendship, where they exist, rather than something from which these two must be subtracted. In *Either/Or*, Judge William is made to say: 'He who regards friendship ethically sees it as a duty. I might therefore say that it is every man's duty to have a friend.'[57]

There are two problems with this, however. First, how can friendship and natural ('pathological') love 'conform' to spirit when the latter appears to require the elimination of features essential to the former? Thus Haufniensis remarks in *Anxiety* that 'in spirit there is no distinction in man or woman'.[58] If so, then conformity of the sexual with the spirit would seem to *exclude* sexuality. Second, where the 'neighbour' is one for whom we feel only repulsion, it will not be possible to talk of a sympathy that draws its warmth from natural love, or even friendship, for these are *ex hypothesi* absent. With what loving resources, then, does one confront a person when there is neither love nor friendship for 'neighbour' to build on? In the case of friendship, for instance, is it really possible, as Judge William appears to imply, to establish such a resource just by obeying the injunction to 'have a friend'?

With respect to the first problem, one can reasonably suppose that by conforming the sexual to the spiritual Kierkegaard means no more than that one's actions, including sexual ones, be conducted in such a way that the persons involved are *also* regarded as persons independently of their sexual specification and that the latter specification is subordinate to the universal category of 'neighbour'.

Kierkegaard's argument seems to be that it is only if natural ('pathological') love is subordinated to the strict standards of Christian love, that this identification of the other person as another self takes place. One way in which, when left on its own, natural love fails to comply with these standards is indicated in Kierkegaard's remarks on the 'duplication' of selves — a point discussed earlier.

> One who is burning with love can never, because of or by virtue of this burning, endure the duplication which would here require the relinquishing of love, if the object of love required it.[59]

For there to be a bond of friendship or love in any proper sense, there must genuinely be another for whom one is sympathetically concerned. Unless one is ready to give up one's love in the loved one's interest, the loved one is not genuinely acknowledged as another self, and therefore not as one of those who can be nearest, the neighbour being, we recall, 'the one who is nearer you than all others . . . but not in a predilectory sense'. To conceive another person as your neighbour is to satisfy the condition that there be an acknowledged diversity of selves, while to fail to add the neighbour-dimension is not to satisfy it. To be personally *close* to another, one has first to acknowledge that person's separateness. A neighbour is someone whose presence as another self with its own interest is genuinely acknowledged. The underlying principle here, as before, is that concern based purely on preferential appeal fails to 'reach' that other self, and is at root a concern for benefactor rather than beneficiary.

But there is another side to it, too. Kierkegaard says that if two or more persons are *merely* friends or natural lovers and not also mutual 'neighbours', they in effect form a coalition of (not properly differentiated) selves, two, three, or more as the case may be, from which all others are excluded.[60] So there are two aspects of selfishness in an emotional tie: first, the failure to acknowledge the other (or others) *in* that tie in the sense of being willing to 'let the other be' if the other required that; and second, the failure of the two or more coalesced in that tie to acknowledge the existence of others outside it. The passion of mutual concern is matched by a corresponding indifference to, even a positive rejection of, those who have no part in that concern. If we think of emotional ties beyond those of erotic attraction, for example those binding such larger groupings as families, football teams, their supporters, nations, races, in fact any grouping that falls short of universal humanity, the moral force of the concept of neighbour becomes apparent. As the concept of the other (*any* other) for whom both forms of failure to acknowledge duplication are absent, 'neighbour' signifies an ideal of undiscriminating concern, of general but particularized good will. So our question of whether one person can be simultaneously neighbour and also either friend or loved one may be reformulated as the question of whether ties of friendship and/or natural love are always alliances involving an infringement of that ideal.

It would be easy to read into Kierkegaard's remark that one who is 'burning with love can never . . . endure the duplication' an affirmative answer, to this question, at any rate in the particular case of love. But that may not be necessary. If love and friendship are not wholly distinguishable from one another, and if Kierkegaard could accept that there were forms of both which were sufficiently lacking in ardour to tolerate duplication and to coexist with a general good will, it might be possible for him to conceive of neighbour-love as a development of natural human love and friendship which retains some of the essential features of these latter.

But there is still the question of the source of the bond in the 'love' one is supposed to have even of one by whom one is, in Kant's words, 'repelled by a natural and unconquerable aversion'. Love and friendship surely presuppose some tie of sympathy, at least a fair measure of agreement in interests and values — a common pool of sympathies and ideals in the midst of differences — friendship perhaps having the advantage over a more ardent relationship in that in its case the pool is larger if not so deep. Our question is, what possibility is there for love when the pool runs dry, as is supposedly the case when there is only aversion?

Well, on Kierkegaard's view, there is always something in common, an interest which, if it does not resolve, at least overrides all other particular differences in sympathies and aims: namely the universal interest in becoming a 'whole man'. This, according to Climacus, is every individual's ethical task. Though not everyone may admit to this interest, those who do will recognize its universality and accept that they share it also with those who do not. They will acknowledge an interest which transcends ordinary differences, just as the sharing of interests in the ordinary way can transcend the presence or absence of merely physical appeal. Perhaps the sharing of this interest can be a basis for the transference of interest from one's own benefit to that of others which is essential to neighbour-love?

Whether we accept this or not, there are other factors to take into account. First, we must bear in mind the *self*-edifying function Kierkegaard ascribes to a practical loving attitude: that it opens the moral agent's eyes to hidden value, so that what is at first naturally and unconquerably repulsive is seen in another, more sympathizable light. Aversion to someone may, after all, be due to the petty-mindedness of the beholder, and a decision to look upon that person in an open-hearted way — i.e. charitably, or lovingly — may result in the beholder's seeing in the person's 'peculiarity' a possibility of the latter's self-fulfilment.

Second, in terms of its *other*-edifying function, the appropriate model for Kierkegaard's neighbour-love is surely, as suggested earlier, that of parental love. Here it is precisely the *possibility* of self-fulfilment that is the object of loving concern, not some actual set of characteristics to which the concerned person may respond immediately either with aversion or natural warmth and sympathy. Furthermore, parental love comprises a much wider range of expressions than warmth and sympathy. Kierkegaard writes that he learned from his own father 'what fatherly love is and so was given the same idea of divine fatherly love, the one unshakeable thing in life, the true Archimedean point'.[61] In terms of this model, neighbour-love would be not so much an effective response to its object as an active occupation with the latter's realization of a shared ideal of fulfilment. The bond is established by the bestower's decision to treat the other as a proper candidate for that fulfilment. In one passage Kierkegaard reserves Christian love for the persons who 'will allow themselves to be saved', rather than for the human race as a whole,[62] which perhaps indicates that he does in fact think of such love as a form of sympathy based, as in natural love and friendship, on ties of mutual interest.

Finally, the possibility of a dutiful love is less easily dismissed than many writers, including Kant, assume. To them it seems easy because they see it as a question of whether a power to be appealed to can, in the absence of the appropriate stimulus, be exercised by force of will. In these terms the impossibility of loving (or hating) someone in obedience to a command is as evident as that of obeying the instruction to enjoy a dish that you know very well turns your stomach. Certainly, feelings may in some cases be overcome by instant action (taking a cold shower or trying *The Times* crossword), and perhaps even elicited or redirected in the longer term, say by psychoanalysis or aversion- or reinforcement therapy; but they cannot be willed instantly into existence when dispositions are not there. But this is not the question. We should ask not: Can love as 'tender sympathy' be commanded?, but: Can anything that can be commanded, by any reasonable stretch of the logic of the term, be called 'love'? Neighbour-love, for Kierkegaard, is not the unfolding of something implicit, but not fully realized, in natural love and friendship; it is a radically new phenomenon, the concept of which provides a perspective, confusedly anticipated in the latter phenomena (e.g. 'immediate love contains the eternal in the form of a beautiful fantasy'), from which the latter phenomena are to be seen in a new light, and in accordance with which they should be 'reshaped'.[63] Kierkegaard says the ideal of universal love requires a 'turning up-side-down' of the 'natural man's ideas and concepts'.[64] The concept of 'neighbour' itself is not a concept of nature, and the 'reduplication' of selves it calls for is not a matter simply of a normal command of the personal pronouns and of an ability to conjugate verbs. 'Neighbour', whatever its affinity with token-reflexive terms, is a moral notion, not a grammatical one.

5   The transcendent source of value

'Worldly wisdom takes love to be a relationship between man and man', says Kierkegaard, but 'Christianity teaches that love is a relationship between man—god—man — that is, that God is the middle term [*Mellem-Bestemmelsen*] '.[65]

The suggestion above was that Kierkegaard would say that it is possible to love persons in the face of an 'immediate' aversion to them because the primary target of this love is not personal peculiarity itself but the potential self-educative achievements of those who exhibit it. But now he claims that practical love is a triadic relation with God in the mediate position. If I am to love my neighbour, God has to be interposed. It looks, then, as if God was the primary target.

In saying that God occupies the mediate position Kierkegaard does not mean, however, that in morally (truly) loving another person one must really be loving God instead, or that in being morally (truly) loved by another person, it is really God that is loving you and not the other person.[66] It is not the love itself that must be directed at God, or comes from God, but the question of whether the love actually directed at another amounts to what is required of *moral* love.

We noted earlier the important reservation Kierkegaard places on the possibility of a quasi-Hegelian transition from an ethics of duty to an ethics of love: that however much the moral agent's attitude to the law 'Love thy neighbour' may change as he or she becomes more 'conversant' with it, the content and status of the law itself remain unchanged. Being willingly agapeistic does not mean that what was earlier conceived as stemming from external

authority is now more adequately understood as rooted in consciousness itself — or, even more naturalistically, as merely an
instrument of socialization in the hands of rational man. The
ethical remains transcendent: man does not appropriate God's
law-giving functions. Consequently, moral agents can never themselves either specify moral goals or judge moral performance — a
point underlined by Abraham's example in *Fear and Trembling*.
In other words, Kierkegaard denies that moral agents are able to
identify genuine cases of practical love, either as bestowers or as
recipients. He argues in effect that because such identifications
can only be made by answering questions like, 'How much sacrifice
and devotion does so-and-so require before he will acknowledge
that he is being loved?', they do not have the absoluteness required
of moral principles. Such questions and their answers are confined
to the realm of contingent human demands and satisfactions. It is
always possible, therefore, to ask whether it is *right* to identify a
given display of sympathetic concern as moral love — i.e. practical,
'true', 'moral', or neighbour-love.[67] Yet this latter question cannot
be answered, either, by specifying any further requirements, for
wherever we turn for these we are still bound by human, therefore
variable and not absolute, criteria of satisfaction. Not being a positivist Kierkegaard does not conclude that the question has no sense.
Instead, he accepts that an answer exists but is not available. This
may be seen as a further aspect of the idea noted in the previous
chapter, that the moral enterprise is not based in time and experience, that moral experience is, in fact, the influx into time of a
transcendent, timeless order, and that moral action is in some
sense action on behalf of and in the spirit of that order and as such
requires a spiritualization of the temporal self. Similarly with the
identification of genuine moral practice, specifically moral love. If
such love cannot be identified with whatever meets the demands
and satisfaction I or anyone else specify for it, but love does nevertheless make demands (and if there is to be love these must be
met), then the demands must be conceived as stemming from, and
the satisfactions as belonging to, a transcendent moral arbiter and
agent, namely God. The criterion of whether one person's love of
another is moral or not is therefore a divine criterion; no moral
yardstick is available to human beings.[68] So if the recipient of love
makes demands he must not make them of the giver but of God.
He must treat the demands he makes of the love another bestows
on him as demands God would make of him, the recipient, for his,
the recipient's love. To be satisfied that the requirements have
indeed been met, in other words actually to *be* loved by another,
is 'to be helped by another person to love God'.[69] To be the

271

bestower of moral love is, correspondingly, to help the other person to love God, for again the demands the bestower must satisfy are not any particular demands the recipient might make of him, but whatever is required for loving God. It is what God demands as a *receiver* of love that provides the standard for what counts as *bestowing* love upon another person.

The interposition of God has a further function. In the case of love and friendship the middle term is preference.[70] Kierkegaard clearly means that by substituting God for preference the object of one's love is transposed into the neighbour, and thus potentially everyone: 'If you love God higher than anything, then you also love your neighbour, and in your neighbour everyone.' In occupying the mediate position God is not standing in for the other person as the target of one's love, but representing the latter as an intrinsically valuable 'other' to be loved as such and not loved because preferred. The idea of God as the middle term is, in short, that of the other being loved as a representative of universal humanity, and thus of universal humanity as the concrete objective of a moral action. Kierkegaard says in the same context that love of God is also moral love of oneself. He appears to mean that in trying to satisfy the absolute requirements for moral love, one is in effect assuming one's own right to demand similar satisfaction. For the following reason: in accepting that there *is* an absolute standard of moral love (which, incidentally, is logically independent of its being also a transcendent standard), one is assuming the correctness of a principle on which such a standard is based, namely the intrinsic value of human beings as such. The notion of love of God can therefore be interpreted as an expression of this principle, as a way of symbolizing it (rather than conceiving it, since for Kierkegaard, like Kant, there is no concept of God — God is to be related to, not conceptualized).[71] On this interpretation it is not necessary to construe God as a triangulating intruder in the interpersonal relationship. It is rather that love of God is accepted as the legitimate analogue of love of persons in general, and so for the attribution of value to human beings and therefore also to oneself. In saying love of God is love of oneself Kierkegaard is obviously not going back on what he has said elsewhere by sanctioning selfishness. He points out that there is a right and a wrong way of loving oneself. When one is willing to accept on behalf of anyone else the demands of love one makes on behalf of oneself, then one is loving oneself correctly: 'Loving oneself in the right way and loving one's neighbour correspond absolutely to one another, are basically one and the same.'[72]

There is yet another aspect to the notion of God as middle term;

namely that of God as law-giver. This is connected with Kierke-gaard's anti-intuitionism, his view that objective true moral prin-ciples must be accepted on authority because human cognitive resources are insufficient to identify (or analyse) them. Kant, too, is an anti-intuitionist. But whereas for him the authority appears to reason in the form of the categorical imperative, which functions as moral-truth dispenser (for Kant 'God' is only an idea that one comes by in rational reflection on the possibility of moral experi-ence), for Kierkegaard the authority rests directly in God. God, apart from being the judge of the standards required of genuine moral practice, also prescribes the norms themselves. It would be wrong to interpret this in a conventionally anthropomorphic way. The notion of God as a moral prescriber is not, for Kierkegaard, part of an explanation (a necessarily inadequate explanation) of how moral principles originate; it is a way of symbolizing the absoluteness and transcendency of the principles themselves. To say that God *is* love can be interpreted as saying that love is an absolute and transcendentally given norm.

The notion of God as love has, however, another aspect. 'The law [of God] takes, or to put the relation more exactly, the law makes demands, [but] love gives.'[73] But love's giving is not the correlate of the law's taking; that must be love's being *obedient* to the law. Such love, as we know, is selfless and does not count on receiving anything in return, though, of course, it may. But the moral agent must count on receiving something. Otherwise there would be no point in the giving that *is* the correlate of the law's taking, namely the obedience to the law, the carrying out of the duty (to give or love). What is it that is hoped for in return for the obedience, but which (remembering the message of the previous chapter) must not be conceived as an *incentive*, or the *aim* of the giving? We noted a moment ago that Kierkegaard said of immediate love that it 'contains the eternal in the form of a beautiful fantasy'. He goes on to say that because such love is 'not consciously grounded on the eternal . . . it can be changed'[74] and '[e]ven if it does not change, it still retains the possibility of change, for it is a matter of fortune'. It seems, then, that the ideal of the eternal in love is that in which change is, if not impossible, at least depen-dent on the will. Kierkegaard speaks passionately of this ideal: 'Only when it is a duty to love, only then is love eternally secure against every change; eternally emancipated in blessed indepen-dence. . . .'[75] The security provided by, and only by, principled, willed love obviously speaks decisively in its favour. Kierkegaard values the fact, as he sees it, that such love − 'sterling love' − is not only eternally secure against change,[76] but that it is free,[77] amongst other things of anxiety;[78] that it requires no tests, oaths, promises or other forms of symbolic renewal.[79] Equally, the fact that natural love fails to give such security, or that whatever security it provides depends on uncontrollable factors outside the will — is left to 'fate' — and is therefore a merely contingent security,[80] is a decisive shortcoming of that form of love.

That a reward awaits fulfilment of the ethical ideal is part of Kierkegaard's position, although the position requires that no thought of a reward must operate as an inducement to its fulfilment. Properly conceived, we argued earlier, the reward cannot so operate, for it has to be 'homogeneous' with the good which is 'eternal', and therefore cannot be identified with specific temporal benefits. Which left us with the problem of conceiving *anything* that might count as a reward. Nevertheless, if there is something that can be the reward it would be intelligible within the Kierkegaardian framework to describe it as a manifestation of God's love; as what the moral agent *receives* for giving what God's law exacts. The passages cited indicate what that 'something' might be: namely fundamental advantages (security, freedom) which can *only* be achieved by an act of will, by a mutual or unilateral resolution, made unconditionally. In fact, this is a principle underlying all Kierkegaard's writings. In the *Postscript* we saw it in connection with the certainty, or certitude, that can only be achieved by risking everything. In *Stages on Life's Way* we find it again, in a context analogous to that of *Works of Love*, where Kierkegaard contrasts a union in which a couple decide to live together as long as it works with one, a genuine marriage, based on a mutual resolution to create a bond come what may. In the latter case, as with risking everything, the decision underlying the subsequent association is based on eternity.[81] Similarly with love itself. Kierkegaard describes the 'poetic' love in which a couple 'swear *with their love* to want to love one another forever', instead of 'swearing *with eternity* to love one another'.[82] It is only when it is unconditional, and therefore an act of obedience to law, and has thus 'undergone the transformation of eternity',[83] that it secures itself against the influence of change. Such security is a kind of freedom — from those influences and from the possibility of change. It is something worth having, a possible reward.

But in what way can this reward be conceived (by the moral agent) as 'homogeneous' with eternity? The answer might be as follows. Suppose there was something we believed intrinsically worth doing, but which was nevertheless difficult to do. It might be philosophy. Now the reward for persisting in this activity, in spite of the difficulties, might be (1) that it became easier, or

(2) that it seemed even more worthwhile, or even (3) that in doing it the value of the activity seemed to outweigh the inherent, even increasing, difficulties; in short, that one felt a certain satisfaction in having persisted, and a sense of the confirmation of the hope one had that it was, in spite of the difficulties, a worthwhile occupation. Provided the contentment and confirmation are in respect of the activity itself and not in respect of one's personal achievements in that activity, one might readily acknowledge that the satisfaction was homogeneous with the activity. It comes as a result of the activity, and not as the expected or hoped for fulfilment of an ulterior goal. It is perhaps not even something that *could* be an ultimate goal. For until one appreciates that the activity *is* worthwhile, and *then* one has the reward, its worthwhileness cannot be a goal that one can envisage (as opposed, say, to the further goal of purely psychological well-being that might be *envisaged* to ensue from finding a tedious occupation one is stuck with worthwhile). Now, the description of this 'outer' realm case seems to fit the kinds of examples Kierkegaard hints at when he talks of consequences of, or the reward for, successfully or truthfully willing the good. In fact, we can convert it into an inner realm case by simply substituting the ethical activity of loving one's neighbour for the presumably, on Kierkegaard's view, non-ethical activity of philosophizing. In *Purity of Heart* Kierkegaard talks of a 'crown of honour laid aside for each of those that have in truth willed only one thing', and seems to be saying that this consists not in any kind of formal recognition, but in 'willing the same in eternity'.[84] The security that only dutiful love can bring is not *guaranteed* by bringing one's loving practices under the regime of the will. In fact, strictly it cannot be guaranteed at all, either as a theoretical possibility — which in turn is something one can only accept by a personal resolution, 'risking everything', including one's 'thought' — or as what is due. It is a *possible* product of actually obeying the commandment to love one's neighbour, the sense that in doing so, one is doing something absolutely right, and being *willing* to continue: a sense one would not properly have unless one was succeeding in obeying the commandment.

VIII

Equality and Association

Equalization . . . is the false anticipation of the
eternal life, which people have done away with as a
'beyond' and want to realize here *in abstracto*.[1]

1 Equality and politics

At the beginning of his 'Two "Notes" Concerning My Activity as
an Author', Kierkegaard voices the familiar complaint that 'nowadays everything is politics'.[2] His point is not the usual one,
however, that certain activities should be politically neutral, that
people should be able to stake out at least some area (home life,
sport, culture, personal religion) where they can carry on unham-
pered by the party lines that otherwise divide them. That is, he is
not saying: *not* everything should be politics, though he might also
want to say that; his point is rather that in his own time everything
is *only* politics. Kierkegaard is saying not that certain activities are
wrongly regarded as political, but that the large and important
range of activities properly regarded as political are improperly
regarded as being no more than that.

What more does he think they should be? Readers of Kierkegaard's
pseudonym Johannes Climacus will detect in what Kierkegaard
says here an application of the principle that temporal goals should
be made relative to absolute ones. First there is the assumption
that political goals are inherently temporal. That may reasonably
be granted, like everyone else politicians try to preserve or improve
upon relevant states of affairs in the world, and everything that
occurs there occurs in time: there is a sense in which the achievements of politicians can *necessarily* be dated. Second, there is the
assumption that no temporal goals can be absolute. That, too, can

be granted, since the category of time is that of history and change while the absolute, traditionally conceived, transcends both time and change. But Hegel, of course, denied that time and eternity, finite and infinite exclude one another. In the present context this denial has significant implications. In the first place, it allows that finite social forms, political institutions and the like, can be expressions of the absolute or Spirit. Second, it means that the absolute need not be sought where Kierkegaard believes it can alone be found, in the 'inner' realm of individual ethics. In the 'Two "Notes" ' Kierkegaard is criticizing politicians for leaving out the infinite, which is in effect what they do whether they reject it altogether or, as Hegelians, see it in the world around or ahead of them. In either case they busy themselves with the incalculable host of measures which the time calls for (*fordrer*), instead of with the one thing it really needs (*behøver*), the eternal.[3] It is the 'misfortune' of the age, he says, that it operates solely within time. This one-dimensionality leads politicians to distort their goals and to convert them into impossible demands. How, asks Kierkegaard, can the political dream of equality (*Lighed*) be realized in time, the very 'medium of differentiation'? What politicians fail to see, in their 'impatience' with the eternal, is that absolute equality not only cannot be achieved but cannot even be conceived in worldly terms. True equality (*Menneske-Lighed*, human sameness) and humanity (*Menneskelighed*) can only be achieved in 'the religious'.[4] However 'impractical' it may seem to a politician, 'the religious is eternity's transfiguration [i.e. true representation] of [his] fondest dream'.[5]

These remarks of Kierkegaard's on the notion of human equality give one pause. Do they not suggest the political outlook of an extreme reactionary? Kierkegaard seems not only to be rejecting something basic to social justice as fraudulent, he appears to offer as the 'true' equality something we nowadays all too easily diagnose as a fraud — an equality (in the eyes of God) open to all whatever their mutual standing, an illusory consolation for the disadvantaged, and in the hands of the advantaged a means for preserving a selectively beneficial *status quo*.

It has become something of an orthodoxy to write Kierkegaard off in the political context, to see him, as someone has put it, as 'for all practical purposes a *Homo apoliticus*'.[6] That itself can be a kind of indictment: a serious irrelevance would attach to Kierkegaard's views if no political consequences at all could be seen to follow from them. But it would be even worse if, as the above quotations seem to hint, there were political implications but unacceptable ones.

277

The crucial questions here are: does Kierkegaard deny the importance of social justice in favour of an abstract 'religious' equality that takes no account of human distress? Or does he accept its importance but deny that political measures are the appropriate means for establishing social justice? Or is it rather that he denies that political measures *alone* (i.e. without a concern for the eternal dimension) are sufficient? The aim of this chapter is to show that Kierkegaard does not, either explicitly or by implication, deny the importance of social justice, and that he does at least intend his religious notion of equality to have political implications. Roughly, the political framework which Kierkegaard envisages, though without concerning himself with its practicability or details, is one in which social harmony is a function of respect for individual autonomy, a respect which is in its turn exclusively an expression of such autonomy.

The view that Kierkegaard is an apolitical writer is not shared by all commentators. For instance, *Works of Love* has been described as an (anticipatory) answer to the *Communist Manifesto* which came out the following year.[7] Kierkegaard himself says that one section of his book is an attack on Communism.[8] The section in question contends, among other things, that if all human suffering were remedied but without compassion, then this, the absence of compassion, 'would be a greater misery than all temporal need'.[9] Note that there is no suggestion here that temporal need should not be provided for, only that what is more significant from an eternal point of view than the actual providing for it, or the ability to provide for it, is the presence of compassion, or the will to provide for it. Calling *Works of Love* a Christian counter-manifesto is misleading if it suggests the presentation of an alternative political programme to that of Marx and Engels, but not if the purpose of Kierkegaard's work is seen as that of elaborating in detail (rather than providing rational support for) such theses as, first, that the basic social unit is interpersonal relationship and not group membership (this might even be interpreted as an attack on 'false' socialism parallel to that of the *Communist Manifesto*, but from a point of view which has the allegedly 'true' Marx—Engels version of socialism as its target); second, that sociality is in the first instance an ethical, not a political problem, and thus *in any case* a matter for the individual will; and third, that ethics (and, in Kierkegaard's Kantian view, therefore religion) is an autonomous, i.e. irreducible, category not to be explained anthropologically, as for instance in terms of the basic, historically constant need to establish and maintain the material conditions of life.

It is at least true that *Works of Love* is concerned with a theme some view on which is presupposed by any political doctrine, namely sociality — or the mode of interpersonal relationship. It is significant that the term 'sociality' is one Kierkegaard himself uses to specify the topic of *Works of Love*.[10] As it happens, this comment comes in response to the criticism that hitherto in his writings, and particularly in his recent *Edifying Discourses in Different Spirits*, which include the one on purity of heart, Kierkegaard has shown no real understanding or knowledge of the social. Although calling his critics 'fools', Kierkegaard admits there is something by which fools can easily be led astray. It is only when one side of something has been 'clearly and distinctly brought out' that the 'relevance of the other side comes correspondingly to the fore'.[11] *Works of Love* is thus supposed to be Kierkegaard's account of this other side, namely the element of sociality implicit in purity of heart. We must, of course, think of sociality here in a broad sense of the term, and not as designating some particular form of social organization.

We saw that for Kierkegaard the content of the moral (and therefore unified) will is unselfish concern for others. This concern is already an exercise of sociality in the broad sense of that term. But it might also be claimed to be an exercise of sociality in a more precise sense: in so far as the unselfishness of the concern immunizes it from partiality, it might reasonably be said to be itself an actual embodiment of social harmony. Even in its limited social orbit an act of neighbour-love constitutes a kind of realization, in the form of the will, of the ideal of a social whole. One might intelligibly, if audaciously, go on to claim that the ideal would be realized if all acted with a similar concern. But even if that claim were false, the presence of impartiality in an act of neighbour-love already gives it something one might call a 'universal' content. Kierkegaard says that 'the neighbour is the equal' and that loving one's neighbour, unlike predilection in love or friendship, is an equitable act or activity; it is an expression of 'eternal equality', for 'equality is simply not making a distinction, and eternal equality is unconditionally making not the slightest distinction'.[12]

This is one way in which the eternal may be said to affect interpersonal relationships. But what does this impartiality mean in practice; how, in Kierkegaard's terms, does equality bear on human misery and need? These questions arise even more acutely in view of Kierkegaard's polemic against equalization, to be discussed in what follows. If the ethical thing to do is to treat people equally, why should it be wrong to *make* them equal?

The polemic occurs in Kierkegaard's single essay on social problems, the long section of *A Literary Review* entitled 'The

Present Age' (the whole work is translated under the title *Two Ages*).
It is there that we shall look for answers to these questions.

2 Authority and the individual

As a theoretical backcloth to his discussion, Kierkegaard employs
an evolutionary framework similar to that in *Anxiety*. What evolved
there was the idea of the source of value, our notion of good and
evil; in *Two Ages* it is the idea (and exercise) of authority.
Kierkegaard's use of this framework shows fairly clearly that he
assumes that 'true' (religious) equality will manifest itself in a
society of politically free individuals. There are, predictably, three
stages.

The first involves a politically primitive form of society, what
we would call a fascist society, in which authority rests with
outstanding individuals set apart from the 'generation' (or broad
collectivity of their contemporaries). Their exceptionality is their
assumed possession of a social asset, namely an ability to catch the
ebb and flow of fate.[13] In such a society the common run of people
surrender their autonomy (if only in a manner of speaking, since
in effect they have never had it) in order to enjoy the protection
of those believed to be invested with the special power to give it.
It is crucial that their authority be recognized,[14] in other words
that their facility with fate be seen to be a fact. The social formation
is organic, both parties realizing that this mutual dependence is a
condition of the survival of the society as a whole.[15] Kierkegaard
says that such a formation is 'dialectical in the direction of eminence
[*Fremragenhed*] ', 'the great individual — and then the crowd, one
[who is] free — and then those in bondage'.[16]

In intermediate position comes the contemporary 'Christian'
society with its conception of authority as power vested in a
representative of the formerly bound majority. Here the right to
command is based on the voluntary agreement of equals to submit
to leaders they themselves choose, i.e. the 'democratic' system as
we know it (a system whose connection with Christianity can, in
fact, be traced to its origin in Calvinist doctrine). The 'generation'
is now 'liberated' by its recognition 'in a form of self-awareness'
that authority is no longer alien to it but exercised on its behalf.
Such a society is 'for the time being [*indtil videre*] dialectical in
the direction of representation'.[17] Authority in this society is not
yet vested in the members of the generation individually, it lies
only with the generation as such, or more exactly with the majority
of the generation.

The transition to individual autonomy occurs, and it is a painful process, with the leap into religiousness (Climacus's religiousness B).[18] Here, however, the notion of authority undergoes a radical change. It ceases to be the exercise of an *external* control over the members of the generation, and ceases to represent them *qua* their membership of the generation. When the individual is distinguished from the generation in the new, autonomous way, this individual is not, as in ancient society, a leader whose social function depends on his individuality, on his exceptionality, on his *difference* from the 'generation', being publicly recognized, on his 'eminence', and whose 'danger' is therefore that it should not be so recognized. On the contrary, if 'men of excellence' are to function here as 'leaders' they must disclaim all pretension to authority.[19] Leadership must now take a Socratic form if it is to have effect. For now the function of leadership is to prompt a final abandonment of the idea of an external authority representing people as members of the generation, and acceptance of a notion of authority according to which authority rests in individual choice. If others are to achieve the same 'excellence', or distinction from the generation, as that already achieved by the 'true' individual, then, whatever the counterpressures, they must achieve it on their own. The prompting cannot, therefore, take the form of direct assistance, advice, or instruction, for that would be to deprive others of their autonomy and so amount to dereliction of the leader's role; it would be to 'dabble in the shortsighted ingenuity of human sympathy', and thereby precisely to *prevent* others from making the freedom-constituting leap themselves.[20] Kierkegaard refers to the new leaders as 'the unrecognizable' (*Ukjendelige*).

What this development seems intended to show is a gradual appropriation *by the individual* of the authority, whatever its nature, needed to maintain society: from being an authority exercised over him as a member of the generation, it becomes an authority vested in himself as an individual. The development might, of course, be interpreted from a different point of view, as showing how the individual gradually appropriates the autonomy needed to become a true individual, irrespective of the consequences for society. The context, however, is one in which Kierkegaard discusses, and seeks to diagnose, the *social* ills of his time. The former interpretation seems therefore plausible. But in any case it is clear from a number of places in Kierkegaard's authorship that he regards both goals, the establishing of a harmonious society on the one hand and the fulfilment of true individuality on the other, as closely interwoven, even logically connected.

Still, the three-stage schema leaves very unclear the relationships which autonomous individuals are supposed to have to one another, either within a true community or prior to its establishment. Is, for example, the distinction between leader and led just a necessary expedient in present society where so few individuals have attained their autonomy, but dispensable in the true community; or is it also essential to that community? Are the ideals of social justice and freedom automatic consequences of the autonomy of (enough, or is it enough well-placed, i.e. politically influential) individuals? Or is the autonomy of individuals no more than one necessary condition among others of the achievement of these ideals? Or perhaps the ideals themselves have to be realized *before* individuals can begin appropriating authority?

Kierkegaard does not help us here. But it would be wrong to suggest that the ideals in question are ones that he either disregards or denies. Of his own, the 'present', age he says that it is 'dialectical in the direction of equality' (*Ligelighed*, equity or proportional equality, a notion more closely linked to justice or fairness than is 'Lighed', a word Kierkegaard uses more rarely in this context and which means similarity, or equality in the sense of plainly *being alike*).[21] He does not intend this as a criticism of his age. He does, indeed, criticize people who have this ideal for misunderstanding it, as we shall see. The kind of people his age needed, however, the 'unrecognizable ones', do understand it. Indeed, they choose to remain unrecognizable just because they do grasp 'how the notion of equal standing before God applies to people in general' (*det Almene i Ligeligheden for Gud*).[22] Kierkegaard's meaning here may be clarified by an entry in the *Journals* which says in effect that where a widely accepted ideology is true the only leadership needed is the kind that prompts a personal understanding of it, and that cannot be done by a leader recognized as such.[23] The central points, however, are that Kierkegaard consistently links the idea of equality before God with that of the equality of all people,[24] and that he claims the latter only makes sense in terms of the former.

At times Kierkegaard talks of the combination of these equalities as constituting an ideal end-state, the true community, or 'divine totality', which comprehends 'everyone individually' and in which *alone* 'equality' becomes 'fulfilment'.[25] At others, however, as when he talks of the single individual's being willing 'to learn to be satisfied with himself in the essentiality of religiousness before God . . . because it *expresses* equality before God and the equality of all people',[26] the end-state is referred to merely as an idea in the individual's mind. It is tempting, and consistent with what Kierkegaard says in a number of places, to interpret him as believing *both* that the end-state's being in the minds of some individuals is at least a necessary condition of its being eventually realized in fact, *and* that entering (properly) into the religious life is at least a necessary condition of anyone's having the idea of that end-state in mind in such a way as to dispose him to act in ways likely to bring it into being. But in any case, what cannot be doubted is that Kierkegaard envisages, in however vague a way, a total community in which generally accepted social ideals such as freedom and justice are achieved. It seems true, nevertheless, and consistent with the Kantianism pervading Kierkegaard's ethics, to say that his thinking is concentrated on the conditions in which the end-state can be 'expressed' in the single individual's life, in anticipation of it, as it were, rather than on the details of the end-state itself or on how its expression in the individual's life can in fact contribute causally to its eventual realization.

3 Levelling 1

Granted that Kierkegaard envisages positive social consequences from his ideal of human equality, what form or forms, in his view, do the prevailing misconceptions of this ideal take? The 'most consistent implementation' of his own age's misunderstanding of its dialectical tendency towards equality, he says, is 'levelling'. And the 'profound significance' of levelling is the 'ascendance of the category of the generation over that of individuality'.[27] What does this mean? Kierkegaard illustrates his claim with some examples. They give point to a version of the logicians' fallacy of division, the error of assuming that what goes for a collectivity can also be assumed to go for its members individually, or 'distributively'. The possibility which invalidates the inference is that of the whole being, either in fact or in effect, more than the sum of its parts. Kierkegaard castigates his own age for assuming a particular version of this possibility. In this version the 'more' is a myth. It consists in the *idea* of a collectivity being spuriously given the status of a *thing*.

Different kinds of case can be used to demonstrate the fallacy of division. The most common are of actions a group can perform but which its members cannot perform individually, either because the action or achievement is, as a matter of logic or of conceptual fact, reserved for groups (e.g. winning the Football League Championship), or because in point of brute fact individuals distributively cannot do what they can accomplish collectively (e.g. push the stalled car). This, however, is not what Kierkegaard has in mind. He refers to people willing to face death, give their wealth to a good cause, steep themselves unconditionally in sensuality, or devote themselves with uninhibited enthusiasm to

something, but only in association with others similarly willing.[28]
Here too, in order to capture Kierkegaard's meaning, we must
distinguish carefully between two possibilities. Either the people
are willing to do these things only if others lend their 'moral'
support by showing themselves willing to do the same, the enabling
effect in this case being the provision of greater strength of purpose,
or they will only do them if the actions are prescribed or at least
permitted by the constitutive rules of the group of which they are
members. In the former case they need the numerical support of
similarly motivated associates in order to generate sufficient
determination to act in the ways in question; in the latter they
need the social sanction, over and above whatever determination
they themselves have to act in those ways.

Kierkegaard's examples are clearly to be construed under the
second of these two kinds. He is thinking of people under the
influence of the belief that they must always act as members of a
group or association on behalf of group aims; that is, he is not
thinking, primarily at least, of people who have insufficient
motivation to act at all in the ways in question unless at least some
relevant others proclaim their intention to act similarly. In the
case of those who decide together to face death with equanimity,
to give everything they possess to charity, or themselves to sensual
love or some enthusiasm, Kierkegaard says that the fact that in his
own time this would *not* be to say that these persons would decide
to do these things on their own, is not necessarily due to any *lack*
of courage, to any irresoluteness, or fear of the personal consequences (e.g. death, penury, social disgrace), on their part; it is
because, over and above any such qualms, they fear the 'judgement
of reflection'; they are afraid of reflection's indictment of them
for venturing something *as individuals*.[29]

This overriding respect for reflection's judgment is linked to the
notion of association by an assumption of Hegelian philosophy
which we have already noted: namely that rationality, as the
foundation of human action, growth, and freedom, is embodied in
man's collective institutions. The fundamental principle is that
such institutions are not obstacles to individual freedom, but its
vehicles, even when the participants do not at first understand
them as such — according to Hegel the state harmonizes the limited
and more or less selfish interests of individual agents into a whole
in which their separate interests are mutually served even before
this fact is recognized. This bears witness, in Hegel's view, to
reason's 'cunning'.[30] The modern 'age of reflection', which
Kierkegaard criticizes, could be described as one in which reason's
'cunning' has been translated into conscious ideology; people now

consciously accept that they *must* act as members of associations, and conclude therefore that free, rational, in short properly *human* action, is necessarily collective action. The idea of association thus assumes the status of, as Kierkegaard says, a 'positive principle'. The idea of sociality is 'idolized',[31] and individuals are subjected to the idea that they count only in respect of their group affiliation, not in respect of whatever ability they have to venture something as individuals. As he says, in his time

> the individual does not belong to God, to himself, to the
> beloved, to his art, to his scholarship; no, just as a serf
> belongs to an estate, so the individual is conscious of belonging
> part and parcel to an abstraction under which reflection
> subordinates him.[32]

The levelling Kierkegaard is opposed to here could be called a reduction of the individual to the ranks: not, however, in the sense of simple demotion, or levelling down, but in the sense of reduction from the status of an individual to that of a replaceable member of a set. Kierkegaard says that in antiquity the collectivity of individuals made its own assessment of the outstanding individual's worth, but that now 'the currency standard has changed' and by means of a straightforward mathematical calculation 'it takes more or less so-and-so many persons to make an individual'.[33] If we think of the ranks in the above sense as social and political collectivities, and these as providing their members with corresponding social and political roles and functions, and then assign to these roles and functions the liberating 'spiritual' significance given them by Hegel, we can discern in outline the target of Kierkegaard's attack. On Hegel's view political maturation is a part of spiritual growth in general, and the latter a 'world-historical' process which the life and consciousness of the individual in an essential respect merely reflect, according to the individual's location in the process, not an ethical task to be undertaken and completed by the individual itself. It is true, and Kierkegaard seems often to be less than cognizant of this fact, that Hegel himself gives individual interests, especially the demand for rights, a central role in his theory of spiritual fulfilment as social participation: this provides a kind of input which eventually, by reason's cunning, gives rise to the rational state. Nevertheless, for Hegel the process of fulfilment does not take place *within* the category of the individual; on the contrary, in terms of spiritual growth the category of the individual is for Hegel a limited, because subjective, one and individuals are destined in the process to become more than individuals, they are destined to become harmoniously integrated in a society in which they find that the opposition between particular (the individual) and universal (the state) is overcome. That is where society and politics come in. Spiritual growth calls for the incorporation of the individual within the state. For Hegel the representative form of government is inferior precisely because those represented are represented *merely* as individuals, and not, as for Kierkegaard, because authority in such a form of government is still not properly vested *in* the individual. Indeed, only by actually taking part in affairs of government does a person properly emerge, as Hegel believes a person should, from the narrow, abstract confines of individuality, of particularity, and of subjectivity, and achieve his or her inherent sociality and thereby freedom and spiritual fulfilment.

In attacking levelling, Kierkegaard is not attacking Hegel directly. Nor is he criticizing the conscious application of Hegelian political theory in his time. What he is condemning is the general spirit of his age, a spirit of which Hegelian speculative philosophy is just as much a symptom as a cause or constituent. What is wrong with the age is a kind of loss of enthusiasm, a retreat into generalities, even a spiritual cowardice, what Climacus diagnoses as fear of being an individual.[34] Levelling is, at ground level, a kind of evasion, a refusal to accept the claims of individuality, which Kierkegaard sees as the primary principle of personal fulfilment. He also sees these claims, in a way interestingly parallel to Hegel's conception of the cunning of reason, as manifesting a kind of insistence and strategy even before people become fully conscious of them, and as actually making use of levelling. 'In its eternal truth', says Kierkegaard, 'the principle of individuality *uses* the abstraction and equality of the generation as levellers and thereby religiously develops the co-operating individual into an essentially human being.'[35] Levelling involves a flight into abstraction; it is 'an abstract power and is abstraction's victory over individuals'.[36] In levelling, Kierkegaard writes, 'the dialectic turns away from inwardness and wants to render equality in the negative; so that those who are not essentially individuals constitute an equality in external association . . .'.[37] He says that levelling involves the 'negative unity' of the individual's 'negative mutuality'. The negative unity is the unity of association. It is negative because it places sociality in the external and temporal instead of the subjective and eternal. 'Instead of the relation of inwardness another relation supervenes.'[38] Similarly, negative mutuality is the mutuality of an overriding commitment to common rules of association. Equality in this context is simply a matter of parity of commitment, of shared duties and rights, under an associative umbrella which covers all associates indiscriminately, and protectively. Following Kierkegaard's typology of societies, this represents a false transition from ancient society to modern. It simply transfers authority from the outstanding individual to the generation, with a consequent eclipse of the role of the individual, instead of reconstituting the generation as a society of individuals. The age needs Socratic leadership, leaders who disown authority and help the individual, less by attraction than by repulsion, to become autonomous.[39] But because it is an age of reflection, the present age has got it wrong. It sees fulfilment and freedom in the idea of a universal affiliation. It fails to see that more important than agreement with one's affiliates is agreement with oneself, satisfaction with oneself and one's God-relationship.[40] Equality becomes fulfilment only when 'everyone, individually, is essentially within the divine totality'.[41]

According to the passage which is this chapter's motto, equalization, or levelling, is 'a false anticipation' of the divine totality. It is so because it conceives universal social harmony in terms of membership of the group of all human groups. Kierkegaard says that the idea of this superordinate association, of 'pure humanity' (*den rene Menneskehed*), is a 'higher negativity'.[42] Higher, that is, than that of any of its subordinate collectivities, such as nationality, membership of a family, etc. It is, he thinks, a typical fabrication of the age of reflection, enabling people to suppose quite spuriously that they possess potential personal and social identities simply by virtue of being human beings. This illusory supposition is supported by the myth of 'the public', a 'monstrous abstraction', for which he says journalists are mainly responsible.[43] The public is the political equivalent of pure humanity: it is the 'phantom', or 'mirage', which gives this 'all and nothing'[44] apparent substance in the field of social action, and allows the most comprehensive and destructive form of levelling, 'genuine, purely abstract levelling',[45] to take effect.

It is important to note that Kierkegaard distinguishes the purely abstract notion of the public from forms of association in which people can and do genuinely acquire personal identity through a social commitment. The latter forms of association, because they in turn support (*understøder*) the individuals who compose them, not just politically but also personally, in a sense exploited by modern psychologists (for example, Erikson), are 'concretions' or substantial unities, not myths.[46]

A generation, a people, a general assembly, a community,
a man [, all of these] still have a responsibility to be something,
can show shame for fickleness and treachery. . . . A people,
a general assembly, a man can change in such a way that it can
be said they are no longer the same.

But not so the public: 'the public can become the very opposite and is still the same — the public'.[47] What pure levellers do is draw the wrong conclusion from the undeniable fact that people acquire personalities, or 'become themselves', by being members of collectivities. They see 'concretions' as immature forms of an emerging pan-social consciousness; not, as Kierkegaard would insist, as immature forms of an emerging individual autonomy.

As we have just noted, Kierkegaard nevertheless finds in real, i.e. abstract, levelling something positive. Although levelling may initially be linked with the passionate pursuit of ideals (in its revolutionary origins levelling is the attempt to neutralize the power of the eminent individual by strengthening the union [Foreningen] of those upon whom he exerts it),[48] its principle of association is in fact inherently 'sceptical' and non-passionate. The freedoms people acquire in their groups generate opposition, divisiveness, partisanship, and cross-purposes which are inconsistent with the goal of total social harmony. So the true leveller insists that people divest themselves of these divisive forms of association in order to identify themselves with their pure humanity as members of the public, an absolute affiliation which 'consumes' all relative unities.[49] However, since the general public is an abstraction which cannot give its members specific duties or commitments, the process, if carried out, leaves the individual bleached of all identity — a bare individual. This none the less has a Socratically edifying effect.

> And so when the generation which has itself wanted to level,
> has wanted to be emancipated and to revolt, has wanted
> to do away with authority, and has thereby, with the scepticism
> of associationism generated the desolating forest fire of
> abstraction, when the generation has [in this way] done away
> with individual personalities and all organic forms of
> association [organiske Concretioner], has put humanity in
> their place and established a numerical equality between
> man and man; when the generation has thus for a moment
> diverted itself with the broad vista of an abstract infinity
> undisturbed by the limitation of even the slightest elevation
> . . . then begins the work, where individuals must help
> themselves, each on its own.[50]

The positive role which Kierkegaard assigns to levelling parallels that of anxiety. Like the latter, 'pure' levelling puts the individual in a position where a radical choice can no longer be avoided: levelling can be 'the starting-point for the highest life', because the abstract totality 'by its very repellancy helps [the individual] to be absolutely constituted'. The alternative is to perish, to vanish as an individual. Echoing the theme of 'the pupil of possibility' in *Anxiety*, Kierkegaard says it 'will [nevertheless] be genuinely educative to live in the age of levelling',[51] for there people are forced to face 'the judgement of abstraction's infinite equality' alone.[52] There is even a hint that levelling is just as indispensable as anxiety for spiritual growth. A similar parallel is to be found in Kierkegaard's account of irony (see Chapter III, above). In his dissertation he writes of the 'abstract measure' by which irony 'levels everything', i.e. drains the temporal world of all value, of how 'total' irony 'razes all eminences', and of how 'controlled' irony nevertheless 'chastens and punishes'.[53]

Levelling, then, is something which in certain rather typical circumstances should be promoted. It is a tool in the hands of the unrecognizable leader in his efforts to prompt people into accepting that authority is an individual and internal matter, not a collective and external one — though Kierkegaard says it is 'only in a *suffering* act that [one] will dare to promote levelling', and the suffering of one's act is at the same time a condemnation of the tool.[54] Absolute levelling, even in its scepticism and the absence of passion, is, in the right hands, an instrument of salvation. In an age of despair most people fail to be 'separated out' by their own inner development. The failure of this development to occur gives rise, says Kierkegaard, to a 'friction' which in turn induces that 'self-combustion' of the human species which is pure levelling. By 'consuming everything' levelling provides sluggish developers with an 'examen rigorosum' which can prompt them into 'winning the essentiality of religiousness in themselves'.[55]

Kierkegaard denies categorically that 'the idea of sociality or of community will save the age'.[56] But it can help negatively. By relieving individuals even of their passionate group-involvements, it places them in a situation where each individual can learn 'to be satisfied with himself in the essentiality of religiousness before God, to be satisfied with ruling over himself instead of the world'.[57] This individual autonomy is what Kierkegaard thinks *alone* can save the age.

4   Levelling 2

Not everything in Kierkegaard's attack on levelling is anti-Hegelian. In *Two Ages* we find, in fact, two distinct conceptions to which Kierkegaard is opposed. Besides the Hegelian idea of human fulfilment as a 'levelling' of the individual by absorption into the group, with its correlative ideal of equality as parity of group commitment,

Kierkegaard attacks another kind of levelling to which Hegel was also opposed. This is the idea that personal differences, of talent, interest, and authority, should play no role in politics. The ideal of equality corresponding to this conception is that of absolute uniformity. Levelling in the former sense involves a merging of the individual with the collectivity, a suspension of the category distinction between the individual and the group. Levelling in the latter sense involves the eliminating of politically relevant differences between the group's individual members. The two conceptions are not logically related: a collection of true individuals might be as uniform as you please but still be individuals, and a group of persons who had surrendered their individual status in the former sense need not be levelled in the latter sense. This latter levelling, applied to the group of all human beings, was the official programme of the French Revolutionaries. Hegel himself points out that they regarded 'all differences in talent and authority as being superseded',[58] and criticizes their aim of forcibly eliminating differences, not only these but all other differences, in their attempt to establish what Kierkegaard, playing again on the ambiguity of 'Lighed', calls 'Verds-lighed',[59] i.e. sameness in temporal or worldly categories, time being the very 'medium of differentiation'.[60] Like Kierkegaard, Hegel sees this as a perverse denial of the fact of diversity and of particularity.

It was also part of the same revolutionary programme to identify people with the state. If this identification is allied to the second kind of levelling, all personal differences will be politically relevant and therefore prone to the egalitarian scythe. So there will be no limit, in principle, to the elimination of difference. Hegel objects to this, too. On the grounds that people with special qualifications are required to administer the modern state, he distinguishes sharply between the people, or civil society, on the one hand, and the state on the other.[61] The latter exercises a necessary control over the social life of the former.

Kierkegaard has very similar targets in view. In *Two Ages* he deplores the lack of passion characteristic of the age of reflection. In it, he says,

> [t] he coiled springs of life-relationships, which owe their nature
> to qualitatively distinguishing passion, lose their resilience;
> the qualitative expression of the distance between those who
> differ from each other is no longer the law for a relation
> of inwardness between them in their relationship. . . . Instead
> of . . . inwardness there enters another relation: the disparates
> do not relate to what distinguishes them but stand there,

as it were, keeping an eye on each other, and *this tension
is really the cessation of their relationship*. This is not that
cheerful, outspoken admiration, quick to express appreciation,
which [can] take off its hat to distinction [but also be]
shocked by its pride and arrogance; neither is it the opposite
relation, no, not at all — admiration and distinction become
pretty well a pair of courteous equals keeping a close eye
on each other. This is not the citizen who with cheerful
loyalty [can] pay homage to his king [but also become]
embittered by his tyranny, no, by no means — being a citizen
has come to mean something else, it means to be a *third-party*.
The citizen doesn't relate himself in the relation but is a
spectator computing the problem of the relation between
a king and his subject; for time passes in appointing committee
upon committee, at least so long as there are still enough
people who are interested, with full passion and each for
himself, in being this definite thing [e.g. a king's subject] he
is supposed to be: but in the end the whole age becomes a
committee. This is not the father who in indignation
concentrates his fatherly authority in a single curse or the
son who defies him, a rift which may still end in the inwardness
of reconciliation. No, [their] relation as such is irreproachable,
for it is about to come to an end in any case, inasmuch as
they do not relate essentially to each other in the relation,
the relation itself being now the problem in which, like rivals
in a game, the parties watch each other instead of 'relating'
to each other. . . . This is not the difficult adolescent who
nevertheless quakes and trembles before his schoolmasters.
No, the relation is rather that of a certain equality in a mutual
exchange between teacher and pupil on how to run a good
school . . . .
What should one call such a relation? A tension perhaps . . .
but one in which life is exhausted and in which there vanish the
fervour, enthusiasm, and inwardness that make the chains of
dependency and the crown of dominion light, that make the
child's obedience and the father's authority happy, that make
the humility of admiration and the eminence of distinction
open-hearted and frank, that give the teacher's position
its unique validity and thus the pupil the opportunity to learn,
that unite the frailty of the woman and the strength of the
man in the equal [*lige*] intensity of devotion. The relation still
indeed remains, but without the resilience to concentrate
itself in inwardness so as to bring about a harmonious
union. . . .[62]

Kierkegaard, too, is arguing for the preservation of difference. But not with Hegel's administrational preoccupations in mind, with their emphasis on the state as the controlling centre of social life. What Kierkegaard wants to save are personal relations of responsibility, accountability, and concern quite generally, in the private as well as the public sphere, and between these. He, too, attacks the identifying of the private with the public, but again, not with Hegel's considerations in mind. Predictably, in terms of the distinction between private and public, Kierkegaard's focus is on the former. For Hegel social life can only be maintained by an enlightened and responsible civil service (the instrument *par excellence* of rationality and therefore of social conciliation on Hegel's view). For Kierkegaard it is in the private sphere, indeed the individually private sphere, that the conditions for a harmonious social life are first to be established. The distinction ('disjunction') Kierkegaard focuses on is that between inner and outer, subjectivity and objectivity, a distinction which he considers essential for *all* authentic social intercourse,[63] but which he says has disappeared in passionless chatter and gossip.[64]

An interesting sidelight can be thrown on the different perspectives from which Hegel and Kierkegaard criticize egalitarianism by comparing the reasons they have for nevertheless finding some virtue in it. Hegel saw in the revolutionary programme an expression of what he considered a true principle: namely that society should be founded on reason and objectivity, and therefore must be understood in the categories of thought. For him the French Revolution was an attempt to reconstruct society on the basis of the *idea* of universal justice and equality; its error was to fail to see that individual rights had to be safeguarded by law and administrative control. For Kierkegaard, on the other hand, the virtue of the Revolution was its demonstration of collective passion.

A passionate, tumultuous age wants to overthrow everything, reject everything. [While an] age that is revolutionary but also reflecting and devoid of passion transforms the expression of strength into a dialectical trick: letting everything remain the same but subtly draining it of meaning. . . .[65]

Collective action sustained by passion has a substance; *it* is not based on an abstract 'all and nothing'. We noted that Kierkegaard accepts the value of associative links in which people preserve and even strengthen their individual identities. In the same spirit he acknowledges both the existence of such 'full-blooded individual associations of agents' as 'the people and political parties', *and* their liberating role:[66] it is 'no empty abstraction when an energetic people levels'. Perhaps they are not really levelling either, for Kierkegaard describes that as being indeed a matter of empty abstraction. In the case of full-blooded group action, aimed at neutralizing the oppressive power of an eminent individual or a group, the inherent abstractional character of levelling is still anchored in a substantial unity, something passionate and therefore concrete, namely the group commitments of collaborating individuals.[67] Kierkegaard would probably have approved of the October revolution, though he would have deplored also *its* aftermath.

5   Equality in difference

If Kierkegaard's targets in *Two Ages* are, on the one hand, levelling as the merging of the individual with the group and, on the other, levelling as the eliminating of grades of authority and responsibility within and between groups, what kind or kinds of political structure could Kierkegaard positively envisage? If we take attitudes and approaches to equality as indicators of specific political theories, we can address this question first by asking, just what kinds of political theory view human differentiation favourably, and then second, what sense, if any, can they give to the notion of human equality.

The term 'inequality' becomes relevant in a political context, one might say, when differences between human beings manifest themselves in uneven distributions of humanly essential or, more widely, desirable possibilities. The differences which come naturally to mind are those we label 'injustices'; that is to say, undeserved undercapacities and overcapacities, particularly where a functional dependence exists between the two, for instance where undeserved undercapacities are due to direct or indirect exploitation by those with undeserved overcapacities, and again specifically with regard to those differences in capacity which are due to political and economic factors rather than to plain natural endowment, though most people would consider the alleviation of, or compensation for, 'natural injustice' a proper addition to any programme designed to rectify political and economic injustice. The attempt to put people on an equal footing in respects in which it is felt to be both unfair and unfortunate that they are not, is a widely accepted political ideal.

Social democrats believe that extensive control of economic life is necessary to ensure a minimum of justice, and that in order to ensure the individual's control over the factors determining whether or not it is unjustly situated, there should be equality of opportunity to influence political decisions. The framework allows room for disagreement, for instance on whether equal achievement, that is equality in the result, should be a measure of the avoidance of injustice, or whether equal opportunity is enough. But the emphasis, in any case, is on a general equalization of political and economic status, supported by an assumption, perhaps basic for all democrats, that apart from its providing the individual with an effective defence against injustice, the principle of *political* equality is an intrinsic ideal, while the principle of *economic* equality, apart from its possible connection with political equality, stands because there appears to be no self-sufficient reason why some people should enjoy economic privileges which are denied to others.

In contrast, political conservatives have a cavalier attitude to the principles of political and economic equality. They point out, as does Hegel, that the special talents needed to run a modern society are not, and cannot be expected to be, a common possession. Though their lack can be due in some cases to social injustice, this is not always so. And in all cases such comparative overcapacities must be cultivated and rewarded. In this respect, they are not undeserved. Some undercapacities are not undeserved either, in so far as they follow from failure to meet life's challenges. Other undercapacities, for example lack of opportunity and natural disability to meet challenge, are no doubt ethically unacceptable, but their amelioration should be left to individual beneficence or the indirect benefits of a prosperous, free-market economy, not administered centrally and financed in such a way as to reduce the rewards, and hence motivation, for socially beneficial individual achievement. Apart from their belief in the social benefits of individualism, moreover, political conservatives often tend to see in individual distinction a measure of intrinsic personal superiority. For them, in contradistinction to social democrats, there appears to be no self-sufficient reason why some people should not enjoy economic privileges which are denied to others.

Where does Kierkegaard stand in respect of these alternative paradigms? If we recall his observation that it is absurd to try to impose equality (*Lighed*, sameness) in the 'medium of differentiation' and add to this his critique of the second kind of levelling, it is natural enough to characterize him as a conservative in the mould of Hegel. True, Hegel's belief in the necessity of difference goes with his belief in the need for, and the needs of, centralization, while in a Kierkegaardian society of autonomous individuals the centres of control are ultimately, in some ill-defined way, the individuals themselves. True, too, that the differences Kierkegaard wishes to retain are not intended as guarantees of effective external administration, but as positions from which people can enter into relations of personal responsibility, accountability, and concern. Nevertheless it appears that a society of autonomous individuals in Kierkegaard's sense is not necessarily, and perhaps is even necessarily not, a society of social, political, and economic equals; or if it were, the 'coiled springs of life-relationships' would have to be provided elsewhere. And even if Kierkegaard esteems such inequalities for reasons other than Hegel's, so long as they are the same inequalities the same justification exists for labelling him a political conservative.

But there are three significant deviations from the paradigm. First, although Kierkegaard does not directly criticize the state apparatus as such, this is not because he assumes that its social and political functions are inevitably favourable. Rather he sees in the apparatus a framework which can play host to a more fundamental, but also socially important, set of alternatives, namely the ethical maturity or otherwise of its incumbents and clients. As far as the former are concerned, as long as they conceive themselves not as instruments of the reason which Hegel claimed to be embodied in the political organs of society, nor as having any other *ex officio* moral or political status, but as individuals accountable personally for their bureaucratic actions and political decisions, the framework can be allowed to stand, or so Kierkegaard seems in many places to imply. The same applies to those over whom social and political authority is exercised. In the *Journals* he writes, for instance, that from a Christian point of view people should be satisfied with the position they are given by birth, class, circumstances, education, and living conditions.[68] Again, his view seems to be that there is nothing *inherently* right or wrong about such differences of status; what matters is whether they take effect in a Christian or an un-Christian way. To deny that such differences are acceptable is to suppose that there is some blueprint, 'the pure human being', which provides a model for everyone. But 'Christianity is too serious to rave on about the pure human being . . . it simply wants a person not to damage his soul by abusing [the] difference'. However, the abuse Kierkegaard refers to here is not social oppression but the tendency of social status, low and high alike, to make a person abandon the idea of personal salvation.[69] A rather special context, and one should not jump to the conclusion that Kierkegaard is unconcerned with the oppressive consequences of differences in social status. In the passage concerned he is questioning the particular assumption, no doubt voiced loudly in his time, that it is only those in power who abuse this difference, and that the lowly situated are 'justified in doing anything to obtain equality [*Ligelighed*]'. In the same place

Kierkegaard writes, 'just as once the powerful refused to recognize in the humble their neighbour, so now one wants to teach the humble to see in the powerful only their enemy. Surely that isn't the way to approach Christian equality [*Lighed*]!' His point is that it would be just as unwarranted to justify the depriving of those in power of their special status in terms of a conceptual political ideal ('pure humanity') as it would be for them to exercise their power in the belief that they are instruments of reason. In both cases the only valid appeal is to whatever moves individual agents to their accountable choices.

Second, it is a radical deviation from the conservative paradigm on Kierkegaard's part that he denies that those governing a society should expect rewards for their special responsibilities. Here we begin to see the full extent of the requirements of the ethical maturity Kierkegaard ambitiously expects of his rulers, what he thinks is really needed to introduce the dimension of eternity into political affairs.[70] There is nevertheless some unclarity. A general point here is that according to Kierkegaard's strongly Kantian ethical views, moral action must be its own reward. Moral *leadership*, as we have noted, can even involve 'acts of suffering'. The question is whether Kierkegaard believes politicians to be capable, *qua* politicians, of *moral* leadership, for we remember both that political goals are temporal ones and that moral leaders in the proper sense must disown authority. Since it is certainly Kierkegaard's general view that a harmonious society depends first of all on its moral centre, and that individuals are that centre's only proper location, this also engenders a certain unclarity about Kierkegaard's actual attitude to the corporate state and its organs. Does he, or would he, believe that the corporate state must eventually go? Or even that it must go immediately? In his preparatory notes to 'A Cycle of Ethico-religious Treatises', he does indeed say that it should go. He says that once all the turmoil is over (he is writing in 1848, a time of political upheaval in Europe as well as of actual warfare in the dispute over Schleswig-Holstein, and two years after the publication of *Two Ages*), politicians will have to be replaced by what he calls the 'Fourth Estate', by which he does not mean established religion (among the 'tyrants' the Fourth Estate is to replace are popes and Jesuits, along with 'emperors, kings, generals, and diplomats'), but people unconditionally obedient to God. When the time comes for the Fourth Estate to establish itself, and that is *not* when the services of the corporate state are no longer required, as in the Marxist theory of the withering away of the state, but when it is finally clear that the functions in question cannot be *served* by the corporate state, by politicians and ministries, that is when it is clear that what is needed is a moral revolution led by a minority who are 'in truth' and prepared for the 'certain' victory of martyrdom;[71] when that time comes, says Kierkegaard, its rulers, far from enjoying their power, as those now in power do 'however much work and responsibility [their worldly rule] involves', will look upon their positions as 'the opposite of an advantage' and even as a punishment.[72]

Third, there is the question of equality. As a professed adherent of the principle of equality, Kierkegaard should surely side with the social democrats against the conservatives. We have seen, however, that he dismisses institutionalized equality (which must also encompass political and economic equality) as a misguided attempt to secularize the properly religious notion of human equality; he calls it 'a false anticipation of the eternal life'.[73] But how can he have it both ways? That is, how can he profess the democratic principles of equality and at the same time accept real inequalities in human existence? More particularly, how can he accept both of these without subscribing to a reactionary political theory?

A first rejoinder is that 'equality' as such is by no means synonymous with 'justice'. Suppose that 'equality before the law' is interpreted in legal practice as enjoining like punishment for like crimes; and suppose, further, that the only form of punishment permitted is forfeiture of goods or a fine. Since the punishment is designed to fit the crime and not the pocket, a poor offender will be treated unjustly in relation to a rich one, and conversely. The biblical injunction to the Jews, 'Ye shall have one manner of law, as well for the stranger as for one of your own country: for I am the Lord your God',[74] makes a similar concession to inequality within equality. It says in effect that the unlike (in given respects) should be *treated* alike. It says that the difference here should be ignored. In this case the ignoring of the difference would be considered to favour justice. In both cases the likeness resides not in those whom the law affects, but in the implementation of the law, in the legal action. Consider also Kant's picture of the kingdom of ends in which every rational being is a legislating member, that is, himself makes the laws to which he is subject. Kant says that this ideal is arrived at by '[abstracting] from the personal differences of rational beings, and likewise from all the content of their private ends . . .'.[75] But then what if the differences *here* include injustices? Does this not mean that they are simply allowed to remain? No, not in principle, because the idea of abstracting from personal differences is not to direct attention elsewhere (upon

297

God or the prospects of an after-life), but to lay a consensual basis for legislating away the differences that are unjust; the legislator ignores his own 'difference' thus gaining in impartiality; he does not ignore differences among people in general. As for differences in general, however, these are not simply to be eliminated without further ado. It is only where they amount to injustices, and hence constitute disrespect for persons, that differences should be eliminated. According to Kant, all persons deserve respect, because, whatever else distinguishes them, they are (whatever their actual political and economic status, or for that matter whatever their actual intellectual capacities) rational and free. A person, according to Kant, is *as such* entitled to respect, to be treated, as he says, as an end and not just as a means, and is therefore entitled to his individuality, to his special talents and interests. But by the same token he is entitled to redress when other people's interests impinge disrespectfully on his, as other people are when his impinge on theirs. In Kant's conception there is, then, the idea of a kind of guarantee that the inequalities that survive or ensue from equal treatment do not amount to injustices.

Similarly with Kierkegaard's notion of equality as Christian equality. He says that it 'watches over' difference.[76] That is, it prevents it from becoming injustice. As to what this equality is in practice, it is 'loving one's neighbour'.[77] This notion, like Kant's, provides people, not just as incumbents and clients of a corporate state, but in whatever interpersonal relationships they are involved, with a basis for the mutual furtherance of others' interests. It allows these interests to develop in individual ways, but aims to protect the relationships from personal exploitation by making the elimination of selfishness and partiality a condition of its genuine practice. Kierkegaard's moral rule is directed not at the individual's rationality and freedom, but at the 'infinite reality' which on his view belongs to each.[78] The effect, or purpose, however, is the same: to locate in the person as such, and thus in all persons equally, a basis for the belief in the inherent value of the individual, a primary value, furthermore, in the sense well captured by Rawls's remark that 'to respect persons is to recognize that they possess an inviolability founded on justice that even the welfare of society as a whole cannot override'.[79]

As far as his own society is concerned, Kierkegaard thinks that in it persons fail even to respect themselves. They are *afraid* of being individuals. What society needs first of all is that they begin to face their own individuality and the questions it gives rise to. Levelling, as we saw, eventually forces them precisely to do that, because the ultimate goal of levelling, identification with the 'all and nothing' of 'pure humanity', leaves them without affiliation and thus with the problem of deciding what their true identities, in all eternity, are. The same happens, says Kierkegaard, when people begin to show a generalized disrespect for the state. If they want to rule themselves and show themselves dissatisfied with 'the State, the Church, and everything connected with them (art, science, etc., etc.)', they must eventually 'resolve themselves into atoms'. Their notion of equality in that case, instead of being, as it once was, a matter of balance between groups or between the group and the eminent individual, is translated into uniformity, a likeness between individuals. Kierkegaard caricatures this equality in what he calls its two 'diametrically opposed' interpretations:

> Communism which says: the proper thing in secular terms
> is . . . that there must be no difference at all between
> people; wealth, art, science and government etc., etc. are
> evil, all people should be like workers in a factory or the
> inmates of a poorhouse, clothed alike, eating the same food
> made in one big pot, at the same time, in the same amount,
> etc., etc.: and Pietism which says: the proper thing in
> Christian terms is that there must be no difference between
> people, we should be brothers and sisters, own everything
> in common; wealth, position, art, science, etc. are evil;
> all people should . . . be clothed alike, pray on schedule, get
> married by drawing lots, go to bed at the same time, eat the
> same food from one dish, in a definite rhythm, etc., etc.[80]

Kierkegaard's individual *is*, in a sense, an atom, an isolated unit in society; that is a necessary part of the individual's autonomy, of what it means to deny Hegel's assumption that the category of the individual is limited and must be transcended if the individual is to be fulfilled; and also, on Kierkegaard's view, a presupposition of the sociality that can and must emerge from the individual will (as opposed to being institutionalized in the organs of society). But this sociality is not to be conceived in terms of likeness, of what is had or done in common. On the contrary, it has to spring out of what cannot coherently be thought collectively at all, namely the 'infinite' reality which is to be attributed to each individual.

It does not follow, of course, that because Kierkegaard thinks that respect for the organs of state sustains personal identity at the immature level of group-identification, then these organs cannot be valued for other reasons. It could be, for example, that in a society of autonomous individuals the organs of state provided apt avenues for individual diversity in talent, authority, and personality in general, instead of refuges for persons (as in one typical picture of the bureaucrat) unwilling to become autonomous individuals. But they could also continue to be valued for their practical functions. It is important to note that Kierkegaard admits, in passing but quite explicitly, that in relation to *material* interests the 'principle of association' can indeed have its 'validity'.[81] Considering the wide range of human activity in which these interests are pursued, ever more so in our own time, this is a large concession. The crucial point, however, is that, even where association is 'valid', Kierkegaard believes it must be based upon the already individually constituted morality of the associates. Kierkegaard says that, before there can be talk of genuine association, individuals must first acquire 'a moral attitude in defiance of the whole world'. Without a basis in individual morality human associations are as 'unseemly and corrupting as child-marriages', 'evasions', 'diversions', 'illusions' which, though they strengthen individuals numerically, nevertheless weaken them morally.[82]

There are residual unclarities about Kierkegaard's view with regard to familial or civil groupings in this respect (e.g. would he allow that the family was one group in which the ethical attitude of the individual was fostered rather than — and it would certainly be odd to have to say this — presupposed?). But, again, the important point is the denial that the principle of association has any validity other than in respect of its serving material interests. The issue, once more, is with Hegel, or more immediately with Hegelian optimism and complacency. Associations are not, Kierkegaard insists, collective aspects of spirituality, such that active membership of them implies participation in a greater spiritual unity. They are no more than external arrangements to be justified by their practical utility. As against Hegel, Kierkegaard is, if you like, a social nominalist, denying that collective categories, the family, civil society, the corporate state, provide successively more adequate social media for a spirit naturally bent upon its social fulfilment. The spirit 'finds itself' not in the outward forms of sociality but in the social content of the individual will. Acquiring a will with that content is *not* a world-historical process. Neither is it a social process. Nor a natural one. In fact, it is not a process at all but an activity, a 'self-activity' whose various stages are marked by an awareness, not of the aptness of the organs of society to express true human nature, but of the inability of the external, finite world to provide the conditions of human fulfilment at all.

The positive response to this latter insight, when it finally dawns, is the leap of faith, and Kierkegaard believes it is only from this that genuine sociality, in the form of each person's unselfish concern for the interests of any other — hence in principle for all others — emerges. In this light the evil of levelling is the assumption of levellers that sociality is to be found in increasingly comprehensive forms of *external* association, an instance of what Kierkegaard constantly remarks upon as the general and Hegel-inspired evil of his time, namely the blurring of the distinction between inner and outer, a theme also discussed at some length in *Two Ages*.[83] For Hegel, as we saw earlier, subjectivity and objectivity do not represent true opposites. The sense that an individual has that its freedom is incompatible with social and political participation is based on an inadequate grasp of the nature of human fulfilment. 'The absolute ethical whole', says Hegel, 'is nothing else than a people.'[84] For him the individual's spiritual maturity is a matter of convergence, in fact and in consciousness, with this whole, the 'abstract' notion of freedom of conscience giving way to a 'concrete' grasp of subjective freedom as part of a whole. Kierkegaard believes this ethical whole to be pure myth, as is any whole about which all that can be said about its being more than the sum of its individual parts is that it corresponds to an idea. The *ethical* whole is no more than the sum of its ethical parts and *they* are individuals. The myth, the 'idea' of sociality and community (*Menighed*), is in fact an obstacle to true sociality and community. It gets in the way. As the humorist Climacus says in the *Postscript*, 'the infiltration of the idea of the state, of society, of community, and association' makes it no longer possible for God to get hold of the individual. Whatever the extent of God's wrath, 'the punishment . . . has to be transmitted through all the due processes of the objective order'. 'In this way, in the most courteous and appreciative of philosophical language, God has been manoeuvred adroitly into the outside [i.e. the finite] world.'[85] Unlike Hegel, and Marx too, Kierkegaard believes the objective order obscures, and Kierkegaard also thinks people *use* it to obscure, the basic question of human and social responsibility, the question of what the individual's fundamental needs are. Not wanting to know these needs is part and parcel of not wanting to be the kind of entity that has them. In the 'Notes' on his authorship, written some two years after *A Literary Review*, and which we quoted at the beginning, Kierkegaard says that anyone with an eye for the state of the times will

> unequivocally oppose [the] immoral mystification which, philosophically and socially, aims at demoralizing 'the individuals' with the help of 'humanity' or imaginary association-identities, a mystification which wants to teach an ungodly scorn for that which is the first condition of all religiousness: being an individual.[86]

The 'Abstract' Individual

'The individual' is the category through which, in a
religious respect, this age, history, the human race
must pass.[1]

1   Kierkegaard and Marx

Marcuse says of Kierkegaard's work that it is 'the last great attempt
to restore religion as the ultimate organon for liberating humanity
from the destructive impact of an oppressive social order'.[2] The
compliment is back-handed. While acknowledging the seriousness
of Kierkegaard's attempt, Marcuse sees it as vainly drawing upon
a now definitely outdated tradition. Social liberation, as Marcuse
points out, is the problem *par excellence* of post-Hegelian philosophy. He divides this philosophy into two main types: one,
represented by Feuerbach and Kierkegaard, which fastens upon
'the isolated individual', and the other, represented by Marx, which
'penetrates to the origins of the individual in the process of social
labour'. Marcuse speaks, of course, for the latter type: that is, for
a point of view from which the ethico-religious concepts and
principles central to Kierkegaard's concept of the single individual
are interpreted as ideological expressions of states of the social
and political order, and these in turn as expressions of the prevailing type of the process of social labour. So although he concedes
that 'Feuerbach's materialism and Kierkegaard's existentialism . . .
embody many traits of a deep-rooted social theory', Marcuse
dismisses both because, as he says, 'they do not get beyond earlier
philosophical and religious approaches to the problem'.[3] In
nominating Kierkegaard to at least an honorary place in the
pantheon of social philosophers, Marcuse is at the same time

recommending that the social philosophy itself be relegated to the museum.

The traditional charge levelled at Kierkegaard, as at existentialism generally, by Marxists amongst others, is 'abstraction'. The charge assumes both a strong and a weak form and the Marxist charge is sometimes a combination of both. The strong form is suggested by the Marxist idea just mentioned, that ethico-religious concepts and principles simply reflect temporal political and economic processes. According to this, Kierkegaard's fixation on the individual would be abstract, not just because it ignored such limitations as those imposed upon individual fulfilment, say, by the social environment, but also because in assuming the irreducibility of the ethico-religious concepts and principles in terms of which he analyses individual fulfilment, Kierkegaard is claiming for ethics and religion an area immune to explanation in terms of natural and social facts. But, of course, this will appear to constitute a 'fatal' limitation only to those convinced of the naturalist assumptions upon which the criticism is based.

The weak form of the charge may well command wider support. Here the objection is simply that Kierkegaard's notion of human fulfilment fails to take account of certain important aspects of human development, namely those aspects the failure of which to develop can at least partly be traced to the presence of an 'oppressive social order'. Doubtless most people would nowadays agree in calling a view of human fulfilment abstract, or at any rate seriously deficient, if it denies the existence or the importance of social sources of selective deprivation. But fewer would also claim that it was abstract simply because it postulated an ideal of fulfilment for the attainment of which the elimination of these injustices was not sufficient, or — to come closer to the specifically Marxist idea — because it held its ideal of human fulfilment to be in certain respects historically inviolable and not something which would be radically modified when the processes causing selective deprivation were mastered and rectified.

The problem of human fulfilment, in the terms of post-Hegelian philosophy, can be roughly described as that of man's appropriation of his essence. Correlative to this idea are those, first, of man's estrangement from what is necessary to that essence and, second, of the need to free himself from a state which has brought that estrangement about. Thus the terms 'fulfilment' and 'liberation' in this tradition are interchangeable. In Marcuse's view Kierkegaard's 'fixation' on the individual involves 'adopting an abstract approach' to the problem.[4] To call an approach to this problem 'abstract' is, from the point of view of the same tradition, to charge it with lack of insight into what is in fact necessary to human essence. Hegelians themselves would put this by saying that an abstract approach is one that fails to grasp essential connections between what mis-leadingly appear to be mutually exclusive terms. The terms in this case are the individual and society. It was, as we saw, Hegel's own view that the conception of the individual as an isolated being, for whom sociality and community life are unessential qualifications, is due to just such a lack of insight. Like Aristotle before him and Marx after him, Hegel believed, as Marcuse puts it, that 'the fullest existence of the individual is consummated in his social life'.[5] And not just the approach, but also the individual itself, can be abstract in this sense. According to Hegel one who feels himself isolated from (or in) society, or even one who feels self-sufficient without it, has not yet acquired an insight into his own essentially social nature. For Hegel this insight consists in a sense of the universal, and the isolated individual is one who, because of the lack of this sense, cannot see beyond the fact of being a distinct and particular being for whom social life and its institutions are at best irrelevant and at worst alien constraints. For such persons any social categories in terms of which it might be suggested their activities should be, or are really, constrained, are themselves in turn grasped in a merely abstract way. From the Hegelian point of view it is exactly these categories, however, that form the real and the concrete, and the view that social categories are abstract is the view of an abstract person, that is, not a notional or theoretical person but a real person actually abstracted in thought and action from the social life in which his or her existence is most fully consum-mated.

It is important to see how on this point Marxists see themselves as at once both Hegel's true heirs and his most pertinent critics. They agree with Hegel that the individual is not essentially isolated in the sense that the social context is just an incidental setting for human fulfilment; like Hegel they claim that the social context provides (logical, not merely causal) conditions essential for that fulfilment. Their difference with Hegel is that they analyse human isolation as a hard fact to be remedied by conscious control of the process of social labour, and not as an illusion of the understand-ing to be remedied by forming the relevant sense of the universal (though one should not forget that for Hegel, too, the appropriate social and political organs have to come into being). 'Genuine community', says the young Marx, 'does not originate through reflection, mere thinking; it emerges through the *need* and *egoism* of individuals.'[6] Because the rejected view represents for Marx a merely 'philosophical' and not a 'practical' approach to the problem, it is to be dismissed as outdated.

Let us note straightaway the points on which the early Marx and Kierkegaard agree and disagree. First, they agree that genuine community is not something that emerges through the 'movement' of thought. But then, second, Kierkegaard does not believe, as both Marx and Hegel do, that genuine community emerges through the 'need' and 'egoism' of individuals. On the contrary, for Kierkegaard genuine community emerges only when the egoism of individuals has been transformed into unselfish benevolence. As for needs, we saw that Kierkegaard believes that also here, whatever social co-operation may be called for, social affiliation never in itself provides the conditions of community; indeed, unless individuals are already 'socialized' to the extent that they have acquired moral wills, the co-operatives they form will be corrupt and, in respect of 'humanity' or mankind as a whole, divisive. In this respect the problem of the emergence of genuine community is for Kierkegaard, as it is for Marx, a practical and *not* a theoretical, or in this sense 'philosophical', one. But Kierkegaard does not believe, as Marx does, that the practical problem is that of arriving at some 'external' solution which allows the needs and egoism of individuals to harmonize. Let us dwell a little longer on these two points.

First, both Kierkegaard and Marx can, and do, direct the charge of abstraction at Hegel himself. If the establishing of genuine community is a task, and an abstract approach is one which conceives this task in a way which takes no account of the factors which actually determine whether or not the task can be successfully carried out, then for the Marxist an abstract approach will be one which disregards the function of the social factors which constitute and maintain the forms of social labour. The abstract concept of a person from this point of view will be one which does not see possession of genuine sociality as a practical problem requiring knowledge and control of the process of social labour for its solution; and one who adopts an abstract approach will be one who does not see that people have been and are deprived of their essential sociality by limitations imposed upon their practical possibilities of fulfilment by past and prevailing forms of social labour.

Similarly for the Kierkegaardian. Indeed, a plausible rendering of Kierkegaard's critique of Hegelian abstractionism can be generated by making a simple substitution in a succinct formulation by Marx himself of the distinctively Marxist twist to the thesis of the practicality of the problem of human liberation. Marx says that the task is for individuals 'to bring under their own conscious control the material conditions of life, conditions which have previously been left to chance and which have thus acquired an independent existence over against individuals'.[7] It would not be too far-fetched to say that on Kierkegaard's view the task requires individuals — but no, to stress both the particularity of the individual and the idea that the problem is not one to be solved collectively, let us rather say *the* individual — to bring under its own conscious control the *psychological* conditions of life — conditions which if abandoned to chance acquire an independent existence over against the individual. True, the substitution of 'psychological' for 'material' marks a radical shift in topic, but there is no doubt that the project of becoming a self which Kierkegaard takes, in some sense, to be necessary, and even — though initially this must seem less credible — sufficient, for the liberation of the individual is a thoroughly practical project, both in itself and in its implications, and that any view of human fulfilment which ignores the factors that count for the integration of personality and for the self's failure or success in coming to terms with itself, is open to the charge of abstraction.

In the previous chapter we saw that, in effect, Kierkegaard himself directs the charge at those who see human fulfilment and freedom in the idea of universal affiliation, in an agreement with mankind instead of with oneself. We interpreted this as a critique of the optimistic Hegelian view that association is an integral part of spirituality and that active membership of associations implies participation in a greater spiritual unity. But Kierkegaard would no doubt have felt justified in directing a similar charge at Marx. In spite of Marx's unexceptionable insistence on the need to understand and control the material conditions of life if genuine community is to emerge, there is something analogous to the background assumption of the ideal of pure levelling in the idea that genuine community *emerges* from individual need and egoism. That is to say, there is a strong trace here of the Hegelian belief that the achievement of community is somehow the realization of a general truth about mankind, and therefore about each human being *as such*, and not an achievement of the individual will in spite of whatever may be true of human beings in general. So before exposing Kierkegaard to the charge of abstraction levelled by Marxists at his 'fixation' upon the 'isolated' individual, we should first go rather more closely into the assumptions upon which Marxists base their charge.

2   Marx on Feuerbach

The passage in which Marx denies that genuine community emerges through mere thinking, and claims instead that it emerges through the need and egoism of individuals, continues as follows: 'It is not up to men whether community exists or not; but as long as man does not recognize himself as man and organize his world humanly, this community will appear in the form of estrangement.'[8] There is a hint here that genuine community exists potentially in all forms of social life, and that those forms in which it is not realized, i.e. where there is estrangement, are in effect distortions of a genuine community somehow lurking beneath the surface. The hint becomes an explicit thesis in another passage where Marx writes of human integrity — of being a 'whole' man — in terms of the 'appropriation' by man of his 'manifold essence' in an 'all-sided way', this essence consisting of specifically human capacities — 'the organs of his individuality (perceiving, sensing, feeling, wishing, acting, loving, etc.)' — which are 'immediately communal in form'.[9]

However, Marx seems himself to have become aware of an element of abstraction in this view and later to have made what he considered the necessary adjustments. A source of this reappraisal, and the classic text for the criticism of the 'abstract individual', is the sixth of Marx's 'Theses against [*gegen*] Feuerbach'. There Marx observes that Feuerbach's '[resolution of] the religious essence into the *human* essence' involves an incomplete analysis. First, it '[abstracts] from the historical process . . . [, establishes] religious feeling as something self-contained, and [presupposes] an abstract — *isolated* — human individual'. Second, it '[views] the essence of man merely as "species", as the inner, dumb generality which unites the many individuals *naturally*'. Now the latter could be an apt enough description of just what Marx himself had earlier assumed in respect of man's inherent, i.e. naturally given, capacity for genuine community. What Marx is saying here is that although Feuerbach had analysed religious essence into human essence, he had stopped short of an analysis of the latter; which is just what he, Marx, had earlier done in respect of man's 'manifold' and 'communal' essence. Had Feuerbach carried his critique further he would have found what Marx himself now saw, that 'the essence of man is no abstraction inhering in each single individual [but is in] its actuality . . . the ensemble of social relationships'.[10]

This, particularly in the context of an appraisal of the respective merits of Marxist social theory and one which 'fixates' upon the individual, calls for careful interpretation. The characterization of the essence of man as the ensemble of social relationships easily invites the riposte that here it is Marx who reduces the individual to a mere abstraction. For what does this say but that individuals are the vanishing foci of their relationships to the social worlds around them? Abstraction *par excellence*, surely; with the concrete individual reduced now to circumstances hardly less straitened than those of an extensionless point, identifiable only in terms of something which by definition it is not. Combined with the thesis, also sometimes attributed to Marx, that the social world — what corresponds, on this picture of relationships converging on a proximal point, to the distal terms in the relationships — is subject to dialectical laws which dictate its changes with all the rigour of the laws of matter in motion, the resulting view would make the concept of the individual doubly redundant. For according to this, even if there were individuals in some attenuated sense, they could only be helpless, 'abstract' observers of their own social fates. So that even if they were permitted 'private' sectors in which to exercise active roles, their transactions in these would be altogether unrelated to social events.

It seems safe to say, however, that whatever the attributions of his more obtuse followers and less sympathetic critics, Marx's own view bears no resemblance to this travesty of a social theory. And there is, indeed, no need to interpret the Sixth Thesis as reducing the individual to punctual abstraction or social impotence. If we understand 'human essence' as potential human capacity, and contrast this with the actual, practical abilities of concrete human beings, then we can read the thesis as the claim that human beings simply do not contain in themselves, irrespective of specific social time and place, the possibility of fulfilment. To talk of a capacity corresponding to human fulfilment as though it were a property of the individual as such is to introduce an abstraction, a 'dumb generality', into the analysis of the concrete individual; and, more importantly, to obscure thereby the fact that the capacity in question has first to be established by creating an appropriate social context. (Here we might see a parallel with Kierkegaard's view that the capacity is to be established by the individual's changing his 'given' nature.) Seen in this light the Sixth Thesis presents not so much a reduction of the notion of human essence to a mere constellation of social relationships, as an attempt to give a more faithful account of the possibilities pertaining to given individuals in particular social times and places. Far from eliminating the individual — whom, it is important to stress, Marx nowhere denies, whose egoism and needs we have already seen him appealing to, and indeed whose existence, according to Engels,

308

was Marx's 'first premise'[11] — the Sixth Thesis looks more like an attempt to say what that individual, that *concrete* individual, essentially is — that individual without whom there could be no social relationships and whose socially effective agency (which must in most cases call for collective rather than single-handed action), we must surely assume, is specifically required for the changing of the social context. Surely what Marx is saying here is simply that in order to identify human essence you must look not at the individual as such, but at the factors which prompt, modify, and limit the individual's aspirations and capabilities. Then you will see, as Feuerbach did not, and as Marx puts it in the Seventh Thesis, that ' "religious feeling" is itself a social product and that the abstract individual he [Feuerbach] analyses belongs to a particular form of society'.[12]

Ignoring for the moment the question of with what justification Marx might (as Marcuse does) regard Kierkegaard's 'religious' approach as open to the same charge of abstraction as Feuerbach's 'philosophical' one, let us proceed a little further with our examination of the accusation of the abstractness of views which 'fixate' upon the individual. If we are right in our interpretation of Marx, then acceptance of the category of the individual is not in itself enough to substantiate the charge of abstraction, for on this interpretation Marx himself accepted it. Presumably, the basis must lie in how this category is understood. What, then, could be an abstract understanding of the category of the individual?

If the answer we wanted was Marx's own, we would have to raise a host of exegetical questions which take us far beyond our present terms of reference. Instead we can adopt as our guideline a fairly widely accepted interpretation of Marx, which, even if it is wrong, represents a philosophically interesting point of view. According to this interpretation the mature Marx would regard any approach to the problem of liberation as abstract if it postulates a 'given' human nature, in the sense of a nature not subject to alteration in history. Again this is not as clear as one would wish. Understood in one way it might be a very radical but altogether implausible thesis based, as before, on the Sixth Thesis. According to this it would be claiming that the only determinants of human nature are social forces. But not only would it be implausible, it would also contradict the Marxist thesis that the social forces are themselves to be understood in terms of man's 'timeless' need to work and produce. Moreover, Marx and his disciples have interpreted the operations of these forces as tending towards a specific goal, genuine community. So there is both an essential pushing and an essential pulling in the Marxist scheme — one might call them the 'poles' of human nature — which are indeed 'given' in so far as the theory postulates them as necessary conditions of all human life. However, what proponents of the view may more plausibly and consistently be assumed to claim is that human nature is indeterminate in at least the two following respects: first, between the two poles (and whatever additional constants might consistently be included) human nature is indeterminate in the sense that the actual standards and forms of human satisfaction and excellence are not 'given' but are governed by, perhaps amongst other this-worldly factors, the forms taken by the processes of social labour; and second, the poles or constants themselves are also unfixed, in so far as the actual forms taken by work, production, and whatever else, and the actual nature or content of the goal of genuine community, also undergo change and for the same reasons.

This interpretation offers an initially plausible basis for dismissing as abstract a certain *way* of fixing upon the individual. On the assumption that human nature is to be specified in terms of actual human needs and aspirations, it would seem to be a patent abstraction to fixate exclusively upon the constant features of human nature and to ignore the variety; particularly when, as Marx himself says, the variety contains novelty and the novelty can provide an enrichment of the human species in the form of 'new powers and ideas, new modes of intercourse, new needs and new language'.[13]

3   Methodological abstraction

It might seem, on this interpretation, that far from being guilty of abstractness, Marx himself has arrived at a rational and enlightened basis for convicting others, including maybe Kierkegaard, of abstractness. Let us spell out that seemingly rational and enlightened basis in more detail. Let us say that, according to it, an abstract approach would be one which exemplified one or more of the three following characteristics:

(1)   It fails to concentrate on the essential. In this case the essential is not the characteristics and capacities of an individual independently of its specific social time and place, but the factors governing the kinds of performance open to, or the kinds of behaviour exhibited by, the individual *in* its social time and place. 'Essence', if you like, is not so much a matter of unchanging natural kind, to be contrasted with variable 'accident', as of 'essential' underlying forces or elements, factors accessible to the appropriate scientific vantage-point, amenable to formulation in general laws (for example, in Marxist theory, laws of the relationship of labour and

wages), and forming an underlying and not immediately discernible reality, to be contrasted, therefore, not now with 'accident' but with (social) 'appearance'. The former view of essence is abstract precisely because it ignores what *is* essential, namely the under-lying and determining forces. Indeed, it treats these essential factors as accidental and so generates a distorted view of human affairs. Take, for example, the notion of human freedom. If one wishes to explain this notion, the view forces one to focus on something 'constant', but when one searches for it nothing constant can be found. So freedom becomes a mere postulate, and human beings are then simply *said* (depending on one's vested metaphysical interests) either to be uniformly free in the sense of being sources of absolute initiatives, or to be uniformly unfree. The view is a distortion precisely because it 'abstracts' from the variety of the scope and even nature of the actual initiatives human beings take, and from the fact that this variety is determined by the social context in which the individual is placed. It obscures the fact that what seem to be, and perhaps in some limited sense really are, the initiatives of isolated first causes are in fact expressions of a social process that bears the possibly freely but more or less ineffectually gesticulating individual along – the freedom, as it has been put, of a man to walk east on a boat going west.[14] In practical terms the distortion means that persons are actually deprived of an insight into the circumstances which limit the satisfaction of their real interests, and so also of the possibility of changing those cir-cumstances so that their full satisfaction becomes possible. An inability to bring these circumstances (what Marx calls the material conditions of life) under conscious control means that they are left to chance and are, in fact, conceived as the operation of processes into which it is neither possible nor indeed necessary to intervene. On this view the task of liberation or fulfilment cannot even begin.

(2)   In ignoring the essential, an abstract approach easily generates distorted accounts of human possibilities by assigning to the isolated agent all that is needed to realize such possibilities. That agent, the solitary individual, is then exaggeratedly invested with qualities which do not, in fact, belong to individuals as such, but at best only to individuals by virtue of their favourable social times and places. One assumes, for instance, and as Marx himself appears earlier to have done, that the notion of human essence applies to individuals in general. If this notion is assumed already to contain that of human community, the essence of man is then linked logically to a form of unity in which each individual as such can already know itself concretely as sharing membership of the

human species — a possibility sometimes thought to be both inherent in and dependent upon the specifically human capacity to be aware of oneself as a specimen of the species. Thus Feuerbach assumed that the species-faculties of sensing and feeling, in their different ways, bridge the gap between the individual's particular existence and the world outside, the world of nature on the one hand, and the existence of other individuals as *particulars* (i.e. not merely in general terms as co-members of the same species) on the other: giving access in sensation to the objective world of nature, and in feeling — especially love — to other particular individuals.[15] It is then assumed that every being classifiable as human possesses a human essence in exactly the same sense. Consequently, one believes, as did Feuerbach, that every individual, irrespective of social time and place, is in possession of all that is needed to constitute humanity. The social world is conceived accordingly as a mere medium for the expression of an *inherent* communal capacity; not as providing only the materials for the actual *constitution* of that capacity. Social forms are then regarded as either preventing or permitting the free unfolding of a constant, if only latent, human essence, but not as creating either that essence itself or any of its essential modes. On this abstract view the task of liberation is not a productive or creative but a deprophylactic one; it is confined to the elimination of obstacles to free social expression.

(3) Ascription to the isolated individual of an inherent capacity to appropriate its humanity encourages a correlative tendency to misconceive that goal in terms which make its attainment by that individual a practically possible project. A tendency, in other words, to conceive the genuinely essential factors as irrelevant, except in so far as they impede the individual's assumed capacity to attain the goal on its own. In some superabstract conceptions even this latter qualification may be rendered idle. For Hegel the goal is partly specified as the awareness that what seem impediments in this respect are not really so, though for Hegel there is also the additional safeguard against the intervention of social factors that the task is assigned, not to finite individuals placed in time but to spirit, which exists through time. Since spirit is by definition not confined to any particular social time and place, it escapes location in any situation in which social factors may actually and not merely illusorily intrude upon an innate capacity to attain fulfilment. But the same general tendency is found in any conception of human fulfilment which conceives that fulfilment in an intellectual rather than a practical goal, which locates freedom in thought rather than action and thus brings it within

potential reach of the individual irrespective of social time and place. Such conceptions are typified in the form (*Gestalt*) of consciousness Hegel calls 'Stoicism', which we saw earlier was the attempt of spirit to achieve freedom by conceiving itself as 'the simple essentiality of thought'.[16] (Much post-Hegelian criticism of Hegel, it seems, can be construed as rightly or wrongly assigning the whole of Hegel's philosophy to what he himself understood to be the limited viewpoint of the Stoic.) The fact that these conceptions abstract from the essential factors may sometimes be explained by their being expressions of conditions of dependency and unfreedom. Hegel himself understood Stoicism in this way, though in his case not in terms which make conscious control and manipulation of the factors in question a requirement for further development. An abstraction similar in principle is to be found in Feuerbach's (and, it is suggested, the earlier Marx's) view that the problem of the individual's appropriation of its humanity is that of providing inherently human capacities — including an inherently communal capacity — with their natural and social outlets. For even though it is allowed that the manipulation of material conditions may be needed for providing these outlets, the task is still understood restrictively in terms of what is given as essential to all human beings irrespective of social time and place. However, the paradigm of this aspect of abstraction, it is claimed, is the even more restrictive *religious* conception of human fulfilment. Here the task is seen (at least in the first instance) as that of establishing a relationship, whether of fear, love, obedience, or some other form of dependency, with a transcendent being; admittedly a practical rather than a purely intellectual goal, but typically one which calls for the actual stifling of inherently human, including communal, capacities rather than their encouragement or cultivation. In this case, there are perhaps special grounds for suspecting a link, perhaps various kinds of link (for example, politico-ideological and patho-psychological), with social oppression and/or neurosis.

The three characteristics sketched here can be regarded as criteria of abstraction in the investigation of human nature. It is appropriate, therefore, to call them criteria of methodological abstraction. They can be briefly summarized as follows: an investigation into human nature is abstract, first, if it fails to take account of the factors or processes determining what individual human beings are capable of; second, if it attributes to all individuals an inherent capacity of fulfilment, in relation to which the state of the individual's environment is an extraneous factor, at best a medium for the expression of an inherent sociality; and third, if it

313

makes of human fulfilment something other, typically less, than the realization and expression of natural, manifold human capacity.

4 Defending Kierkegaard

At first sight it looks as if Kierkegaard must be convicted of abstractionism on all three counts. First, we have Climacus's statement that 'every human being must be assumed to be in essential possession of what essentially belongs to being a human being',[17] a statement that can be interpreted as claiming that every person possesses the real possibility of being a genuine, that is, in some sense a fulfilled human being. Second, there is the claim that the ethical goal of becoming a whole man can be attained by anyone anywhere (it is an 'ethical presupposition that every man is born in such a condition that he can become one').[18] Third, this goal is to be attained by subordinating all temporal goals, that is all personal and social objectives, to an absolute goal.[19] Furthermore, the concept of spirit in terms of which Climacus understands human fulfilment is for him, unlike Hegel, an irreducibly religious, and not even a philosophical, concept. Just for that reason Kierkegaard's may seem an even more primitive, outmoded, and 'mystifying' approach than Hegel's. We noted earlier that both for Hegel and for Marx the religious form of consciousness represents an immaturity of the spirit, a 'dialectical narrow-mindedness [*Borneret hed*]' as Climacus puts it on behalf of Hegelians.[20] True, Hegelians and Marxists have conflicting interpretations of this immaturity: the latter see maturation as marked by the translation of religion into ideology — that is, into an awareness of religion as an instrument of social oppression, and, from the point of view of the oppressed, as the source of a substitute fulfilment outside social life; while Hegel himself saw it more immodestly as marked by the translation of religion into Hegelian philosophy — that mode of spiritual self-consciousness wherein in principle nothing at all surpasses human understanding. True, also, that while Marxists, following Feuerbach, flatly deny the existence of an Infinite Being that can in any literal sense be conceived as the source either of things in time or of their value (we saw earlier that Feuerbach regarded the finite and particular as ontologically primary and infinity as in some sense a structural property of the finite,[21] and for Marx eternity is a quality of temporal conditions, their unchangeableness — e.g. the process of social labour as an 'eternal' condition of human life),[22] Hegel's own view of the philosophical truth of which religion is the inadequate expression, namely that Infinite Being is not distinct from the finite but is necessarily manifested in it,[23] precisely presupposes the primacy and irreducibility of Infinite Being. But despite these disagreements, the crucial point remains the same: the idea of a transcendent Infinite Being, necessarily not manifested in the finite, and furthermore conceived as the extra-human source of human value and perfection, is diversionary. It deflects attention away from social life as the necessary locus of human fulfilment, and thus also from an adequate conception of the nature and also the conditions of that fulfilment.[24]

The issue, however, is not so clear-cut. There are a number of points that can be raised on Kierkegaard's behalf. Let us begin by recalling that Marx's objection to Feuerbach's view was that it conceived the social world as a mere medium for the expression of an innate communal capacity. What is wrong with this, according to Marx, is that it fails to see that this capacity has to be generated in man through a socio-historical process. But Marx still seems to believe that exercise of this generated capacity will be a direct (in some sense a 'natural') consequence of the working out of that process, that is, that genuine communality will be an effect having completion of the process as its sufficient cause. He seems not to consider the possibility that the cultivation of the individual's disposition or intention to act communally also plays a necessary part. Either he assumes that the will to act communally is part of basic human equipment (though recall Marx's remark about the role of the individual's needs and *egoism*), or he believes it is generated by the process. One who rejects these assumptions will find Marx's account correspondingly abstract; perhaps even accuse Marx of simply replacing the dumb generality which unites the many individuals naturally with another which unites them socially — as if natural mankind magically transforms itself into a social whole once the conditions of social oppression are removed. The same could not be said of Kierkegaard: not because he rejects the ideal of genuine community, but because for him the unity which the notion of genuine community implies must first be a characteristic of the will. If wills are not individually unified, individuals cannot be unified collectively; social harmony and 'to will one thing' go together.[25] True, Kierkegaard seems to hold that no other intention than that of unity of will is needed; and further that any other intention, e.g. class-struggle, will be self-defeating: 'all group solidarity is partisanship against universal humanity',[26] claims which may or may not be valid or immune to charges of abstraction, but there can be little doubt that Kierkegaard's reference to the function of the will represents a socio-psychological advance upon both Feuerbach and Marx. Feuerbach believed that mankind can be united by the proper exercise of natural love guided by reason. But if this were to be true it would have to be by dubious virtue of some socio-psychological parallel to the Invisible Hand theory in economics, the theory that in intending one's own gain one is, as the author of the theory put it, 'led by an invisible hand to promote an end which was no part of one's intention'.[27] The socio-psychological version assumes that a community of free rational agents can be constituted by the unassisted exercise of a natural capacity which Kierkegaard plausibly claims is inherently partial and divisive. Kierkegaard holds that for genuine community to become possible there must be a transformation of the individual's given nature, a radical reorientation of its interests towards an absolute goal. A more pessimistic view than Feuerbach's perhaps, but not the less plausible on that account. Likewise in respect of Marx. Even if the socialization of human institutions is necessary for the generating of the conditions for the real possibility of a genuinely communal life, there is no guarantee that, once the institutions are socialized ('humanized', as it is often put), individuals will be willing or able to avail themselves of that possibility. It may even be doubted whether the conditions for the real possibility of genuine community can ever actually be achieved, let alone exploited, without individuals *first* becoming willing and *thus* able, in principle where it is not yet feasible in practice, to avail themselves of that possibility. If so, Kierkegaard's stress on the will and individual spiritual development ('self-activity') could have importance even for a conception of human fulfilment which, like Marx's, makes that fulfilment the goal of a *social* process.

But Kierkegaard's apologist must do better than this. For Kierkegaard is still open to the objection that, whatever preconditions a theory of human fulfilment specifies for the achievement of human fulfilment in society, a theory like his which makes human freedom a pre-condition (rather than consequence) of the establishment of a just social order is necessarily abstract. This, indeed, is Marcuse's objection when he says that Kierkegaard fails to see that 'individual freedom *presupposes* a free society, and that the true liberation of the individual therefore *requires* the liberation of society'.[28] The accusation is not that Kierkegaard fails to see that the freeing of society is a sufficient condition of human liberation — the view just discussed which so easily invites the counter-accusation that human fulfilment is not simply an unproblematic aspect of social liberation, or one of its logical products — but that he fails to see that it is at least a necessary condition. Marcuse accuses Kierkegaard of the unwarrantable abstraction of conceiving human liberation independently of the elimination of the social sources of human deprivation and disrespect — of assuming, in the face of glaring counter-examples, that an individual's social time and place play no part in determining whether that individual is or can be free or fulfilled. He is saying that Kierkegaard supposes that personal freedom and fulfilment have nothing to do with the forms of political, social, and economic association to which members of a given society are bound. The abstractness of the view is that of our third criterion: because it wants to make individual freedom a necessary pre-condition of social freedom, it has to postulate a form of human freedom, and hence a process of human liberation, that is immune to the kinds of social influence which so clearly govern the nature, range, and distribution of human possibilities. The conception of a 'free' individual corresponding to such a view is not that of a concrete person whose actual possibilities are circumscribed by his or her social context, but the supposed instantiation of an 'essence' or 'species-nature' which transcends all social change.

If it were indeed an implication of Kierkegaard's view that changes in social conditions play no part in the process of human liberation, then it would have to be admitted that the view is scandalously deficient. I say 'an implication' because I know of no passage in his writings where he actually makes such a claim. Before conceding the alleged deficiency of the view, therefore, let us first have recourse to whatever saving possibilities are to be found in the terms of the view itself.

One possibility comes to light with a closer inspection of the notion of liberation. Following Marcuse, who in turn follows Hegel, this notion has so far been linked uncritically with that of fulfilment. We said at the outset that in the tradition to which post-Hegelian philosophy belongs, the terms are interchangeable. And we said that from a post-Hegelian point of view the problem of liberation can be described as that of man's appropriating his essence, what is essential to his humanity. As far as Hegel himself goes, that is certainly correct. According to Hegel's 'philosophical' and 'abstract' (because not 'practical') notion of the goal of history, the appropriation by spirit of *its* freedom is at the same time the concrete realization of its perfection, for the latter is nothing other than spirit's working out of its insight into the ultimate, consoling truth that the idea of reason is consciousness's 'certainty [that it] is all reality'.[29] However, once the notion of spirit is demythologized and fulfilment is conceived as a goal for individuals to strive for in their particular social locations, it becomes less clear that liberation and fulfilment can be spoken of in the same breath. Unlike Hegel's spirit, individuals do not have the field to themselves. In the practical context there are therefore potentially at least three separate problems. There is the familiar problem of a plurality of subjects establishing a situation in which they can all attain fulfilment, or perfection, without frustrating each others' (or their own) possibilities of doing so. This could be called the central problem of social liberation. On each side of it, however, we have another problem: on the far side there is the problem of fulfilment itself, a matter for each individual and still a task when the central problem has been solved; and on the near side there is, for those who admit it, the prior problem of establishing a frame of mind capable of solving the central problem. Let us call the state in which this third problem is solved 'primary fulfilment'.

In the light of these distinctions it would be natural to say that Kierkegaard's works are concerned mainly, or even exclusively, with primary fulfilment. The three stages, or spheres of existence, represent phases in a development the outcome of which is the constitution of the ethical subject, not the establishment of perfection. True, Climacus says that the subjective thinker's task is to become an instrument which 'clearly and decisively expresses in existence what is human',[30] which might be interpreted in Aristotelian fashion as saying that human perfection *consists* in the fulfilment of a function, i.e. in the instrument's use, and not in some further end, or what the instrument might be used to obtain. But that seems to be a misinterpretation. By 'expressing the human' Kierkegaard means not so much 'achieving what is perfectly human' as 'achieving what is specifically human', namely a properly *individual* existence. The task of 'bringing the existential categories into relationship with one another',[31] and that of 'understanding [oneself] in [one's] existence',[32] represent minimum requirements of living in the way appropriate to a human rather than another kind of being. They are not specifications of human perfections, but of (to borrow from a more recent existentialist terminology) human 'authenticity'. A specification of the 'human' here would involve an account of the individual's mode of consciousness, of its having to live in the category of existence, not an account either of perfection or of the highest good, an 'eternal happiness', which only become *possibilities* for one who expresses the human in existence.

How, then, will an interpretation of Kierkegaard's works as concerned with primary fulfilment contribute to a defence of his conception of human fulfilment against the charge that it ignores the 'central' problem of social liberation? We split the Hegelian project of liberation as fulfilment into three distinct components or tasks: primary fulfilment which equips the individual with the ethical, and, perhaps, also socio-political, wherewithal for achieving, second, social liberation which, third, secures a platform of constraints within which the individual can pursue, unimpeded, its own project of fulfilment. Now in order to be able to say that Kierkegaard has not *ignored* the second task we would have to assume that its solution was supposed to be provided as a consequence of fulfilling the first task. But this would surely be a very weak defence. The view that repressive and demeaning social institutions will disappear merely with the exercise of Christian love is, on the face of it, as unrealistic and 'abstract' as the Marxist assumption that the disappearance of these institutions is all that human fulfilment requires. It seems, then, that Kierkegaard's apologist must accept that the problem of social liberation is ignored, and argue instead that there is room for a treatment of it nevertheless. Thus it could be suggested that the elimination of social sources of deprivation and disrespect be assigned to a secondary goal to which Kierkegaardian primary fulfilment stands as a propaedeutic. Kierkegaard's apologist might claim that really there is no compelling reason why Kierkegaard should categorically deny the necessity of social liberation. In spite of his disdain of politics and especially of socialist policies, there is no reason to assume that, where social constraint leads to obvious injustice, Kierkegaard would not regard the removal of the constraint, by group action if need be, as one necessary condition of the full fruition of the humanity of the constrained. It might even be maintained that the absence of any political programme (socialist or otherwise) in Kierkegaard's work is more a matter of focus than of principle. Although there is no doubt that Kierkegaard's 'fixation' on the individual — his insistence that the individual is 'the category through which, in a religious respect, this age, history, the human race must pass'[33] — is indeed a matter of principle and not of focus, and any attempt to deduce or even make room for a *politics* of liberation as part of Kierkegaard's theory of the liberation of the individual can only distort that theory, we nevertheless recall that he does not deny that a science of association can have its 'validity' in respect of material interests. There is a similar concession regarding the principle of majority decision. In a footnote directed at his misinterpreters he writes:

Perhaps I should nonetheless remark once and for all, what is self-evident and as I have never denied, that in respect of all temporal, earthly, worldly goals [a] majority can have its validity, even decisively, as the authority [*Instantsen*]. But of such things I do not speak, as little as I am concerned with

319

them. I speak of the ethical, the ethico-religious, about 'truth',
and about the fact that, from an ethico-religious point of
view, the crowd is untruth when it is assumed to be the
authority on what 'truth' is.[34]

Perhaps if Kierkegaard had engaged himself in economic affairs, or
had lived to read Marx's analyses of capitalist society, he would
have seen the point of certain specific changes in social and economic forms of association.[35] Certain aspects of Marx's analysis and
the conclusion Marx drew from them, however, would certainly
have struck him as misguided, some of them grotesquely so. He
would not have been impressed, for example, by Marx's belief that
it is indeed the forms of association to which people are bound,
and not the people themselves, that are corrupt.[36] And he would
have considered it naïve and obscurantist to suppose that people
have a 'natural' communal capacity,[37] that all that is required to
elicit communality is the replacement of a corrupting social organization by one that gives a spontaneous sociality free rein.

But Kierkegaard's apologist has still another suggestion to make.
In splitting the Hegelian project of liberation as fulfilment into a
primary fulfilment, social liberation, and secondary fulfilment,
there is something rather unsatisfactory about using the word
'fulfilment' for the first task when fulfilment 'proper', so to speak,
must obviously be identified with the objective of the third and
culminating task. The line the apologist may now take is to argue
that the word 'fulfilment' be applied not *also* to the primary
project, but *only* to it. To do this he must offer reasons for rejecting the conception of fulfilment implicit in the idea of the third
task.

That conception is eudemonistic; that is to say, it conceives of
man's ultimate end as a kind of comprehensive contentment
('happiness') in the performance of specifically human activities.
Eudemonists need not consider the range or type of these activities
constant. The claim that they are not constant we saw was part
of the basis of Marx's later rejection of the notion of a fixed human
nature. It is no doubt reasonable to suppose that in the course of
mankind's psychic, social, and technical development the sources
of specifically human satisfaction will increase in sophistication
and diversity; and also that there will be an increase in the chances
of each individual's securing the corresponding contentment. The
idea that fulfilment is the enjoyment of the exercise of both natural
and acquired capacities is an Aristotelian conception of human
perfection, a conception admirably summed up by a present-day
proponent as

an optimum road of human development in terms of felicity or happiness, a way of life that produces men capable of enjoying life to the fullest . . . a life of humane love and creative work, a life that can help us achieve a sense of psychic well-being, a life that can take us into a world of broad and vivid harmonious fulfilling experiences.[38]

Marx's own ideal of fulfilment is clearly eudemonist. Assuming labour or work to be *the* distinctively human capacity by which man masters his environment and gives it value, he envisages the possibility of labour becoming a 'free manifestation of life and an enjoyment of life', the latter then being identified as a central element in psychic well-being, arising only when our products become 'so many mirrors reflecting our nature'. Finally, there is an ensuing general satisfaction, the sense of being confirmed in one's 'individuality [and] in the thought and love of [one's] fellowmen'.[39]

But what if there is a primary human need which cannot be satisfied in the enjoyment of human activity? Kierkegaard says that 'views of life which teach that one must enjoy life' ignore the breach with immediacy and assume that human ideals can be confined to that level.[40] Characteristic of human consciousness is, with its break with innocence, the individual awareness of human finitude as an imperfection which, so literally to speak, *nothing* on earth can alter. Certainly, no conceivable social development will alter it, to whatever enlargement or enrichment of the sources of human satisfaction that development gives rise. No doubt certain forms of satisfaction can lead to a loss of the sense that finitude is an imperfection, and the eudemonist might deliberately cultivate these as ways of avoiding the dissatisfaction he feels at this finiteness. (Though it is hard to see how he could do that except by either ignoring or acquiescing in what he knows to be a fact, neither of which could be justified by the eudemonic principle itself: the first calls for self-deception and the second involves an implicit rejection of the principle. Acquiescing in the cessation of eudemonic contentment can hardly be itself a part of a conception of fulfilment which identifies fulfilment with enjoyment of that contentment.) The would-be consistent eudemonist might even advocate another state of contentment, namely that of being *satiated* in the contentment arising from the exercise of specifically human capacities, but even this form of contentment would have to come to an end. Whatever problems of consistency face the advocate of eudemonism, the fact of finitude and with it the cessation of contentment remain. And quite clearly the states of health, happiness, or harmonious fulfilment prized by eudemonists and the means to the attainment of those states, for instance the enlargement of social, political, and economic opportunities, are quite incapable of altering it.

Of course, Kierkegaard's apologist would have to admit that, even if eudemonism were unable to satisfy all primary human needs, it would be an equally inadequate conception of human fulfilment that placed no value on the sources of satisfaction that do fall within its province. We should recall from *Works of Love*, however, that Kierkegaard does not deny the value of life (or nature), nor *a fortiori* that of human life (or human nature), and that the ethics of selfless love which he advocates is, in fact, presented as an ethics of liberation and the thriving of diversity. It is not that Kierkegaard denies the value of human activities, but that he believes that the fact that they do have value is not to be accounted for by the contentment and satisfaction people derive from them. To say that the value of health and of the cultivation and exercise of natural talent is not to be measured by the amount of enjoyment people can derive from them is not necessarily to say that they should *not* derive enjoyment from them, nor to deny that health or happiness, or psychic well-being in general, are good things. It could be to say that, prior to the enjoyment of specifically human activities, a more basic fulfilment is needed, without which this enjoyment cannot provide the fulfilment — the comprehensive kind of self-confirming contentment — eudemonists claim for it. Furthermore — and this touches a fundamental nerve in Kierkegaard's thought — it might be argued that the amount of value claimed for such enjoyment, or of disvalue claimed for its absence, will be less the more the need for the basic fulfilment is acknowledged. When the finite as such is set against its opposite 'sub specie ironiae' the enjoyment of life acquires the same limitation as life, or existence, itself.[41]

However, suppose it is objected that even if one grants that enjoyment in human activity leaves an important gap unfilled, it is surely the case that for most people the first problem is not to fill that gap but to secure for themselves the material conditions of biological existence and the political conditions of personal self-respect. Surely an interest in an *eternal* happiness can only become central when the more basic problems of social liberation and the fair distribution of scarce material necessities have already been solved? There are finite satisfactions, the satisfaction of basic needs, the reduction of poverty and disease, the securing of the natural expectation of life itself, which must take priority over the luxury of the establishment of a satisfying God-relationship.

To this it may be replied that it is one thing to claim that the individual's spiritual needs are secondary in relation to the satisfaction of basic material (and psychological) needs, but another to claim that a sense of spiritual need is secondary in relation to the establishing of the conditions in which the individual can expect basic needs to be provided for. If the cultivation of individual autonomy — for Kierkegaard a spiritual goal — is a necessary propaedeutic to the goal of eliminating social sources of deprivation and disrespect, the latter claim would be false. As we saw, it appears to be Kierkegaard's view that autonomy of the individual will is necessary for successfully co-operative efforts to secure basic necessities. If so, the provision of one person's basic needs can be said to depend on the *spiritual* development of at least some other persons.

If the effect of a sense of spiritual needs is to lessen the importance attached to eudemonistic forms of fulfilment, and if a sense of such needs is inherently bound up with the cultivation of sociality, the socio-ethical perspective which accords with our three-phase extension of the Hegelian model of human fulfilment becomes foreshortened and we seem to be left again with only one phase. On the one hand, social liberation comes into view as a goal to which it becomes intelligible to ascribe intrinsic value. At least it no longer has importance merely for the individual achievement of contentment in the exercise of specifically human activity. And on the other hand, the weight of the notion of human fulfilment can be seen now to fall, as many will agree it should, on the wide and complex range of problems connected with the cultivation of that effective sense of social values which Kierkegaard clearly intends to be part of the process (or 'self-activity') of becoming an individual.

There are other considerations, too, to be added to the defence. One is that those who advocate eudemonism as a view of life either presuppose an absence of human suffering — and so project the possibility of human fulfilment into a utopian future — or else ask us to ignore such suffering — in which case the view is not ethical. Indeed, it could be claimed that those who are capable of eudemonistic satisfaction betray a lack of insight into the kinds and causes of human (or other) suffering. Eudemonists rashly assume that suffering is a contingent, that is to say uncharacteristic, feature of truly human life, and are thus led to turn their backs on a primary source of moral competence, knowledge of human (and other) suffering.[42]

There is another consideration. Putting the burden of human fulfilment on some form of perfection that presupposes social liberation forces one to project the notion of 'humanity' itself into the future, thus in principle excluding its application to any (except perhaps exceptional) real condition in the present. Humanity then becomes a goal for not yet completely human beings ('defective examples of humanity')[43] to strive for, rather than a mode of fulfilment to which already genuinely human beings can contribute. If to be human has an intrinsic value, that value will not properly belong to members of generations which have so far failed to achieve fulfilment. Moreover, because persons, to the extent that they fall short of fulfilment, can be regarded as not yet fully human, the idea is already born of the duty of unfulfilled generations to contribute to the fulfilment of succeeding generations, with its sinister implication of the right of future successors to claim, through their 'proper' representatives, sacrifices on the part of present predecessors. These are implications of any strict identification of the idea of human nature with that of an historically projected human fulfilment. They are implications, for instance, of Feuerbach's claim that the idea of human species is that of the exercise of man's 'highest powers',[44] but equally of the Marxist view that the process of human liberation (or, for Marx, fulfilment) requires nothing more than the establishment of political justice through a radical reorganization of the economic basis of society. Not only does Kierkegaard's alternative conception of human fulfilment give appropriate recognition to the task of *becoming* social, something to which eudemonists assign merely instrumental value, it recognizes in each individual, in whatever social time or place, perhaps even especially in those of deprivation, the capacity to 'express the human in existence'.

5   Religion as a constant

At the beginning of this chapter we distinguished a weaker and a stronger form of the charge of abstraction. The weaker form charged Kierkegaard with not taking into account certain important aspects of human development the failure of which to develop can be partly, perhaps wholly, traced to the presence of an oppressive social order. If our discussion has not altogether absolved Kierkegaard of this weaker charge, maybe it has gone some way towards correcting some of the misconceptions and non-sequiturs to be found in conventional criticism of Kierkegaard's apoliticality.[45]

There remains the stronger version. This was the charge that Kierkegaard claims for ethics and religion an area immune to explanation in terms of the process of social labour. We took this to rest on the assumption that it is the fact of development that is constant about human nature and not any fixed constellation of inherent capacities and interests. Apart from the need to work and the goal of community there are no constants, and even these change in content according to social time and place.

We referred earlier to Marx's 'Theses against Feuerbach', in which Marx associates an abstract conception of the individual with religion. According to Marx, what Feuerbach failed to see was that ' "religious feeling" is . . . a social product and that the individual he analyses belongs to a particular form of society'. Instead, because he presupposed 'an abstract – isolated – human individual', he saw religious feeling as something 'self-contained'. This criticism follows a now familiar Marxist line of argument, though according to Lukács it goes back to Hegel's criticism of Kant. It points, says Lukács, to the tendency 'to freeze the various moments of modern bourgeois fragmentation, to turn them into absolutes and thus to perpetuate the contradictions in a primitive, rudimentary state in which they can no longer be superseded or transcended'.[46] Feuerbach 'made' religion into an absolute. To be clear abour the manner in which he did so, let us briefly outline Feuerbach's position.

Man, says Feuerbach, is distinguished from other animals by his special form of consciousness. Man's peculiarity is his ability to form an idea of himself. But, on Feuerbach's naturalistic and anthropologizing view, this idea can only be symbolic. Religious concepts are, accordingly, imaginative projections of human feeling, willing, and thinking – these, together with sensing, comprising the modes of human consciousness. In general, religion symbolizes the fulfilment of specifically human needs and wishes. To accept the symbols at their face value is to assume that fulfilment is a divine and not a human notion. It is to deny that fulfilment is a possibility for man; it is to alienate man from the source of human value and project it, as in Hegel's unhappy consciousness, into a Transcendent Being. Instead of expressions of human fulfilment, the symbols thus become expressions of human imperfection, of sin and of the need for renunciation, repentance, and – though it remains only a possibility since it depends on Providence – salvation. Feuerbach calls this 'alienation of the self'. Because he conceives the self abstractly merely as a consciousness, he confines the alienation to consciousness. Overcoming the alienation is therefore a mental operation. The self has simply to re-conceive the symbols as expressions of the fulfilment of the *natural* human species, of possible *human* perfection. When that is done it no longer literally projects its value onto another reality, but interprets the projection as the imaginative transformation of its own value. The object of religion then lies revealed as the *essence of man*, and religion as 'the relation of man to himself'.[47]

By anthropologizing Christian religion Feuerbach meant to restore to man the nature that was really his, to make men, conceived in religion as 'half-animal, half-angel', once more into 'whole men'. But his programme presupposes the absoluteness of the anthropologized form of consciousness: for Feuerbach religion is a fundamental constant in the specifically human life, it is an essentially human mode of self-understanding. This, objects Marx, is an abstraction. Feuerbach is not really giving man his nature back to him, for the nature projected into the notion of a Transcendent Being is not man's true, or at least not man's inescapable, nature. It is not yet the nature of the whole man envisaged by Marx, not the man who appropriates his manifold essence. Feuerbach is mistaken when he fastens on the religious form of consciousness, with its special notion of value and fulfilment, as if it were essential to man as such.

Could Marx have said the same about Kierkegaard? There are significant differences between Kierkegaard's and Feuerbach's views. First, Kierkegaard's ethico-religious concepts and principles are not part of, nor do they appear to commit him to, the idea that man has a 'species-nature'; and it is especially in connection with the assumption of a context-independent species-nature — that is, with the idea of a human essence 'inhering in each single individual' — that Marx objects to the assignation to man of a religious destiny and a natural religious 'feeling'. In fact, one could claim that Kierkegaard's conception of the individual, despite its religious framework, is radically open-ended in its specification of human nature. The idea that the individual should ever come to know itself by virtue of its possession of a set of shared characteristics — which is what the notion of a species-nature implies — is totally alien to Kierkegaard's category of the individual. From within that category the problem of appropriating one's essential humanity is not one of coming to satisfy a certain ready-made description, but of adopting an ethical, or authentically human, attitude in the choice between alternative descriptions.

Second, 'humanity' is not, for Kierkegaard, as it is for both Feuerbach and Marx, a concrete realization of the possibilities of the species, but 'just that each is a single individual'.[48] Although Kierkegaard criticizes Hegel's world-historical conception of spiritual growth for destroying 'the essential unity of what it is to be a human ebing',[49] he does not mean by this unity any fixed constellation of native or acquired capacities. 'Giftedness, learning, and aptitude', he says, 'are after all a "what" ' while the unity of being human consists in the fact, as he sees it, that all humans are capable of acquiring that particular ' "how" in relation to what one is, be it much or little', which is that of the 'absoluteness of relationship to spirit'.[50] Again, although Kierkegaard does in one sense accept the idea of a constant human nature — he insists (as indeed it would be hard even for the most 'dialectical' of thinkers to deny) that there are 'essential characteristics' common to all men — these, thinking (*Forstand*), feeling, and willing (the same traditional triad invoked by Feuerbach to delimit the modes of human consciousness), are faculties or capacities, not specifications of human ideals of development or performance. Kierkegaard calls attention to them merely to oppose what he understands to be Hegel's claim that human nature undergoes qualitative changes in the course of history. The impression that there are such changes is due, says Kierkegaard, to focusing on the species and its history instead of on the category of the individual, a category which underlies these changes. Kierkegaard insists that essential change occurs only *within* the category of the individual, not to it, and changes within the category are not attributable thereby to the species, 'as if', in Climacus's words, 'spiritual development were something that one generation [can] bequeath to another', and as though 'spirit were a character belonging to the race and not to the individual'. The spiritually developed individual

> takes his development with him when he dies. If a succeeding individual is to reach the same development, he will have to do so through his own activity. So he can't be allowed to hop over anything. But now it is of course more convenient, easier, and more comfortable to make a big noise about being born in the nineteenth century.[51]

Third, we can note Climacus's reference to Feuerbach in the *Postscript* as the 'scoffer' who attacks Christianity but 'at the same time explains it so reasonably that it is a pleasure to read him'. In adding that anyone who needs a definitive exposition of Christianity 'might just as well go to him',[52] Climacus implies the absurdity of supposing Christianity to be something that can be expounded at all. According to him, it is not a doctrine but an 'existence communication'.[53] Accordingly, Kierkegaard does not regard religion as a constant in the sense that its *content* undergoes no essential change. As we saw earlier, he conceives different forms of consciousness as providing different expressions of religious interest. His own version of Christianity obviously differs widely from that of his contemporaries. In so far as it was the latter that Feuerbach took as his model, and inasmuch as it was Feuerbach's account of 'the religious essence' that Marx took as his target, it would be rash to draw conclusions about the precise nature of Marx's potential critique of Kierkegaard's views on the matter.

Not many, however, will deny that over and above man's material needs, and even beyond the need, noted by Marx himself, to be confirmed in one's 'individuality' and in the 'thought and love of [one's] fellowmen', or perhaps as part of this latter, human beings *as such* have an additional and overriding need to come to terms with their merely finite existence. In the long run, then, perhaps Kierkegaard's most persuasive counter-claim to Marx's proposition that 'religious feeling' will vanish in humanized conditions of social labour would be that an interest in eternal happiness, in some form or other, is indeed a human constant; and that whatever sources of satisfaction, new forms of excellence, or possibilities of psychic well-being become available in the course of human and social development, none will provide either the eternal happiness itself or any satisfactory substitute for it.

Finally, it will be obvious from the above comments that there is a sense in which it is indeed correct to call Kierkegaard's *concept* of the individual 'abstract'. It is abstract in the sense that it does not specify the individual's own 'peculiarity' (see Chapter VII, above), specific possibilities, or actual tasks. Just as, according to Judge William, ethics tells us we should get married but not with whom,[54] so being told to become an individual is being told to cultivate inwardness in our relation to the infinite, but not what finite things we should cultivate it in connection with. The concept of 'individual', like that of 'neighbour', is a regulative principle; it defines an attitude, an outer limit, as it were, within which individual autonomy must operate. It is analogous in this way to Kant's principle that 'humanity and generally every human nature is an end in itself', which Kant calls 'the supreme limiting condition of every man's freedom of action'.[55] But it will be equally obvious that, like Kant's abstract principle, and as with his own abstract concept of 'neighbour', to call Kierkegaard's concept of the individual abstract is not to say that it is the concept of an abstract individual in the sense or senses adumbrated in this chapter.

X

Unconcluding Postscript

> If, to master one's personal life and adjust to the
> pursuit of worldly goods and gains, one makes that
> life one thing and philosophy another, philosophy
> becomes science and we get the professor of
> philosophy.[1]

The preceding chapters have tried to give a philosophically ampli-
fied presentation of Kierkegaard's thought. I mean by that a
version which emphasizes its over-all unity and logical structure,
as well as the conceptual content of the parts, to a degree and in
a way not found in Kierkegaard's own writings. The advantage of
this approach is that it allows one to form a better idea than one
gathers from the texts themselves of the precise nature and scope
of the subject-matter, as well as of its intellectual content. If
successful, the result will have been to bring Kierkegaard nearer
to the centre of the philosophical stage than a cursory reading of
his own philosophically unamplified version would seem to justify.

But there are problems with this result, both from the point of
view of Kierkegaard himself, whose well-documented scorn of
professional philosophy suggests an unwillingness to be placed
anywhere on the philosophical stage,[2] and from that of those who
currently occupy it, for whom, quite apart from the matter of
style, the religious element in Kierkegaard's thought will seem to
deprive it of any general philosophical relevance.

In conclusion of the book but not of what I think might usefully be said on these matters, I offer some very brief comments
towards a 'mediation' of the opposites in this apparent conflict of
interests.

First, we have already noted, in Chapter I, that Kierkegaard was by no means scornful of philosophy as a 'dialectical' activity, as long as it was divorced from its speculative, system-building pretensions. We saw, too, that he regarded himself as a latter-day Socrates encouraging the return to individual autonomy and a sense of the limits of understanding. And, further, that he recognized in himself a philosophical talent, or 'nature', to which, however, the religious direction of his writing prevented him from giving free rein. In addition to this, towards the end of his life Kierkegaard even expressed the belief that 'intellectually speaking' he would leave a 'by no means insignificant legacy'.[3] As long, that is, as his work did not fall into the wrong hands as he nevertheless feared and expected it would. The wrong hands would be those of the professional philosophers of the time, the Hegelians, for whom anything 'incommensurable' with systematic thought was not worth discussing, the 'incompetents' (*Halvbefarene*) who Climacus, in the last line of the *Postscript*, prays will not 'lay a dialectical hand' on his work but 'let it remain as it now stands',[4] or those 'castrati' (the 'professors') who have 'gelded' themselves, not to qualify for 'the kingdom of heaven', but to 'fit themselves for this world'.[5] In short, what Kierkegaard feared was that his intellectual heir would be that 'figure' so 'exceedingly distasteful' to him, who till then had 'inherited all that [was] best and [would] continue to do so', namely 'the Docent, the Professor'. To which 'sad' reflection Kierkegaard adds a characteristic note:

> And even should the 'Professor' chance to read this, it would not give him pause, would not cause his conscience to smite him; no, this too will be something to hold forth on. Nor, again, would this latter observation, should the Professor chance to read it, give him pause; no, this too would be something to hold forth on. For even longer than the . . . tapeworm [of unusual length, recently reported in a Copenhagen newspaper] . . . longer even than this is the Professor, and there is no human power that can purge a man of this 'Professor' once he is lodged in him.[6]

However, although we may perhaps admit, uneasily, that the image of the philosopher as that perpetuum immobile for whom nothing is importantly said unless it figures as the topic of what Kierkegaard calls an 'unessential reflective refraction',[7] is still very much alive, it does seem fair to say that nowadays philosophers are decreasingly disinclined to consider the kinds of question Kierkegaard was concerned with, even if they are just as insistent as he was that they are not the kinds that can be given traditional philosophical, i.e. quasi-scientific, answers. All in all, given the stress on the individual's power of reasoning in modern philosophy, at least in some quarters, and the range of topics discussed, though not necessarily in the same quarters, but not least the willingness of some modern philosophers to recognize the importance of the subjective view-point, and even its centrality, Kierkegaard would perhaps find less reason in our time than in his to distinguish sharply between his own activity and that of philosophers.

It is less than clear, however, that we can expect a corresponding concession from the other side. The agnostic majority of contem-porary philosophers, when acquainted with Kierkegaard's work, will perhaps at best see in Kierkegaard an important precursor of modern anti-metaphysics. They will see it as unfortunate that the framework within which Kierkegaard operates continues to coun-tenance such erstwhile metaphysical goals as are embodied in his concept of a 'second immediacy', even if these goals are made the individual's own. They may recognize in Kierkegaard's conversion of the Hegelian philosophy into an open-ended, future-looking, action-orientated world-view a revolutionary step in the direction of the modern philosophical consciousness, but they will see it as a merely half-consummated revolution that takes us to the threshold of modern consciousness without passing into it.

The brief comments which follow are made in tentative qualifi-cation of this assessment, both in respect of the religious framework which is axiomatic for Kierkegaard, and in respect, more generally, of the subjective viewpoint.

The first comment has two phases. The first phase is to point out that the goal of a 'second immediacy' envisaged by Kierkegaard is a special kind of goal, and that it might be appropriate to regard it as being, therefore, the goal of a special individual. Marxists and others do this when they try to account for it in terms of the indi-vidual's particular social and economic environment. But here I propose that we look at it more narrowly and more straight-forwardly as a matter of the individual's mode of consciousness. What I mean is well captured in a remark of Wittgenstein's that 'the Christian faith . . . is a man's refuge in [an] *ultimate* torment', and that '[t]he Christian religion is only for the man who needs infinite help, solely, that is, for the man who experiences [this] infinite torment'.[8] The reference to refuge is clearly apt in Kierke-gaard's case. We have noted his talk of the 'security' and 'certainty' afforded by 'choice of' the eternal. In one place, he even refers to eternity as a 'fortress' on 'the other side of the boundary' and in which 'the good man . . . is stronger than the whole world'.[9] It is worth also recalling Wittgenstein's own, much quoted, sentence from the 'Lecture on Ethics' in which he speaks of 'the experience of feeling *absolutely* safe . . . the state of mind in which one is inclined to say "I am safe, nothing can injure me *whatever happens*" '.[10] But what general significance, it will be asked, can we attach to this feeling or to the need that it satisfies? Suppose now, and this is the second phase of our comment, that we look at the obverse side of the claim that the Christian religion is only for the man who needs infinite help and read it as saying, not that it has nothing to say to others, but that if others are to understand what it does say they must acquire the kind of inner life in which the Christian concepts, at least the central ones of sin, faith, and redemption, apply. Then it would be plausible to argue as Hampshire does, that '[e]ntry into a certain "form of life" is a necessary background to using and attaching sense to [the] concepts . . . [which correspond] to the more refined distinctions within the vocabulary of sentiment and emotion'.[11] The form of life Hampshire refers to is the 'adult human form of life', with its habits of controlled expression in both word and deed. But if we regard Kierkegaard's religious world-view as a Wittgensteinian form of life,[12] then Hampshire's argument to the effect that the 'concept of feeling and sentiment' is derived from that of 'inhibited' behaviour, in such a way that 'the order in which a person learns the use of two classes of expression' is also that in which he 'acquires the faculties of mind to which the expressions refer',[13] can be extended, and adapted, to the feelings and sentiments (needs and hopes) of a person about whose form of expression Wittgenstein also says, 'No cry of torment can be greater than the cry of *one* man' ('Ein Notschrei kann nicht grösser sein, als der *eines* Menschen').[14] Now clearly Kierkegaard's concept of spirit, as that of a kind of distancing from the finite world as a whole, is a faculty of mind in the above sense. In order to account for it we must allow for both a widening and a transforming of the contexts in which it makes sense to talk, for instance, of privation (the root sense of the German 'Not' here translated 'torment'), and correspondingly of restitution and refuge. Thus you might say that a concept of privation confined to physical loss is narrower than one that includes also psychological forms of deprivation, and that one that embraces cosmic solitude and lack of security, what in the Hegelian tradition is called loss of essence, is broader than either of the others. In this sense a Kierkegaardian world could be said to be wider than a Hobbesian. And so, beyond the inhibition of natural response, and it is in terms of inhibition that Hampshire accounts for the origin and logical placement of the inner life — 'in conjunction with [the] power to dissociate . . . inclinations from their immediate natural expression'[15] — we must focus on the *expansion* of a person's consciousness which occurs in that same dissociation.

Of course, the solitary individual's cry of torment is not a *natural* expression, in Hampshire's and Wittgenstein's sense. It is a manifestation of a sensibility belonging to an expanded consciousness involved in a many-levelled relationship to its environment. It might, however, be appropriate to call it 'natural', in the sense of 'normal', or 'to be expected', for one whose possibilities of privation, and corresponding needs of refuge, were thus expanded; and their being expanded in that way might in turn be regarded as, in the same sense, 'natural' for a consciousness as astute at seeing through its own deceptions and false identities as Kierkegaard's.

Nothing, of course, follows for the likelihood, or even possibility, of the fulfilment of a need from either its presence or intensity. But a limited conclusion can be drawn with regard to the assessment of the status of a need. In fact, the argument here could be dressed in a way that lends support to Kierkegaard's mistrust of philosophers. Thus, if only those whose inner lives have the necessary depth and range are qualified to identify the needs of someone who seeks or prizes refuge or security in the expanded senses of these terms, and if philosophers cannot be relied upon *ex officio* to be equipped with that amount of inner life, then someone who has those needs cannot be given specifically philosophical reasons for rejecting the conceptual framework in which they are identified.

This provides a cue for our second, and final, comment. Contemporary so-called analytical philosophy, the platform of the present series, can be roughly but usefully carved into a recent anti-subjectivist past and a moderately pro-subjectivist present. In its anti-subjectivist past analytical philosophy (as against phenomenology, which is, of course, also in a sense analytical) tended either flatly to ignore or to call in question the very existence of what had been traditionally and ordinarily referred to as 'consciousness', 'experience', and the like. Talk of such things was sometimes said, under the influence of the later Wittgenstein, to be due to conceptual illusion, fostered by misleading philosophical models, especially that of Descartes's dualism. The task of philosophy itself was seen variously as articulating the language of science or, later but also concurrently, as analysing the structure of ordinary-language concepts. Both conceptions of philosophy, the articulation of the language of science and the analysis of ordinary language, retain elements of Hegel: the former inherits his notion of reality as exhaustively the domain of science, but puts reality in a physical, not as with Hegel a conceptual, setting; the latter adopts the Hegelian assumption that reality and language are in a fundamental way correlative (an extension of the principle of the identity of thought and being), but denies that the reality revealed in, or mirrored by, language, in its representational function and in the way it is used, can be called 'reality' in any 'monolithic' or quasi-scientific sense. Indeed philosophy here is regarded as an alien intruder obscuring our vision of the proper status and function of language itself as well as of the nature of specifically mental phenomena. In both of these analytical styles of the recent past the very idea of subjectivity, as a perspective, point of view, or category of reality, is called in question, or even just plainly passed over.

This is not so in the analytical present. Recently the question of the need to acknowledge the presence of a subjective point of view has been raised and answered affirmatively, in connection, it should be noted, with the felt limitations of behaviourism as a means of access to the reality that is the state of a conscious being's consciousness. Accordingly, one would expect concepts, or categories, like that of 'flow of consciousness', 'experience', 'quality of experience', 'inner life', and 'inwardness' to be given their due place in the scheme of things, and philosophers interested in questions like, 'What is it like to be a tormented individual?', to seek out Kierkegaard as someone who can give answers.

But this, of course, does not reach the crux of the matter. As far as what it may be like to be a tormented individual is concerned, the contemporary philosopher in this style has no reason to find this question any more philosophically interesting than, say, the question, 'What is it like to be a bat?'[16] For him the crux is a matter of methodology, of whether in filling out the map of reality we are entitled at all, in respect indifferently of bats or tormented individuals, to ask questions about the quality of a subject's experience in the expectation of receiving (or in the case of the bat, forming) answers interestingly different from those we address directly to what is assumed to be a physical world shared by bats, tormented individuals, and ourselves alike. In the case of Kierkegaard, however, the question is rather whether a quality of experience can itself be the basis of a description of the scheme of things; or more attenuatedly, whether the quality of a specific experience of *need* can be the basis of a belief in a scheme of things that satisfies it.

In the long run it may be supposed that two conditions have to be satisfied by a philosopher who is willing to embrace Kierkegaard as a colleague in this respect. In the first place, he must answer at least the unattenuated version of the above question affirmatively. That is to say, he must think that what is properly called reality is always, or necessarily, described in a framework whose axiomatic basis is somehow the expression of human interest, and that reality is inescapably in some sense a reality for human beings, rather than, say, for abstract observers of a physical continuum or for bats. It is immaterial whether a philosopher who satisfies this condition interprets the view as expressing a limitation on what human beings are capable of conceiving (i.e. their 'realities' are always parochially human ones) or as expressing, in Hegelian fashion, a specifically human ability to grasp *the* real which happens to be in a fundamental way a human reality. It is enough that he finds an investigation into (to use Kierkegaard's distinction) the 'how' of human experience essential for a specification of what is real, where what the 'how' delivers is something other than the 'what' understood as representing a common, objective world available directly in perception, perhaps even, in their special fashion, to bats.

The second condition our philosopher would have to satisfy is that of believing, deep down and ineradicably, that human beings play a pre-established role in the scheme of things. That is, for better or for worse his point of view must be anthropocentric. The reason for this is that, unless he believes this he cannot accept that a description of human reality from the point of view of the tormented individual, which corresponds to Kierkegaard's account of the individual's determinable situation when properly, i.e. determinately, conceived, can in principle have its counterpart in an undeterminable reality that fulfils the need which occasions the torment. In addition, the view must be anthropocentric not just in the sense that it envisages a pre-established role for human beings collectively, it must see such a role as being pre-established for each human being individually.

From here it may seem but a short step to requiring of our philosopher that he be a Christian. And, indeed, Kierkegaard did regard Christianity as the only non-pagan life-view that appealed to the individual as such. But in the context of a discussion of the specifically philosophical background for Kierkegaard's thought and its basic motivations it may be more revealing to see his basic commitment as being that of the rationalists, that is to the principle that reality is a meaningful, structured whole in which human life (for Kierkegaard each individual human life) plays a significant part. Seen in this light, Kierkegaard's 'torment' would be that of one who knows he will *find* nothing beyond or above the sheer contingency of human life.

Whether it is reasonable to retain the rationalist's commitment when one also denies that there could ever be any 'objective' grounds for accepting the rationalist principle, is, I think, hard to decide. Many people with a large experience of life, not least of suffering, do accept it, even though they know of no objective grounds. But very few of them are professional philosophers. There is at least one not uninteresting conclusion waiting to be drawn here. Kierkegaard would have been quicker and bolder than I to draw it.

References

References to Kierkegaard's writings are to the Collected Works (Søren Kierkegaard, *Samlede Værker*), edited by A. B. Drachmann, J. L. Heiberg, and H. O. Lange, vols 1–20, in the 1962–4 edition, Gyldendal, Copenhagen, and to *Søren Kierkegaards Papirer*, 2nd expanded edition edited by Niels Thulstrup, vols I–XVI, Gyldendal, Copenhagen, 1968–78. The translations are, with a few exceptions, my own. References to *Samlede Værker* are prefixed with the abbreviation 'S.V.', and to *Søren Kierkegaards Papirer* with 'Papirer'. References to the Danish text are followed, for the most part, by references to available English translations. Where the English version in my text departs from the published translation the reference is in italic. The translations referred to are as follows:

Either/Or, vols I and II, translated by Walter Lowrie, with revisions and a foreword by Howard A. Johnson, Anchor Books, Doubleday, Garden City, NY, 1959.

Fear and Trembling, translated with introduction and notes by Walter Lowrie, Anchor Books, Doubleday, Garden City, NY, 1954.

Philosophical Fragments or a Fragment of Philosophy, originally translated and introduced by David F. Swenson, new introduction and commentary by Niels Thulstrup, translation revised and commentary translated by Howard V. Hong, Princeton University Press, Princeton, NJ, 1962.

The Concept of Anxiety: A Simple Psychologically Orienting Deliberation on the Dogmatic Issue of Hereditary Sin, edited and translated with introduction and notes by Reidar Thomte in collaboration with Albert B. Anderson, Princeton University Press, Princeton, NJ, 1980.

Kierkegaard's Concluding Unscientific Postscript, translated by David F. Swenson and completed, with introduction and notes, by Walter Lowrie, Princeton University Press, Princeton, NJ, 1941.

Purity of Heart is to Will One Thing: Spiritual Preparation for the Office of Confession, translated with introductory essay by Douglas V. Steere, Harper Torchbooks, Harper & Brothers, New York, 1958.

Two Ages: The Age of Revolution and the Present Age: A Literary Review, edited and translated with introduction and notes by Howard V. Hong and Edna H. Hong, Princeton University Press, Princeton, NJ, 1978.

The Sickness unto Death, translated with introduction and notes by Walter Lowrie, Anchor Books, Doubleday, Garden City, NY, 1954. (In same volume as *Fear and Trembling*.)

Notes

Chapter I A kind of philosopher

1 S.V. 18 (*The Point of View of My Work as an Author*), p. 125.
2 Josiah Thompson, *Kierkegaard*, Alfred A. Knopf, New York, 1973, pp. 9–10.
3 S.V. 9, pp. 155–6 (*Postscript*, pp. *165–6*). Kierkegaard also complains of being misunderstood by his public. One journal entry (*Papirer* I, A 123, p. 80) says that people failed even to understand his complaint that they did not understand him. Cf. S.V. 18, p. 139.
4 See James Collins, *Interpreting Modern Philosophy*, Princeton University Press, Princeton, NJ, 1972, p. 243.
5 Martin Heidegger, *Sein und Zeit*, 8th edn, Max Niemeyer, Tübingen, 1957, p. 235 n.
6 For most of the biographical information that follows I have drawn on Josiah Thompson's excellent *Kierkegaard*, supplemented by Kierkegaard's journals.
7 See S.V. 18, p. 127; cf. *Papirer* X, 1, A 8, p. 8: 'I have never known the joy of being a child.' Cf. S.V. 18, p. 131: 'To whatever extent I may have lived in other respects, I had in fact humanly speaking skipped over childhood and youth . . . instead of being young, I became a poet, which is youth at one remove [*hvilket er Ungdom anden Gang*].'
8 See *Papirer* I, A 96, p. 69.
9 Ibid., A 75, p. 53. Emphasis removed. The entry is dated 1 August 1835 and reads: 'What matters is to find a purpose, to see what it really is that God wills that *I* should do; the crucial thing is to find a truth which is truth *for me*, to find *the idea for which I am willing to live and die*.' In neither Kierkegaard's nor Mill's case was the disillusionment so radical as to undermine the basic principle of the paternal inheritance. Kierkegaard continued to believe there was a God and Mill remained a utilitarian and a believer in the liberal humanistic morality of which Bentham and Mill's father, James Mill, were the first major philosophical spokesmen.
10 Ibid., A 161, p. 93.

11 *Papirer* II, A 171, p. 88; cf. also ibid., A 549, p. 204: 'My consciousness is at times far too roomy, far too general . . . so large, hanging so loose about me'; and *Papirer* III, A 224, p. 92: 'My head is as dead and empty as a theatre after the performance is over.'

12 *Papirer* II, A 637, p. 232.

13 See *Papirer* VII, 1, A 5, p. 6.

14 *Papirer* II, A 228, p. 106. The entry gives not only the date, 19 May 1838, but also the time, 10.30 a.m.

15 Ibid., A 517, p. 194.

16 *Papirer* X, 5, A 149, p. 159. From 1849.

17 *Papirer* X, 1, A 584, p. 368.

18 *Papirer* VIII, 1, A 163, p. 82. See Thompson, op. cit., pp. 188 ff.

19 S.V. 18, p. 87.

20 Ibid., p. 137.

21 *Papirer* VII, 1, A 4, p. 6; cf. *Papirer* X, 6, B 249, pp. 410–12, which implies that the idea of the priesthood had occupied him even before the feud with *Corsair*.

22 *Papirer* VII, 1, A 229, p. 149.

23 Thompson (op. cit., p. 93) gives $235,000, but some allowance must be made for nearly ten years' inflation since 1973. See ibid., pp. 127–8 where Thompson cites evidence against the theories, once variously extant, that Kierkegaard's fortune went on publishing costs, an idealistic refusal to accept interest on his capital, and giving away money to the poor: 'The fact is that Kierkegaard simply spent his fortune on . . . carriage drives, exquisite furniture, elegant buildings, stuffed lamb, and good wine; 30 bottles of which were found in his apartment at his death.' Thompson's view is that Kierkegaard 'used [his money] up with great deliberation to construct the "cloister" in which he could work fruitfully, without interruption or distraction'. In his review of Thompson's book in the *Observer* (13 January 1974) Philip Toynbee sees it all rather as a sign of 'malicious gluttony, selfishness and self-pity', not to say 'hypocrisy'.

24 See *Papirer* VIII, 1, A 100, pp. 48–9, and Thompson, op. cit., pp. 274 and 278.

25 See Thompson, op. cit., p. 234.

26 Quoted in ibid., p. 233.

27 See ibid., pp. 235 ff.

28 For the influence of Kierkegaard on Heidegger, see, for example, George J. Stack, 'The Language of Possibility and Existential Possibility', *Modern Schoolman*, vol. L (January 1973).

29 Roger Scruton, *From Descartes to Wittgenstein: A Short History of Modern Philosophy*, Routledge & Kegan Paul, London, Boston, and Henley, 1981, p. 190.

30 Collins, op. cit., pp. 242–5.

31 S.V. 18, p. 125.

32 Ibid., pp. 119 ff. and 144. In *Papirer* X, 1, A 116, p. 87, Kierkegaard says his readers will not have 'the time or ability', or 'faith enough' in his work, to see a 'total plan in the whole'; instead they will interpret its

transitions as due to changes in the author's beliefs and interests. Still, it is not at all clear that the coherence which Kierkegaard himself attributes to the whole is one that we should expect to be visible on the semantic surface, even to those lacking these disabilities. He himself says that the fact that 'there is a totality in the whole' and that 'there is truly something more to be said about it than this poor comment that the author changed' is something he 'knows deep within [himself] '. Further useful remarks on the alleged unity of the authorship are to be found in, for example, *Papirer* IX, A 226, p. 123; *Papirer* X, 1, A 300, p. 201; *Papirer* X, 2, A 106, pp. 81 ff. and *Papirer* X, 6, B 4, 3, pp. 14 f.

33 The text here is based on part of my paper, 'A Kind of Philosopher: Comments on Some Recent Books on Kierkegaard', *Inquiry*, vol. 18 (1975), pp. 354–65.

34 *Papirer* X, 1, A 666, p. 421; see also *Papirer* VIII, 1, A 358, p. 161, and *Papirer* VIII, 2, B 81, 1, p. 144, and B 86, p. 168.

Chapter II   Turning Hegel outside-in

1 S.V. 2, p. 204 (*Either/Or*, vol. 1, p. 220). The remark is by the 'author' of the papers making up the first volume of *Either/Or*. See Ch. III below.

2 Johann Georg Hamann (1730–88), often called an 'irrationalist', but more accurately described as a critic of the Enlightenment's concept of reason, which Hamann regarded as abstract and incapable of grasping reality in the round.

3 Jean Wahl, *Études Kierkegaardiennes*, Fernand Aubier, Éditions Montaigne, Paris, 1938, p. 166.

4 See 'The Unhappiest Man' in S.V. 2, pp. 204 ff. (*Either/Or*, vol. 1, pp. 220 ff.). For a discussion of Kierkegaard's familiarity with Hegel's work, see Niels Thulstrup, *Kierkegaard's Relation to Hegel*, trans. George L. Stengren, Princeton University Press, Princeton, NJ, 1980.

5 G.W.F. Hegel, *Phenomenology of Spirit*, trans. A.V. Miller, Clarendon Press, Oxford, 1977, §199, p. 121. I have removed the largely superfluous capitalization that abounds in this as in most translations of Hegel.

6 Ibid., §206, p. 126.

7 Ibid., §§205 and 206, pp. 125 and 126.

8 Ibid., §208, p. 127.

9 See G.W.F. Hegel, *Logic*: Part One of the *Encyclopaedia of the Philosophical Sciences* ('Smaller Logic'), trans. W. Wallace as *Hegel's Logic*, Clarendon Press, Oxford, 3rd edn, 1975, p. 142, *Zusatz*.

10 G.W.F. Hegel, *Faith and Knowledge*, trans. W. Cerf and H.S. Harris, State University of New York Press, Albany, NY, 1977, p. 189. The other representatives discussed by Hegel are Jacobi and Fichte.

11 Hegel, *Phenomenology of Spirit*, §208, p. 127.

12 Ibid.

13 I. Kant, *The Critique of Pure Reason*, trans. N. Kemp Smith, Macmillan, London, 1929, A 107, p. 136. Emphasis added.

14 Hegel, *Phenomenology of Spirit*, §§119 and 204, pp. 121 and 124.

15 G.W.F. Hegel, 'Die Positivität der christlichen Religion' (1795–1796), *Werke* 1, *Frühe Schriften*, Suhrkamp, Frankfurt am Main, 1971, p. 211.
16 Hegel, *Phenomenology of Spirit*, §217, p. 131.
17 See ibid., §232, pp. 139–40.
18 See *Hegel's Logic*, pp. 137 ff. and the discussion in Charles Taylor, *Hegel*, Cambridge University Press, Cambridge, 1975, pp. 114–15 and 240–4.
19 Hegel, *Phenomenology of Spirit*, §230, p. 138 (original emphasis).
20 For a distinction between common and communal goals (between the having a specific goal being instantiated by more than one person and the having a specific goal being instantiated by more than one person for each only by virtue of its also being instantiated by the others), see Jay F. Rosenberg, *One World and Our Knowledge of It*, Reidel, Dordrecht, Boston, and London, 1980, pp. 159–60.
21 Hegel, *Phenomenology of Spirit*, §§210 and 232, pp. 128 and 139.
22 Hegel, *Faith and Knowledge*, p. 58.
23 Ibid.
24 Hegel, *Faith and Knowledge*, p. 59. Hegel says here that construing highest bliss as highest idea is *the* task of 'every' philosophy. See the translator's note to p. 87 of *Hegel's Logic*, pp. 313–14.
25 Hegel, *Faith and Knowledge*, p. 59; cf. Hegel, *Phenomenology of Spirit*, §§538–81.
26 Ibid., p. 58.
27 Ibid., p. 57.
28 Ibid., p. 58 (latter brackets in Cerf and Harris's translation). Hegel says of this 'vision' that it is 'of the absolute and the eternal' (ibid.).
29 Ibid., p. 66.
30 S.V. 18 (*The Point of View of My Work as an Author*), p. 91.
31 Hence it was not, Kierkegaard assures us, because the public was 'unfavourably disposed' to him that he deserted it; nor 'out of pride or arrogance, etc.' (ibid.).
32 Ibid., p. 93 fn. Cf. Ch. I, note 32 above.
33 Cf. S.V. 9, p. 181; S.V. 10, pp. 111 and 170 (*Postscript*, pp. 195, 376, and 439).
34 Hegel, *Phenomenology of Spirit*, §217, p. 131.
35 S.V. 10, p. 102 (*Postscript*, p. 367).
36 S.V. 9, p. 206 (*Postscript*, p. 214).
37 Ibid., pp. 135 and 166 (*Postscript*, pp. 145 and 178).
38 Ibid., pp. 169–70 (*Postscript*, p. 182).
39 Ibid., p. 131 (*Postscript*, p. 141).
40 Cf. S.V. 14, pp. 88–95 (*Two Ages*, pp. 96–104).
41 S.V. 15, p. 96 (*The Sickness unto Death*, p. 173): 'Health is generally speaking to be able to resolve contradictions [*Modsigelser*].'
42 Ibid., p. 77 (*The Sickness unto Death*, p. 150).
43 John xi. 4.
44 S.V. 15, p. 69 (*The Sickness unto Death*, p. 144).
45 Ibid., p. 77 (*The Sickness unto Death*, p. 150).
46 Ibid., p. 77 (*The Sickness unto Death*, p. 151).
47 Hegel, *Phenomenology of Spirit*, §206, p. 126. Cf. note 6, above.

48 Ibid., §205, p. 126. Original emphasis.
49 Ibid., §207, p. 126.
50 S.V. 15, p. 86 (*The Sickness unto Death*, p. *163*).
51 S.V. 10, p. 114 (*Postscript*, p. 381).
52 S.V. 10, p. 241 (*Postscript*, p. 509).
53 Ibid., pp. 113 and 114 (*Postscript*, pp. 379 and 380). See note 59 below.
54 Ibid., p. 118 (*Postscript*, p. *384*).
55 Ibid.
56 S.V. 10, pp. 114 and 116; cf. p. 113 (*Postscript*, pp. 381 and 382; cf. p. 379).
57 'Existents-Sphærer' ('spheres of existence' or 'existential spheres'). See ibid., p. 179 (*Postscript*, pp. 448 and 570 (editor's note 19)).
58 'Existents-Oppfattelser'. See ibid., p. 238 (*Postscript*, p. 506).
59 Kierkegaard uses the expression 'becoming eternal' (see S.V. 10, p. 240 (*Postscript*, p. 508)) and 'becoming infinite' interchangeably.
60 See ibid., p. 240 (*Postscript*, p. *508*).
61 Ibid., p. 239 (*Postscript*, p. 509).
62 Ibid., p. 239 (*Postscript*, pp. 507—8).
63 Ibid., pp. 239—40 (*Postscript*, p. 508).
64 Ibid., p. 238 (*Postscript*, p. 506).
65 Ibid., p. 239 (*Postscript*, p. 507).
66 S.V. 9, p. 212 (*Postscript*, p. 227).
67 S.V. 3, p. 280 (*Either/Or*, p. *309*).
68 Ibid., p. 279 (*Either/Or*, p. *309*).
69 S.V. 10, p. 238 (*Postscript*, p. 506).
70 Ibid., p. 237 (*Postscript*, p. *505*).
71 Ibid., p. 239 (*Postscript*, p. *507*); cf. ibid., p. 229 (*Postscript*, pp. 497—8).
72 Ibid., p. 229 (*Postscript*, p. 507).
73 Ibid., pp. 237—8 (*Postscript*, pp. *505—6*).
74 Ibid., p. 240 (*Postscript*, p. *508*).
75 Ibid., p. 239 (*Postscript*, p. *507*).
76 Ibid., p. 237 (*Postscript*, p. *506*).
77 Ibid., p. 239 (*Postscript*, pp. *507—8*).
78 Ibid., p. 113 (*Postscript*, p. *379*); cf. ibid., p. 240 (*Postscript*, p. 508).
79 S.V. 9, p. 123 (*Postscript*, p. 133).
80 Ibid., p. 101 (*Postscript*, p. 107).
81 Ibid., p. 159; cf. p. 160 (*Postscript*, p. 170; cf. p. 171). Emphasis added.
82 Ibid., p. 102 (*Postscript*, p. 108).
83 I have this useful expression from Martin J. De Nys, 'The Motion of the Universal: Hegel's Phenomenology of Consciousness', *Modern Schoolman*, vol. LVI, no. 4 (May 1979), p. 318.
84 S.V. 15, p. 89 (*The Sickness unto Death*, pp. 164—5).
85 See Hegel, *Phenomenology of Spirit*, §229, p. 137.
86 See G.W.F. Hegel, *The Philosophy of Religion*, vol. I, trans. E.B. Speirs and J.B. Sanderson, London, 1895, p. 200: 'without the world, God is not God'.
87 S.V. 10, p. 113 (*Postscript*, p. *379*). Emphasis added.
88 S.V. 9, p. 18 (*Postscript*, p. *18*); cf. S.V. 10, p. 67 (*Postscript*, p. 330).
89 S.V. 9, p. 19 (*Postscript*, p. *19*).

90 Ibid., p. 51 (*Postscript*, p. *54*).
91 Ibid., p. 106 (*Postscript*, p. 113).
92 Ibid., pp. 51–2 (*Postscript*, p. *54*). Emphasis added.
93 Ibid., p. 189 (*Postscript*, p. *203*).
94 Ibid.
95 S.V. 10, p. 9 (*Postscript*, p. 267).
96 Ibid., p. 13 (*Postscript*, p. 271).
97 Hegel, *Phenomenology of Spirit*, §230, p. 138. Original emphasis.
98 Ibid.
99 See S.V. 10, p. 240 (*Postscript*, p. 508).
100 Ibid., pp. 114 and 115 (*Postscript*, pp. *380* and 381).
101 Hegel, *Phenomenology of Spirit*, §77, p. 49.
102 Ibid.
103 Hegel, *Phenomenology of Spirit*, §798, pp. 485–6. Original emphasis.
104 S.V. 15, p. 73 (*The Sickness unto Death*, p. 146).
105 Ibid., p. 100 (*The Sickness unto Death*, p. *176*); cf. S.V. 9, p. 206 (*Postscript*, pp. 220–1).
106 *Papirer* VIII, 1, A 9, p. 7. ('Enkelthedens Kategorie' can also be translated 'the category of the individual'.) He adds that 'this is precisely the principle of Christianity'. Cf. *The Point of View of My Work as an Author*, S.V. 18, p. 165.
107 Thus 'spirit' in Hegel is a 'mass noun', it cannot take numerical adjectives or the plural form, while Kierkegaard's 'spirit' can do both and is therefore a 'count noun'.
108 S.V. 6, pp. 48 ff. (*Fragments*, pp. 61 ff.).
109 Cf. S.V. 9, p. 169 (*Postscript*, p. 181), and S.V. 10, p. 113 (*Postscript*, p. 379).
110 S.V. 9, pp. 169–70 (*Postscript*, p. 182).
111 Cf. S.V. 6, p. 169 (*The Concept of Anxiety*, p. 72), and S.V. 15, pp. 84 and 91 (*The Sickness unto Death*, pp. 158 and 166).
112 Ibid., p. 113 (*The Sickness unto Death*, p. *190*).
113 Ibid., p. 36 (*Postscript*, p. 296).
114 Hegel, *Phenomenology of Spirit*, §80, p. 51.
115 L. Feuerbach, *Sämtliche Werke*, ed. W. Bolin and F. Jodl, Fromann-Verlag, Stuttgart, 1903–10, vol. II, pp. 229–30 and 232.
116 Ibid., p. 232. Emphasis added.
117 See Marx W. Wartofsky, *Feuerbach*, Cambridge University Press, Cambridge, London, New York, and Melbourne, 1977, pp. 358 ff. and 393 ff., for a discussion of Feuerbach's conception of practical philosophy. Wartofsky claims that Feuerbach's conception verged on but failed explicitly to pass over into the Marxist notion of *praxis*.
118 S.V. 9, p. 131 (*Postscript*, p. 141). Cf. note 39, above.

Chapter III   The knight of faith's silence

1 S.V. 5, p. 102 (*Fear and Trembling*, p. 122).
2 See G.W.F. Hegel, *Phenomenology of Spirit*, trans. by A.V. Miller, Clarendon Press, Oxford, 1977, §§798–800, pp. 485–6.

3 Ibid., §798, p. 485.

4 S.V. 5, p. 73 (*Fear and Trembling*, p. 89).

5 *The Point of View of My Work as an Author*, S.V. 18, pp. 105 and 106. Original emphasis.

6 Ibid., pp. 96, 101, and 105.

7 'En første og sidste Forklaring', S.V. 10, pp. 285–6 (*Postscript*, unnumbered page following p. 550). A note in the Danish edition (Drachmann, Heiberg, & Lange) says that in calling the explanation 'final' Kierkegaard had in mind to stop writing and to apply for a pastorate (ibid., p. 306). See p. 7 above.

8 S.V. 2, p. 19 (*Either/Or*, vol. 1, p. *13*).

9 Ibid., p. 19 (*Either/Or*, vol. 1, p. *14*).

10 Ibid.; cf. S.V. 9, p. 217 (*Postscript*, pp. 227–8).

11 S.V. 3, pp. 310–14 (*Either/Or*, vol. 2, pp. 333–7).

12 See, for example, S.V. 1, p. 253.

13 Immanuel Kant, *Fundamental Principles of the Metaphysic of Morals*, trans. T.K. Abbott, in Kant's *Critique of Practical Reason and Other Works on the Theory of Ethics*, Longmans, Green, London, New York, and Toronto, 6th edn, 1954, p. 55.

14 Ibid., p. 51.

15 See G.W.F. Hegel, *Lectures on the History of Philosophy*, 3 vols, Humanities Press, New York, 1963, vol. I, pp. 387 and fn.; and Charles Taylor, *Hegel*, Cambridge University Press, Cambridge, 1975, p. 376: 'The crucial characteristic of *Sittlichkeit* is that it enjoins us to bring about what already is. . . . With *Moralität* the opposite holds. Here we have an obligation to realize something which does not exist.'

16 See p. 8 above.

17 The Danish is 'det Almeen-Menneskelige'. See, for example, S.V. 3, p. 301 (*Either/Or*, vol. 2, p. 333).

18 Ibid., p. 242 (*Either/Or*, vol. 2, p. 267) Emphasis added.

19 See Chapter VI below.

20 S.V. 3, p. 272 (*Either/Or*, vol. 2, p. 300).

21 Ibid., p. 245 (*Either/Or*, vol. 2, p. 245).

22 Ibid., p. 280 (*Either/Or*, vol. 2, p. *309*). Cf. *Papirer* IV, A 234, p. 92: 'Marriage . . . is the profoundest form of revelation in life.' Cf. *Papirer* IV, A 234, p. 91.

23 S.V. 3, p. 279 (*Either/Or*, vol. 2, p. 309).

24 Ibid., pp. 323–4 (*Either/Or*, vol. 2, p. 355).

25 Cf. S.V. 9, pp. 215–16 (*Postscript*, pp. 230–1). Emphasis added.

26 Ibid., p. 216 (*Postscript*, p. 231). That is, where the ethical, the existing code, *Sittlichkeit*, 'becomes the temptation'.

27 See, for example, G.A. Cohen, *Karl Marx's Theory of History – A Defence*, Princeton University Press, Princeton, NJ, 1978, p. 21.

28 See, for example, G.W.F. Hegel, *Wissenschaft der Logik* ('Greater Logic') (1812–16), ed. G. Lasson, Felix Meiner, Hamburg, 1963, Parts One and Two; cf. Taylor, op. cit., pp. 226, 232 and 258.

29 See Taylor, op. cit., p. 225.

30 S.V. 6, pp. 132, 133, 135 (*The Concept of Anxiety*, pp. 34, 35, and 37).

31 G.W.F. Hegel, *The Philosophy of History*, trans. J. Sibree, rev. edn, Willey Book Co., New York, 1944, p. 17.
32 S.V. 15, p. 74; cf. p. 179 (*The Sickness unto Death*, p. 147; cf. p. 262).
33 See Ch. II, Sect. 4, above.
34 See S.V. 5, p. 193: 'Et religieust Individ . . . hviler i sig selv . . .'
35 *Papirer* V, A 96, p. 36; cf. *Papirer* II, A 379, pp. 150–1.
36 Cf. *Papirer* IV, C 75, p. 401: 'What do I learn from experience? Nothing, or a merely numerical knowledge. Whenever I construct a law from experience, I put more into it than there is in the experience. A product of experience alone would be a statistical report, like the results of meteorological observations . . .' See Ch. IV, note 198 below.
37 *Papirer* II, A 49, p. 41.
38 *Papirer* VII, 1, B 83, p. 277.
39 S.V. 5, p. 118.
40 Ibid., p. 121.
41 Ibid., p. 119.
42 Ibid., p. 121.
43 Ibid., p. 121.
44 Ibid., p. 120; cf. p. 121.
45 Ibid., p. 122.
46 Ibid., p. 122.
47 Ibid., p. 155.
48 Ibid., p. 161. It appears that in his original manuscript Kierkegaard had portrayed the young man's actual achievement of the 'second immediacy' in repetition, i.e. in establishing a relationship with God on whom the possibility of that immediacy depends. But he changed the text on hearing of Regine's new engagement to the man she eventually married. The published ending has the young man rejoicing in having his 'self' returned to him through this 'noble-minded' step on the part of the girl. It has been plausibly conjectured that Kierkegaard made the alteration for personal rather than theoretical reasons: he wished in this way to give Regine's betrothal his blessing. Whatever his reasons, however, there is a prima facie incompatibility between the young man's reference to his supposedly happy state as one of 'repetition' (ibid., pp. 185–6) and the characterization of repetition as a 'transcendence'.
49 Ibid., p. 180.
50 Ibid., p. 176.
51 Ibid., pp. 162 and 161.
52 See S.V. 9, pp. 242–4 (*Postscript*, pp. 256–8); cf. G. Malantschuk, *Kierkegaard's Thought*, Princeton University Press, Princeton, NJ, 1971, pp. 235 and 274 ff.
53 S.V. 5, p. 192.
54 See ibid., p. 191.
55 Ibid., p. 192.
56 Ibid., p. 193.
57 Ibid., p. 192. In *Papirer* IV, A 169, Kierkegaard says that repetition 'is and remains a religious category', and therefore Constantin Constantius cannot come further. He is a wise, an ironist, fights against the (merely) 'inter-

esting', but does not 'notice that he himself is still caught up in it' (p. 63).

58 S.V. 1, pp. 154 and 173.
59 Ibid., p. 328. Original in italic.
60 S.V. 5, p. 193. Emphasis added.
61 S.V. 1, p. 270.
62 L. Wittgenstein, *Tractatus Logico-Philosophicus*, trans. D.F. Pears and B.F. McGuinness, Routledge & Kegan Paul, London, 1961, 6. 45.
63 S.V. 5, p. 10 (*Fear and Trembling*, p. 23); cf. ibid., p. 11 (*Fear and Trembling*, pp. 24–5): 'I prostrate myself in deepest deference before every systematic bag-searcher. This is no system; it has not the slightest thing to do with the system. I call every blessing upon the system and on the Danish shareholders in this omnibus [a reference to the all-embracingness of Hegel's system but also to a newly instated public transport system] . . . .'
64 S.V. 5, p. 13 (*Fear and Trembling*, p. 26).
65 S.V. 5, p. 64 (*Fear and Trembling*, p. 79).
66 S.V. 3, p. 310 (*Either/Or*, vol. 2, p. *342*).
67 *Papirer* IV, A 133, p. 50 (Hong trans.).
68 Ibid., A 107, p. 43 (Hong trans.).
69 S.V. 3, pp. 280 and 302 (*Either/Or*, vol. 2, pp. 309 and 336).
70 S.V. 5, p. 51 (*Fear and Trembling*, pp. 64–5).
71 *Papirer* I, A 42, p. 19 (dated 23 December 1834).
72 S.V. 5, p. 55 (*Fear and Trembling*, p. *69*). Cf. S.V. 1, pp. 275 and 284, for comments on the tragic hero also in connection with Socrates, whom in *Fear and Trembling* Kierkegaard calls an 'intellectual tragic hero' (S.V. 5, p. 105 (*Fear and Trembling*, p. 126)).
73 Ibid., p. 55 (*Fear and Trembling*, p. 69).
74 See Genesis xxii.
75 S.V. 5, p. 55 (*Fear and Trembling*, p. 70).
76 *Papirer* IV, A 77, pp. 29–30.
77 S.V. 5, p. 56 (*Fear and Trembling*, p. 70).
78 Cf. ibid., p. 51 (*Fear and Trembling*, p. 65).
79 Ibid., p. 55 (*Fear and Trembling*, p. *69*).
80 Ibid., p. 51 (*Fear and Trembling*, p. 64).
81 Simply because the notion of a τέλος is conceived from the point of view of ethics as belonging exclusively *to* ethics.
82 Ibid., p. 65 (*Fear and Trembling*, p. 80).
83 Cf. ibid., p. 65 (*Fear and Trembling*, p. *80*), where the possibility of the ethical's acquiring 'a quite different expression, the paradoxical' is mentioned.
84 *Papirer*, X, 2, A 594, pp. 425.
85 S.V. 5, p. 52 (*Fear and Trembling*, p. 66).
86 Ibid., p. 51 (*Fear and Trembling*, pp. 64–5).
87 Ibid., pp. 85 ff. (*Fear and Trembling*, pp. 103 ff.).
88 Ibid., p. 86 (*Fear and Trembling*, p. 104).
89 Ibid., p. 87 (*Fear and Trembling*, p. 105).
90 Ibid., p. 89 (*Fear and Trembling*, p. 108).
91 Ibid., p. 90 (*Fear and Trembling*, p. *109*).

92 Ibid., pp. 88–9 (*Fear and Trembling*, pp. 106–7).
93 Ibid., p. 89 (*Fear and Trembling*, p. 107).
94 Ibid., p. 90 (*Fear and Trembling*, p. *109*); cf. p. 89 (p. 107).
95 S.V. 7, e.g. pp. 153 ff. (*Stages on Life's Way*, e.g. p. 166).
96 S.V. 3, p. 199 (*Either/Or*, vol. 2, p. 218); cf. pp. 198 and 200 ff. (pp. 217 and 219 ff.).
97 S.V. 5, p. 55 ('et reent privat Foretagende') (*Fear and Trembling*, p. 70).
98 See Malantschuk, op. cit., p. 238.
99 S.V. 10. p. 119 (*Postscript*, p. 386).
100 S.V. 5, p. 90 (*Fear and Trembling*, p. 109); cf. pp. 101 and 103 (pp. 122 and 124).
101 Ibid., p. 52–3 (*Fear and Trembling*, p. 66).
102 Ibid., p. 66 (*Fear and Trembling*, p. *81*).
103 Hegel, *Phenomenology of Spirit*, §97, p. 60. Emphasis added.
104 S.V. 5, pp. 56 and 102 (*Fear and Trembling*, pp. 70 and 122).
105 This thesis can help to throw some light on the extreme 'subjectivity' of the knight of faith, mentioned at the beginning of this chapter, and associated with the idea of solitariness or isolation. One way of understanding the isolation would be to see the knight of faith as, in respect of his relationship to the absolute, supporting an existence as a 'mere' particular below the allegedly particular-dissolving medium of language and general description. According to Johannes, the isolation of the 'true' knight of faith is 'absolute'. Not even the universal 'knight of faith' can 'mediate' his isolation. It is only the 'false' knight who tries to mediate his isolation in this way by becoming 'sectarian' and 'abandon[ing] the narrow path of the paradox in order to become a tragic hero on the cheap' (S.V. 5, p. 73 (*Fear and Trembling*, p. *89*)). By merging the divine with the ethical, the tragic hero 'allows the paradox to be mediated in the universal', i.e. brings it into conceptual, intelligible relation with what is already shared in respect of meaning and understanding, so as to be able to 'sacrifice himself for it' (ibid., pp. 56 and 73 (*Fear and Trembling*, pp. *70* and *89*)). But where the 'sectarian Punchinello . . . has [his] private theatre, i.e. several good friends and companions', who do dubious proxy for the universal, the knight of faith, for his part, *is* the paradox; he is 'the individual, absolutely nothing but the individual, without any connections and attenuations [*Vidtløftigheder*]' (ibid.). Knights of faith cannot 'render aid' to other knights of faith. Each has 'only himself alone' (S.V. 5, pp. 72 and 66 (*Fear and Trembling*, pp. 89 and 82)). Accordingly, in a society of knights of faith the knight of faith is as isolated as he is as a lone recalcitrant in a society of adherents to *Sittlichkeit* ethics. A hard and intuitively anomalous result. Still, another theory of the limits of language, or some interpretation of the one proffered, might soften it, so that certain consequences for communicability could ensue from the fact that knights of faith after all share a common life-view, or even from the fact that their 'God-relationships' all converge on the same intentional object. Unfortunately, Kierkegaard's text does not facilitate the analysis needed to handle these questions with any precision.

106   Ibid., p. 56 (*Fear and Trembling*, p. 70).
107   Ibid., p. 66 (*Fear and Trembling*, p. 81): 'Troens Paradox har tabt det Mellemliggende, dvs. det Almene.'
108   Ibid., p. 51 (*Fear and Trembling*, p. 64). See p. 74, above.
109   S.V. 5, p. 102 (*Fear and Trembling*, p. 122).
110   Ibid., p. 90 (*Fear and Trembling*, p. 108). There is an apparent complication here. In saying, at the place cited, that he cannot understand Abraham, Johannes concedes that he *can* understand the 'movements' of the merman, because the latter 'comes precisely through the paradox to want to realize the universal' (ibid.). This suggests that it is Abraham's absolute indifference to the universal that 'repels' Johannes and causes the 'shudder of thought', not any implication of the notion of faith itself, which would clearly implicate the merman too. However, Johannes's discriminating between them can be interpreted as an illustration of the point just made: namely that Johannes can only 'explain' faith in the way in which he concedes it cannot be explained, by appeal to the universal. In this respect the merman's action (intention) *seems* intelligible, though in having faith as a necessary antecedent it must, strictly speaking, be just as repellent to thought as Abraham's action (intention).
111   Ibid., p. 56 (*Fear and Trembling*, p. 70).

Chapter IV   The dialectic of faith

1   S.V. 10, pp. 169–70 (*Postscript*, p. *438*).
2   S.V. 18, p. 106.
3   See, for example, ibid., p. 107: 'In our times, as often previously, the idea that being an author is to engage in practical activity and that his authorship is therefore part of his personal existence has been totally lost.'
4   Ibid., p. 106.
5   S.V. 6, p. 99 (*Fragments*, p. *139*).
6   S.V. 10, p. 15 (*Postscript*, p. *273*).
7   There is an important footnote in the *Postscript* (S.V. 9, p. 172, and in the English translation, pp. 184–5) in which Kierkegaard acknowledges that in 'tracing the Socratic back to the principle that all knowledge is recollection' he has not bothered with textual questions as to where one should distinguish between Socrates and Plato. He says, however, that he has been guilty of a connected oversimplification: by making Socrates a representative of the 'pagan-philosophical' he has failed to do justice to Socrates' insistence that the philosopher is *qua* philosopher an existing individual. Socrates' 'accentuation' of existence and of its link with 'inwardness' puts him 'fundamentally in advance of speculative philosophy', in which the philosopher, in order to begin, has to 'forget the most important thing, what it is to exist'.
8   Ibid., p. 245 (*Postscript*, p. 260).
9   S.V. 10, p. 286 (*Postscript*, second unnumbered page after p. 550).
10   See, for example, S.V. 9, p. 201 (*Postscript*, p. 216).

11 G.W.F. Hegel, *Logic*: Part One of the *Encyclopaedia of the Philosophical Sciences* ('Smaller Logic'), trans. W. Wallace as *Hegel's Logic*, Clarendon Press, Oxford, 3rd edn, 1975, p. 3.
12 Ibid., p. 4.
13 Ibid., p. 7.
14 See Josiah Thompson, *Kierkegaard*, Alfred A. Knopf, New York, 1973, pp. 48 and 221.
15 *Papirer* X, 2, A 155, p. 117; cf. S.V. 6, p. 10 (*Fragments*, p. 5).
16 S.V. 9, pp. 247–8 (*Postscript*, p. *262*). First emphasis added.
17 S.V. 6, p. 98 (*Fragments*, pp. *137–8*).
18 Ibid., p. 98 (*Fragments*, p. 138); cf. *Papirer* V, B 1, 2, p. 53.
19 See Paul Dietrichson, 'Introduction to a Reappraisal of *Fear and Trembling*', *Inquiry*, vol. 12 (1969), p. 245, note 10.
20 S.V. 6, p. 9 (*Fragments*, p. 3).
21 'Bedre godt hengt end slet gift', a Danish rendering of the German translation of the clown's 'many a good hanging prevents a bad marriage' from *Twelfth Night*.
22 S.V. 9, p. 9 (*Postscript*, p. *3*).
23 See note 19 above.
24 See Henry Chadwick's article on Lessing (Gotthold Ephraim) in Paul Edwards (ed.), *The Encyclopedia of Philosophy*, Collier-Macmillan, London, 1967, vol. 4 p. 444.
25 G.E Lessing, 'Uber den Beweis des Geistes und der Kraft' (1777), *Gesammelte Werke*, vol. 8, Auflau-Verlag, Berlin, 1956, p. 12. See S.V. 9, p. 80 (*Postscript*, p. 86) where Kierkegaard writes 'eternal' (*evige*) for 'necessary'.
26 See *Papirer* V, B 1, 3, p. 53; cf. S.V. 9, p. 84 (*Postscript*, p. 90).
27 Ibid., p. 84 (*Postscript*, p. 90).
28 Following Bernard Williams's discussion in 'Deciding to Believe', in Bernard Williams, *Problems of the Self: Philosophical Papers 1956–1972*, Cambridge University Press, Cambridge, 1973, pp. 136–51.
29 See ibid., p. 150.
30 Hegel does not deny that historical truths have 'contingent and arbitrary aspects . . . which have no necessity'. See *Phenomenology of Spirit*, trans. A.V. Miller, Clarendon Press, Oxford, 1977, §41, p. 23.
31 S.V. 6, p. 69 (*Fragments*, p. *93*).
32 Ibid., p. 68 (*Fragments*, p. *91*). First emphasis added.
33 Ibid., p. 69 (*Fragments*, p. 93).
34 Ibid., p. 76 (*Fragments*, p. 103); cf. p. 77 (*Fragments*, p. 105).
35 Ibid., pp. 74 and 75 (*Fragments*, pp. 100 and 101).
36 Ibid., p. 71 (*Fragments*, p. 78).
37 Ibid., pp. 72–3 (*Fragments*, pp. *97–9*).
38 Cf. ibid., p. 74 (*Fragments*, p. 100).
39 Ibid., p. 73 (*Fragments*, p. *99*).
40 Ibid., pp. 74–5 (*Fragments*, pp. *100–1*).
41 Cf. note 48 below.
42 S.V. 6, p. 76 (*Fragments*, p. *103*).
43 See, respectively, ibid., p. 57 (*Fragments*, p. 75) and p. 58 (*Fragments*,

p. 76); and S.V. 10, p. 241 (*Postscript*, p. 509): 'All historical science [*Viden*] and knowledge [*Kundskab*] . . . is only an approximation, even at its maximum.' In the *Postscript* Kierkegaard says: 'the knower cannot know an historical reality before it has been dissolved into a possibility' (ibid., p. 22 (*Postscript*, p. *280*)). See p. 153, below.

44 Ibid., p. 240 (*Postscript*, p. 508).

45 S.V. 6, pp. 16—17 (*Fragments*, p. 14).

46 Ibid., p. 16 (*Fragments*, p. *13*) (the addition in brackets is taken from S.V. 10, p. 240 (*Postscript*, p. 508)).

47 Ibid., p. 245 (*Postscript*, p. 513).

48 S.V. 6, p. 68 (*Fragments*, p. 91); see Thulstrup's commentary (ibid., p. 237, in the English translation) on the origin of the formula in Hegel's *Science of Logic*.

49 S.V. 6, p. 93 (*Fragments*, p. *130*).

50 S.V. 9, p. 174 (*Postscript*, p. 187).

51 See Ch. II, p. 39, above.

52 S.V. 6, p. 79 (*Fragments*, pp. 107—8) (original emphasis).

53 On the etymology of αἰώνιος see W. Barclay, *New Testament Words*, SCM Press, London, 1964, pp. 33 ff. Barclay suggests that Plato may have coined αἰώνιος, formed from αἰών, which in classical Greek has the three main meanings, 'life-time', 'age' or 'generation', and 'a very large extent of time', 'to denote that which has neither beginning nor end, and that is subject to neither change nor decay, that which is above time, but of which time is a moving image [a reference to the *Timaeus*, 37d] ' (ibid., p. 34). He adds that '[t]he essence of the word . . . is that it is the word of the eternal order as contrasted with the order of this world; it is the word of deity as contrasted with humanity' (ibid., p. 35). See also William C. Kneale's article on 'Eternity' in *The Encyclopedia of Philosophy*, ed. Paul Edwards, Collier-Macmillan, London, 1967, vol. 3, pp. 63—6, which also discusses Parmenides' concept of 'the One'.

54 See p. 31, above.

55 S.V. 6, p. 44 (*Fragments*, p. 55); cf. p. 40 (*Fragments*, p. 49).

56 Kierkegaard (Climacus) writes: 'What then is the unknown? It is the limit one repeatedly arrives at, and for that matter, when the category of movement is replaced by that of rest, the different, the absolutely different.' The connection between these two categories and the epistemological side of the absolute difference can be grasped in terms of the static representation of reality unavoidable in reducing reality to concepts and the dynamic aspect which Hegel thought he could account for by reference to the 'movement' characteristic of speculative reason. That aspect cannot be represented in thought, according to Kierkegaard, either in its conceptual products or in the manner of its producing these. Here, however, by the dynamic aspect we may understand the 'movement' of the world regarded as an action involving the project initiated by the paradox. A movement based on a paradox will be doubly unintelligible from the point of view of a medium confined to static *and* non-paradoxical forms. (Ibid., p. 44, (*Fragments*, p. 55).)

351

57 Ibid.
58 Ibid., p. 45 (*Fragments*, p. 57).
59 Ibid.
60 Ibid., p. 46 (*Fragments*, p. 58); cf. pp. 18 ff. (*Fragments*, pp. 17 ff.).
61 See S.V. 10, p. 239 (*Postscript*, pp. 507–8).
62 This is my own gloss on the relevant passage at S.V. 6, p. 46 (*Fragments*, p. 58).
63 Ibid.
64 *Papirer* IV, A 62, pp. 23–4 (my emphasis). Cf. the related passage in S.V. 6, p. 45 (*Fragments*, p. 56). On p. 60 (ibid. (*Fragments*, pp. 79–80)), Kierkegaard (Climacus) says that the servant-form was no disguise or deception. Jesus was not an emissary or special agent of the eternal, whose 'true' divinity was hidden by a guise of humbleness. The paradox is that the eternal became a human being and equal with the humblest of human beings.
65 S.V. 6, pp. 46–7 (*Fragments*, p. 59).
66 See ibid., p. 84 (*Fragments*, p. 116) on sin-consciousness as a condition of understanding the eternal.
67 There seems to be another paradoxical element not mentioned by Kierkegaard: the idea that the unknowable adopts the totally alien guise of the knowable in order to be understood. But it may be that *Kierkegaard* should be understood as intending that the unknowable *become* known (in a sense) by appearing 'polemically' in that guise. The sense of 'known' here could be related to a practical grasp of the divine intention rather than to knowledge *that* such an intention had been formed. It is relevant in this context to mention the claim, sometimes made, that the absolute paradox is not 'absolute', in the sense that the situation described as paradoxical in the pseudonymous works is not so regarded in the acknowledged works. This contention has been supported by statistical investigation of the occurrences of the expressions 'Paradoxe' and 'Absurde' in the two genres. But the (virtually) total absence of these expressions in the acknowledged works is more satisfactorily explained, to my mind, by seeing the acknowledged works as presupposing acceptance on the reader's part of the reality of the situation denoted by the paradox, in spite of its paradoxicality, and not as written from a point of view from which the barriers to understanding have been surmounted. See, for example, Benjamin Daise, 'Kierkegaard and the Absolute Paradox', Journal of the History of Philosophy, vol. 14 (1976), pp. 63–8, and Alastair McKinnon, 'Kierkegaard's Pseudonyms: A New Hierarchy', *American Philosophical Quarterly*, vol. 6 (1969), pp. 116–25, and esp. p. 121.
68 S.V. 6, p. 48 (*Fragments*, p. 62).
69 Ibid., pp. 48–9 (*Fragments*, p. 62).
70 Ibid., p. 48 (*Fragments*, p. 63). See also fn. (*Fragments*, fn. 5) on the same page.
71 Ibid., p. 49 (*Fragments*, p. 63).
72 Ibid., p. 50 (*Fragments*, p. 64).
73 Ibid., p. 90 (*Fragments*, p. 125).

74 Ibid., p. 90 (*Fragments*, p. 125); cf. p. 62 (*Fragments*, p. 81).
75 Ibid., p. 56 (*Fragments*, p. 72).
76 Ibid., pp. 64 and 65 (*Fragments*, pp. 85 and 87).
77 Ibid., p. 56 (*Fragments*, pp. 72–3).
78 Ibid., pp. 59 and 60 (*Fragments*, pp. 77 and 79).
79 Ibid., p. 47 (*Fragments*, p. 59).
80 S.V. 9, p. 175 (*Postscript*, p. 188).
81 S.V. 6, p. 59 (*Fragments*, p. 77).
82 Ibid., p. 52 (*Fragments*, p. 67).
83 Ibid., p. 84 (*Fragments*, p. 116).
84 S.V. 15, p. 136 (*The Sickness unto Death*, p. 213); cf. pp. 173 and 180 (*The Sickness unto Death*, pp. 255 and 262). Kierkegaard (Anti-Climacus) cites Romans xiv. 23: 'whatsoever is not of faith is sin.'
85 S.V. 6, p. 60 (*Fragments*, p. 79).
86 Ibid., p. 58 (*Fragments*, p. 76).
87 Ibid., p. 99 (*Fragments*, p. 139); cf. p. 61 (*Fragments*, p. 80).
88 S.V. 10, pp. 31 and 32 (*Postscript*, p. 290).
89 S.V. 6, p. 56 (*Fragments*, p. 72).
90 Blaise Pascal, *Pensées sur la religion et sur quelques autres sujets*, §§418 and 213. (English translation of the Louis Lafuma annotated edition (Paris, 1962) by Martin Turnell, entitled *Pensées*, London, 1962.)
91 For Pascal 'God' is just as incomprehensible a notion as the 'absolute paradox'.
92 Although this may sound plausible enough, there are possible objections. Thus one might ask: If the question facing the 'understanding' in its encounter with the paradox is whether religious satisfaction is possible, given that it rests on a contradiction, how can the choice be construed as one *between* the alternatives? The prior problem is whether there is an alternative. However, there is no illogicality here since, although the possibility of the satisfaction is the logically prior alternative, the option with which a person who wants to be able to maintain an interest in the satisfaction is primarily concerned is its actual availability. Such a person wants to kill the two birds with one stone. He answers the question: Is it logically possible? by affirming: It is true! Another, related objection would be that the irrational step required to envisage this alternative withdraws pre-emptively whatever licence the above argument gives us to call Kierkegaardian belief rational. However, there seems no prima facie reason why Pascal's argument should not apply just as much where the satisfaction-sensitive alternatives are 'a contradictory claim can be true' and 'a contradictory claim cannot be true' as where they are 'God exists' and 'God does not exist'. Indeed, it is probably wrong to suppose that Pascal's believer is not required to make exactly the same step, since the (on Pascal's view) incomprehensibility of God is fully analogous to the paradox in respect of being an affront to reason (understanding), thus making reason itself an obstacle to anyone who wants to accept that God exists. Third, it may be asked, What is the difference between Pascal's case where believing is assumed to be a necessary condition of satisfaction, if the belief is true, and the

case of choosing to believe rather than disbelieve simply because it is more comforting to do so? Of both cases it can be said that the satisfaction depends on the belief. Should they not then be considered equally rational, or if not that, equally irrational? In whichever way this question is settled, there is at least one difference to which a relevant significance might be attached. In the Pascal case the satisfaction is only, as Hegel might say, an advantage in principle; it is not a known advantage; the Pascalian believer is offering a hostage, if not to fortune, at least to the unknown (which is not to deny that he may be enjoying a present satisfaction, based on what he does know, e.g. that he has at least not, by disbelieving, deprived himself of the possibility on which the primary satisfaction depends). The other believer's satisfaction is not in this way contingent on unknown circumstances; it is an attempt to have and enjoy things as he wants them, as if the satisfaction was not just in principle, but in fact. Where the Pascalian envisages a reality beyond human experience which determines the validity of religious belief, just as experience determines that of empirical belief, this other believer treats truth as though it were subject to his will, and that *is* irrational.

93   S.V. 10, p. 113 (*Postscript*, p. *379*). See Ch. II, p. 40, above.
94   Ibid., p. 118 (*Postscript*, p. 384). See Ch. II, p. 36 above.
95   Ibid., p. 233 (*Postscript*, p. 501). Kierkegaard also talks of the need to endure 'the crucifixion of the understanding' (ibid., p. 232 (*Postscript*, p. 500)).
96   'Nympholepsy, n. Ecstasy or frenzy caused by desire of the unattainable' (*Concise Oxford Dictionary of Current English*, 1956).
97   Kierkegaard's criticism is focused on those who retain the interest without facing up to the paradox, and on those who disclaim the interest on rational grounds without having faced the issue as a clear-cut choice, and without having been genuinely motivated by the interest. The group of those whom Kierkegaard calls the 'unhappy lovers' (S.V. 6, p. 28 (*Fragments*, p. 31)) falls outside his range. In the *Postscript* (S.V. 9, p. 82 (p. 87)) he says that the choice as posed by Christianity is between an eternal happiness and an eternal unhappiness, 'the decision to be in time'.
98   S.V. 6, p. 98 (*Fragments*, p. 137).
99   S.V. 170 (*Postscript*, p. 182).
100 See note 25, above.
101 S.V. 9, p. 23 (*Postscript*, p. *24*).
102 Ibid., p. 24 (*Postscript*, p. 25).
103 Ibid., p. 26 (*Postscript*, p. 27).
104 Ibid., p. 34; cf. 28–9 (*Postscript*, p. *35*; cf. pp. 29–30).
105 Ibid., p. 28 (*Postscript*, p. 29).
106 Ibid., p. 44 (*Postscript*, p. 45).
107 Ibid., pp. 30 and 46 (*Postscript*, pp. 31 and 47).
108 Ibid., p. 23 (*Postscript*, p. 24).
109 Ibid., p. 46 (*Postscript*, p. 50). See ibid., p. 258 (note for p. 46), for an explanation of the term 'bittweise'.

110 Ibid., pp. 46 ff. (*Postscript*, pp. 49 ff.).
111 Ibid., p. 51 (*Postscript*, p. 54).
112 Ibid., p. 51 (*Postscript*, p. *54*).
113 Ibid., p. 51 (*Postscript*, p. 55).
114 Ibid., p. 24 (*Postscript*, p. 25). Original emphasis.
115 Ibid., p. 170 (*Postscript*, p. *182*).
116 Ibid., p. 217 (*Postscript*, p. *232*).
117 Ibid., p. 244 (*Postscript*, p. *259*).
118 S.V. 10, pp. 272–3 (*Postscript*, p. *540*), original emphasis; cf. S.V. 9, p. 63 (*Postscript*, p. 68).
119 In spite of occasional passages (e.g. S.V. 9, p. 217, and S.V. 10, p. 42) that might be read as suggesting otherwise. From an appropriately elevated philosophical vantage-point *Inderlighed* can in a way, be connected with the idea of a direction inwards. The notion of 'turning Hegel outside-in', outlined at the end of Chapter II, was that in order to pose and answer Hegel's problems properly one should turn attention away from the objective, public domain and 'in' towards the subjective domain. This is a methodological proposal to the effect that one should take note of such phenomena as inwardness in accounting for human reality.
120 In S.V. 15 (*The Sickness unto Death*).
121 S.V. 9, p. 170; cf. p. 116 (*Postscript*, p. *182*; cf. p. 126).
122 See Ch. II, note 41.
123 S.V. 9, p. 8 (*Postscript*, p. 8).
124 Ibid., p. 169 (*Postscript*, p. 181).
125 See Hegel, *Phenomenology of Spirit*, §230, p. 138.
126 S.V. 9, p. 169 (*Postscript*, p. 181).
127 See Hegel, *Phenomenology of Spirit*, §217, p. 131.
128 S.V. 9, p. 166 fn. (*Postscript*, p. *178* fn.).
129 S.V. 10, p. 28 (*Postscript*, p. *287*).
130 S.V. 9, p. 170 (*Postscript*, p. 183).
131 Ibid., pp. 169–70 (*Postscript*, p. *182*).
132 See ibid., p. 166 fn. (*Postscript*, p. *178* fn.).
133 Ibid., p. 166 (*Postscript*, p. *178*).
134 Ibid. Emphasis removed.
135 Paul Edwards, 'Kierkegaard and the "Truth" of Christianity', in P. Edwards and A. Pap (eds), *A Modern Introduction to Philosophy*, 3rd edn, Free Press, New York, 1973, pp. 513–14. Original, slightly longer version in *Philosophy*, vol. 46, 1971.
136 S.V. 9, p. 167; cf. p. 166 (*Postscript*, p. 179; cf. p. 178).
137 Ibid., p. 168 (*Postscript*, p. *180*).
138 Ibid., p. 168 (*Postscript*, p. 180).
139 Ibid., p. 167 (*Postscript*, p. 179).
140 S.V. 10, pp. 66–7 (*Postscript*, p. 330).
141 S.V. 9, p. 168 (*Postscript*, p. *180*); cf. ibid., pp. 204–5 (*Postscript*, p. *219*): 'All paganism consists in God's being related directly to man, as the remarkable in relation to the amazed. But the spiritual relationship to God in truth – i.e. inwardness – has as its prior condition the

breakthrough of inwardness, which corresponds to that divine elusiveness in which God is nothing remarkable, is indeed so far from being able to be remarked that he is invisible, so that it can by no means occur to one that he exists, while his invisibility is again his omnipresence.'

142 *Papirer* X, 2, A 299, p. 217.

143 S.V. 9, p. 173 (*Postscript*, p. 185).

144 Ibid., p. 145; cf. p. 144 (*Postscript*, p. 155; cf. p. 154). Swenson-Lowrie mistranslates 'yderligere' as 'outward'. Kierkegaard does talk of 'inner' proof (see *Papirer* X, 1, A 481, pp. 307 and 308), but not in the sense in which a proof is an objective guarantee. The Swenson-Lowrie translation suggests that an 'inner' proof will be analogous to an 'outer' one, while the word 'further' stresses that one should not be looking for that kind of thing at all. Cf. S.V. 16 (*Practice in Christianity*), pp. 97 f.

145 *Papirer* X, 1, A 481, p. 308.

146 S.V. 5, p. 91 (*Fear and Trembling*, p. 109).

147 S.V. 9, p. 170 (*Postscript*, p. *183*).

148 Ibid., p. 19 (*Postscript*, p. 19).

149 S.V. 6, p. 99 (*Fragments*, p. 139).

150 L. Wittgenstein, *Culture and Value*, trans. Peter Winch, ed. G.H. von Wright, Blackwell, Oxford, 1980, p. 32e. Original emphasis.

151 Hegel, *Phenomenology of Spirit*, §97, p. 60. Original emphasis; cf. Ch. III, note 103, above.

152 *Hegel's Logic*, p. 38; cf. p. 31. Emphasis added.

153 S.V. 9, p. 203 (*Postscript*, p. *217*).

154 Ibid., p. 217 (*Postscript*, p. 232).

155 *Papirer* VII, 1, A 186, pp. 122–6; cf. A 187–200, pp. 127–35.

156 S.V. 10, pp. 55–6 (*Postscript*, p. *317*). Another passage says that the influence of speculative philosophy on the interpretation of Christianity 'is rooted much more deeply in the whole tendency of the age ... and the vast increase in knowledge'. Ibid., p. 202 (*Postscript*, p. *216*).

157 Ibid., p. 51 (*Postscript*, p. *313*).

158 Cf. ibid., p. 53 (*Postscript*, p. *315*).

159 Ibid., p. 9; cf. p. 15 (*Postscript*, p. *267*; cf. p. *273*).

160 Ibid., p. 10 (*Postscript*, p. *268*).

161 Ibid., p. 52 (*Postscript*, p. *314*). Emphasis added.

162 Ibid., p. 55 (*Postscript*, p. *316*).

163 See ibid., p. 85 (*Postscript*, p. *350*): 'Existence is composed of infinitude and finitude, the existing [individual] is infinite and finite.'

164 Ibid., p. 10 (*Postscript*, p. *268*).

165 Ibid., p. 52 (*Postscript*, p. *313*).

166 Ibid., p. 14 (*Postscript*, p. *272*).

167 *Papirer* IV, A 164, p. 61.

168 S.V. 10, p. 14 (*Postscript*, pp. *272–3*).

169 Ibid., p. 15 (*Postscript*, p. *273*).

170 Ibid., p. 50 (*Postscript*, p. *311*).

171 Ibid., p. 51 (*Postscript*, p. *312*).

172 Ibid., p. 52 (*Postscript*, p. *314*).

173 Ibid., p. 56 (*Postscript*. p. *318*).

174 Ibid., p. 33 (*Postscript*, p. 292). 'The dubiousness of [Hegel's] "Method" can already be seen in Hegel's relation to Kant. A scepticism that lays an embargo on thought cannot be answered by *thinking* it through, since this has to be done by the very thought that has been outlawed [*som er paa Oprørerens Side* — Lit. 'which is on the side of the rebel'] . [Scepticism] must simply be broken with. To answer Kant in the fanciful shadow-play of pure thought is precisely not to answer him. — The only *An-sich* which cannot be thought is to exist, which thought has nothing to do with at all. But how could pure thought possibly remove this difficulty when pure thought is abstract and what pure thought abstracts from is existence; that is to say, the very thing it is supposed to explain.' See note 183, below.

175 S.V. 10, p. 36 (*Postscript*, p. *296*).

176 Ibid., p. 36 (*Postscript*, pp. *296–7*).

177 Ibid., p. 12; cf. p. 19 (*Postscript*, p. 270; cf. p. 277).

178 Ibid., p. 57 (*Postscript*, p. 319); cf. S.V. 9, p. 100 (*Postscript*, p. 107). Somewhere Kierkegaard refers amusingly to the 'waltz time' of Hegelian philosophy. In *Anxiety* he talks of the 'tirelessly active negative', and of the 'masters of movement' that have made Hegel's logic a 'miracle' and given 'logical thoughts feet to walk on'. S.V. 6, p. 112 fn. (*Anxiety*, p. 12 fn.).

179 S.V. 10, p. 19 (*Postscript*, p. *277*).

180 See S.V. 9, pp. 101 ff. (*Postscript*, pp. 107 ff.).

181 Ibid., pp. 104–5 (*Postscript*, p. *111*).

182 Ibid., p. 96 (*Postscript*, p. 102).

183 Ibid., pp. 97–8 (*Postscript*, pp. 103–4). In point of fact Hegel distinguishes between the abstraction that is the result of 'the elimination of all character' and that of 'the original featurelessness which precedes all definite character and is the very first of all'. It is, he says, the latter 'we call Being', and it is in this sense of 'abstract' that Hegel wants us to understand him when he says: 'The Absolute is Being . . . [this] is (in thought) the absolutely initial definition, the most abstract and stinted' (*Hegel's Logic*, p. 125). Kierkegaard might therefore be accused of misrepresenting the Hegelian position in saying that the immediacy with which Hegelian logic is supposed to begin is 'that most abstract [content] that remains after an exhaustive abstraction'. But he might well have argued that Hegel's notion of an original and preceding featurelessness could only be arrived at by just such a process of abstraction, and that what Hegel does is simply assign to the product of this process a special kind of logically generative status.

184 S.V. 9, p. 95 (*Postscript*, pp. *101–2*). See *Hegel's Science of Logic*, trans. A.V. Miller, Routledge & Kegan Paul, London, 1969, p. 76: '[The beginning] is mediated because pure knowing is the ultimate, absolute truth of consciousness.' It is relevant to note that Kierkegaard's first, and uncompleted, Climacian work, *De Omnibus Dubitandum est*, takes up the assumption held by contemporary Hegelians that philosophy begins in doubt and that that means that it is free of presuppositions. See *Papirer* IV, B 1, pp. 116–50.

185   S.V. 9, p. 137 (*Postscript*, p. *147*).
186   Ibid., p. 213 (*Postscript*, p. *228*).
187   Ibid., pp. 137–51 (*Postscript*, pp. 147–61).
188   Ibid., p. 141 (*Postscript*, p. *151*).
189   Ibid., p. 66 (*Postscript*, p. 71).
190   Ibid., p. 63 fn. (*Postscript*, p. *68* fn.).
191   Ibid., pp. 63–4 fn. (*Postscript*, p. *68* fn.).
192   Ibid., p. 64 (*Postscript*, p. *69*).
193   Ibid., p. 65 (*Postscript*, p. 70).
194   Cf. ibid., p. 63 fn. (*Postscript*, p. 68 fn.).
195   See *The Point of View of My Work as an Author*, S.V. 18, p. 91.
196   See Ch. I, note 9.
197   S.V. 1, pp. 34 and 35–6. Carl Daub was a contemporary theological writer whose work Kierkegaard comments upon, for example, in *Papirer* II, A 72, p. 48, 74, 79, p. 49, and 97, p. 61.
198   See *Papirer* V, A 74, p. 29, and 75, pp. 29–30, in connection with Adolf Trendelenburg's account of Aristotle, and *Papirer* IV, C 75, p. 401, in connection with inductive inference.
199   S.V. 1, pp. 34–5. In *Papirer* II, A 77, p. 50, Kierkegaard writes that philosophy is a mistaken attempt to elaborate a purely humanist *Weltanschauung* ('den reen [menneskelige] Verdens Anskuelse – det *humane* Standpunkt').
200   *Papirer* IV, C 105, p. 414.
201   Ludwig Wittgenstein, *Tractatus Logico-Philosophicus*, trans. D.F. Pears and B.F. McGuinness, Routledge & Kegan Paul, London, 1961, 6.432; cf. S.V. 9, pp. 205 and 206 (*Postscript*, p. 220).
202   Wittgenstein, *Tractatus*, 6.421: 'It is clear that ethics cannot be put into words.'
203   This is an unnumbered remark in the manuscript of the *Prototractatus*. In its entirety it reads: 'How everything stands is God. God is how everything stands.' *Prototractatus: An Early Version of Tractatus Logico-Philosophicus*, ed. B.F. McGuinness, T. Nyberg, and G.H. von Wright, trans. D.F. Pears and B.F. McGuinness, Routledge & Kegan Paul, London, 1971, p. 239; cf. Wittgenstein, *Notebooks 1914–1916*, ed. G.H. von Wright and G.E.M. Anscombe, trans. G.E.M. Anscombe, Blackwell, Oxford, 2nd edn, 1979, p. 79e (1.8.16).
204   Wittgenstein, *Tractatus*, 6.41.
205   Ibid., 6.521.
206   Ibid., 6.43; cf. *Notebooks*, p. 79e (2.8.16); cf. p. 78e.
207   Letter to Fricker, *Prototractatus*, p. 16. The German original is given on p. 15.
208   Wittgenstein, *Tractatus*, 1 and 6.373.
209   S.V. 10, p. 247 (*Postscript*, p. *515*).
210   Ibid., pp. 22 and 31 (*Postscript*, pp. 280 and 291).
211   Ibid., p. 22 (*Postscript*, p. 280).
212   Ibid., p. 42 (*Postscript*, p. *302*).
213   Ibid., p. 22 (*Postscript*, p. *280*).
214   Ibid., p. 42 (*Postscript*, p. *302*).

215 Ibid., p. 43 (*Postscript*, p. *304*).
216 Ibid., p. 27 (*Postscript*, p. *286*).
217 Ibid.
218 S.V. 10, p. 57 (*Postscript*, pp. *319–20*).
219 S.V. 9, pp. 208 and 209 (*Postscript*, pp. 223 and *224*).
220 S.V. 10, p 179 (*Postscript*, p. *448*); cf. p. 181 (*Postscript*, p. 450):
     'Irony is the cultivation of the spirit [*Aandens Dannelse*].' It grasps
     'the contradiction between the way in which [one] exists inwardly
     and the fact that [one] does not express it outwardly.'
221 *Papirer* IV, C 105, p. 414. Emphasis added.
222 *Papirer* II, A 140; cf. A 111, 138 ff.
223 See Niels Thulstrup's commentary in the English translation of *Frag-
     ments* by Swenson, revised by Howard V. Hong, Princeton University
     Press, Princeton, NJ, 1962, p. 148; *Papirer* II, A 335, p. 138; 'Hegel is
     a Johannes Climacus who, unlike the giants who storm heaven by
     putting mountain upon mountain, enters it with his syllogisms.'
224 S.V. 10, pp. 169–70 (*Postscript*, pp. *438–9*).

Chapter V Pathology of the self

 1 S.V. 15, p. 90 (*Sickness*, p. *165*).
 2 Cf. S.V. 6, p. 169 (*Anxiety*, p. 81).
 3 Ibid., pp. 119–20 (*Anxiety*, p. 21).
 4 Cf. S.V. 10, pp. 47–8 (*Postscript*, p. 309).
 5 S.V. 6, p. 113 (*Anxiety*, p. *14*).
 6 Ibid., p. 114, (*Anxiety*, p. 15).
 7 Ibid., p. 119 (*Anxiety*, p. 21).
 8 Ibid.
 9 Ibid., p. 120 (*Anxiety*, p. 22).
10 Ibid., p. 120 (*Anxiety*, p. 21).
11 Ibid., p. 202 (*Anxiety*, p. *118*).
12 For the notion of a 'whole person [*et Heelt Menneske*]' see S.V. 10,
     p. 48 (*Postscript*, p. 309).
13 *Papirer* III, A 5, p. 8.
14 Cf. S.V. 6, p. 150 (*Anxiety*, p. 58).
15 'Syndens Trældom'. Ibid., p. 203 (*Anxiety*, p. 118).
16 Ibid., p. 203 (*Anxiety*, p. *119*).
17 Ibid., p. 176 (*Anxiety*, p. 88).
18 Ibid., p. 162 (*Anxiety*, p. 72).
19 Cf. ibid., p. 138 (*Anxiety*, p. 44).
20 'Ethvert Menneskeliv er lagt religieust an.' Ibid., p. 191 (*Anxiety*,
     p. 105).
21 Ibid., pp. 135, 156, and 186 respectively (*Anxiety*, pp. 41, 65, and 96).
22 Ibid., p. 138; cf. p. 142 (*Anxiety*, p. 44; cf. p. 49).
23 Ibid., p. 136 (*Anxiety*, p. 42).
24 Ibid., p. 138 (*Anxiety*, p. 44).
25 Ibid., p. 153 (*Anxiety*, p. 61).

26 Ibid., p. 136; cf. p. 153 (*Anxiety*, p. 42; cf. p. 61). Emphasis removed.
27 Ibid., p. 137 (*Anxiety*, p. *43*).
28 Ibid., p. 197 (*Anxiety*, p. 112).
29 Ibid., p. 198 (*Anxiety*, p. 113).
30 Cf. ibid., pp. 202 ff. (*Anxiety*, pp. 118 ff.).
31 'En anet Forestilling.' Ibid., p. 145; cf. p. 153 ('en Complexus af Ahnelser') (*Anxiety*, p. 53; cf. p. 61).
32 Ibid., p. 138; cf. p. 200 (*Anxiety*, p. 113; cf. p. 116).
33 'ikke blot en Liden.' S.V. 15, p. 117 (*Sickness*, p. 196).
34 Ibid., p. 117 (*Sickness*, p. 195).
35 Cf. S.V. 6, p. 168 (*Anxiety*, p. 79).
36 Of his own relationship to the pseudonyms Johannes Climacus and Anti-Climacus, Kierkegaard writes that he would place himself 'higher than' the former but 'lower than' the latter. *Papirer* X, 1, A 517, p. 332.
37 Cf. S.V. 15, p. 116 (*Sickness*, p. 194).
38 'som væsentligt forskjelligt fra Omverdenen'. Ibid., p. 110 (*Sickness*, p. 188).
39 Ibid.
40 Ibid., pp. 112—13 (*Sickness*, p. 190).
41 S.V. 6, p. 197 (*Anxiety*, p. 113).
42 Cf. S.V. 3, pp. 198—9 (*Either/Or*, vol. 2, p. 217): 'That which I choose I do not posit, for in case this were not [already] posited, I could not choose it.'
43 'Psychology is what we need', says Kierkegaard, 'and above all adequate knowledge of human life, and sympathy for its interests. . . . Without [these] there can be no question of completing a Christian view of life.' *Papirer* V, B 53, 29, p. 119.
44 'den spionerende Uforfærdethed'. S.V. 6, p. 114 (*Anxiety*, p. 15). The translation here is Lowrie's.
45 Ibid.
46 Ibid., pp. 113 and 114 (*Anxiety*, pp. *14* and 15). Lowrie's translation in the latter phrase is preferred here.
47 S.V. 15, p. 76 (*Sickness*, p. 150).
48 S.V. 6, pp. 114 (*Anxiety*, pp. 14—15).
49 Ibid.
50 Ibid., p. 115 (*Anxiety*, pp. 16—17).
51 Ibid., p. 120 (*Anxiety*, p. 22).
52 Ibid., p. 118 (*Anxiety*, pp. 19—20).
53 Ibid., p. 127 (*Anxiety*, pp. 31—2).
54 G.W.F. Hegel, *Phenomenology of Spirit*, trans. A.V. Miller, Clarendon Press, Oxford, 1977, §216, p. 130.
55 Ibid., §233, p. 140.
56 L. Feuerbach, *The Essence of Christianity*, trans. George Eliot, Harper Torchbooks, Harper & Row, New York, Evanston, and London, 1957, p. 37.
57 Ibid., p. 46.
58 Ibid., p. 48.
59 Ibid., p. 47.

60 Ibid., p. xxxvii.
61 L. Feuerbach, *Das Wesen der Religion*, Alfred Körner Verlag, Leipzig, 1846, p. 170, quoted by Karl Barth in his introduction to the English edition of *Essence*, p. xi.
62 Cf. S.V. 15, p. 123 (*Sickness*, p. 202).
63 S.V. 6, p. 106 (*Anxiety*, p. 8).
64 Ibid., p. 152 (*Anxiety*, p. *61*).
65 Ibid., p. 173 (*Anxiety*, p. *85*). Emphasis added.
66 Ibid., p. 176 (*Anxiety*, p. 88).
67 Ibid., p. 218 (*Anxiety*, p. *136*).
68 Ibid., p. 177 (*Anxiety*, p. 89). Kierkegaard remarks here on the connection between the Greek conception of eternity as the past and Plato's doctrine of recollection, which, as we saw earlier, Kierkegaard finds inapplicable from the point of view of human existence.
69 Ibid. 'The instant is that ambiguity [*hiint Tvetydige*] in which time and eternity touch one another, and the concept of *temporality* is thereby posited, in which time constantly intercepts eternity and eternity constantly penetrates time. Only now does the division in question — the present, the past, the future — get its meaning.'
70 Ibid., p. 178 (*Anxiety*, p. 90).
71 Ibid., pp. 175 and 177 (*Anxiety*, pp. 87 and 89).
72 Ibid., p. 178 (*Anxiety*, p. 90).
73 Ibid., p. 176 (*Anxiety*, p. *88*).
74 Ibid.
75 Ibid., pp. 135 and 137–8 (*Anxiety*, pp. 41 and *43*).
76 Ibid., p. 156 (*Anxiety*, p. *65*).
77 Ibid., p. 136 (*Anxiety*, p. 42). Haufniensis says a little later (ibid., p. 166 (*Anxiety*, p. 77)): 'If [anxiety's] object is a something such that, viewed essentially, i.e. in regard to freedom, it means something, then we have, not the leap, but a quantitative transition which throws every concept into confusion.'
78 Ibid., p. 136 (*Anxiety*, p. *41*). The Lowrie translation transposes the subject and object terms, thus rendering the sentence unintelligible in the context.
79 Ibid., p. 136 (*Anxiety*, p. *42*).
80 Ibid., p. 153 (*Anxiety*, p. *61*). Haufniensis also says that although the 'later' individual has a ' "more" in relation to Adam, and again a "more" or a "less" in relation to others, it nevertheless holds true that the object of anxiety is a nothing' (ibid., p. 166 (*Anxiety*, p. 77)); also (ibid., pp. 145–6 (*Anxiety*, p. *53*)) that 'anxiety in the later individual is more self-conscious [*reflekteret*] as a result of its participation in the history of the race', since 'anxiety now enters the world also in another sense. [It is not just that] sin came into [the world] with anxiety, but sin again brought anxiety along with it. The reality of sin . . . has no endurance. On the one hand [its] continuity is its being possible, which causes anxiety; on the other, the possibility of a salvation is again a nothing, which the individual both loves and fears; for this is always the relation of possibility to individuality. Only in the instant when salvation is

really posited is this anxiety [i.e. in regard to salvation] overcome'. The individual is first anxious in the face of the possibility of sin *before* sin is posited, then about not gaining salvation once it *is* posited. The former anxiety is 'left behind' (not 'annihilated') with the positing (of the real possibility) of sin.

81 See ibid., p. 141 (*Anxiety*, p. 48).
82 Ibid., p. 153 (*Anxiety*, p. *61*).
83 Ibid.
84 S.V. 6., p. 132 (*Anxiety*, p. 37).
85 'Som aandløs bestement er Mennesket blevet en Talemaskine.' Ibid., p. 182 (*Anxiety*, p. 95).
86 Ibid., p. 183 (*Anxiety*, p. *96*).
87 Ibid., p. 184 (*Anxiety*, p. 96).
88 Ibid., p. 184 (*Anxiety*, p. *97*).
89 Ibid., p. 190 (*Anxiety*, p. 104).
90 Ibid., p. 190 (*Anxiety*, pp. *104–5*).
91 Ibid., p. 188 (*Anxiety*, pp. *101–2*).
92 Ibid., p. 193 (*Anxiety*, pp. 106–7).
93 Ibid., p. 193 (*Anxiety*, p. 108).
94 Ibid., p. 194 (*Anxiety*, pp. *108–9*).
95 Ibid., pp. 183 and 189 (*Anxiety*, pp. *96* and *103*).
96 Ibid., pp. 142 and 160 (*Anxiety*, pp. 49 and *69*). Emphasis added.
97 Ibid., p. 142 (*Anxiety*, p. 49). Cf. Marx's remark that history is man's act of coming into existence in *Economic and Philosophical Manuscripts, 1844*, ed. with intro. by Dirk J. Struik, International Publishers, New York, 1982, p. 145.
98 Cf. S.V. 6, p. 184 (*Anxiety*, p. 97).
99 Ibid., p. 160 (*Anxiety*, p. *69*).
100 Ibid., p. 185 (*Anxiety*, p. *97*).
101 Ibid., p. 169 (*Anxiety*, p. *80*).
102 Ibid., p. 162 (*Anxiety*, p. 72).
103 Ibid., pp. 179, 138, and 142 (*Anxiety*, pp. *82*, 40, and *44*).
104 Cf. ibid., pp. 166 and 234 (*Anxiety*, pp. 76–7 and 155).
105 Cf. ibid., p. 231 (*Anxiety*, p. 151 f.).
106 Ibid., p. 235 (*Anxiety*, p. *156*).
107 Ibid., p. 142 (*Anxiety*, p. 49).
108 Ibid., pp. 235–6 (*Anxiety*, pp. 156–7).
109 M. Heidegger, *Was ist Metaphysik?*, 6th edn, V. Klostermann, Frankfurt-aM, 1951, see pp. 9 and 25.
110 Ibid., p. 19.
111 S.V. 6, p. 237 (*Anxiety*, p. 158).
112 See M. Heidegger, *Sein und Zeit*, 8th edn, Max Niemeyer, Tübingen, 1957, pp. 188 and 187.
113 S.V. 6, p. 237 (*Anxiety*, p. *159*).
114 Heidegger, *Sein und Zeit*, p. 266.
115 S.V. 6, p. 237 (*Anxiety*, p. *159*).
116 Ibid., p. 234 (*Anxiety*, p. *155*).
117 Ibid., p. 153 (*Anxiety*, p. *61*). Emphasis added.

118 Ibid., p. 196 (*Anxiety*, p. *111*). Emphasis added.
119 Ibid., pp. 197–8 (*Anxiety*, pp. *113–14*).
120 Ibid., p. 202 (*Anxiety*, p. 118).
121 Ibid., pp. 201–2 (*Anxiety*, pp. 117–18).
122 Ibid., p. 205 (*Anxiety*, p. 109).
123 Ibid., pp. 231–3 (*Anxiety*, pp. 151–4).
124 Ibid., p. 228 (*Anxiety*, pp. 146–7).
125 Ibid., p. 168 (*Anxiety*, p. 79).
126 S.V. 15, p. 73 (*Sickness*, p. *146*).
127 Ibid.
128 Ibid. Emphasis added.
129 Ibid., p. 73 (*Sickness*, p. *147*). In Hegel equilibrium and peace reside in the notion of self-sufficiency. From Hegel's standpoint the notions of a transcendent infinity and self-sufficient individuality represent correlative extremes of a false opposition. False in view of the individual's possibility of conceiving its oneness with the unchangeable, and thus appropriating to *itself* the infinite value it had previously been forced to conceive as an 'unattainable beyond'. Rediscovering itself as the source of its own essence is part of spirit's confirmation of itself as freedom. In his lectures on the *Philosophy of History* Hegel writes: 'It is a result of speculative philosophy that freedom is the sole truth of spirit. . . . Spirit may be defined as that which has its centre in itself. [Unlike matter it] has not a unity outside itself, but has already found it; it exists in and with itself. Matter has its essence out of itself. Spirit is self-contained existence. Now this is freedom exactly. For if I am dependent, my being is referred to something else which I am not; I cannot exist independently of something external. I am free, on the contrary, when my existence depends on myself. This self-contained existence of spirit is nothing other than self-consciousness — consciousness of one's own being' (*The Philosophy of History*, trans. J. Sibree, rev. edn, Willey Book Co. New York, 1944, pp. 17–18). For Kierkegaard the individual cannot be spirit in this sense, for from the finite point of view to which the individual is inescapably bound the infinite from which the notion of its essence stems is necessarily transcendent. Nevertheless, as will be more apparent in the next chapter, the idea of a psychologically self-contained existence does apply to Kierkegaard's concept of the self. And towards the end of *Repetition*, Constantius says that 'a religious individual . . . rests in itself and disdains all childish tricks' (S.V. 5, p. 193).
130 S.V. 15, pp. 121 ff. (*Sickness*, pp. 200 ff.).
131 Ibid., p. 122 (*Sickness*, p. 202).
132 Ibid., pp. 98–9 (*Sickness*, p. *175*).
133 Ibid., p. 75 (*Sickness*, p. *148*).
134 S.V. 10, p. 110 (*Postscript*, p. *376*), original emphasis; cf. S.V. 15, p. 88 (*Sickness*, p. 163).
135 S.V. 15, p. 75 (*Sickness*, pp. *148–9*).
136 Ibid., p. 74 (*Sickness*, p. *147*).
137 Ibid., p. 105 (*Sickness*, p. 182).

138 Cf. ibid., p. 106 (*Sickness*, p. 184).
139 Ibid., p. 116 (*Sickness*, p. 194), and *passim*.
140 Ibid., p. 107 (*Sickness*, p. 184).
141 Ibid., p. 108 (*Sickness*, p. 185).
142 Ibid., pp. 107–8 (*Sickness*, p. 185).
143 Ibid., p. 109 (*Sickness*, p. 186).
144 Ibid., p. 110 (*Sickness*, p. 187).
145 Ibid., p. 110 (*Sickness*, p. *188*).
146 Ibid., pp. 110–11 (*Sickness*, pp. 188–9).
147 Ibid., p. 111 (*Sickness*, p. 188).
148 Ibid.
149 S.V. 15, p. 111 (*Sickness*, p. 189).
150 Ibid., p. 112 (*Sickness*, p. 190).
151 Ibid.
152 Ibid., p. 115 (*Sickness*, p. 193).
153 Ibid., p. 113 (*Sickness*, p. 190).
154 Ibid., pp. 113–14 (*Sickness*, pp. 191–2).
155 Ibid., p. 115 (*Sickness*, p. *193*).
156 Ibid., p. 115 (*Sickness*, p. *194*).
157 Ibid., p. 116 (*Sickness*, p. *194*).
158 Ibid., pp. 116–17 (*Sickness*, p. 195).
159 Ibid.
160 Ibid., p. 118 (*Sickness*, p. 196).
161 Ibid.
162 Ibid., p. 117 (*Sickness*, p. *196*).
163 Ibid., p. 118 (*Sickness*, pp. 196–7).
164 Ibid., p. 120 (*Sickness*, pp. 198–9).
165 Ibid., p. 121 (*Sickness*, p. *200*).
166 Ibid., p. 120 (*Sickness*, p. 199).
167 Ibid., p. 121 (*Sickness*, p. 199).
168 Ibid., p. 122 (*Sickness*, p. 202); cf. note 131 above.
169 S.V. 15, p. 74 (*Sickness*, pp. 147–8).
170 S.V. 1, p. 118.
171 S.V. 6, p. 236 (*Anxiety*, p. 157).

Chapter VI   Purity of heart

1 S.V. 11, p. 35 (*Purity of Heart*, p. *61*). The Danish for 'despair', *Fortvivlelse*, contains in *tvi* the notion of 'two' (e.g. -mindedness), as also does *Tvivl*, the Danish for 'doubt'. Cf. Josiah Thompson, *Kierkegaard*, Alfred A. Knopf, New York, 1973, pp. 154–5.
2 Cf. S.V. 5, pp. 88–9 (*Fear and Trembling*, p. 107). In a footnote we read: 'Aesthetics sometimes treats something similar with its customary coquetry. The merman is saved by Agnete, and the whole thing ends in a happy marriage. A happy marriage! How convenient! If ethics, on the other hand, were to deliver the speech at the wedding ceremony I imagine it would be a quite different thing. Aesthetics casts the cloak

of love over the merman, and so everything is forgotten. It is also care-
less enough to suppose that at a wedding it all goes as at an auction,
where everything is sold in the condition that it is in when the hammer
falls. All it cares for is that the lovers get one another, it doesn't trouble
about the rest. If only it saw what happened afterwards . . .'

3 In his retrospective 'glance' at his own 'producer's' production, Climacus
observes that Kierkegaard had noted in his prefaces to his 'edifying
discourses' that they were not intended as 'sermons'. The reason offered
by Climacus is that their ethical universe was still that of 'immanence',
while a religious sermon proper would have to employ the 'doubly
reflected religious categories in the paradox' (S.V. 9, p. 214 (*Postscript*,
p. 229)). Two comments: first, presumably the later 'Christian discourses' employ the latter categories, but it seems clear that, due to the
need for 'double reflection' and the consequent indirectness of the
communication, as well as (or in connection with this) the inappropriate-
ness of presenting oneself as an 'authority' (see Chapter VIII below),
Kierkegaard would not want to call these discourses sermons either;
second, the earlier 'edifying' discourses may be seen as linked essentially
with the project, noted at the beginning of Chapter III, of leading the
reader 'back' from the aesthetic to a true conception of Christianity,
this being the specific task of the aesthetic (pseudonymous) production.
Perhaps the difference between the pseudonymous and the non-
pseudonymous works in respect of this task can be pinpointed in the
absence of any 'cheating' in the latter (see Chapter III above).

4 See note 3 above.

5 Cf. *Papirer* VIII, 1, A 6, pp. 6–7.

6 S.V. 15, p. 133; cf. p. 164 (*Sickness*, p. 210; cf. p. 245).

7 Ibid., p. 133 (*Sickness*, p. 210).

8 Ibid., p. 164 (*Sickness*, p. 245).

9 S.V. 9, pp. 18–19; cf. S.V. 10, p. 278 (*Postscript*, p. 19; cf. p. 545).

10 There is an ambiguity in the notion of a highest good, both in Aristotle,
from whom it stems, and subsequently. In some contexts it refers to
the highest good in a hierarchy: the good better than which there is
none. In others it refers to the only intrinsic good: something in respect
of which alone anything else can be called a good. In Kierkegaard we
find instances where the highest good is spoken of as the most worthwhile goal, i.e. the best in a hierarchy, and instances where it is treated
as the notion of an intrinsic good, implying the correlative notion of an
extrinsic good, in particular virtue as (misleadingly, claims Kierkegaard)
contrasted with the reward for virtue, i.e. the highest good.

11 S.V. 9, p. 20 (*Postscript*, p. 20).

12 I. Kant, *Critique of Practical Reason*, in T.K. Abbott's translation,
*Kant's Critique of Practical Reason and Other Works on the Theory of
Ethics*, Longmans, Green, London, New York, and Toronto, 6th edn,
1954, p. 207.

13 Cf. ibid., p. 212.

14 Ibid., p. 211.

15 S.V. 9, p. 19 (*Postscript*, p. 19).

16 Ibid., pp. 44—5 (*Postscript*, p. *46*).
17 Ibid., p. 51 (*Postscript*, pp. *53—4*).
18 Ibid., pp. 107—8 (*Postscript*, p. *116*).
19 S.V. 10, p. 116 (*Postscript*, p. *382*).
20 See, for example, ibid., p. 229 fn. (*Postscript*, p. 497 fn.).
21 S.V. 11, p. 13 (*Purity of Heart*, p. 27).
22 St James's Epistle iv. 8. See S.V. 11, p. 30 (*Purity of Heart*, p. 53).
23 See S.V. 11, p. 139 (*Purity of Heart*, p. *217*).
24 Ibid., p. 41 (*Purity of Heart*, p. 69).
25 Ibid., p. 43 (*Purity of Heart*, p. 72).
26 Ibid., p. 43 (*Purity of Heart*, pp. 72—3).
27 Ibid., p. 41; cf. p. 44 (*Purity of Heart*, p. 69; cf. p. 75).
28 Ibid., p. 44 (*Purity of Heart*, p. 74).
29 Ibid., pp. 116—17 (*Purity of Heart*, p. 183). Emphasis added.
30 Ecclesiastes iii. 11. See S.V. 11, p. 18 (*Purity of Heart*, p. 36). The passage in the Danish bible translates into 'hath set eternity [*Evigheden*] in their heart', while the Authorized Version has 'hath set the world in their heart'. Kierkegaard has not taken liberties with the text, as the translator of *Purity of Heart* supposes (see ibid., p. 219).
31 Cf., for example, S.V. 11, p. 44 (*Purity of Heart*, p. 74).
32 E.g. ibid., p. 42 (*Purity of Heart*, p. 72).
33 S.V. 9, p. 114 (*Postscript*, p. *123*).
34 S.V. 11, p. 44 (*Purity of Heart*, p. 74).
35 Quoted by M. O'C. Drury in *Acta Philosophica Fennica*, vol. 28, nos 1—3 (1976), (*Essays on Wittgenstein in Honour of G.H. von Wright*), North-Holland Publishing, Amsterdam, 1976, p. 397.
36 See S.V. 11, p. 41 (*Purity of Heart*, p. 70).
37 Ibid.
38 Ibid., p. 42 (*Purity of Heart*, p. 72).
39 Kant, op. cit., p. 179. Original emphasis.
40 S.V. 11, p. 60 (*Purity of Heart*, p. 99).
41 Ibid., pp. 60—1 (*Purity of Heart*, pp. *99—100*).
42 Ibid.
43 Ibid., p. 62 (*Purity of Heart*, pp. 101—2).
44 Ibid., p. 63 (*Purity of Heart*, p. 103).
45 Ibid., p. 63 (*Purity of Heart*, p. 104).
46 Ibid., p. 76 (*Purity of Heart*, p. 122).
47 Cf. ibid., p. 69 (*Purity of Heart*, p. 112).
48 Ibid., pp. 63—4 (*Purity of Heart*, p. *104*). Original emphasis.
49 Ibid., p. 66 (*Purity of Heart*, p. *108*). Original emphasis.
50 Ibid., p. 69 (*Purity of Heart*, pp. 111—12).
51 I. Kant, *Fundamental Principles of the Metaphysic of Morals*, in *Kant's Critique of Practical Reason and Other Works on the Theory of Ethics*, p.10.
52 Ibid., p. 59.
53 Ibid., p. 59.
54 Ibid., p. 63. Original emphasis.
55 Ibid., p. 61. Original emphasis.

56 Ibid., p. 63. Original emphasis.
57 Ibid., p. 60. Original emphasis.
58 Ibid., p. 59.
59 Ibid., p. 20.
60 Ibid., p. 4.
61 Ibid., p. 22.
62 S.V. 15, p. 91 (*Sickness*, p. 166).
63 See ibid., p. 87 (*Sickness*, p. 162), where Anti-Climacus correlates an increase of consciousness *both* with an increase of selfhood *and* with an increase of will.
64 S.V. 11, p. 113 (*Purity of Heart*, p. 178).
65 S.V. 10, p. 116 (*Postscript*, pp. 382–3).
66 S.V. 11, p. 113 (*Purity of Heart*, p. 178).
67 S.V. 10, p. 233 (*Postscript*, p. 501).
68 Ibid., p. 225 (*Postscript*, p. 494).
69 Ibid., pp. 237 and 225 (*Postscript*, pp. 505 and 494).
70 Ibid., p. 239 (*Postscript*, p. 507).
71 Ibid., pp. 229–30; cf. p. 238 (*Postscript*, p. 498; cf. p. 506).
72 Kant, *Critique of Practical Reason*, p. 214.
73 Ibid., p. 132. Original emphasis removed.
74 Kant, *Fundamental Principles of the Metaphysic of Morals*, p. 83.
75 Ibid., p. 60.
76 S.V. 10, p. 48 (*Postscript*, p. 309).
77 Ibid., p. 48 (*Postscript*, p. 309). Emphasis added.
78 S.V. 11, p. 34 (*Purity of Heart*, p. 59). Original emphasis.
79 Ibid., p. 34 (*Purity of Heart*, p. 60).
80 For an interesting parallel in Kant, see the latter's claim in the *Critique of Practical Reason* (p. 214) that 'the inclinations change [and] grow with the indulgence shown them, and always leave behind a still greater void than we had thought to fill'.
81 Cf. Jon Elster, *Logic and Society: Contradictions and Possible Worlds*, John Wiley & Sons, Chichester, New York, Brisbane, and Toronto, 1978, pp. 96 ff. Elster discusses two main types of 'social contradiction', one in which 'unintended consequences . . . stem from uncoordinated actions' ('counterfinality'), and another, related to the game-theoretical situation known as the Prisoner's Dilemma, and which he calls 'sub-optimality'.
82 S.V. 10, p. 51 (*Postscript*, p. 312).
83 See *Papirer* IV, B 117 (on *Repetition*) in connection with evolving concepts of 'freedom', especially p. 281. The notion of *conceptual* development (or development in the individual's grasp of some central category or concept) is abundantly illustrated in the first part of *Either/Or*. The development is portrayed as beginning in a diffuse conception and ending in a clear concept, consciously wielded and acted upon. An example is the concept of desire. In a passage concerned with the 'immediate stages of the erotic', Kierkegaard illustrates three stages by means of figures from characters in Mozart's operas. A dreaming stage of desire, desire which is not yet desire, is personified in the Page

in *Figaro*; desire as a yearning without specified object in Papageno in *The Magic Flute*; and full-blooded, explicit desire in the figure of Don Giovanni, an exponent of the consciously aesthetic life (S.V. 2, pp. 47 ff. (*Either/Or*, vol. 1, pp. 46 ff.)).

84 In *Either/Or*, vol. 1, in the section on 'the unhappiest man', the latter is described in these words: 'Left to himself he stands in the wide world. He has no contemporary time he can unite himself with, no past he can yearn back to, since his past is yet to come, no future to hope for, since his future is already past. Alone he has the whole world opposite him as the "thou" with which he is in conflict; for the entire rest of the world is only one person to him, and this person, this inseparable importunate friend, is a misunderstanding. He cannot become old, for he has never been young; he cannot become young, for he has already become old; in a way he cannot die, for he has not lived; in a way he cannot live, for he is already dead; he cannot love, since love is always in the present, and he has no present time, no future, no past . . . he has no passion, not because he lacks it, but because at the same instant he has the opposite [passion]. He has no time for anything, not because his time is occupied with something else, but because he simply has no time at all . . .' (S.V. 2, pp. 207—8 (*Either/Or*, vol. 2, p. 224)).

85 See Ch. V, note 43, above.

86 Bernard Williams, 'A Critique of Utilitarianism', in J.J.C. Smart and Bernard Williams, *Utilitarianism. For and Against*, Cambridge University Press, Cambridge, 1973, pp. 116—17.

87 See ibid., p. 116.

Chapter VII   Love of one's neighbour

1 S.V. 11, pp. 131—2.

2 Deuteronomy vi. 5.

3 Matthew xxii. 37; cf. Luke x. 25 and 27.

4 I. Kant, *Critique of Practical Reason*, in T.K. Abbott's translation, *Kant's Critique of Practical Reason and Other Works on the Theory of Ethics*, Longmans, Green, London, New York, and Toronto, 6th edn, 1954, p. 176.

5 S.V. 12 (*Works of Love*), p. 29.

6 Ibid., p. 357.

7 See *Papirer* VIII, 1, A 293, p. 139, on the difference between a 'deliberation' and an 'edifying discourse'.

8 See the Preface to S.V. 12, p. 9.

9 Ibid., p. 56. Emphasis removed.

10 Ibid., p. 58.

11 Cf. ibid., pp. 25 and 27.

12 Ibid., p. 26.

13 Cf. I. Kant, *Fundamental Principles of the Metaphysic of Morals*, in *Kant's Critique of Practical Reason and Other Works on the Theory of Ethics*, p. 47.

14 William Shakespeare, Sonnet CXVI.
15 S.V. 12, p. 162. Emphasis removed.
16 Ibid., p. 26.
17 Ibid.
18 As, for example, 'I'll give you all the pretty things you think you need
———— as long as I can keep this cornet up to my mouth'. *Louis Armstrong and His Hot Five*, Fontana TFR 6003, Joker SM 3742, etc.
19 See S.V. 11, p. 62 (*Purity of Heart*, pp. 101–2).
20 Kant, *Fundamental Principles*, pp. 15–16.
21 Ibid., p. 60.
22 I. Kant, *Metaphysical Elements of Ethics*, in *Kant's Critique of Practical Reason and Other Works on the Theory of Ethics*, p. 312.
23 Matthew xxii. 39; cf. S.V. 12, p. 23.
24 Kant, *Critique of Practical Reason*, p. 176.
25 Ibid.
26 Kant, *Metaphysical Elements of Ethics*, p. 313.
27 Kant, *Critique of Practical Reason*, p. 176.
28 Kant, *Fundamental Principles*, pp. 16–17.
29 Kant, *Critique of Practical Reason*, p. 175. Original emphasis.
30 Ibid., p. 176. Emphasis added.
31 S.V. 12, pp. 274–5.
32 Ibid., p. 276; cf. S.V. 14, p. 72 (*Two Ages*, p. 78).
33 S.V. 12, p. 275.
34 Ibid., p. 281.
35 Ibid., pp. 277 ff.
36 S.V. 11, pp. 131–2.
37 Kant, *Fundamental Principles*, p. 15.
38 G.W.F. Hegel, 'The Spirit of Christianity', in *Early Theological Writings*, trans. T.M. Knox and Richard Kroner, Chicago University Press, Chicago, 1948, p. 212.
39 Ibid., p. 218.
40 S.V. 3, p. 246 (*Either/Or*, vol. 2, p. 270). Emphasis added.
41 S.V. 5, p. 72 fn. (*Fear and Trembling*, p. 88 fn.).
42 I John iv. 12. Emphasis added.
43 S.V. 12, p. 357.
44 Cf. ibid., p. 156.
45 Ibid., p. 357.
46 S.V. 9, p. 106 (*Postscript*, p. 113).
47 Kant, *Fundamental Principles*, p. 49. Emphasis added.
48 S.V. 12, pp. 262–3.
49 Ibid., pp. 260–1.
50 Cf. ibid., pp. 259–60.
51 Just as Kant's principle that rational beings be regarded as ends in themselves delimits the scope of free action, so Kierkegaard's principle of neighbour-love may be said to delimit the area in which human growth (and natural growth in general, see ibid., p. 259) may not be interfered with.
52 Cf. S.V. 12, pp. 24–5 and 56.

53 Ibid., p. 25.
54 Ibid., p. 61.
55 See S.V. 6, p. 169 (*Anxiety*, p. *80*).
56 See S.V. 10, p. 50 (*Postscript*, p. 311).
57 S.V. 3, p. 296 (*Either/Or*, vol. 2, p. 327).
58 S.V. 6, p. 161 (*Anxiety*, p. 63).
59 S.V. 12, p. 27.
60 Ibid., p. 60.
61 *Papirer* III, A 73, p. 36.
62 S.V. 12, p. 112; cf. *Papirer* IV, A 104, p. 40.
63 S.V. 12, pp. 36 and 112.
64 Ibid., p. 30; cf. ibid., p. 110, where the life of Christ is described as 'a fearful confrontation with the purely human idea of what love amounts to'.
65 Ibid., p. 106. Emphasis removed.
66 Cf. a remark in *Fear and Trembling*: 'Duty becomes duty by being referred to God, but in the duty itself I do not come into relation with God. Thus it is a duty to love one's neighbour. As such it is referred to God, but in the duty I enter into a relation, not with God, but with the neighbour that I love. If I say in this connection that it is my duty to love God, I really only utter a tautology, in so far as "God" here is taken in the altogether abstract sense of "the divine", i.e. the universal, i.e. duty' (S.V. 5, p. 63 (*Fear and Trembling*, p. 78)).
67 Cf. a remark in *Papirer* (IV, C 82, pp. 403—4, from 1842—3): 'The reason why man becomes blessed through belief and not through deed, or rather in faith . . . is that even if man himself effected the good, he cannot know that, since to do so he would have to be omniscient. Thus no one can dispute with Our Lord. Even the most exalted, the humanly speaking most noble of deeds I dare not call a good deed, for I must constantly say: "After all, God alone knows if it was so." So it is impossible to base my happiness on it.'
68 Cf. S.V. 3, p. 316 (*Either/Or*, vol. 2, p. 347), on assuming one knows that one has done what one can.
69 S.V. 12, p. 107. Emphasis removed.
70 Ibid., p. 62.
71 Cf. S.V. 6, p. 60 (*Fragments*, p. 78): 'God cannot be conceived', or, more exactly, 'cannot be imagined, or represented'. Earlier, however, we read (ibid., p. 41 (*Fragments*, p. *51*)) that 'God is a concept [*Begreb*], not a name'. The sense in which Kierkegaard allows that there is a concept of God is one in which we are able to say, as he points out it has been suggested in the case of the idea of God's existence (the ontological proof of God's existence), that the idea of God's deeds cannot be separated from the idea, or perhaps one should rather say notion, of God — as the deeds of Napoleon *can* be identified independently of our knowledge of the fact that Napoleon performed them. In this sense we have a conception of the logical anatomy of the notion of God, but not such as to enable us to have an idea, in the sense of a representation (*Forestilling*), of God which would make God a possible intruder in an act of neighbour-love.

72 S.V. 12, p. 28.
73 Ibid., p. 106.
74 Ibid., p. 36. Original emphasis.
75 Ibid., p. 34. Emphasis removed.
76 Ibid., pp. 37 and 39.
77 Ibid., pp. 42 f.
78 Ibid., pp. 34 and 44 f.
79 Ibid., pp. 35 and 36.
80 Ibid., p. 37.
81 S.V. 7 (*Stages on Life's Way*), pp. 93 ff. See R.F. Holland, 'Morality and the Two World Concept', in his *Against Empiricism: On Education, Epistemology and Value*, Blackwell, Oxford, 1980, pp. 76–8.
82 S.V. 12, p. 36. Original emphasis.
83 Ibid., p. 37.
84 S.V. 11, p. 34 (*Purity of Heart*, p. 59).

Chapter VIII   Equality and association

1 *Papirer* VII, 1, B 135, p. 338. This passage was deleted from the final draft of *En literair Anmeldelse* (*Two Ages*).
2 S.V. 18 ('Appendix. "The Individual". Two "Notes" Concerning My Activity as an Author'), p. 149; cf. *Papirer* IX, B 24, p. 326.
3 S.V. 18, p. 150; cf. S.V. 9, p. 120 (*Postscript*, p. 129).
4 S.V. 18, pp. 149–50; cf. *Papirer* IX, B 10, pp. 309 and 310–11; cf. notes in *Papirer* X, 5, B 167, p. 360, and *Papirer* IX, B 21, p. 318.
5 S.V. 18, p. 149.
6 Herbert Spiegelberg, 'Equality in Existentialism', in *Nomos*, vol. IX, Atherton Press, New York, 1967, p. 194.
7 See Gregor Malantschuk, *Den kontroversielle Kierkegaard*, Stjerne-bøgernes Kulturbibliotek, Vinten, 1976, p. 20. 'It is interesting that *Works of Love* came out in the very autumn that Marx and Engels took on the task of preparing the Communist Manifesto, which was published the following year. *Works of Love* thus stands as a programme for a life-view diametrically opposed to that expressed in the Communist Manifesto.' My translation.
8 *Papirer* VIII, 1, A 299, p. 141.
9 S.V. 12, p. 312.
10 *Papirer* VIII, 1, A 4, p. 6.
11 Ibid.
12 S.V. 12, pp. 64 and 62.
13 See S.V. 14, p. 80 (*Two Ages* (henceforth cited as *TA*), p. 87): 'The outstanding person in the direction of eminence and the dialectic of Fate'. Kierkegaard also says: 'In modern times levelling is reflection's equivalent to Fate in antiquity' (ibid., p. 78 (*TA*, p. 84)). I interpret this enigmatic remark as saying that the idea of authority on which levelling is based places authority outside the individual, as did the old idea of authority as Fate. The case for this interpretation should emerge below.

371

14 S.V. 14, p. 97 (*TA*, p. 107).
15 Ibid.
16 Ibid., p. 78 (*TA*, p. *84*).
17 Ibid. Cf. S.V. 2, pp. 83 ff. (*Either/Or*, vol. 1, pp. 86 ff. where Kierkegaard relates the figure of Don Juan to the Christian era, and so to the Middle Ages, which are 'on the whole the idea of representation, part consciously, part unconsciously; the whole is represented in the single individual, but in such a way that only one side is given as being the whole and now comes to view in a single individual who is therefore both more and less than an individual').
18 See S.V. 14, p. 80 (*TA*, p. 87).
19 Ibid., p. 97 (*TA*, p. 107).
20 Ibid., pp. 98–9 (*TA*, p. *108*).
21 Ibid., p. 78 (*TA*, p. *84*).
22 Ibid., p. 97 (*TA*, p. 107); cf. *Papirer* VII, 1, B 199, p. 382: 'at finde Ligeligheden i det Almene, i hvad der er Felles for ethvert Menneske som Menneske', and B 200–4, pp. 383–5.
23 *Papirer* X, 4, A 558, pp. 377–8. In this entry Kierkegaard tries to explain why *he* had made himself recognizable by assuming responsibility for the 'aesthetic foreground' of his authorship.
24 See S.V. 14, p. 81 (*TA*, p. 89).
25 *Papirer* VII, 1, B 135, p. 338.
26 S.V. 14, p. 81 (*TA*, p. 89) (emphasis added): 'fordi det udtrykker Ligheden for Gud og Ligheden med Alle . . .'.
27 Ibid., p. 78 (*TA*, p. 84).
28 See ibid., pp. 78–9 (*TA*, p. *85*); cf. *Papirer* VIII, 1, A 77, pp. 37–8 for further examples, also of Kierkegaardian irony: 'Never enter alone into discussion with God, in case you venture too far; make sure your God-relationship is just like others', so someone can help you when God leaves you in the lurch'; and *Papirer* IX, B 24, pp. 325–6.
29 S.V. 14, p. 78 (*TA*, p. 85).
30 See G.W.F. Hegel, *Philosophy of Right*, trans. T.M. Knox, Oxford University Press, Oxford, 1942, pp. 392 f.
31 S.V. 14, p. 79 (*TA*, p. 86).
32 Ibid., pp. 78–9 (*TA*, p. *85*).
33 Ibid., p. 78 (*TA*, pp. 84–5).
34 See S.V. 10, pp. 55–6 (*Postscript*, p. 317); cf. ibid., p. 57 (*Postscript*, pp. *318–19*): 'the peculiarity of our age is that the fools are not even content to confuse themselves with some great man, but identify themselves with the age, with the century, with the contemporary generation, with mankind'; cf. also ibid., p. 223 (*Postscript*, p. 492): 'to thrust oneself under the category of the species is evasion'.
35 S.V. 14, p. 82 (*TA*, p. *89*). Emphasis added.
36 Ibid., p. 78 (*TA*, p. 84).
37 *Papirer* VII, 1, B 135, p. 338; cf. S.V. 9, p. 73 (*Postscript*, p. 78).
38 S.V. 14, p. 72 (*TA*, p. *78*).
39 Ibid., pp. 97–9 (*TA*, pp. 107–9).
40 Ibid., p. 84 (*TA*, p. 92).

41 *Papirer* VII, 1, B 135, p. 338.
42 S.V. 14, p. 80 (*TA*, p. 87).
43 Ibid., p. 83 (*TA*, p. 90).
44 Ibid., p. 85 (*TA*, p. 93).
45 *Papirer* VII, 1, B 123, p. 325.
46 See S.V. 14, pp. 83 and 84 (*TA*, pp. 90 and 92); cf. ibid., pp. 58—9 (*TA*, pp. 62 f.).
47 Ibid., p. 84 (*TA*, p. 92).
48 See *Papirer* VII, 1, B 123, p. 326.
49 S.V. 14, p. 84 (*TA*, p. *92*). The principle of association's link with scepticism is to be found in the failure of Hegel's philosophy to allow the passionate, personal problem of truth even to arise. See S.V. 9, pp. 32—3 fn. (*Postscript*, p. 34 fn.).
50 S.V. 14, p. 98 (*TA*, pp. *107—8*).
51 Ibid., p. 81 (*TA*, p. *88*); cf *Papirer* VII, 1, B 122, p. 325.
52 S.V. 14, p. 97 (*TA*, p. *107*): 'medens Abstraktionens uendelige Ligelighed dømmer hvert individ, examinerer det i dets Isolation'; cf. *Papirer* VII, 1, B 125, p. 329.
53 S.V. 1, pp. 130, 154, and 328. Emphases removed.
54 S.V. 14, p. 99 (*TA*, p. *109*).
55 Ibid., p. 80 (*TA*, p. *87*).
56 Ibid., p. 96 (*TA*, p. 106). The Hongs translate 'Menighedens Idee' as 'the idea of association', but 'Menighed' should be distinguished from 'Selskab' or 'association' in the way that the German 'Gemeinschaft' is distinguished, as it notably was by Ferdinand Tönnies, from 'Gesellschaft', and as we distinguish in English between 'community' and 'society'.
57 Ibid., p. 81 (*TA*, p. 88—9).
58 Hegel, op. cit., §5, p. 227. See Z.A. Pelczynski (ed.), *Hegel's Political Philosophy: Problems and Perspectives*, Cambridge University Press, Cambridge, 1971, for relevant discussions, especially J.-F. Suter, 'Burke, Hegel, and the French Revolution'.
59 S.V. 18, p. 150.
60 See note 4, above.
61 Hegel, op. cit., §301.
62 S.V. 14, pp. 72—4 (*TA*, pp. *78—80*); cf. *Papirer* VII, 1, B 118, pp. 322—3.
63 S.V. 14, p. 90 (*TA*, pp. *98—9*).
64 Ibid., p. 91 (*TA*, p. 100).
65 Ibid., p. 71 (*TA*, p. 77).
66 *Papirer* VII, 1, B 126, p. 330.
67 Ibid., B 123, p. 325.
68 *Papirer* VIII, 2, B 31, 20, p. 86. Here Hegel would not agree.
69 Ibid.
70 See note 3, above; cf. *Papirer* IX, B 19, and B 20, pp. 316—17.
71 *Papirer* IX, B 10, p. 311, and B 20, p. 317, and A 4, p. 6; cf. ibid., B 24, p. 324, and S.V. 15 (*Two Minor Ethico-religious Treatises*), p. 46. Unlike Dr Stockman, Ibsen's 'enemy of the people', Kierkegaard does not claim that the minority is always right, only that in the prevailing circumstances those who have the truth will be in the minority.

72 *Papirer* IX, B 22, pp. 319–20; cf. ibid., B 10, pp. 308 ff.

73 *Papirer* VII, 1, B 135, p. 338; cf. *Papirer* IX, B 10, p. 311, for Kierke-gaard's ironical comment on attempts to make 'a round-shouldered watchman and a bow-legged journeyman smith into the equal human being'.

74 Leviticus xxiv. 22; see Emanuel Rackman, 'Judaism and Equality', in *Nomos*, vol. IX. The author makes the interesting observation that despite its notion of equal dealing, biblical Hebrew has no word for 'equality'. See ibid., p. 154.

75 I. Kant, *Fundamental Principles of the Metaphysic of Morals*, in Kant's *Critique of Practical Reason and Other Works on the Theory of Ethics*, Longmans, Green, London, New York, and Toronto, 6th edn, 1954, p. 51.

76 *Papirer* VIII, 2, B 31, 20, p. 86.

77 Ibid., B 71, 9, p. 125; cf. ibid., B 71, 10, p. 125; cf. S.V. 12, pp. 64 and 62.

78 *Papirer* IX, A 91, p. 48.

79 John Rawls, *A Theory of Justice*, Harvard University Press, Cambridge, Mass., 1971, pp. 3–4.

80 *Papirer* IX, B 22, p. 320.

81 S.V. 14, p. 96, (*TA*, p. 106).

82 Ibid., pp. 96–7 (*TA*, p. *106*).

83 See ibid., pp. 88–95 (*TA*, pp. 96–104) where Kierkegaard sees in 'chatter', 'formlessness', 'superficiality', 'philandering', and 'loquacity' a 'nullifying' of the distinction between subjectivity and objectivity, internal and external.

84 G.W.F. Hegel, *Sämlicht Werke* (20 vols), ed. G. Lasson, Felix Meiner, Leipzig, 1923–30, VII, p. 368.

85 S.V. 10, p. 215 (*Postscript*, p. *484*). Kierkegaard uses a selection of the same terms ('Socialitetens, Menighedens Idee') in *A Literary Review* (S.V. 14, p. 96 (*TA*, p. 106)). The Swenson-Lowrie translation of *Postscript* omits the crucial word 'idea' in the sentence about the infiltration of the idea of the state, etc. It also renders 'Menighed' as 'congregation', but Kierkegaard does not intend the religious connotation here.

86 S.V. 18, p. 161.

Chapter IX   The 'abstract' individual

1 S.V. 18 (' "The Individual": Two "Notes" Concerning My Activity as an Author'), p. 162.

2 Herbert Marcuse, *Reason and Revolution: Hegel and the Rise of Social Theory*, Beacon Press, Boston, 1941, 1960 edn, p. 264.

3 Ibid., p. 263.

4 Ibid.

5 Ibid., p. 262.

6 *Writings of the Young Marx on Philosophy and Society*, ed. Loyd D. Easton and Kurt H. Guddat, Anchor Books, Doubleday, New York, 1967, p. 272, original emphasis; cf. p. 281.

7   Karl Marx and Friedrich Engels, *The German Ideology* (1845—6), International Publishers, New York, 1963, p. 75.
8   *Writings of the Young Marx*, p. 272.
9   Ibid., p. 307.
10 Ibid., pp. 400—2. The title is usually translated 'Theses on Feuerbach'.
11 Friedrich Engels, 'Ludwig Feuerbach and the End of Classical German Philosophy' (1886), in *Marx-Engels Selected Works*, vol. II, Progress Publishers, Moscow, 1958, p. 609; Marx and Engels, op. cit., p. 31; see also Karl Marx, *Grundrisse: Foundations of the Critique of Political Economy* (1857—8), Penguin Books, Harmondsworth, 1974, pp. 83 ff.
12 See note 10, above.
13 Marx and Engels, *Grundrisse*, p. 494.
14 The remark is attributed to Samuel Beckett by Peter Mew in 'The Liberal University', *Inquiry*, vol. 21 (1978), p. 245. I do not have the original reference.
15 Ludwig Feuerbach, *The Essence of Christianity*, trans. George Eliot, Harper Torchbooks, Harper & Row, New York, Evanston, and London, 1957, pp. 1 ff.
16 G.W.F. Hegel, *Phenomenology of Spirit*, trans. A.V. Miller, Clarendon Press, Oxford, 1977, §199, p. 121.
17 S.V. 10, p. 56 (*Postscript*, p. *318*).
18 Ibid., p. 48 (*Postscript*, p. 309).
19 Cf. ibid., p. 97 (*Postscript*, p. 364).
20 Ibid., p. 60 (*Postscript*, p. *323*).
21 See Ch. II, Note 115, above.
22 Karl Marx, *Capital* (1867 etc.), vol. I, Progress Publishers, Moscow, 1961, Ch. 10, Sec. 3, etc.
23 Cf. G.W.F. Hegel, *The Philosophy of Mind*, trans. W. Wallace and A.V. Miller, Clarendon Press, Oxford, 1971.
24 See *Writings of the Young Marx*, p. 250.
25 See S.V. II, pp. 131—2.
26 Ibid.
27 Adam Smith, *The Wealth of Nations*, Bk IV, Ch. 2; edited by E. Cannon, Methuen, London, 1961 cdn, vol. I, pp. 477—8.
28 Marcuse, op. cit., p. 263. Emphasis added.
29 See Hegel, *Phenomenology of Spirit*, §230, p. 138.
30 S.V. 10, p. 56 (*Postscript*, p. *318*); cf. p. 144 above.
31 S.V. 10, p. 58 (*Postscript*, p. 320).
32 Ibid., p. 52 (*Postscript*, p. 314). Emphasis removed.
33 See S.V. 18 (' "The Individual": Two "Notes" Concerning My Activity as an Author'), p. 162.
34 Ibid., pp. 151—2 fn.
35 As a matter of interest, it has been surmised that Kierkegaard may well, if unwittingly, have read at least one of Marx's works, an article entitled 'Luther als Schiedsrichter zwischen Strauss und Feuerbach' by 'Kein Berliner', a pseudonym adopted by Marx, and to be found in a collection called *Anekdota zur neuesten deutschen Philosophie und Publicistik*, ed. Arnold Ruge, Zürich, 1843. See G. Malantschuk, *Den kontroversielle*

Kierkegaard, Stjernebøgernes Kulturbibliotek, Vinten, 1976, p. 62.

36 *Writings of the Young Marx*, p. 231.

37 See ibid., p. 281, where Marx, in an unpublished note (1844), writes of being 'confirmed and realized in [one's] true human and social nature'. Emphasis removed.

38 James R. Flynn, 'Do We Really Want a *Moral* Justification of Our Basic Ideals?', *Inquiry*, vol. 17 (1974), p. 167.

39 *Writings of the Young Marx*, p. 281. Emphasis removed.

40 S.V. 3, p. 171 (*Either/Or*, vol. 2, p. 187); cf. ibid., pp. 169–74 (*Either/Or*, vol. 2, pp. 184–90).

41 See p. 72, above.

42 Kierkegaard writes: 'He who has not suffered under human bestiality will not become spirit.' *Papirer* XI, 1, A 407, p. 313.

43 S.V. 10, p. 48 (*Postscript*, p. 309).

44 Feuerbach, op. cit., p. 3.

45 See, for example, Theodor W. Adorno, 'On Kierkegaard's Doctrine of Love', *Zeitschrift für Sozialforschung* (*Journal for Social Research*), vol. 8 (1939), pp. 413–29; later published as an appendix to the 1962 edition of Adorno's *Kierkegaard: Konstruktion des Ästhetischen*, 1933, pp. 267–91. Adorno claims that Kierkegaard's positive claims about sociality lack significance unless 'interpreted in terms of social critique' (ibid., p. 423), where the terms of this critique are not Kierkegaard's. He also criticizes Kierkegaard's notions of 'individual' and 'neighbour' for being 'abstract', as well as his concept of 'equality' for obscuring actual inequalities. Adorno's criticism, which stems from the same source as Marcuse's ('Critical Theory'), takes for granted certain fundamental assumptions to which Kierkegaard would be deeply opposed.

46 Georg Lukács, *The Young Hegel*, trans. Rodney Livingstone, Merlin Press, London, 1975, p. 150.

47 Feuerbach, op. cit., p. 14.

48 *Papirer* VIII, 1, A 9, p. 8.

49 *Papirer* IV, C 78, p. 402. Kierkegaard says here that 'whatever advances are made in understanding, religion can 'never be done away with'.

50 S.V. 10, p. 212 (*Postscript*, p. *481*).

51 Ibid., pp. 47–8 (*Postscript*, p. *309*).

52 Ibid., p. 275 (*Postscript*, p. *543*).

53 See ibid., p. 228 (*Postscript*, p. *497*).

54 See Ch. III, note 22, above.

55 See I. Kant, *Fundamental Principles of the Metaphysic of Morals*, in *Kant's Critique of Practical Reason and Other Works on the Theory of Ethics*, Longman, Green, London, New York, and Toronto, 6th edn, 1954, p. 49.

Chapter X   Unconcluding postscript

1 *Papirer* X, 5, A 113, pp. 125–6, somewhat freely rendered.

2 For a sampling of Kierkegaard's disparaging remarks about academics see *Papirer* X, 4, A 236, p. 130; A 450, p. 277; A 503, p. 323; A 614,

pp. 430—1; A 628, pp. 443—4; and A 629, p. 444; and *Papirer* XI, 1, A 136, p. 95; A 412, p. 316; A 473, p. 364; and A 581, p. 439.

3 *Papirer* X, 4, A 628, p. 443.

4 S.V. 10, p. 289.

5 *Papirer* X, 4, A 450, p. 277; cf. S.V. 16 (*Practice in Christianity*), p. 111.

6 *Papirer* X, 4, A 629, p. 44.

7 See Ch. V, note 46, above.

8 Ludwig Wittgenstein, *Culture and Value*, trans. Peter Winch, ed. G.H. von Wright, Blackwell, Oxford, 1980, p. 46e, original emphasis.

9 S.V. 11, p. 60 (*Purity of Heart*, p. 98).

10 Ludwig Wittgenstein, 'Lecture on Ethics', *Philosophical Review*, vol. LXXIV (1965) p. 8, second emphasis added.

11 Stuart Hampshire, 'Feeling and Expression', in J. Glover (ed.), *The Philosophy of Mind*, Oxford University Press, London, 1976, p. 81.

12 As proposed, for example, by Stanley Cavell in 'Kierkegaard's *On Authority and Revelation*', in S. Cavell, *Must We Mean What We Say?*, Cambridge University Press, Cambridge, London, New York, and Melbourne, 1976. See p. 172.

13 Hampshire, op. cit., p. 82.

14 Wittgenstein, *Culture and Value*, p. 45e. The emphasis added to the English translation. Winch translates 'eines' as 'solitary'.

15 Hampshire, op. cit., p. 82.

16 The title of a paper by Thomas Nagel, which appears as Chapter 12 of his *Mortal Questions*, Cambridge University Press, Cambridge, London, New York, and Melbourne, 1979.

Index